T0305234

Wellbeing at Work in a Turbulent Era

IN A TURBULENT ERA SERIES

These are turbulent and changing times. The longer-term effects of phenomena such as pandemics, the climate crisis, disruptive technologies, war, rising inequality, and shifts in global influence and power, on business, the economy and geo-politics are still unknown. Given these rapidly changing economic and social norms, businesses, organisations and institutions must be nimble to thrive. Focusing on one area at a time, this series seeks to investigate best practice, cutting-edge research and new ways of operating in this turbulent era.

For a full list of Edward Elgar published titles, including the titles in this series, visit our website at www.e-elgar.com.

Wellbeing at Work in a Turbulent Era

Edited by

Paula Brough

Professor of Organisational Psychology and Director, Centre for Work, Organisation and Wellbeing, Griffith University, Australia

Gail Kinman

Professor of Occupational Health Psychology, Birkbeck Business School, Birkbeck, University of London, UK

IN A TURBULENT ERA SERIES

Edward Elgar
PUBLISHING

Cheltenham, UK • Northampton, MA, USA

Published by
Edward Elgar Publishing Limited
The Lypiatts
15 Lansdown Road
Cheltenham
Glos GL50 2JA
UK

Edward Elgar Publishing, Inc.
William Pratt House
9 Dewey Court
Northampton
Massachusetts 01060
USA

A catalogue record for this book
is available from the British Library

Library of Congress Control Number: 2024936914

This book is available electronically in the **Elgar**online
Business subject collection
http://dx.doi.org/10.4337/9781035300549

ISBN 978 1 0353 0053 2 (cased)
ISBN 978 1 0353 0054 9 (eBook)

Printed and bound in Great Britain by
TJ Books Limited, Padstow, Cornwall

Contents

Contributors

Amanda Biggs is a Lecturer at the Department of Employment Relations and Human Resources, Griffith Business School, Griffith University, Australia

Jo Billings is a Clinical Professor of Psychological Trauma and Workplace Mental Health with University College London, UK

Paula Brough is a Professor of Organisational Psychology, and the Director of the Centre for Work, Organisation and Wellbeing (WOW), at Griffith University, Australia

Xi Wen (Carys) Chan is a Senior Lecturer at the Department of Employment Relations and Human Resources, Griffith Business School, Griffith University, Australia

Andrew J. Clements is a Lecturer in Work & Organisation with Aston University, Birmingham, UK

Kevin Daniels is a Professor in Organizational Behaviour with the Employment Systems and Institutions Group, Norwich Business School, University of East Anglia, UK

Cristina Di Tecco is an Occupational Psychologist and Researcher with Istituto Nazionale Assicurazione contro gli Infortuni sul Lavoro (INAIL), Italy

Rodrigo Rodriguez Fernandez is a Global Health Advisor for Mental Health and Wellbeing at International SOS, UK

Sheetal Gai is a Research Fellow with the Centre for Work, Organisation and Wellbeing (WOW), Griffith University, Australia

Christine Grant is an Associate Professor with the Centre for Healthcare and Communities, Coventry University, UK

Peter J. Jordan is a Professor of Organizational Behaviour with the Griffith Business School, Griffith University, Australia

Gail Kinman is a Professor of Occupational Health Psychology with Birkbeck, University of London, UK

Rachel Lewis is a Managing Partner with Affinity Health at Work and Birkbeck, University of London, UK

Karen Maher is a Lecturer in Work & Organisation with Aston University, UK.

Almuth McDowall is a Professor of Organisational Psychology with Birbeck, University of London, UK

Rachel Nayani is an Associate Professor with the Norwich Business School, University of East Anglia, UK

Phong T. Nguyen is a Lecturer with The Business School, RMIT University, Saigon South Campus, Vietnam

Karina Nielsen is a Professor with the Sheffield University Management School, University of Sheffield, UK

Ida Bagus Gede Adi Permana is a PhD Researcher at the Griffith Business School, Griffith University, Australia

Alannah E. Rafferty is an Associate Professor with the Griffith Business School, Griffith University, Australia

Emma Russell is a Reader in Occupational and Organisational Psychology (Management) with the University of Sussex Business School, UK

Sudong Shang is a Lecturer at the Department of Employment Relations and Human Resources, Griffith Business School, Griffith University, Australia

Olga Tregaskis is a Professor with the Employment Systems and Institutions Group, Norwich Business School, University of East Anglia, UK

Ashlea C. Troth is a Professor of International HRM with the Griffith Business School, and the Assistant Director of the Centre for Work, Organisation and Wellbeing (WOW), Griffith University, Australia

Michela Vignoli is an Associate Professor with the University of Trento, Italy

Sophie Walker is a Research Consultant with Affinity Health at Work, UK

David Watson is a Senior Lecturer in Organisation Studies and HRM at the University of Essex, UK and a Research Partner with the Norwich Business School, University of East Anglia, UK

Matthew J. Xerri is a Senior Lecturer at the Department of Employment

Relations and Human Resources, Griffith Business School, Griffith University, Australia

Jo Yarker is a Managing Partner with Affinity Health at Work and a Professor in the Birkbeck Business School at Birkbeck, University of London, UK

1. Will work ever be the same? Future trends for wellbeing at work

Paula Brough and Gail Kinman

OUR TURBULENT WORKPLACES

We have produced this book in recognition of the vast changes which occurred to numerous aspects of our working lives during and after the COVID-19 pandemic. In many cases, the changes experienced during the pandemic were accelerated pathways of work progression that were already underway, albeit at a much slower pace. Thus, for example, as Chan and Kinman discuss in Chapter 4, the progression to normalize full-time remote working for so many people was experienced in weeks, instead of years or decades as was anticipated. In the UK, national statistics show that 1.5 per cent of people worked from home in 1981, only rising to 5.7 per cent in 2019 (Felstead, 2022). The ability to work at home was often seen as a 'perk' or a privilege that was reserved for the favoured few. Prior to the pandemic, achieving the flexibility to work from home for one or two days a week was often a hard-fought battle with employers, and was generally perceived by employers to be their only 'consideration' of a flexible work option to assist new parents in their return to work. It is significant that the tumultuous period of the pandemic meant that common obstacles cited *against* such remote working arrangements – including a lack of suitable technology, internet connectivity problems, and a distrust of workers to work without close supervision – often disappeared in a very short time, to maintain some (any!) level of work performance and productivity. The pros and cons of remote working for wellbeing and productivity continue to be the subject of intense public scrutiny, with the 'positions' taken by various groups polarized and often politicized. It is generally agreed, however, that remote working can benefit wellbeing, work–life balance, and productivity, provided the potential challenges are recognized and appropriate measures are in place to support workers (Mutebi & Hobbs, 2022). How long would such widespread remote working arrangements, that have benefited so many, have taken without the stimulus of the pandemic?

1

Similar rapid progression occurred in other aspects of work during and after the pandemic, and we have chosen 12 key topics to feature in this book. The impact of the pandemic upon workers' mental health and wellbeing is, of course, very well publicized, and is a common theme to be found in each of the 13 chapters in this book. The direct impact of occupational stress experienced during the pandemic on different groups of workers, including healthcare workers, non-essential workers, working parents, female workers, younger workers, remote workers, and gig workers, is discussed by Biggs, Brough, and Gai in Chapter 2.

Moral injuries, describing the distress resulting from actions (or inactions) that violate an employee's moral or ethical code, were observed more frequently during the COVID-19 pandemic and its aftermath, in response to the compromised care that many frontline health and social care workers were obliged to provide, and the difficult decisions or actions they were obliged to take. In Chapter 3, Billings provides a highly pertinent review of managing the symptoms and outcomes of moral distress, and of the burnout, compassion fatigue, and work trauma that these frontline workers encountered during this time. Billings also includes a comprehensive discussion of post-traumatic stress disorder (PTSD), which typically has a prevalence rate of between 10 per cent to 40 per cent amongst these high-risk workers. Also discussed is the occurrence and management of the 'compassion satisfaction' and the post-traumatic growth (or resilience) that these workers can experience. This type of satisfaction can, to some extent, attenuate the negative effects of working in occupations with a high risk of stress and burnout, and can help explain why many workers choose to remain in such jobs. Nonetheless, stress and burnout are common reasons for the high turnover in health and social care, which is a serious concern considering the global staffing crisis.

How to prevent, treat, and manage occupational stress and employee wellbeing effectively is a long-established problem that is challenging and increasingly expensive. We include two chapters in this collection which provide refreshingly new and incisive perspectives on this issue. In Chapter 9, Watson, Nayani, Tregaskis, and Daniels discuss a 'strategic and dynamic approach to workplace wellbeing'. They observe how organizations rarely adopt a rational planning approach for the implementation of workplace health and wellbeing strategies. They suggest that organizations adopt a dynamic, ongoing programme of different health and wellbeing strategies, some of which will be successful and become widespread, while others will remain in the background and be rarely used. The implementation and delivery of these strategies are crucial to embedding such programmes as actual organizational practices over time. Importantly, Watson et al. also discuss the impact of the pandemic upon organizational health and wellbeing programs where, in some cases, initiatives were entirely derailed, due to the employer's primary focus on the economic survival of their organization and the physical health of their workers. They identify how lessons learned from this focus shift can be applied to the sustainability of workplace health and wellbeing strategies in the future.

Similarly, in Chapter 13, Nielsen, Di Tecco, Yarker, and Vignoli draw on three case studies to present their 'integrated organizational mental health resilience framework' as a best-practice strategy for managing work-related stress and wellbeing. This framework helps ensure that stress intervention practices occur at each of primary, secondary, and tertiary levels. Also emphasized is the need for job-related stress to be prevented and treated for workers who are currently seeking to return from sick leave caused by long COVID, as well as those who are currently attending work. Nielsen et al. discuss the responsibilities for these intervention practices within each structural level (i.e., worker, team, manager/leader, and organizational levels), but emphasize the need to carefully *integrate* these levels and approaches to produce the best outcomes in safeguarding employee mental health.

As noted above, the rapid developments in technology were a defining feature of the pandemic, particularly in terms of software advances, enabling virtual meetings to occur more easily and personal connections to be maintained. In the aftermath of the pandemic, we are now experiencing a significant 'digital transformation' of our workplaces, with the introduction of multiple artificial intelligence (AI) technologies creating new working platforms, for example, via the development of work 'metaverses' and 'digital twins' of workers (Loy et al., 2023). In Chapter 10, Russell and Grant discuss these and other developments in work technology. They emphasize how work technology and tools enable us to function as 'agile workers', which is a step beyond merely working in remote locations. The use of digital technology enables seamless communications between employers and workers, meaning that workers are (in theory) constantly available, accessible, and contactable: that is, agile. Importantly, the technology that facilitates agile working also enables employment to become more inclusive, offering increased work opportunities to sectors that have been traditionally marginalized, including workers with neurodivergence and/or disability and/or of a low socio-economic status. The potential drawbacks associated with this constant connectivity to work are, however, also acknowledged in this chapter, echoing the concerns about levels of employee wellbeing raised previously and the need for careful boundary management. Russell and Grant's final point is highly pertinent: 'In increasingly turbulent, fast paced, and challenging times, where the nature of work has changed dramatically, the optimization of digital tools to aid timely and inclusive adjustments is now more relevant and important than ever before'.

Echoing these points, McDowall in Chapter 5 also discusses how the pandemic and its aftermath have increased awareness of the need to support the wellbeing of an increasingly diverse workforce, including intersectional workers, and the advantages of doing so. McDowall defines intersectionality as when 'a person can have more than one marginalising identity or "occupy multiple disadvantage statuses" (Brown & Moloney, p. 94)' and highlights research showing that such individuals can be at higher risk of poor wellbeing than those who are non-intersectional. McDowall discusses the common 'disadvantage statuses' of workers including disability, neurodiversity, gender identity, age, health, and racial identity. Findings that people who are neuro-divergent, for example, can respond to work-related stress in different ways to those who are neurotypical are particularly important, highlighting the need for organizations to offer support that is tailored to individual needs. Importantly, McDowall proposes a conceptual model for intersectionality and wellbeing, to inform the appropriate data collection and workplace practices to support the wellbeing and retention of these workers.

In Chapter 7, Troth, Jordan, and Rafferty discuss how workers' emotional experiences influence their wellbeing and job performance, specifically their emotional reactions to changes caused by the pandemic and its turbulent after-math. These discussions draw heavily on research on occupational stress and organizational change. Troth et al. identify how daily events at work, such as customer interactions, can directly impact a worker's emotional reactions and their subsequent decision-making abilities, as well as their overall wellbeing. Changes in work conditions, such as those caused by COVID, are perceived to be intense affective events, and employees rely on their managers to guide them through these changes and resolve any uncertainty. In situations where managerial support is low and/or ineffective, levels of anxiety are likely to increase amongst workers, while their morale and sense of organizational justice will typically decrease. Troth et al. highlight research findings indicat-ing that employees with higher levels of emotional intelligence can generally manage organizational changes better by, for example, having greater insight into the emotions of all involved, and seeking collaborative solutions to best suit everyone. This reasoning implies that when employees' emotional intel-ligence is low and they receive insufficient managerial support and guidance, their reactions to organizational changes will be particularly aversive.

Chapter 6 by Nguyen, Rafferty, and Xerri discusses organizational change in greater detail, focusing especially on differing outcomes resulting from either emergent (unplanned) or planned organizational changes. Most changes experienced during the pandemic were emergent, developing *in situ* as our understandings of the pandemic and its implications grew over time. Nguyen et al. present a conceptual model explaining the associations between the change event characteristics (e.g., the degree of effective communication about the change, and the frequency and scale of the change), employee perceptions of psychological uncertainty and job insecurity resulting from this change, and key individual outcomes (such as employee job satisfaction, work-related wellbeing, and work attachment). The authors argue that emergent organizational changes are likely to increase levels of uncertainty and anxiety for employees and impact their subsequent wellbeing, to a far greater extent than planned changes. An important implication of this discussion is for employers to recognize the increased benefits resulting from *planned* organizational changes. When emergent changes are unavoidable, however, the implementation of positive change processes, such as high-quality communications and employee participation, will reduce the risk of negative outcomes, and assist with the successful implementation of this change.

How changes experienced during and after the pandemic influenced the structures and cultures of our workplaces is the focus of Chapter 12, written by Permana, Shang, and Jordan. They consider how organizations initiate structural change as a way of adapting to external experiences of turbulence, and subsequently re-shape their culture, impacting employees' wellbeing. This process is pertinent, as changing the culture of an organization is traditionally a slow and difficult undertaking. In our post-pandemic workplaces, many workers are settling into different expectations and norms regarding their work outcomes and processes, and these new working norms can often require new skills and competencies. Permana et al. provide examples of new workplace norms and expectations, such as the use of new technology, a widespread move to remote working, and employees' different perspectives of their work. Providing opportunities for workers and employers to co-design our emerging post-pandemic workplaces is a recommended route to embedding organizational structural and cultural changes, and promoting employee wellbeing.

Issues surrounding changing organizational structures since the pandemic are explored in further depth in Yarker, Lewis, Walker, and Fernandez's chapter, which focuses on the implications of changing working patterns for employee wellbeing (Chapter 11). The authors provide a very relevant review of how post-pandemic work patterns have changed for three groups of workers: business travellers, remote rotational workers (such as fly-in-fly-out site-based workers), and hybrid workers. Their review is directly informed by their own empirical data collected from these three groups of workers, with the authors recommending a toolkit of 'Evidence-based Wellbeing at Work' as an efficient means by which employers can improve employee wellbeing. The authors make a pertinent point that, despite repeated acknowledgments that employee wellbeing interventions are not sufficiently evidence-based (for a detailed discussion, see Burgess et al., 2020), both practitioners and employers need reminding of the value of utilizing evidence-based practices in producing meaningful, long-term improvements in employee health and wellbeing. Yarker et al. emphasize that the use of evidence-based processes enables highly effective, targeted guidance, and can generate recommendations for employees, managers, and organizations.

Finally, Kinman, Clements, and Maher's chapter discusses the need for the post-pandemic workplace to implement effective methods to manage employees' sickness absence behaviours (Chapter 8). An important lesson learned from the pandemic was of the risks and adverse impacts caused by employees who work when they are unwell. Kinman et al. recommend ways for organizations to adopt a 'healthy' sickness absence culture, highlighting the need to ensure that organizations' attempts to reduce sickness absence do not inadvertently encourage dysfunctional presenteeism. Growing evidence that remote workers are at greater risk of presenteeism is discussed, and the need for organizations to implement mechanisms to manage this risk emphasized. The authors call for regular multi-level risk assessments to identify workers most at risk of presenteeism, and to identify those who would most benefit from targeted support. Also considered is how the pandemic and its aftermath have influenced organizational culture and social norms regarding sickness absence, with a particular focus on workers experiencing long COVID, and how they can be supported to return to work in an efficient but sustainable way.

FUTURE TURBULENCE

As we return to our changed but increasingly settled workplaces during this post-pandemic period, we begin to look ahead. Many workers strive for normality (albeit a 'new normal') and wish to focus on simply earning their living once again; but we also face some ongoing uncertainty. Will another pandemic occur, and will we have to endure lockdowns once again? Will increasingly more virulent viruses appear that threaten our physical health and ability to work? Will most workers eventually return to the Monday to Friday 9 am to 5 pm working week, or will hybrid working patterns become a permanent option (and even an expectation) for some workers? Has the meaning of work permanently changed for some people? We discussed these points in a recent paper (Brough et al., 2021), and this book serves to advance these discussions within a post-pandemic, turbulent working environment.

It is apparent that the pandemic has changed the core meaning of the value of work for some employees, and now we watch to see how entrenched these changes will be over the next few years. We noted in 2021, for example, how the enigmatic concept of work–life balance is perpetuated by a stigma which thwarted access to available parental leave for many workers, especially to new male parents. This is evident in the marked under-utilization of relevant human resource initiatives by employees who are entitled to access parental leave and flexible work policies. Moreover, the turbulence caused by the pandemic, as some of the authors of chapters in this book have observed, led to a recognition by many employees that work can fit around our lives and our interests, rather than the prior single-minded focus on work, careers, and advancement, to the detriment to other aspects of our lives. The extent to which this attitude shift is sustainable remains to be seen over the coming years, but we suspect it will depend on several factors such as global economics and demographic trends, as well as other public health threats such as a new pandemic. To monitor this sustainability objectively, careful assessment is needed of the uptake of human resource work–life balance policies in organizations, and who is most and least likely to utilize them.

In our 2021 paper we also discussed how many of our workplaces are entrenched in, as Berdahl et al. (2018) describe, 'masculinity contest cultures'. These competitive, hierarchical cultures have a focus on the personal gains and advancement of individual employees at the expense of others, adopting an informal 'mine's bigger than yours is' contest for the favourable allocation of workloads, working hours, and work resources. We noted how the prevalence of such toxic cultures directly hinders an employee's utilization of their work–life balance policies, by informally stigmatizing their uptake. We also discussed how masculinity contest cultures are likely to encourage increased reports of workplace sexual harassment, sexual discrimination, and pregnancy discrimination, as well as the growth in unequal unpaid labour that has been observed over the last two decades in Australia, Europe, and the US. We noted the unacceptable levels of lip service that some employers continue to apply to workplace equity legislation, which allows such practices to continue. We hope that increasing recognition that inclusive workplace cultures – that promote equality, and value diversity in background, knowledge, skills, and experiences – have major benefits for organizations as well as individuals will encourage change in the post-pandemic workplace.

For many workers, the pandemic reinforced a realization that chasing career advancement and monetary gain was not the only way to gauge one's personal value and achievements. An increasing trend has been observed towards valuing family, personal interests, and other aspects of our lives over work, and is reflected by many post-pandemic work practices. Thus, for example, growing interest in the four-day work week, 'quiet quitting', and the increased use of digital AI technology to support our work has exploded in our post-pandemic working lives, as people strive to balance work needs with other aspects of their lives more equally. Again, it will be pertinent to observe how sustainable these changes in work attitudes engendered by the pandemic will be. It will be particularly interesting to observe whether the major disadvantages of organizational cultures that encourage informal masculinity contests, and discourage equality, diversity and inclusion, will continue to be realized. It is our hope that the pandemic has indeed caused enough turbulence to provide opportunities for our workplaces to become safer and fairer domains for all workers.

Finally, although the notion of generation changes in workers' attitudes is an oft repeated but not wholly accurate idiom, there is an increased sense that a 'life beyond work' is valued more highly by our younger generation of workers. These workers acutely experienced the pandemic lockdowns and its restrictions and physical health risks, at a key developmental stage in their lives. They have also witnessed the often intense juggling act performed by their parents and other older workers in an attempt to succeed in their work, family, and personal lives. The rise in experiences of work-related stress, mental ill health, and burnout amongst workers reported *before* the COVID-19 pandemic attests to damaging effects of this intense juggling of multiple life demands. For many of our younger workers, therefore, the notion of 'having it all' has limited appeal, replaced perhaps by a 'live for now' maxim. As these younger people move through their working lives, it will be interesting to observe how their attitudes and career expectations disrupt, shape, and transform the cultures within which they work.

CONCLUSION

The current period of post-pandemic recovery has restored some functions of our working lives to their pre-COVID states. However, turbulence remains in other components of our working lives, especially as regards perceptions of the fundamental value of work and how it adds to or detracts from workers' health and wellbeing. This book is a collection of 12 works from key scholars around the globe discussing the enduring aspects of this post-pandemic turbulence, and how these work components impact employee wellbeing. It is certainly clear that our working lives will continue to experience turbulence over the coming years, especially in terms of how advances in digital technology will broaden employment to different groups of workers, will create new job roles, and will reinforce remote working opportunities for some employees. We hope you enjoy these discussions, and that they assist you in your own contemplations of the changing aspects of our work lives.

REFERENCES

Berdahl, J. L., Cooper, M., Glick, P., Livingston, R. W., & Williams, J. C. (2018). Work as a masculinity contest. *Journal of Social Issues, 74*(3), 422–448.
Brough, P., Kinman, G., McDowall, A., & Chan, X. C. (2021). "#Me too" for work-life balance. *British Psychological Society Work-life Balance Bulletin, 5*(1), 4–8.
Burgess, M. G., Brough, P., Biggs, A., & Hawkes, A. J. (2020). Why interventions fail: A systematic review of Occupational Health Psychology interventions. *International Journal of Stress Management, 27*(2), 195–207. https://doi.org/10.1037/str0000144
Felstead, A. (2022). *Remote working: A research overview*. Routledge.

Loy, J., Novak, J., & Diegel, O. (2023). *3D printing for product designers: Innovative strategies using additive manufacturing.* Taylor & Francis.

Mutebi, N., & Hobbs, A. (2022). *The impact of remote and hybrid working on workers and organisations.* UK Parliament. https://post.parliament.uk/research-briefings/post-pb-0049/

2. Occupational stress and wellbeing: key considerations for improvements

Amanda Biggs, Paula Brough, and Sheetal Gai

INTRODUCTION

The COVID-19 pandemic and its aftermath have produced remarkable transformations in how we live and work (World Health Organization, 2020). The adverse impact of these disruptions on employees' wellbeing and job performance has been highlighted in numerous studies, with the most notable impacts occurring for employee wellbeing experiences (Brough et al., 2021; Wang et al., 2020). As many employees continue to navigate the shift to hybrid work models, numerous challenges arise, including difficulties in disengaging from work responsibilities, and experiencing feelings of isolation when working from home. Additionally, many remote-working employees are confronted with expanded work hours and heavier workloads (Chan et al., 2022; Griffiths et al., 2022). The economic instability that continues to reverberate post-pandemic has produced increased experiences of job insecurity, salary reductions, and redundancies, further compromising employees' wellbeing (e.g., Basyouni & El Keshky, 2021; Brough et al., 2022b). This chapter discusses the implications for workers' experiences of occupational stress and wellbeing in the current aftermath of the COVID-19 pandemic.

IMPACTS OF COVID-19 ON EMPLOYEE WELLBEING

Numerous studies have demonstrated that the changes brought about by the COVID-19 pandemic have had significant implications for employee wellbeing and work outcomes. With the boundaries between work and home having become more blurred, many workers have experienced significantly increased emotional, psychological, and physical strain, exacerbated by amplified information and communication technology use (Kim & Chon, 2022). Managing work and non-work demands has become more challenging, with some workers finding it increasingly difficult to 'switch off' from work when working at home, hindering adequate psychological recovery (Chan et al.,

2022; Morgan, 2020). Other reports identified that high levels of occupational stress experienced during the pandemic were attributed to career instability, remote work practices, exhaustion from video conferencing, impacts of disrupted (work and personal) social support mechanisms, and imbalance between work and non-work domains (Gao et al., 2020). In addition, the uncertainty surrounding employment during the pandemic has been linked to lower work satisfaction, lower organisational commitment, and higher turnover intentions reported by many workers (Brough et al., 2020). The psychological toll of the pandemic, including heightened levels of fear and depression, exacerbates these outcomes.

To gain a comprehensive understanding of the effects of these changes on employees, it is necessary to first understand the concept of wellbeing and its key associations (Brough et al., 2020). Defining wellbeing encompasses the dynamic state in which individuals have the opportunity to cultivate their strengths, function successfully and innovatively, establish meaningful and high-quality connections with others, and make useful contributions to their communities (Ruggeri et al., 2020). In a recent study by Grandi et al. (2022), for example, it was found that the COVID-19 pandemic had a significant negative impact on employee wellbeing and work outcomes – with the most severe impact affecting employees working in education, research, and healthcare services; this included increased reports of depression, stress, isolation, burnout, anxiety, and reduced attachment to work. These changes were attributed to pandemic-induced changes in job patterns, remote working, and social isolation of workers, as well as the broader uncertainty and economic implications associated with the outbreak (Ng et al., 2021). Similarly, Makabe et al. (2015) reported high levels of work–life imbalance, and a decrease in job satisfaction, among healthcare workers in Japan.

As is discussed in other chapters in this book, the Conservation of Resources (COR) theory posits that individuals are driven to safeguard and keep their resources, which include physical, emotional, and cognitive resources (Hobfoll, 1989). Adopting this framework, it is apparent that the pandemic jeopardised resources (related to health, income, work identification, and sociability) for many workers, resulting in increased strain (e.g., Sun et al., 2022). For many female workers especially, the loss of the resource of their *time* was a very noticeable consequence of the pandemic, especially the loss of working time for female workers who juggled simultaneous childcare and/ or child schooling demands (Brough et al., 2022b). This point is discussed in further detail below.

It is important to recognise that the COVID-19 epidemic also produced some positive consequences, primarily relating to reduced travel time (commuting) for work; increased telecommuting practices (i.e., remote working and the widespread adoption of video conferencing meetings), which meant more time at home and with family; and increased work flexibility and scheduling for a large proportion of workers (Chen, 2021). The increased time spent with family was also attributed to *increases* in reported wellbeing for many workers (Brough et al., 2022b). For some workers, surviving through a potentially fatal pandemic also elicited a form of 'existential crisis', where their life values, including the proportion of time spent at work and with their family, were reconsidered, and major life changes were undertaken. These changes included, for example, relocating jobs and homes, changing work hours, and buying a pet (Brough, et al., 2020; Chan et al., 2022). There are also some reports that the pandemic resulted in an increased birth rate in 2021, at least in some Western countries – termed the 'COVID-19 baby bump' (Bailey et al., 2022; Molina, 2022). However, the sustainability of this increase has apparently not been maintained in the post-pandemic period (Sobotka et al., 2023).

UNIQUE EFFECTS ON WORKERS

Although some benefits have been highlighted, the rapid and unprecedented changes instigated in response to the COVID-19 pandemic compromised the wellbeing of the vast majority of workers, irrespective of their circumstances. Nonetheless, research has demonstrated that the wellbeing of certain groups of employees was uniquely impacted; this section of the chapter focuses on the varying experiences of these different employee groups. This includes: the unique challenges faced by healthcare workers, other essential workers, and non-essential workers; by employees, particularly mothers, with caring responsibilities; by women; and by younger workers. It is important to note at the outset that the disparities between employee groups observed in COVID-19 research reflect long-standing societal inequalities, reinforced by prevailing power structures that pre-date the pandemic. However, conditions created by COVID-19 either intensified the disparities, or reversed the progress that had been previously made in addressing these inequalities (Ramos et al., 2020).

Healthcare Workers, Other Essential Workers, and Non-Essential Workers

In response to COVID-19, and prior to the development of vaccines, many countries imposed lockdown measures as a means of minimising population-level exposure to the virus. According to the International Labour Organization (ILO, 2023), 80 per cent of the world's population resided in countries with lockdown restrictions initiated in March 2020. Fundamental to the lockdowns was the mandate that 'non-essential' workers remain at home, while 'essential' workers continue working, albeit with additional safety measures imposed (primarily consisting of social distancing, personal protection equipment, and enhanced cleaning protocols). The distinction between essential and non-essential work was seldom made explicit, and varied substantially between jurisdictions; hence, the definition of essential work also varies within the literature. According to the ILO (2023), essential workers provide goods and services necessary to ensure optimal societal functioning; such workers represent approximately 50 per cent of the workforce, and include eight key occupational groups: food production and systems, healthcare, retail, security, manual labour, cleaning, transportation, and technicians/clerical workers. Similarly, Chowdhury et al. (2022, p. 1) defined essential workers as 'those who conduct a range of operations and services that are typically essential to continue critical infrastructure viability'. Most importantly, research identified differential impacts on wellbeing for essential and non-essential workers during the lockdown periods.

Essential workers continued working during the pandemic, exposing themselves and their loved ones to a greater risk of infection for the benefit of the wider population (Chowdhury et al., 2022; Ramos et al., 2020). Research conducted during this period demonstrated, unsurprisingly, that most essential workers experienced elevated physical and psychological health risks during the pandemic (Bell et al., 2020; ILO, 2023). In terms of physical wellbeing, essential workers experienced a greater risk of infection and higher rates of mortality from COVID-19, in comparison to non-essential workers (ILO, 2023). With respect to psychological wellbeing, essential workers also experienced heightened levels of anxiety and strain, primarily driven by three mechanisms: (1) fear of COVID-19 exposure for themselves and their families; (2) high demands (e.g., due to high numbers of chronically unwell patients) and scarce resources, exacerbated by the increased burden placed on essential services during the pandemic (e.g., supply-chain disruptions, staff shortages, intensified cleaning protocols); and (3) an escalation in violent and abusive behaviour from the public, primarily caused by high levels of distress from both patients and family members due to contact restrictions. Bell et al. (2020), for instance, argued that healthcare workers were exposed to many of the same stressors as the wider population but, due to the nature of their work, they experienced these stressors at a greater frequency and intensity.

The adverse impact of COVID-19 on wellbeing also differed across these groups of essential workers. For instance, the ILO (2023) reported that essential workers with (1) access to personal protective equipment, (2) collective representation (e.g., unions), and (3) greater job security (e.g., formal employment contracts), fared better than those without access to these resources. For example, despite healthcare workers having greater exposure to COVID-19, transport workers experienced higher mortality rates, as they had less access to such protections (ILO, 2023). Similarly, Ramos et al. (2020) argued that risks to the wellbeing of essential workers in agriculture and food-related industries were enhanced during COVID-19, as this form of work is typically conducted by employees who lack access to economic resources and social power.

Several researchers argued that healthcare workers are distinct from 'other essential services' (e.g., Bell et al., 2020). Ramos et al. (2020), for example, observed that healthcare workers were more visible during the pandemic, and were generally awarded higher social status, support, protections, and greater economic resources, relative to other essential workers. Indeed, much of the earlier research on worker wellbeing during COVID-19 lockdowns focused on healthcare workers. This research established that healthcare workers generally experienced increased psychological ill-health symptoms during COVID-19, such as anxiety, depression, and insomnia (e.g., Spoorthy et al., 2020; Vizheh et al., 2020); burnout (McCormick et al., 2023); and stress related to increased exposure to high workloads, intense work hours, work-related violence, and abuse (e.g., Byon et al., 2022; McGuire et al., 2022).

Interestingly, similar outcomes of increased stress and poor wellbeing were also reported in samples of other essential workers. Chowdhury et al. (2022), for example, assessed 32 pandemic-related outcomes in samples of essential workers, excluding healthcare workers. They reported increased depression, anxiety, stress, and other mental health issues, experienced by most other essential workers, primarily caused by the concern about passing the COVID-19 infection onto their own family members. However, these other essential workers typically lacked the training, resources, and sources of supports, to enable them to best manage these COVID-19 risks.

In a rare comparison of these different occupational groups, Bell et al. (2020) conducted a study on the psychological wellbeing of healthcare, other essential, and non-essential workers in New Zealand. The findings indicated that healthcare workers experienced the worst wellbeing consequences due to COVID-19. Overall, each of the three categories of these workers reported poorer psychological health (anxiety, distress, and wellbeing), demonstrating a general adverse effect of COVID-19 on the wellbeing of all workers. However, Bell et al. (2020) noted that healthcare employees and other essential workers were at 71 per cent and 59 per cent greater risk respectively of reporting at least moderate levels of anxiety, compared to non-essential workers; healthcare workers were also at 13 per cent greater risk of experiencing adverse wellbeing. The rates of healthcare workers reporting *high* levels of wellbeing were also lower (3.9 per cent), as compared to other essential workers (9 per cent), and to non-essential workers (7.5 per cent). The types of stressors experienced by the categories of workers also differed: healthcare workers expressed higher levels of stress about the broader health and economic consequences of COVID-19. All essential workers reported increased workload compared to non-essential workers; however, non-essential workers reported higher levels of stress relating to their finances and employment prospects.

Workers, Particularly Mothers, with Caring Responsibilities

Some of the greatest work-related wellbeing impacts of COVID-19 were experienced by parents of young (0 to 5 years) and school-aged children. As the lockdown requirements for many jurisdictions included childcare and school closures, many parents were put in a position where they were simultaneously required to complete their own work tasks and supervise the care and/or home-schooling of their children. Furthermore, COVID-19 created a great deal of uncertainty due to, for example, sudden unemployment, work-from-home arrangements, and schedule changes (e.g., Schmidt et al., 2021; Wang et al., 2021). A study comparing the subjective wellbeing of parents before and during the pandemic demonstrated that wellbeing was substantially lower during the pandemic, and was disproportionately impacted by the COVID-19 lockdown restrictions (Westrupp et al., 2021). In addition, while adverse wellbeing effects were observed for parents overall, working mothers were particularly impacted during the pandemic (e.g., Graham et al., 2021).

The double burden faced by working mothers has long been acknowledged: although women have become increasingly engaged in paid work outside of the home, they retain a disproportionately high responsibility for unpaid domestic duties, such as cleaning, food preparation, childcare, and the mental load associated with running a household (Brough et al., 2008; Dean et al., 2022). This double burden, reflecting long-standing division of labour norms, makes it difficult for women to effectively balance their work and non-work lives. This, coupled with insufficient supports (e.g., flexible work arrangements, high-quality and affordable childcare), leads to disparate rates of workforce participation, and widens the gender pay gap, a situation referred to as the 'motherhood penalty' (Budig & England, 2001). Reports indicate that these ongoing challenges for working mothers were exacerbated by the lockdowns associated with the COVID-19 pandemic (Yildirim & Eslen-Ziya, 2021), creating a 'COVID motherhood penalty' (Couch et al., 2021).

Williams et al. (2020), for example, calculated that female workers spent significantly more of their time on childcare during lockdown, compared to their male spouses, especially 'non-developmental' care (e.g., washing and feeding of children). Male workers, however, were more likely to engage in developmental activities with their children (e.g., home-schooling, playing, and reading). One in three women (34 per cent), compared with one in five men (20 per cent) reported that the burden of childcare had a negative impact on their wellbeing; and the consequential decline in work productivity by female workers has been widely observed (Brough et al., 2021).

Yildirim and Eslen-Ziya (2021) conducted a survey of academics in several countries (Norway, Sweden, Italy, France, Germany, the US, and the UK), and found that having children was the most significant predictor of perceived changes in work and housework during COVID-19. Importantly, an examination of gender differences on the impact of becoming parents found little difference between male academics with and without children (although this result would likely differ for single-parent fathers), while the most negative perceptions were held by female academics with children. Women reported greater perceived change in housework routines, and a greater proportion of their time being absorbed by housework. Similarly, a study by Graham et al. (2021) found that women working from home with children experienced greater perceived stress compared to men working from home with children. Based on their study, and previous research, the authors argued that responsibilities for unpaid domestic and caring work, and for home-schooling, were disproportionately assumed by working mothers – increasing their workload, work–family conflict, and stress; and in turn, adversely impacting their wellbeing and job performance.

Women

As noted above, working conditions initiated by COVID-19 impacted women differently to men, which has been attributed to (1) pervasive and persistent division of labour norms (as discussed above), and (2) the more precarious nature of work disproportionately performed by women. In addition to childcare demands, Couch et al. (2021) argued that women were more adversely impacted during COVID-19 because they are over-represented in (1) precarious employment (less seniority, and more part-time or contract-based work); (2) industries and occupations more likely to be deemed 'non-essential' and, therefore, subject to business closures during lockdown periods; and (3) employment that could not be conducted remotely, and had higher levels of exposure to COVID-19 infection. Similarly, the ILO (2022b) reported that women tend to be disproportionately represented in vulnerable work exhibiting the following characteristics: shorter working hours; one-way flexibility, where work is available at short notice; greater engagement in unpaid work; work in family-based businesses (involving lower pay and greater unpaid work hours); and lower social and maternity protection. A review of studies on the impact of COVID-19 on the wellbeing of non-health essential workers also found that women reported higher levels of psychological ill health, including anxiety, stress, depression, and burnout (Chowdhury et al., 2022).

Together, the impacts of COVID-19 for women are expected to have a long-lasting effect on their labour force participation, career progression, and wellbeing. In academia, for example, the data is clear and sobering: female academics' research outputs during the pandemic dropped significantly compared to their male counterparts (e.g., Gabster et al., 2020). The long-term implications for this productivity decline, in terms of female career opportunities and progression, is still being observed. For example, considering that female students preparing to enter the workplace during COVID-19 also experienced greater disruption to their studies in comparison to male students, the gendered labour force participation and pay gap are expected to widen further in coming years (unless directly addressed), unravelling previously made progress addressing this prevailing societal issue (ILO, 2022b).

Younger Workers

Younger workers who were preparing to enter the workforce, or who were in the early stages of their career during COVID-19, were uniquely impacted by the pandemic. This category of workers includes students completing secondary or tertiary education, recent graduates, trainees, and apprentices. Younger workers are particularly vulnerable during periods of crises, as they are disproportionately impacted by the associated rising unemployment, economic and labour market downturns, and diminished training and development opportunities (Muehlemann et al., 2020). This trend was observed during the COVID-19 pandemic: globally, rates of youth employment decreased by 34 million between 2019 and 2020, and a higher percentage loss in employment occurred for people specifically aged between 15 and 24 years, in comparison to those aged 25 years and above (ILO, 2022a).

This disparity is driven by numerous complex factors associated with COVID-19 that resulted in younger people experiencing higher rates of job loss, or failing to successfully enter the workforce. For example, government-enforced lockdowns, and closure of non-essential businesses, made it difficult for younger workers to seek and secure employment, as recruitment for new positions ceased in favour of retaining existing employees (ILO, 2022a). Furthermore, younger workers typically hold more precarious employment, and possess less seniority, skills, and experience, that make them more vulnerable to job losses that occurred during the pandemic (ILO, 2022a).

Unfortunately, as with female workers, the adverse pandemic-related employment conditions for younger workers are expected to have a long-lasting impact. ILO projections indicate that less than half the global youth unemployment deficit in 2020 has been recovered to date, and the recovery of jobs for youth is likely to be slower than for adults, especially in low- and middle-income countries (ILO, 2022a). The ILO also reported that, irrespective of a country's economic status, young people beginning their careers during periods of crises are more susceptible to 'scarring':

> Young people who lose their job or fail to obtain one are particularly vulnerable to "scarring," the phenomenon whereby future labour market outcomes are worse than those of their peers even when macroeconomic conditions improve again. They may

end up accepting a job for which they are overqualified, which risks trapping them in an employment trajectory that involves informality and low pay. (ILO, 2022a, p. 16)

In addition to these short- and long-term consequences of unemployment, COVID-19 also limited essential learning and skill-development opportunities for people preparing to enter the workforce. It is estimated that the education of 1.6 billion people worldwide was impacted by closures of educational institutions (ILO, 2022a). The lockdowns resulted in disrupted, delayed, and lost opportunities to engage in authentic, hands-on learning experiences. Hospital-based placements for medical students, for example, were terminated to reduce the spread of COVID-19, and to avoid placing an additional burden on the healthcare system (Stout et al., 2021). The availability of apprentice-ships also declined as a result of the pandemic (e.g., Muehlemann et al., 2020). Furthermore, the transition to fully online learning, combined with increased financial pressure, made engaging in education and learning logistically and economically challenging for many young people (ILO, 2022a).

According to the ILO, COVID-19 initiated a spike of 1.5 per cent in the rate of young people not in employment, education, or training (NEET), the highest levels observed in at least 15 years: 'The 282 million young people who were in this situation in 2020 missed out on a crucial early stage of their personal development and risk facing severe disadvantages in the labour market in the future' (ILO, 2022a, p. 27).

Studies conducted with university students and younger workers demon-strated that those in the early stages of their careers experienced unprece-dented levels of anxiety about future career prospects, given the adverse impact of COVID-19 on the economy and labour market (Dodd et al., 2021). The adverse employment-related conditions, and increased pressures placed on emerging and early-career workers during COVID-19, is a particularly important issue from a stress and wellbeing perspective, given the age group is particularly vulnerable to mental ill health.

OCCUPATIONAL STRESS AND WELLBEING POST-PANDEMIC

The consequences of the pandemic highlight four key challenges for consid-eration in order to advance the health and performance of workers, and we discuss these below. These challenges build on the 'decent work' agenda of the Sustainable Development Goals of the United Nations (UN). This agenda, for example, identifies that fairly paid, equitable work conditions are essential to enable workers to earn a reasonable living, free from unfair discrimination and emotional or physical harm (Brough et al., 2022a).

Workers in Essential Services

First, COVID-19 demonstrated the vital, yet completely undervalued, role of essential services within society. In 2023, the ILO published an extensive report citing concerns about the sustainability of essential services, calling for greater international efforts to invest in essential work sectors, as well as enhanced support and remuneration for essential workers, commensurate with their contribution and value to society (ILO, 2023). A detailed discussion of the challenges recruiting and retaining health and social care professionals is presented in Chapter 8 of this book by Kinman et al. Furthermore, this ILO (2023) report noted that many essential services have long been exposed to poor work conditions, such as elevated physical and psychological risks inherent within job tasks, long and irregular working hours, more tenuous employment contracts, and low pay. While the pandemic intensified these issues, they are recognised to have existed prior to the onset of COVID-19. This 'call to action' to policymakers must also be reflected in occupational wellbeing research, as many of the occupations deemed to be essential, such as hospitality and retail, are significantly under-represented in the literature.

Remote Working

Second, the requirement for non-essential workers to undertake their work from home, enacted to offset the adverse impact of the pandemic on the global economy, sparked intense and continuing debate on the issue of work flexibility. The unprecedented shift to remote working and working from home, initiated by the pandemic, identified potential benefits and limitations of flexibility in work time and location; and numerous opinions about how such arrangements should be maintained post-COVID-19 have been voiced in the media. Working remotely from home, largely avoiding presenteeism and the office culture, and, most of all, increasing workers' control over their work hours and how they intertwine with non-work responsibilities, has been both challenging and enlightening for many workers. The permanence of these changed work situations post-COVID-19 continues to be discussed.

Some reports are indicating that remote work is likely to increase across most industry sectors, encouraged by the escalating digital transformation of our workplaces (Brough et al., 2021). The steadfast barriers erected to prevent telecommuting and work hours flexibility (for those workers who desired this) have disintegrated in many sectors, although the permanence of this disintegration remains to be seen. Some organisations prefer their workers to be visible, on site, and accessible during work hours, for at least part of the work week (Chan et al., 2022). The advantages of regularly bringing workers together physically, for some of the work week at least, is associated with the re-building of organisational cultures, improving inter-personal connections and support provisions, facilitating people management, and enhancing work creativity and collaborations (Brough et al., 2022a). Consequently, most organisations seem to have at least reverted to a hybrid work model of both on-site and remote-working days each week (Chan et al., 2022).

Importantly, there is an increasing division between workers able/not able to work remotely, based primarily on their type of work. That is, knowledge workers and office-based workers have greater access to remote and hybrid work models, compared to frontline healthcare, emergency services, hospitality, and retail workers, who typically have less choice of their work location. Low-paid, younger, and/or female employees also tend to be over-represented in these occupational groups with less flexibility over work location. It will be interesting to observe the long-term impacts of this division of workers due to work location, specifically in terms of staff supervision, training, career opportunities, performance, and wellbeing.

Gig Work

Third, the freelance, or independent worker, 'gig work' economy rapidly expanded as a result of the COVID-19 pandemic. The wellbeing of these often precariously employed gig workers is highlighted, primarily because their health and wellbeing is typically not subject to any formal organisational policies and practices, or legal frameworks. The pandemic encouraged an increase in gig work, primarily due to its flexibility of work hours and location, work–life balance opportunities, and access to income for individuals who might not otherwise have been able to work for various reasons (Williams et al., 2022). It is estimated that approximately 20 per cent of workers have undertaken work through digital platforms, including those who participate in gig work as a 'side hustle' to elicit secondary employment income (Williams et al., 2022).

The key wellbeing considerations for gig workers focus upon working long and unsociable hours, personal safety risks, the unpredictability of available work, low pay, confirming to specific platforms' controls, penalties for non-availability, and time pressures for task completion. Thus, many of the perceived benefits of gig work – for example, the flexibility of choosing personal work hours – can be eroded by the demands of the digital platform, thereby negatively impacting worker wellbeing. The lack of corporate responsibility currently offered by these digital platforms for the health and wellbeing of their gig workers thus exposes these workers to significant risks, and to significant inequity when they work alongside colleagues employed on formal contracts.

Formal Wellbeing Strategies

Fourth, and more broadly, the mental health burden associated with the COVID-19 pandemic has emphasised the importance of formal strategies for protecting employees' psychological wellbeing. Thus, workers' wellbeing is increasingly being formalised and addressed via governmental legislation, organisational policies and practices, and individual actions (Brough et al., 2022b). This coordinated action in the form of policy, legal, and organisational instruments is unprecedented. This multi-layered activity also directly addresses the systemic disadvantage experienced by sub-groups of workers who are defined by a disadvantage in relation to income, job security/safety, and physical/mental abilities.

This increasing emphasis, on the inclusion of all types of workers, is informed by the UN's Sustainable Development Goal referred to earlier, of decent work for all; and is enacted by advances in workplace technologies that offer work opportunities to (mainly disabled) people previously deemed (informally) to be unemployable. Such workplace technologies, for example, allow for the capture and interpretation of data relating to worker health and performance, and are driven by artificial intelligence, which guides machines, robots, leaders, and managers to alter the performance of employees through minute adjustments (nudges) to work allocation or social interactions (Brough et al., 2022b). The positive and negative impacts of this employee monitoring – and especially the increasing use of surveillance technologies to assess, for example, workloads, breaks from work, and time spent typing on a keyboard – are increasingly being recognised, especially in terms of their impacts for employee wellbeing and retention (e.g., Rohwer et al., 2022).

CONCLUDING THOUGHTS

The long-term impacts of the COVID-19 pandemic are predicted to be most difficult for those workers hit hardest by the economic and social turbulence of the pandemic lockdowns. Thus, working mothers with young children, young workers, and essential healthcare workers are anticipated to experience the most difficulties post-pandemic, primarily due to work availability (i.e., work shortages), work performance declines, and/or enduring occupational stress experiences. The pandemic has thus, for some workers, produced a significant toll impacting careers and wellbeing.

On the positive side, the pandemic has also produced sustained changes to the work practices of many workers, including increased autonomy of work location and hours, and reduced work commuting. It will be of considerable interest to monitor the success of calls for workers to return to physical work locations, currently being aired by some organisations in this post-pandemic era. We anticipate that worker preference will occur here, with those workers who prefer remote-working conditions moving to organisations that offer this flexibility. This trend would mirror the similar preference observed by working parents who prioritise employment with organisations offering flexible parental leave provisions (Brough & O'Driscoll, 2015). Thus, the issue of flexible work provisions to accommodate employees' work–life balance preferences is anticipated to remain a key consideration for those organisations experiencing difficulties in attraction and retention – of skilled workers, especially.

A final sustained change to work practices produced by the pandemic is the use of technology. Forthcoming developments in digital technology, especially the increase in virtual work (e.g., Tarafdar & Stich, 2021), augmented reality, and the metaverse (e.g., Triono et al., 2023), will continue to revolutionise the ways in which we work – for example, by producing an increased flexibility of work location for some workers, and an increase in the diversity of workers able to be employed. It will be pertinent to observe the ability of this forthcoming digital technology to reduce the inequalities reported above for those workers adversely impacted by the COVID-19 pandemic. It is hoped that the negative impacts of 'techno-stress' (e.g., O'Driscoll et al., 2010) are offset by the positive potential impacts that the work technologies can provide for employees, including those who experienced and are continuing to experience inequalities arising from the pandemic.

REFERENCES

Bailey, M. J., Currie, J., & Schwandt, H. (2022). The Covid-19 baby bump: The unexpected increase in US fertility rates in response to the pandemic. *National Bureau of Economic Research Working Paper Series*, No. w30569. https://doi.org/10.3386/w30569

Basyouni, S. S., & El Keshky, M. E. S. (2021). Job insecurity, work-related flow, and financial anxiety in the midst of COVID-19 pandemic and economic downturn. *Frontiers in Psychology, 12*. https://doi.org/10.3389/fpsyg.2021.632265

Bell, C., Williman, J., Beaglehole, B., Stanley, J., Jenkins, M., Gendall, P., Rapsey, C., & Every-Palmer, S. (2020). Challenges facing essential workers: A cross-sectional survey of the subjective mental health and well-being of New Zealand healthcare and "other" essential workers during the COVID-19 lockdown. *BMJ Open, 11*. https://doi.org/10.1136/bmjopen-2020-048107

Brough, P., Daniels, K., & Gardiner, E. (2022z). Introduction. In P. Brough, E. Gardiner, & K. Daniels (Eds.), *Handbook on management and employment practices* (pp. 1–12). Springer.

Brough, P., Holt, J., Bauld, R., Biggs, A., & Ryan, C. (2008). The ability of work–life balance policies to influence key social/organisational issues. *Asia Pacific Journal of Human Resources, 46*(3), 261–274. https://doi.org/10.1177/1038411108095758

Brough, P., Kinman, G., McDowall, A., & Chan, X. C. (2021). "#Me too" for work-life balance. *British Psychological Society Work-life Balance Bulletin, 5*(1), 4–8.

Brough, P., & O'Driscoll, M. P. (2015). Integrating work and personal life. In R. J. Burke, K. M. Page, & C. L. Cooper (Eds.), *Flourishing in life, work, and careers: Individual wellbeing and career experiences* (pp. 377–394). Edward Elgar Publishing.

Brough, P., Timms, C., Chan, X. W., Hawkes, A., & Rasmussen, L. (2020). Work-life balance: Definitions, causes, and consequences. In: T. Theorell (Ed.), *Socioeconomic determinants of occupational health: From macro-level to micro-level evidence* (pp. 2–15). Springer.

Brough, P., Wall, T. Z., & Cooper, C. L. (2022b). Organizational wellbeing: An introduction and a future gaze. In: T. Z. Wall, C. L. Cooper, & P. Brough (Eds.), *The SAGE handbook of wellbeing in organisational life* (pp. 1–6). SAGE.

Budig, M. J., & England, P. (2001). The wage penalty for motherhood. *American Sociological Review*, *66*(2), 204–225.

Byon, H. D., Sagherian, K., Kim, Y., Lipscomb, J., Crandall, M., & Steege, L. (2022). Nurses' experience with Type II workplace violence and underreporting during the COVID-19 pandemic. *Workplace Health & Safety*, *70*(9), 412–420. https://doi.org/10.1177/21650799211031233

Chan, X.W., Shang, S., Brough, P., Wilkinson, A., & Lu, C.-Q. (2022). Work, life and COVID-19: A rapid review and practical recommendations for the post-pandemic workplace. *Asia Pacific Journal Human Resource*, *61*, 257–276. https://doi.org/10.1111/1744-7941.12355

Chen, Z. (2021). Influence of working from home during the COVID-19 crisis and HR practitioner response. *Frontiers in Psychology*, *12*, 710517. https://doi.org/10.3389/fpsyg.2021.710517

Chowdhury, N., Kainth, A., Godlu, A., Farinas, H. A., Sikdar, S., & Turin, T. C. (2022). Mental health and well-being needs among non-health essential workers during recent epidemics and pandemics. *International Journal of Environmental Research and Public Health*, *19*(10), 5961. https://doi.org/10.3390/ijerph19105961

Couch, K. A., Fairlie, R. W., & Xu, H. (2021). The evolving impacts of the COVID-19 pandemic on gender inequality in the U.S. labor market: The COVID motherhood penalty. *IZA Discussion Papers*, No. 14811. Institute of Labor Economics (IZA).

Dean, L., Churchill, B., & Ruppanner, L. (2022). The mental load: Building a deeper theoretical understanding of how cognitive and emotional labor overload women and mothers. *Community, Work & Family*, *25*(1), 13–29.

Dodd, R. H., Dadaczynski, K., Okan, O., McCaffery, K. J., & Pickles, K. (2021). Psychological wellbeing and academic experience of university students in Australia during COVID-19. *International Journal of Environmental Research and Public Health*, *18*(3), 866. https://doi.org/10.3390/ijerph18030866

Gabster, B. P., Van Daalen, K., Dhatt, R., & Barry, M. (2020). Challenges for the female academic during the COVID-19 pandemic. *The Lancet*, *395*(10242), 1968–1970.

Gao, J., Zheng, P., Jia, Y., Chen, H., Mao, Y., Chen, S., Wang, Y., Fu, H., & Dai, J. (2020). Mental health problems and social media exposure during COVID-19 outbreak. PLoS ONE, *15*(4). https://doi.org/10.1371/journal.pone.0231924

Graham, M., Weale, V., Lambert, K. A., Kinsman, N., Stuckey, R., & Oakman, J. (2021). Working at home: The impacts of COVID 19 on health, family-work-life conflict, gender, and parental responsibilities. *Journal of Occupational and Environmental Medicine*, *63*(11), 938.

Grandi, A., Zito, M., Sist, L., Martoni, M., Russo, V., & Colombo, L. (2022). Wellbeing in workers during COVID-19 pandemic: The mediating role of self-compassion in the relationship between personal resources and exhaustion. *International Journal of Environmental Research and Public Health, 19*(3), 1714. https://doi.org/10.3390/ijerph19031714

Griffiths, D., Sheehan, L., Van Vreden, C., Petrie, D., Whiteford, P., Sim, M. R., & Collie, A. (2022). Changes in work and health of Australians during the COVID-19 pandemic: A longitudinal cohort study. *BMC Public Health, 22*(1), 487. https://doi.org/10.1186/s12889-022-12897-4

Hobfoll, S. E. (1989). Conservation of resources: A new attempt at conceptualizing stress. *American Psychologist, 44*(3), 513–524. https://doi.org/10.1037/0003-066X.44.3.513

International Labour Organization. (2022a). *Global employment trends for youth 2022: Investing in transforming futures for young people.* https://doi.org/10.54394/QSMU1809

International Labour Organization. (2022b). *The gender gap in employment: What's holding women back?* https://www.ilo.org/infostories/en-GB/Stories/Employment/barriers-women#intro

International Labour Organization. (2023). *World employment and social outlook 2023: The value of essential work.* https://www.ilo.org/wcmsp5/groups/public/---dgreports/---inst/documents/publication/wcms_865332.pdf

Kim, K. H., & Chon, M.-G. (2022). When work and life boundaries are blurred: The effect of after-hours work communication through communication technology on employee outcomes. *Journal of Communication Management, 26*(4), 386–400. https://doi.org/10.1108/JCOM-06-2022-0073

Makabe, S., Takagai, J., Asanuma, Y., Ohtomo, K., & Kimura, Y. (2015). Impact of work-life imbalance on job satisfaction and quality of life among hospital nurses in Japan. *Industrial Health, 53*(2), 152–159. https://doi.org/10.2486/indhealth.2014-0141

McCormick, E., Elder, E., Crilly, J., Greenslade, J., & Brough, P. (2023). Measuring occupational stress in Emergency Departments. *Emergency Medicine Australasia, 35*(2), 234–241. https://doi.org/10.1111/1742-6723.14101

McGuire, S. S., Gazley, B., Majerus, A. C., Mullan, A. F., & Clements, C. M. (2022). Impact of the Covid-19 pandemic on workplace violence at an academic emergency department. *American Journal of Emergency Medicine, 53*, 1–285. https://doi.org/10.1016/j.ajem.2021.09.045

Molina, R. L., Tsai, T. C., Dai, D., Soto, M., Rosenthal, N., Orav, E. J., & Figueroa, J. F. (2022). Comparison of pregnancy and birth outcomes before vs during the COVID-19 pandemic. *JAMA Network Open, 5*(8), e2226531.

Morgan, R. (2020). *Working from home during COVID-19: Many Australians experiencing difficulty switching off from work.* https://www.roymorgan.com/findings/hard-to-switch-off-work-for-many-australians-working-from-home

Muehlemann, S., Pfeifer, H., & Wittek, B. H. (2020). The effect of business cycle expectations on the German apprenticeship market: Estimating the impact of COVID-19. *Empirical Research in Vocational Education and Training, 12*(1), 8. https://doi.org/10.1186/s40461-020-00094-9

Ng, M. A., Naranjo, A., Schlotzhauer, A. E., Shoss, M. K., Kartvelishvili, N., Bartek, M., Ingraham, K., Rodriguez, A., Schneider, S. K., Silverlieb-Seltzer, L., & Silva, C. (2021). Has the COVID-19 pandemic accelerated the future of work or changed its course? Implications for research and practice. *International Journal of Environmental Research and Public Health, 18*(19), 10199. https://doi.org/10.3390/ijerph181910199

O'Driscoll, M., Brough, P., Timms, C., & Sawang, S. (2010). Engagement with information and communication technology and psychological well-being. In P. L. Perrewé and D. C. Ganster (Eds.), *New developments in theoretical and conceptual approaches to job stress* (pp. 269–316). Emerald.

Ramos, A. K., Lowe, A. E., Herstein, J. J., Schwedhelm, S., Dineen, K. K., & Lowe, J. J. (2020). Invisible no more: The impact of COVID-19 on essential food production workers. *Journal of Agromedicine, 25*(4), 378–382.

Rohwer, E., Flöther, J. C., Harth, V., & Mache, S. (2022). Overcoming the "dark side" of technology: A scoping review on preventing and coping with work-related technostress. *International Journal of Environmental Research and Public Health, 19*(6), 3625.

Ruggeri, K., Garcia-Garzon, E., Maguire, Á., Matz, S., & Huppert, F. A. (2020). Well-being is more than happiness and life satisfaction: A multidimensional analysis of 21 countries. *Health and Quality of Life Outcomes, 18*, 192. https://doi.org/10.1186/s12955-020-01423-y

Schmidt, A., Kramer, A. C., Brose, A., Schmiedek, F., & Neubauer, A. B. (2021). Distance learning, parent–child interactions, and affective well-being of parents and children during the COVID-19 pandemic: A daily diary study. Developmental Psychology, 57(10), 1719–1734. https://doi.org/10.1037/dev0001232

Sobotka, T., Zeman, K., Jasilioniene, A., Winkler-Dworak, M., Brzozowska, Z., Alustiza-Galarza, A., Németh, L., & Jdanov, D. (2023). Pandemic roller-coaster? Birth trends in higher-income countries during the COVID-19 pandemic. *Population and Development Review*. https://doi.org/10.1111/padr.12544

Spoorthy, M. S., Pratapa, S. K., & Mahant, S. (2020). Mental health problems faced by healthcare workers due to the Covid-19 pandemic: A review. *Asian Journal of Psychiatry, 51*, 102119. https://doi.org/10.1016/j.ajp.2020.102119

Stout, R. C., Roberts, S., Maxwell-Scott, H., & Gothard, P. (2021). Necessity is the mother of invention: How the COVID-19 pandemic could change medical student placements for the better. *Postgraduate Medical Journal, 97*, 417–422. https://doi.org/10.1136/postgradmedj-2021-139728

Sun, Y., Wang, P., & Tang, J. (2022). Impact of mental health, job insecurity, and COVID-19 symptoms on protective behavior changes among White, Black, and other minorities in the US. *Frontiers in Psychology, 13*, 1040413. https://doi.org/10.3389/fpsyg.2022.1040413

Tarafdar, M., & Stich, J.-F. (2021). Virtual work, technology and wellbeing. In T. Z. Wall, C. L. Cooper, & P. Brough (Eds.) (2021), *The SAGE handbook of organizational wellbeing* (pp. 159–169). SAGE.

Triono, T. A., Roostika, R., Muafi, M., & Nursyamsiah, S. (2023). Impact of immersive technology and virtual work environment on innovative work behaviour. In A. Hamdan, A. Harraf, A. Buallay, P. Arora, & Alsabatin, H. (Eds.), *From Industry 4.0 to Industry 5.0: Mapping the transitions* (pp. 77–88). Springer Nature.

Vizheh, M., Qorbani, M., Arzaghi, S. M., Muhidin, S., Javanmard, Z., & Esmaeili, M. (2020). The mental health of healthcare workers in the COVID-19 pandemic: A systematic review. *Journal of Diabetes and Metabolic Disorders, 19*, 1967–1978. https://doi.org/10.1007/s40200-020-00643-9

Wang, M., Henry, D. A., Del Toro, J., Scanlon, C. L., & Schall, J. D. (2021). COVID-19 employment status, dyadic family relationships, and child psychological well-being. *Journal of Adolescent Health, 69*(5), 705–712. https://doi.org/10.1016/j.jadohealth.2021.07.016

Wang, C., Pan, R., Wan, X., Tan, Y., Xu, L., Ho, C. S., & Ho, R. C. (2020). Immediate psychological responses and associated factors during the initial stage of the 2019 coronavirus disease (COVID-19) epidemic among the general population in China. *International Journal of Environmental Research and Public Health, 17*(5), 1729. https://doi.org/10.3390/ijerph17051729

Westrupp, E. M., Stokes, M. A., Fuller-Tyszkiewicz, M., Berkowitz, T. S., Capic, T., Khor, S., Greenwood, C. J., Mikocka-Walus, A., Sciberras, E., Youssef, G. J., Olsson, C. A., & Hutchinson, D. (2021). Subjective wellbeing in parents during the Covid-19 pandemic in Australia. *Journal of Psychosomatic Research, 145.* https://doi.org/10.1016/j.jpsychores.2021.110482Williams, P., McDonald, P., & Mayes, R. (2022). The growing "gig" economy: Implications for the health and safety of digital platform workers. In P. Brough, E. Gardiner, & K. Daniels (Eds.), *Handbook on management and employment practices* (pp. 769–808). Springer.

Williams, T., Mayhew, M., Lagou, M. & Welsby, M. (2020). *Coronavirus and home-schooling in Great Britain: April to June 2020.*

World Health Organisation. (2020). *Mental health and COVID-19.* https://www.who.int/teams/mental-health-and-substance-use/covid-19

Yildirim, T. M., & Eslen-Ziya, H. (2021). The differential impact of Covid-19 on the work conditions of women and men academics during the lockdown. *Gender, Work & Organization, 28,* 243–249. https://doi.org/10.1111/gwao.12529

3. Managing workplace trauma and moral distress

Jo Billings

INTRODUCTION

Many frontline organizations, by definition, place their workers at high risk of exposure to traumatic events. Such high-risk occupational roles include, although are not limited to, workers in health and social care, mental health, and the emergency services, as well as military and security personnel, analysts, civil servants, and journalists. In this chapter, we discuss the nature of trauma experienced in the workplace, explore the impact of trauma at work, and examine the current state of the evidence for supporting staff exposed to trauma and moral injury in the line of their occupational duties.

The risk inherent in many frontline roles is not novel; however, the current turbulent era has highlighted, and in many cases increased, the demands placed on frontline workers. The COVID-19 pandemic has undoubtedly had a profound impact on the frontline workforce worldwide, coupled with climate crises, international conflict, domestic unrest, and the cost-of-living crisis. All of this has occurred within the context of reduced relative investment in frontline services in many countries, which long preceded these crises but continued despite them. The UK, like many countries, is currently facing a recruitment and retention crisis in its frontline services, with poor mental health the most common reason for many frontline workers to reduce their hours, take career breaks, or leave their jobs (Health and Safety Executive [HSE], 2023). The resulting limitations in resources and staff shortages have impacted not only on frontline staff, but also the public they provide vital services for. The unprecedented industrial action seen in the UK amongst frontline services in recent times is testimony to the reality that many frontline workers have reached breaking point.

This is also an era in which frontline workers have been portrayed as both heroes and villains. In the UK, we stood on our doorsteps during the peak of the COVID-19 pandemic and clapped for health and social care workers. However, only a few months later, general practitioners and hospital staff were being vilified for lack of access to their services and waiting times for treatments. Despite the pandemic highlighting the critical importance of frontline workers to the international economy, a survey of 70,000 people across 36 countries in Europe showed that frontline workers were more likely to report feeling that they did not receive the recognition they deserved for their work, compared to other occupational groups (Eurofound, 2022). Similar themes have also been seen globally (Berkhout et al., 2022). Public trust in the police and other public services has also waned in the aftermath of the death of George Floyd and police violence in the US, which gave rise to the Black Lives Matter movement, and public outrage at several high-profile controversies involving officers within the Metropolitan Police in the UK. Public support and trust in frontline services currently hangs in the balance, exacerbating the current turbulent climate for frontline workers.

Within the context of this turbulent and uncertain era, in this chapter we will review research and practice from the UK and across the world, to consider how we can support frontline workers faced with trauma and moral injury in the workplace. We will also consider how to best equip these workers to work more effectively in what is likely to be a continuing period of turbulence and uncertainty. Doing so is vital to tackle the recruitment and retention crisis of workers in crucial frontline services, and ensure that workers are supported to thrive at work. Much of the research available, catalysed by the COVID-19 pandemic, is on health care workers, but we will also draw on findings from other high-risk settings, and consider what knowledge may be transferrable to and from other occupational groups. This chapter sets out a framework for supporting frontline workers in high-risk roles, but also highlights current gaps in our understanding, and potential next steps for research and practice.

THE NATURE OF TRAUMA AT WORK

A traumatic incident could be experienced in any workplace, as it can be outside of a work setting. Such traumas might include an industrial accident, or a natural disaster such as a fire or flood, which would be considered unexpected and outside of the realms of normal experience. However, for most frontline workers, exposure to traumatic events in the line of their occupational duties is often anticipated, and is arguably even inevitable. Health and social care workers will be routinely exposed to illness, injury, and death. Emergency service workers will have to deal with accidents, disasters, and interpersonal violence. Military personnel will be involved in armed conflict. Analysts, investigators, and journalists will see distressing material. When it is your job to deal with such traumatic experiences, shift after shift, a worker's experience of trauma in the workplace is very different from an unexpected and single-incident trauma.

These different types of traumas have been termed Type I and Type II traumas. This distinction was originally made in relation to childhood trauma (Terr, 1991), but has since been applied to adult trauma and is equally applicable to workplace trauma. Type I trauma describes single-incident traumas, whereas Type II trauma captures repeated or prolonged trauma. Frontline workers are arguably at greater risk of exposure to not only trauma, but also more complex Type II traumas.

The prevalence of exposure to trauma in frontline occupations has, however, not been clearly established. Results of global epidemiological surveys in the general population suggest that 70.4 per cent of people will be exposed to a traumatic event in their lifetime, with most people experiencing a mean of 3.2 traumas (Kessler et al., 2017). Whilst exposure to trauma in the general public may be high, both the proportion of workers exposed to trauma and the number of traumas experienced is likely to be much higher in frontline roles. This also intersects with other traumas that workers may be exposed to outside of their workplace roles. For example, during the COVID-19 pandemic, frontline health and social care workers were working directly with large numbers of seriously ill patients and exposed to high rates of mortality, but at the same time they were also potentially exposed to stress, illness, and bereavement in their personal lives (Rabow et al., 2021). Frontline workers who have worked on traumatic incidents in their local communities, which have affected them personally as well as professionally, have been shown to suffer more adverse outcomes in terms of their mental health, as evidenced by research on 9/11 (Boscarino et al., 2004) and Hurricane Katrina (Culver et al., 2011; Lambert & Lawson, 2013).

Frontline workers may also be exposed directly, or indirectly, to trauma at work. For example, a firefighter entering a burning building would be considered to be directly exposed to trauma, whereas the exposure for a mental health professional hearing about childhood abuse from their clients in therapy sessions would be classified as indirect trauma. This latter type of exposure has been termed secondary traumatic stress (Stamm, 1995) or vicarious trauma (McCann & Pearlman, 1990). These two constructs have different origins and slightly differing conceptualizations (Sutton et al., 2022), but both describe a further potential impact of trauma on many frontline workers.

The distinction between direct and indirect trauma in occupational settings is arguably somewhat redundant since the *Diagnostic and Statistical Manual of Mental Disorders* (DSM-5) included 'indirect exposure in the line of professional duties' in its definition of a traumatic event to which a diagnosis of post-traumatic stress disorder (PTSD) could be given. Examples include first responders viewing human remains, or police officers repeatedly exposed to details of child abuse (American Psychiatric Association, 2013). Nevertheless, if we consider the (likely underestimated) degree of exposure to secondary traumatic stress in frontline settings, in addition to direct exposure to trauma, then it is highly probable that most frontline workers are confronted with multiple, complex, protracted, and cumulative traumas over the course of their careers.

The way frontline workers experience trauma in the line of their work is also likely to be qualitatively different from trauma experienced by the general population. Frontline workers have knowingly signed up for an occupation which places them at direct risk of harm, physically and/or psychologically. Frontline workers walk directly toward trauma, whilst the rest of us may run away. The sense of purpose and responsibility that frontline workers bring to their jobs can be protective (Billings et al., 2021c), but it can also be a risk factor when lives cannot be protected or saved.

This brings us on to 'potentially morally injurious events' (PMIEs) which might also be experienced by frontline staff in the line of their work. During the COVID-19 pandemic, well-documented PMIEs amongst health and social care workers included stretched staff having to provide less-than-optimum care, making impossible decisions about who should receive resources, and dealing with bereaved families who were prevented from being with their loved ones in their final moments by social restrictions, which had to be further enforced by staff. Such experiences can result in a 'moral injury', which is discussed further below.

THE IMPACT OF TRAUMA AT WORK

Whilst the risk of exposure to trauma and PMIEs in frontline occupational roles is almost certain, the impact of it is hard to quantify. We know, from wider research on the general population outside of workplace settings, that the impact of trauma can be multifarious. Exposure to trauma can also *not* have a negative impact on those exposed, and may engender compassion and satisfaction, and in some instances can even lead to post-traumatic growth. Frontline workers are, for the most part, very resilient people (Brooks et al., 2020) who find effective ways to cope with physically, psychologically, and morally challenging experiences in the line of their work (Koubra et al., 2023). Nevertheless, repeated and prolonged exposure to traumatic experiences and PMIEs can come at a cost.

Anxiety and Depression

Common mental disorders are highly prevalent in the general population, with one in six working-age adults in the UK estimated to experience anxiety, depression, or stress-related problems at any one time (McManus, et al., 2016). The World Health Organization (WHO, 2022) argued that rates of common mental disorders in the general population increased markedly during the peak of the COVID-19 pandemic, with data from the Global Burden of Disease survey indicating that, in 2020, there was a 27.6 per cent increase in cases of major depressive disorder, and a 25.6 per cent increase in cases of anxiety disorder, worldwide (Santomauro et al., 2021). This increase was argued to be related to fear of infection, loneliness, grief, and financial worries, concomitant to constraints on people's ability to work, access social support, and engage with their local communities (WHO, 2022), with those who had experienced mental health difficulties before the pandemic hit hardest (Mind, 2021).

Estimated prevalence rates of anxiety and depression in frontline workers vary greatly across different studies, largely as a result of inconsistencies in measurement methods, tools, timings, and cut-off points. Prior to the pandemic, a systematic review and meta-analysis of global prevalence rates of mental health problems in police personnel, including 272,463 officers across 67 studies and 24 different countries, found pooled prevalence rates of 14.6 per cent for depression, and 9.6 per cent for generalized anxiety, amongst police personnel worldwide (Syed et al., 2020). In a systematic review and meta-analysis of 27 studies on 30,878 ambulance workers, Petrie et al. (2018) found estimated pooled prevalence rates of 15 per cent for depression, and 15 per cent for anxiety, although they noted rates of 27 per cent for general psychological distress. During the COVID-19 pandemic these rates were notably higher, with a systematic review and meta-analysis of common mental disorders amongst 8,096 first responders across 17 studies during COVID-19 (including police, paramedics, and emergency service personnel) finding pooled prevalence rates of 31 per cent for depression and 32 per cent for anxiety (Huang et al., 2022).

Despite a proliferation in research on healthcare staff during COVID-19, there is surprisingly little good-quality research prior to the pandemic from which we can make comparisons. Mental health problems in the healthcare workforce prior to COVID-19 were noted (i.e., Carrieri et al., 2018) but not systematically reviewed. Bell and Wade (2021), in their rapid review and living meta-analysis of the mental health of clinical staff working in epidemic and pandemic health emergencies (including Ebola, H1N1 influenza, Middle East respiratory syndrome [MERS], severe acute respiratory syndrome [SARS], and COVID-19), noted that high exposure to epidemic and pandemic work incurred only a small additional burden in relation to common mental health problems, compared to low-exposure work. However, they concluded that baseline rates of poor mental health were already high in this population.

In response to the COVID-19 pandemic in the UK, early research indicated that levels of anxiety and depression were high amongst frontline healthcare workers. Findings from an online survey of 1,194 frontline health and social care workers from across the UK, with baseline measures taken during the peak of the first wave of COVID-19, indicated 47 per cent initially met the threshold for clinically significant levels of anxiety, and 47 per cent for depression, based on clinical self-report measures (Greene et al., 2021). These findings were corroborated by similar studies in the early waves of COVID-19 in the UK (Gilleen et al., 2021; Greenberg et al., 2021).

Most early research on COVID-19 was, however, by necessity cross-sectional, reliant on convenience samples and self-report measures, and therefore at some risk of inflating true prevalence rates. This is illustrated by the findings of a two-phase cross-sectional study, where Scott et al. (2023) completed diagnostic interviews with a sub-sample (N = 243) of UK National Health Service (NHS) survey respondents (N = 23,462), and found prevalence rates of anxiety and depression were 14.3 per cent and 13.7 per cent respectively, and combined prevalence of anxiety and depression was 21.5 per cent, when measured by diagnostic interview. This compared to 52.8 per cent of respondents in the wider survey meeting thresholds for common mental disorders based on self-report measures.

It is also challenging to determine to what extent rates of common mental disorders in frontline workers are attributable to traumatic and potentially morally injurious experiences at work. Risk factors for anxiety and depression amongst healthcare workers during COVID-19 included pandemic-specific factors, such as fear of being infected and infecting others, and not having reliable access to personal protective equipment (PPE), but also included non-pandemic-specific factors such as feeling stigmatized, and not feeling able to talk to a line manager (Greene et al., 2021). Qualitative research has also highlighted the nuanced relationship between traumatic stress and other contextual factors at work. A systematic review and meta-synthesis of 46 qualitative research studies published on epidemics and pandemics prior to and including the early stages of COVID-19 identified workers' concerns about their own and others' safety, which were exacerbated by inadequate PPE and poor communication, as a source of anxiety. However, distress was also related to insufficient resources and inconsistent information, as well as complicated relationships with families, colleagues, organizations, media, and the wider public, which could be experienced as sources of support, but also concomitantly as sources of stress (Billings et al., 2021a).

Similar findings have been seen in other frontline roles. In a systematic review of 13 quantitative studies on depression in journalists, MacDonald et al. (2023) found that those most at risk of experiencing depressive symptoms had experienced greater exposure to work-related and personal trauma, including threats to themselves or their family, but that depression was also associated with non-work-related factors including lower levels of family and peer support, social acknowledgement, and education.

Post-Traumatic Stress Disorder

Despite high rates of exposure to trauma in the general population, conversion rates to developing PTSD are relatively low. Whilst most people might experience distress and intrusive memories in the first few days and weeks after a traumatic experience, most will recover naturally over time (Layne et al., 2007). Based on data from the WHO World Mental Health Survey, the cross-national lifetime prevalence rate of PTSD was 5.6 per cent amongst those with reported exposure to trauma (Koenen et al., 2017).

Estimated rates of PTSD amongst frontline workers again vary considerably across studies due to methodological inconsistencies, although they are notably higher than general population norms. In a systematic review of 31 studies, Lee et al. (2020) found that reported PTSD amongst staff who had experienced work-related trauma varied from 8.4 to 41.1 per cent. Rates varied amongst studies due to differences in definitions of PTSD, methods of measurement, types of traumatic events, time since exposure, and occupational group. The systematic reviews and meta-analyses by Syed et al. (2020) and Petrie et al. (2018) found global pooled prevalence rates for PTSD of 14.2 per cent amongst police officers and 11 per cent in ambulance personnel, respectively. In contrast, Greinacher et al. (2019) explored secondary traumatic stress in a systematic review of 31 studies on first responders (police officers, fire fighters, paramedics, and search and rescue personnel) and concluded that levels were low. However, the authors acknowledged that rates varied considerably between studies, and low rates could also be accounted for by under-reporting, social desirability constraints, and job-loss concerns.

Amongst healthcare workers, cross-sectional surveys of PTSD symptoms during the early stages of COVID-19 in the UK estimated that rates were potentially high. Greene et al. (2021) reported that 22 per cent of workers met clinically significant levels of PTSD symptomatology, based on standardized self-report measures, in the first wave of the pandemic in the UK. Similarly, Gilleen et al. (2021) found 14 per cent of 2,773 healthcare workers met criteria for severe PTSD. Greenberg et al. (2021) estimated that 40 per cent of 709 healthcare workers in UK intensive care units (ICUs) met cut-offs for probable PTSD, which is higher than other studies; but arguably ICU staff had the greatest exposure to the highest rates of morbidity and mortality during the peak of the pandemic. Internationally, similar rates were also indicated in systematic reviews and meta-analyses (Marvaldi et al., 2021; Pappa et al., 2020).

Scott et al. (2023) again urge caution about deriving prevalence scores from self-report measures, and argue that, based on a sub-sample of 94 healthcare workers from their larger NHS Check cohort in the UK, PTSD prevalence was 7.9 per cent when measured by diagnostic interview, as opposed to estimates of 25.4 per cent based on self-report measures across the wider sample from

the same study. However, Wild et al. (2022) also conducted structured diagnostic interviews with 103 healthcare workers during the peak of the pandemic
in the UK and found that rates of PTSD were actually slightly higher than those
estimated by self-report measures. Notably, Wild and colleagues (2021) found
that, although the participants in their sample were working directly with
COVID-19 and had experienced a number of COVID-related deaths, most
index events identified were not related to COVID-19 and pre-dated the pandemic; albeit for some participants, onset had been delayed and precipitated
by COVID-19. This reiterates the likelihood of frontline workers experiencing
a range of occupational and personal traumas, as well as the complex interplay
between cumulative trauma exposure and PTSD in frontline workers.

Complex PTSD

Complex PTSD (CPTSD) was included as a formal diagnosis in the International
Classification of Diseases (11th Edition) (ICD-11; WHO, 2018). CPTSD
includes, in addition to the symptoms of PTSD, a triad of further difficulties
in relation to affect dysregulation, negative self-concept, and interpersonal
disturbances. A few studies have explored CPTSD in frontline occupational
groups to date, with a small but growing body of literature on military veterans, police, and healthcare workers. Murphy et al. (2020) assessed the rates of
PTSD and CPTSD amongst treatment-seeking military veterans in the UK and
found that, of those seeking help for mental health problems, 14 per cent met
criteria for PTSD, whilst 56.7 per cent showed signs of CPTSD. The presence
of CPTSD was also associated with higher rates of childhood adversity, more
experiences of emotional or physical bullying during their military careers,
greater comorbidity, more functional impairment, and delayed help-seeking
(Murphy et al., 2021).

Brewin et al. (2022) looked at rates of PTSD and CPTSD in an online survey
of 10,401 serving police officers in the UK who had identified as having been
exposed to at least one traumatic event. The prevalence rate of PTSD was 8
per cent and CPTSD was 12.6 per cent, with the authors suggesting that the
cumulative impact of exposure to trauma may result in the higher likelihood
of CPTSD. In contrast, Steel et al. (2021) looked at rates of PTSD and CPTSD
in a cross-sectional study of 2,444 police officers working in high-risk roles in
the UK, who were regularly monitored as part of a mental health surveillance
programme. In this sample, 3 per cent met criteria for PTSD and 2 per cent for
CPTSD. In this study, higher work stress and lower manager support increased
the odds of CPTSD, but not PTSD. Personal trauma history increased the risk
for both PTSD and CPTSD. This sample may however be atypical of all police
officers, as they were a highly select group working in particularly high-risk
roles with extensive support and ongoing screening.

Amongst healthcare workers in the UK during the first peak of the COVID-19 pandemic, 8.3 per cent met criteria for probable PTSD and 14.2 per cent for CPTSD (Greene et al., 2023). In line with previous findings on military and police samples, this corroborates the above findings that frontline workers are more likely to present with CPTSD than PTSD, which is perhaps unsurprising given the frequency, severity, duration, and cumulative impact of trauma exposure in this population.

Moral Injury

The concept of 'moral injury' was initially coined by Shay (1994) in response to the Vietnam War, and comprises three parts: when (1) there has been a betrayal of what is considered morally correct, (2) by someone who holds legitimate authority, and (3) in a high-stakes situation. Numerous definitions have since arisen, although most refer to Litz and colleagues' (2009) definition of a moral injury as arising from 'perpetrating, failing to prevent, or bearing witness to acts that transgress deeply held moral beliefs and expectations' (2009, p. 695). It is noteworthy that 'betrayal' is less prominent in Litz's definition, a point which we return to below.

Conceptual confusion has arisen, as a 'moral injury' is often used to describe an individual's *exposure* to an event, and/or the resulting psychological *injury* arising from it. Here, we have referred to PMIEs as an exposure, and moral injury as a psychological harm which may be experienced as a result. Nonetheless, there continues to be some confusion in the field which is reflected in differing definitions, conceptualization, and measurement.

Moral injury is not classified as a mental health diagnosis (although there is debate about whether it would be helpful or not to classify it as such), but is an associated risk factor for anxiety, depression, and PTSD (Williamson et al., 2018). Notably, the concept of 'moral distress' preceded moral injury, and was used in the 1980s to describe psychological conflict arising amongst nurses experiencing 'ethical dilemmas' (Jameton, 1984). Research and clinical attention then turned away from healthcare settings, and most research on 'moral injury' in the intervening generations has been conducted in military settings, with interest in moral distress or injury in healthcare contexts only being rekindled 40 years later during the COVID-19 pandemic. A small but growing body of literature has also more recently explored moral injury in other occupational groups, including journalists (Backholm & Idås, 2015), police (Papazoglou & Chopko, 2017), and veterinarians (Crane et al., 2015; Williamson et al., 2022b, 2023b), which has showed that these groups were also at risk of exposure to PMIEs and associated psychological distress, similar to military personnel.

We currently lack standardized treatment protocols and clinical consensus on how best to treat moral injury, although some promising approaches are emerging, including Murray and Ehlers's (2021) adapted cognitive therapy model of moral injury in PTSD, and the development of an innovative treatment protocol for moral-injury-related mental health difficulties in military personnel, which focuses on psychoeducation about such injury, self-acceptance, and self-compassion (Williamson et al., 2022a).

The COVID-19 pandemic has brought our attention back to the potential relevance of moral injury as a way of understanding health and social care workers' experiences, with nearly a third of healthcare workers in the UK reported to have experienced PMIEs at work (Williamson et al., 2023a). Notably, research with healthcare workers has shown that PMIEs, in response to witnessing others' wrongful actions and feeling betrayed or let down by figures of authority, were more commonly reported than perceived self-transgressions, with betrayal-related PMIEs being the most significant predictor of PTSD or CPTSD symptoms (Greene et al., 2023). This raises the question of whether interventions targeted at self-acceptance and self-compassion are appropriate for aggrieved healthcare workers, who are less likely to be experiencing guilt, shame, and self-blame, and more likely to be experiencing emotional responses consistent with feeling betrayed, such as anger, frustration, and loss of trust. Exposure to PMIEs, and the incidence of moral distress and moral injury, are unlikely to abate following the pandemic, and in light of financial and human resource challenges experienced by many frontline professions worldwide.

Burnout and Compassion Fatigue

Burnout and compassion fatigue are not unique to frontline roles, but are certainly experienced extensively within them. Burnout has been defined as a phenomenon resulting from chronic work-related stress, with symptoms typically classified into three constituent parts: emotional exhaustion, increased mental distance or feelings of cynicism or negativity towards one's job, and reduced professional efficacy (WHO, 2018). Burnout was included in the ICD-11 although not as a medical condition, and is referred to as specifically occurring in an occupational context (WHO, 2018). Compassion fatigue was originally characterized by Figley (1995) as the 'reduced capacity of, or interest in, being empathic' (Figley, 1995, p. 7), and, although conceptually slightly distinct, is often used interchangeably with the terms 'burnout' and 'secondary traumatic stress' (Sutton et al., 2022).

Precise rates of burnout and compassion fatigue in frontline roles prior to the COVID-19 pandemic are elusive, although consistently reported as high across different frontline sectors, and countries, in years preceding the pandemic. Since the pandemic, burnout in frontline workers has received much more research attention, with several reviews and meta-analyses reporting on rates amongst healthcare workers since 2020. For example, Ghahramani et al. (2021) conducted a systematic review and meta-analysis of 30 observational studies, and found an overall pooled prevalence rate of 52 per cent of healthcare workers worldwide who experienced burnout during the COVID-19 pandemic. Notably, the authors also found that non-frontline COVID-19-exposed healthcare personnel also reported high burnout, and that rates were highest in low- and lower-middle-income countries. Similarly, Macaron et al. (2023) conducted a systematic review and meta-analysis of 45 observational cross-sectional studies and found the overall pooled prevalence estimate was 54.6 per cent. They found studies conducted in earlier waves of the pandemic reported higher rates of burnout compared to those conducted in the late pandemic period, and that, geographically, burnout was highest amongst Middle East and African studies, followed by Europe, and then South America. Prevalence of burnout was comparable between physicians and nurses.

Without reliable meta-analyses of rates of burnout prior to the pandemic, it is difficult to establish pre-existing levels in the healthcare workforce. The studies included in these reviews are also subject to the same criticism as previously discussed, in that cross-sectional studies using self-report measures, and relying on convenience samples, only provide an unreliable snapshot of one point in time, and may inflate true prevalence rates. Nevertheless, indications that half of the healthcare workforce worldwide might have been subjectively burned-out during the pandemic are certainly concerning, and undoubtedly a key factor in current retention crises.

Self-Harm and Suicidality

Rates of self-harm and suicidality have been noted to be high in the general public. Pre-pandemic results of the British National Psychiatric Morbidity Survey, a randomized cross-sectional survey of 8,580 members of the UK public, found that one in six people had considered suicide, and 4.4 per cent of the total sample had attempted suicide, at some time (Bebbington et al., 2010). The COVID-19 pandemic precipitated significant concerns of an increase in suicidality in the general population. In a systematic review and meta-analysis of 38 studies including 120,076 participants, Farooq et al. (2021) found that the global pooled prevalence of suicidal ideation across studies during the early waves of COVID-19 was 12.1 per cent, with loneliness, mental health difficulties, and social restrictions being contributory factors to suicidal ideation. The authors concluded that suicidal ideation in the general population was higher than in studies published prior to COVID-19, but that it was not yet possible to determine whether COVID-19 had any effect on actual suicide rates.

High rates of suicidality have also been recognized in frontline workers prior to the COVID-19 pandemic. In their systematic review and meta-analysis of mental health problems in police personnel worldwide, Syed et al. (2020) found 8.5 per cent of respondents across studies reported suicidal ideation. Of additional concern was the finding that 25.7 per cent of participants across the studies admitted drinking to hazardous levels. In a systematic review and meta-analysis of 61 studies of physicians conducted prior to the outbreak of COVID-19, Dutheil et al. (2019) found that 17 per cent of doctors reported suicidal ideation, and 1 per cent reported having made a suicide attempt. The UK's Office for National Statistics (ONS) reported that the suicide rates amongst healthcare professionals between 2011 and 2020 was 24 per cent higher than the national average, which was largely accounted for by elevated rates of suicide amongst female nurses, female doctors, and male paramedics (ONS, 2021).

With respect to healthcare workers during the pandemic, Greenberg et al. (2021) noted that in their sample of 709 ICU staff, 13 per cent reported frequent thoughts of being better off dead, or of hurting themselves, in the previous two weeks; and 7 per cent admitted problematic alcohol use. Wild et al. (2022) in their sample of 103 healthcare workers reported that 29 per cent endorsed thoughts of self-harm or suicidal ideation.

Compassion Satisfaction and Post-Traumatic Growth

Compassion satisfaction is considered the opposite to compassion fatigue, and has been defined as pleasure and satisfaction derived from helping others through your work (Stamm, 2005). Research has established that frontline workers can experience positive outcomes after exposure to traumatic experiences. For example, in their review of the literature, Brooks et al. (2018) describe how workers have reported finding their work in response to crises and disasters to be meaningful and rewarding – valuing their life more, and strengthening their sense of personal and professional competency.

Whilst many, perhaps even most, frontline workers may demonstrate remarkable resilience when frequently confronted with trauma and PMIEs, positive experiences are also frequently experienced alongside the more negative and potentially pernicious impacts of exposure to trauma. For example, in a survey of 253 specialist trauma therapists from across the UK, 70 per cent were found to be at high risk of secondary traumatic stress, and 25.8 per cent at high risk of burnout; however, 38.8 per cent also reported high compassion satisfaction (Sodeke-Gregson et al., 2013). This illustrates the potentially positive outcomes that can come with this work, concurrent to burnout and traumatic stress.

In a qualitative research study with 28 mental health professionals who rapidly stepped up to provide support for frontline health and social care workers during the peak of the COVID-19 pandemic in the UK, nearly all reported a strong sense of purpose and derived satisfaction from this work, with many experiencing professional growth. However, this work also came at a cost, as mental health professionals took on additional responsibilities and increased workloads, whilst often neglecting their own health and well-being. Many were also professionally isolated, and affected vicariously by the traumas and moral injuries which health and social care staff discussed in their therapy sessions (Billings et al., 2021b).

Post-traumatic growth is defined as positive psychological change that can occur as a result of trauma or adversity (Tedeschi & Calhoun, 2004). Growth does not arise directly from exposure to trauma, but from individuals integrating traumatic events into their belief systems and worldviews, or modifying prior beliefs, resulting in positive meaning-making, and growth in one or more of five main areas: deeper relationships with others, new perspectives on life, appreciation of life, a greater sense of personal strength, and spiritual development (Tedeschi & Calhoun, 1996). Post-traumatic growth may arguably be more prevalent than PTSD in response to trauma (Tedeschi & Calhoun, 1996), and has been documented in systematic reviews of the literature amongst occupational groups including military personnel (Mark et al., 2018), workers in disaster-exposed organizations (Brooks et al., 2020), and healthcare workers (Melinte, 2023). It can be impacted by numerous work and non-work-related factors (O'Donovan & Burke, 2022). There is less research so far on positive outcomes after exposure to PMIEs, but this will be an interesting avenue for future research.

Impact on Families

Exposure to traumatic experiences and PMIEs not only affects frontline workers themselves, but can also have a knock-on effect on the people around them, notably their families and close friends. Historically, most research on the impact on family members of those working in high-risk roles has focused on military families, with consistent findings of negative outcomes in (mostly female) spouses of (mostly male) military personnel and veterans with PTSD. Previous research has highlighted poor mental health in partners, behavioural problems in children, and high rates of intimate partner violence. For example, in a qualitative study of eight female partners of male military veterans, Murphy et al. (2017) found that partners reported feeling subordinated in the relationship, living in a volatile environment, and experiencing emotional distress and social isolation. In a qualitative study of 30 male military veterans, Williamson et al. (2023c) found that veterans who had experienced PMIEs reported greater social withdrawal, and more risk-taking behaviours. This was highly distressing for family members, and could create a tense, volatile home environment that was challenging for family members to navigate (Williamson, et al., 2023).

In a qualitative study with family members of healthcare workers during the COVID-19 pandemic in the UK, Tekin et al. (2022) explored the experiences of 14 family members (including partners, siblings, parents, and a close friend), and found that they were very proud of their loved ones and motivated to support them. However, family members also experienced intense anxiety and emotional burden due to worrying about their loved one's work, and felt that the sacrifices they made as a family were overlooked by society. Participants also described being vicariously traumatized by hearing about their family members' work, and feeling that healthcare organizations failed to meet the needs of healthcare workers' families, which negatively affected all family members.

These findings are supported by the results of a meta-analysis on the crossover of workplace traumatic stress symptoms between partners (Wang et al., 2022). In a meta-analysis of 276 articles, the authors found that employees' traumatic distress was often transmitted to their partners. The relationship between employee PTSD/distress and spouse PTSD/distress was as strong as the relationship between employee trauma exposure and employee PTSD/distress, suggesting that workers' PTSD/distress is as distressing for partners as the traumatic stressors are for workers encountering them directly.

MANAGING TRAUMA AT WORK

In this section we will explore what can be done to support frontline workers who have been exposed to traumatic experiences and PMIEs in the line of their work, consider the current state of the evidence, and suggest a framework for providing support.

Preventative medicine can provide a useful frame of reference for considering how to support staff in frontline settings. Its application has been suggested in healthcare settings (Tracy et al., 2020), but this can usefully be extended to all high-risk frontline services. Organizations have an ethical and legal duty of care to prevent harm to their workers where possible, or to prepare workers in advance of potential exposure to harm, which would be considered *primary prevention* – interventions delivered in advance of possible exposure to trauma or PMIEs. Inevitably, for many frontline workers, exposure to traumatic experiences or PMIEs is unavoidable. When exposure has occurred, we can therefore think about *secondary prevention* – what interventions can be provided immediately after exposure to mitigate distress. Finally, whilst we would expect most workers to cope, we recognize that some inevitably will struggle, so our responsibility is to identify those individuals and provide early access to appropriate care, which we term *tertiary prevention* – interventions offered after distress has been experienced.

The current state of the evidence for interventions at each of these time-points is presented below, as well as the current gaps and limitations in the existing research. However, in order to provide any mental health support to frontline workers, clinicians and organizations first need to overcome several barriers to doing so.

Overcoming Barriers

Despite much greater awareness and promotion of the importance of mental health in recent years, numerous barriers persist to staff in organizations engaging with mental health support. Shame and stigma about experiencing mental health problems is still pervasive in frontline occupations, and needs to be overcome to better manage trauma and moral injury at work (see also the chapter by Kinman et al. in this collection). Many workers fail to recognize or prioritize their mental health needs, are reluctant to admit that they are struggling, and are unwilling to access help (Billings et al., 2021a). Bell and Wade (2021) in their review and living meta-analysis of the mental health of clinical staff working in epidemic and pandemic health emergencies note: 'It is worth highlighting that formal psychological support was considered useful by clinical staff but that it was least requested and less frequently received by those with higher levels of mental health difficulties' (p. 7). Indeed, even mental health professionals are not exempt from the stigma of help-seeking for mental health problems (Billings et al., 2021b).

Organizations need to secure buy-in from senior leaders, and reduce barriers to accessing support, by protecting time for staff to attend training and support in working hours. Role modelling from managers and senior leadership will be imperative in creating a culture in an organization where it is considered appropriate to talk about the mental health impact of trauma and moral injury at work (Billings et al., 2021c). These barriers need to be considered in any workforce plan to support frontline employee mental health.

Primary Prevention

Organizations have a duty of care to their employees to prevent harm by reducing exposure to psychological hazards where possible. Nevertheless, in many frontline occupations, exposure to trauma and PMIEs is inevitable. So, what then can an organization do to prepare and protect their workers in advance of exposure?

Preparedness and training

Pre-exposure training and preparedness programmes have good face validity for potentially preventing, or minimizing, the mental health impact of exposure to trauma and PMIEs in the workplace. However, supporting evidence is currently somewhat equivocal. In a systematic review of 15 studies that evaluated psychological training or pre-deployment interventions provided for UK military personnel, Harden et al. (2021) found evidence for social benefits such as improved cohesion and improved stress management skills, although substantial mental health wellbeing benefits were not demonstrated, leading the authors to conclude that evidence for the effectiveness of pre-deployment psychological interventions is scant.

In a review of the literature on pre-incident training in first responders, Wild et al. (2020) note a proliferation of training programmes aimed at emergency service workers, but argue that, whilst developed with the best intentions, these programmes vary in efficacy. The authors found no evidence from available literature for psychoeducation delivered as a standalone package, or generic interventions aimed to improve wellbeing or resilience, but they note that specific operational training showed more promise in preventing stress-related pathology. From this we might conclude that pre-exposure training and preparedness programmes may be most beneficial when specific and targeted to the unique operational demands of the role, rather than generic training on wellbeing or resilience. However, this premise warrants further research in high-quality trials.

Trauma-informed workplaces

Trauma-informed care has been advocated in services working with patients affected by trauma, but could arguably be extended to all workplaces where their own employees might also be exposed to trauma and moral injury. A trauma-informed approach essentially focuses on the awareness of trauma and its impacts in all aspects of organizational functioning (Berliner & Kolko, 2016). Incorporating such an approach in high-risk frontline organizations could increase awareness of the impact of workplace trauma, and promote open and honest discussion about the psychological ramifications of this work. Such a cultural shift would require buy-in from senior leaders, and role modelling from those in positions of authority, but could go some way to addressing stigma and willingness to seek help.

Operationalizing and measuring how organizations are trauma-informed with respect to their own workforce warrants further discussion outside the scope of this chapter, but could provide a useful framework for further consideration. The concept of moral-injury-informed services has also yet to be explored, and could be the subject of novel research.

Psychological safety

Safety is a key component of trauma-informed care, and arguably a prerequisite for a workplace culture where staff feel able to disclose and discuss the impact of trauma and morally injurious events. The concept of psychological safety has been explored in organizational psychology, and refers to a shared belief amongst individuals as to whether it is safe to engage in interpersonal risk-taking in the workplace – for example, feeling safe to voice ideas, seek and provide honest feedback, collaborate, take risks, and experiment (Edmondson, 1999). Higher levels of psychological safety have been associated with better team performance and learning, and are critical in enhancing safety and reducing employee errors (Newman et al., 2017).

In a systematic review of 83 papers from a variety of organizational contexts, psychological safety was shown to be enhanced by supportive leadership behaviours, supportive organizational practices, relationship networks, and team characteristics (Newman et al., 2017). In a review of 36 studies on psychological safety in healthcare settings, O'Donovan and McAuliffe (2020) identified several enablers of psychological safety, including priority for patient safety, improvement or learning orientation, support, familiarity with colleagues, and status, hierarchy, and inclusiveness.

How psychological safety can be built and enhanced in frontline organizations certainly warrants further attention, and could be critical to creating a safe and mutually supportive culture where frontline workers are willing and able to talk about the impact of their work.

Secondary Prevention

Recognizing that many workers will, by definition of their frontline roles and responsibilities, inevitably be exposed to traumatic incidents and PMIEs, what then can be done to support them after they have been exposed?

Practical support/needs

In the immediate aftermath of a traumatic event, most workers appear to want practical support to attend to their basic human needs, such as adequate rest and recovery, hydration, and nutrition (Billings et al., 2020; Greenberg & Tracy, 2020). Practical strategies were particularly valued by frontline health care workers during the COVID-19 pandemic – for example, access to hot meals, free parking, areas to rest, and adequate PPE (Billings et al., 2021a). Such interventions appeared to be valued by frontline workers not only in addressing their basic needs, but in that they also conveyed that the organization valued and was committed to its staff (Billings et al., 2021a). We know that getting the 'basics' right is important, and not doing so risks undermining staff value and feeding into the negative cycle of staff burnout and retention problems (Clarkson et al., 2023). Even the best-intended psychological interventions, without basic support structures in place, risk appearing tokenistic and hypocritical.

Early psychosocial interventions

Whether psychological interventions should be offered in the immediate aftermath of a traumatic event has been a contentious subject. 'Psychological Debriefing' became popular in the 1980s and 1990s, but has been contraindicated in subsequent guidelines (i.e., National Institute of Clinical Excellence, 2005, 2018; Phoenix Australia, 2021) due to early evidence from randomized control trials demonstrating some negative results on PTSD (Rose et al., 2003).

In a recent systematic review of 80 research papers and 11 clinical practice guidelines on early psychosocial interventions after traumatic incidents, specifically in workplace settings, Billings et al. (2023) found no harm demonstrated by Critical Incident Stress Debriefing (CISD), Critical Incident Stress Management (CISM), Trauma Risk Management (TRiM), Psychological First Aid (PFA), Eye Movement Desensitization and Reprocessing (EMDR), cognitive behaviour therapy (CBT), and group counselling. However, findings did not conclusively demonstrate significant benefits of these interventions, nor did they establish that any particular intervention was better than others. Some negative outcomes were found for generic debriefing, which often conflated psychological support with operational debriefing. Clinical practice guidelines were inconsistent with the current evidence base, and largely out of date with recent research. Nevertheless, the acceptability of early psychosocial interventions was generally high, with workers valuing support offered by their organizations after a workplace trauma. The quality of research and clinical guidance in this field was notably poor, with more high-quality research needed.

Peer support

Social support has consistently been established as a key protective factor against psychological distress in several meta-analyses (Brewin et al., 2000; Ozer et al., 2003). Peer support from colleagues at work can be crucial (Agarwal et al., 2020), with healthcare workers reporting work colleagues to be their first line of support throughout the COVID-19 pandemic (Billings et al., 2021a). Peer support at work can engender camaraderie, solidarity through shared experiences, normalization of distress, and a culture of mutual support (Billings et al., 2021c). However, peer support in the workplace is often not straightforward. Relationships with peers at work can be positive, but also negative, and having access to peer support is not necessarily effective if organizational culture and stigma prevent workers from utilizing it (Evans et al., 2013). Peer support can also be perceived as taxing, with workers worried about burdening their colleagues, especially if going through the same traumatic event, and feeling burdened by colleagues who lean on them consistently (Billings et al., 2021a).

Peer support can undoubtedly be an efficacious (and cost-effective) form of support for staff impacted by trauma and moral injury in the workplace. However, we need to carefully consider how this can be implemented in a way that is psychologically safe, and not overly burdensome for peers. Careful selection and training of dedicated peer supporters, as well as ongoing supervision and support for them, may be critical in developing an effective peer support programme (Creamer et al., 2012). Peer support also requires organizations to provide time and opportunity for colleagues to interact informally, and create a culture in which disclosure and mutual support are encouraged.

Line management and supervision

Training line managers in mental health awareness can be a cost-effective intervention for improving mental health outcomes for staff (Stevenson, 2017). Conversely, not having a supportive line manager has been demonstrated to be a risk factor for mental distress (Greene et al., 2021). Greenberg and Tracy (2020) highlight the importance of 'psychologically savvy' line managers and supervisors, who are attentive to signs of mental distress and confident in having conversations with their staff about wellbeing. It seems, however, we have some way to go to achieve this goal. In a survey of UK line managers, 69 per cent endorsed supporting employee wellbeing as a core skill, but only 13 per cent reported having received mental health training, and 35 per cent of line managers wished for basic training in common mental health problems (*Mental Health at Work 2019: Time to Take Ownership*; bitc.org.uk).

It is arguably easy to place a lot of responsibility at line managers' doors in addition to the numerous other responsibilities which they already shoulder. Line managers are often overwhelmed and receive little extra recognition or reward for supporting staff, and workers often do not want to burden them. As with other previously discussed interventions, it is imperative for line managers to have dedicated time for training and reward for supporting staff mental health, as well as support for their own wellbeing.

Leadership responses

Clear communication and visible leadership have been identified as key factors in supporting healthcare staff throughout the COVID-19 pandemic (Billings et al., 2021c; Greenberg & Tracy, 2020), although frequent changes in policy and practice, and remote working of many managers due to social restrictions, meant this was not always achieved (Billings et al., 2021a). It is also argued that giving thanks is a simple, but potentially powerful, intervention which leaders can do in recognition of the sacrifices made by their workers (Greenberg & Tracy, 2020). This is supported by previous research, where demonstrations of gratitude, alongside social support, were associated with increased satisfaction and lower symptoms of depression in police officers following Hurricane Katrina (McCanlies et al., 2018).

Programmes in compassionate leadership have been developed within the UK NHS, although their implementation arguably requires a shift in leadership paradigms in traditional hierarchical and threat-focused frontline organizations (de Zulueta, 2015). Their potential impact on supporting trauma-exposed and potentially morally injured staff is yet to be explored. Nevertheless, we might conclude that the expression of gratitude, alongside accessible, authentic, compassionate, and consistent leadership, will be imperative in supporting staff exposed to trauma and PMIEs. This is likely to be critical in establishing psychological safety in trauma-informed workplaces, particularly in order to repair betrayal-related moral injury.

Tertiary Prevention

Given that many frontline workers will, by necessity, be exposed to traumatic and PMIEs in the line of their work, we need to acknowledge that some will inevitably be psychologically harmed by this work. We have a duty of care to support staff who have put themselves in harm's way, with ethical, financial, and reputational repercussions for organizations which fail to do so.

Impact monitoring, health surveillance and screen-and-treat programmes

Identifying individuals who have been negatively impacted by trauma or PMIEs at work in a timely way requires a robust system of impact monitoring of staff wellbeing. Not to be confused with pre-employment screening for selection processes, which has been heavily criticized for being invalid and ineffective (Greenberg & Tracy, 2020; Marshall et al., 2020; Opie et al., 2020), health surveillance refers to a scheme of repeated health checks, which are used to identify ill health caused by work (HSE, 2023). Health surveillance is mandatory in health and safety law for many physical health risks associated with certain occupational roles, but still not officially required for most high-psychological-risk roles.

Health surveillance should be provided by appropriately trained occupational health professionals, although whether any form of impact monitoring should be provided directly by an organization or by an independent clinical provider is debated. Statutory oversight by an organization can help identify staff who might not be safe to continue in their current role, but, concomitantly, this risks staff not being open and honest in reviews. Independent provision can provide more confidentiality and therefore promote transparency from staff, but there are challenges in establishing when information should be disclosed to line managers and organizations if an employee's ability to work is significantly impacted.

Tehrani and Hesketh (2019) provided evidence of the benefits of health surveillance in emergency service responders, including routine clinical surveillance and screening after critical incidents, and argue that these can be a cost-effective and not overly burdensome intervention for often stretched occupational health teams in frontline organizations. 'Screen and treat' programmes refer to specific initiatives established after key traumatic events. For example, Brewin et al. (2010) report on a two-year trauma response programme for both civilians and workers affected by the 2005 London bombings. A systematic and coordinated programme of outreach led to the identification of 910 people who were affected, of whom 596 completed an initial trauma screening questionnaire. Those who scored above cut-off were then invited for a detailed clinician-led assessment, with 217 respondents subsequently referred for specialist trauma-focused psychological therapy. The authors note that case findings relied primarily on outreach rather than standard referral pathways such as via general practitioners, and that effect sizes for treatment exceeded those usually seen in randomized controlled trials (RCTs) for PTSD.

Outreach may be a viable method of identifying the mental health needs of populations affected by specific traumatic events, although this has yet to be evaluated in occupational settings. Such assertive outreach requires organizations to be able to refer individuals on for appropriate, evidence-based intervention, in a timely manner. Identifying need without providing access to appropriate treatment would be a significant ethical concern.

Formal psychological support

It is imperative that employees who have been negatively psychologically impacted by trauma or moral injury at work can access evidence-based interventions, provided by appropriately qualified and experienced mental health professionals. It is also crucial that mental health services are adequately resourced, and the mental health professionals themselves also receive appropriate support (Billings et al., 2021b).

Support for families

Finally, but by no means least, we also have a duty of care to the families of frontline workers, who may also be negatively impacted and vicariously traumatized by their family member's work. We have some way to go to make many occupational roles more family-friendly, but this should be a priority for frontline organizations.

CONCLUSIONS

Working in a frontline role incurs risk of exposure to trauma, and potentially to morally injurious events, which can have multifarious impacts on workers. Frontline workers may, for the most part, be resilient, but high rates of distress and mental health problems are indicative of a workforce in crisis and needing better support. The current recruitment and retention crises in many frontline roles tell us that this increased, targeted support must be a priority.

The COVID-19 pandemic has undoubtedly had a devastating impact on the frontline workforce, one from which workers have had little time or opportunity to recover. However, we have yet to begin to understand the impact of other crises occurring during this uncertain and turbulent era, including civil unrest, climate change, and financial downturn.

Individuals, teams, and organizations have a shared responsibility for the mental health and wellbeing of workers, and longstanding barriers to recognizing and accessing mental health support need to be overcome. If tertiary prevention strategies are built on effective primary and secondary prevention strategies, then we can hope that frontline staff might be more aware of the impact of their work on their mental health, and more willing and able to seek support when needed.

REFERENCES

Agarwal, B., Brooks, S. K., & Greenberg, N. (2020). The role of peer support in managing occupational stress: A qualitative study of the sustaining resilience at work intervention. *Workplace Health & Safety, 68*(2), 57–64.

American Psychiatric Association. (2013). *Diagnostic and statistical manual of mental disorders: DSM-5* (5th ed.). American Psychiatric Publishing.

Backholm, K., & Idås, T. (2015). Ethical dilemmas, work-related guilt, and posttraumatic stress reactions of news journalists covering the terror attack in Norway in 2011. Journal of Traumatic Stress, 28(2), 142–148. https://doi.org/10.1002/jts.22001

Bebbington, P. E., Minot, S., Cooper, C., Dennis, M., Meltzer, H., Jenkins, R., & Brugha, T. (2010). Suicidal ideation, self-harm and attempted suicide: Results from the British Psychiatric Morbidity Survey 2000. *European Psychiatry, 25*(7), 427–431.

Bell, V., & Wade, D. (2021). Mental health of clinical staff working in high-risk epidemic and pandemic health emergencies: A rapid review of the evidence and living meta-analysis. *Social Psychiatry and Psychiatric Epidemiology, 56*, 1–11.

Berkhout, S. G., Billings, J., Abou Seif, N., Singleton, D., Stein, H., Hegarty, S., Ondruskova, T., Soulios, E., Bloomfield, M. A. P., Greene, T., Seto, A., Abbey, S., & Sheehan, K. (2022). Shared sources and mechanisms of healthcare worker distress in COVID-19: a comparative qualitative study in Canada and the UK. *European Journal of Psychotraumatology, 13*(2), 2107810.

Berliner, L., & Kolko, D. J. (2016). Trauma informed care: A commentary and critique. *Child Maltreatment, 21*(2), 168–172.

Billings, J., Abou Seif, N., Hegarty, S., Ondruskova, T., Soulios, E., Bloomfield, M., & Greene, T. (2021a). What support do frontline workers want? A qualitative study of health and social care workers' experiences and views of psychosocial support during the COVID-19 pandemic. *PLOS ONE, 16*(9), e0256454.

Billings, J., Biggs, C., Ching, B. C. F., Gkofa, V., Singleton, D., Bloomfield, M., & Greene, T. (2021b). Experiences of mental health professionals supporting front-line health and social care workers during COVID-19: Qualitative study. *BJPsych Open, 7*(2), e70.

Billings, J., Ching, B. C. F., Gkofa, V., Greene, T., & Bloomfield, M. (2021c). Experiences of frontline healthcare workers and their views about support during COVID-19 and previous pandemics: A systematic review and qualitative meta-synthesis. *BMC Health Services Research, 21*, 1–17.

Billings, J., Greene, T., Kember, T., Grey, N., El-Leithy, S., Lee, D., Kennerley, H., Albert, I., Robertson, M., Brewin, C. R., & Bloomfield, M. A. P. (2020). Supporting hospital staff during COVID-19: Early interventions. *Occupational Medicine, 70*(5), 327–329.

Billings, J., Zhan Yuen Wong, N., Nicholls, H., Burton, P., Zosmer, M., Albert, I., Grey, N., El-Leithy, S., Murphy, D., Tehrani, N., Bloomfield., M. A. P., & Greene, T. (2023). Post-incident psychosocial interventions after a traumatic incident in the workplace: A systematic review of current research evidence and clinical guidance. *European Journal of Psychotraumatology, 14*(2), 2281751.

Boscarino, J. A., Figley, C. R., & Adams, R. E. (2004). Compassion fatigue following the September 11 terrorist attacks: A study of secondary trauma among New York City social workers. *International Journal of Emergency Mental Health, 6*(2), 57.

Brewin, C. R., Andrews, B., & Valentine, J. D. (2000). Meta-analysis of risk factors for posttraumatic stress disorder in trauma-exposed adults. *Journal of Consulting and Clinical Psychology, 68*(5), 748.

Brewin, C. R., Fuchkan, N., Huntley, Z., Robertson, M., Thompson, M., Scragg, P., d'Ardenne, P., & Ehlers, A. (2010). Outreach and screening following the 2005 London bombings: Usage and outcomes. *Psychological Medicine, 40*(12), 2049–2057.

Brewin, C. R., Miller, J. K., Soffia, M., Peart, A., & Burchell, B. (2022). Posttraumatic stress disorder and complex posttraumatic stress disorder in UK police officers. *Psychological Medicine, 52*(7), 1287–1295.

Brooks, S., Amlôt, R., Rubin, G. J., & Greenberg, N. (2020). Psychological resilience and post-traumatic growth in disaster-exposed organisations: Overview of the literature. *BMJ Mil Health, 166*(1), 52–56.

Brooks, S. K., Dunn, R., Amlôt, R., Rubin, G. J., & Greenberg, N. (2018). A systematic, thematic review of social and occupational factors associated with psychological outcomes in healthcare employees during an infectious disease outbreak. *Journal of Occupational and Environmental Medicine, 60*(3), 248–257.

Carrieri, D., Briscoe, S., Jackson, M., Mattick, K., Papoutsi, C., Pearson, M., & Wong, G. (2018). "Care Under Pressure": A realist review of interventions to tackle doctors' mental ill-health and its impacts on the clinical workforce and patient care. *BMJ Open, 8*, e021273.

Clarkson, C., Scott, H. R., Hegarty, S., Souliou, E., Bhundia, R., Gnanapragasam, S., Docherty, M. J., Raine, R., Stevelink, S. A., Greenberg, N., Hotopf, M., Wessely, S., Madan, I., Rafferty, A. M., & Lamb, D. (2023). "You get looked at like you're failing": A reflexive thematic analysis of experiences of mental health and wellbeing support for NHS staff. *Journal of Health Psychology, 28*(9), 818–831.

Crane, M. F., Phillips, J. K., & Karin, E. (2015). Trait perfectionism strengthens the negative effects of moral stressors occurring in veterinary practice. *Australian Veterinary Journal*, 93(10), 354–360. https://doi.org/10.1111/avj.12366

Creamer, M. C., Varker, T., Bisson, J., Darte, K., Greenberg, N., Lau, W., Moreton, G., O'Donnell, M., Richardson, D., Ruzek, J., Watson, P., & Forbes, D. (2012). Guidelines for peer support in high-risk organizations: An international consensus study using the Delphi method. *Journal of Traumatic Stress*, 25(2), 134–141.

Culver, L. M., McKinney, B. L., & Paradise, L. V. (2011). Mental health professionals' experiences of vicarious traumatization in post–Hurricane Katrina New Orleans. *Journal of Loss and Trauma*, 16(1), 33–42.

De Zulueta, P. C. (2015). Developing compassionate leadership in health care: An integrative review. *Journal of Healthcare Leadership*, 8, 1–10.

Dutheil, F., Aubert, C., Pereira, B., Dambrun, M., Moustafa, F., Mermillod, M., Baker, J. S., Trousselard, M., Lesage, F.-X., & Navel, V. (2019). Suicide among physicians and health-care workers: A systematic review and meta-analysis. *PLOS ONE*, 14(12), e0226361.

Edmondson, A. (1999). Psychological safety and learning behavior in work teams. *Administrative Science Quarterly*, 44(2), 350–383.

Eurofound. (2022). Working conditions in the time of COVID-19: Implications for the future. European Working Conditions Telephone Survey 2021 series. Publications Office of the European Union.

Evans, R., Pistrang, N., & Billings, J. (2013). Police officers' experiences of supportive and unsupportive social interactions following traumatic incidents. *European Journal of Psychotraumatology*, 4(1), 19696.

Farooq, S., Tunmore, J., Ali, M. W., & Ayub, M. (2021). Suicide, self-harm and suicidal ideation during COVID-19: A systematic review. *Psychiatry Research*, 306, 114228.

Figley, C. R. (1995). *Compassion fatigue: Coping with secondary traumatic stress disorder in those who treat the traumatized*. Brunner/Mazel.

Ghahramani, S., Lankarani, K. B., Yousefi, M., Heydari, K., Shahabi, S., & Azmand, S. (2021). A systematic review and meta-analysis of burnout among healthcare workers during COVID-19. *Frontiers in Psychiatry*, 12, 758849.

Gilleen, J., Santaolalla, A., Valdearenas, L., Salice, C., & Fusté, M. (2021). Impact of the COVID-19 pandemic on the mental health and well-being of UK healthcare workers. *BJPsych Open*, 7(3), e88.

Greenberg, N., & Tracy, D. (2020). What healthcare leaders need to do to protect the psychological well-being of frontline staff in the COVID-19 pandemic. *BMJ Leader*. https://heeoe.hee.nhs.uk/sites/default/files/bmj_leader_on_psychological_support _during_covid_jan_2021.pdf

Greenberg, N., Weston, D., Hall, C., Caulfield, T., Williamson, V., & Fong, K. (2021). Mental health of staff working in intensive care during Covid-19. *Occupational Medicine*, 71(2), 62–67.

Greene, T., Harju-Seppänen, J., Adeniji, M., Steel, C., Grey, N., Brewin, C. R., Bloomfield, M. A., & Billings, J. (2021). Predictors and rates of PTSD, depression and anxiety in UK frontline health and social care workers during COVID-19. *European Journal of Psychotraumatology*, 12(1), 1882781.

Greene, T., Harju-Seppänen, J., Billings, J., Brewin, C.R., Murphy, D., & Bloomfield, M.A.P. (2023). Exposure to potentially morally injurious events in UK health and social care workers during COVID-19: Associations with PTSD and complex PTSD.

Psychological Trauma: Theory, Research, Policy and Practice. Advance online publication. https://doi.org/10.1037/tra0001519

Greinacher, A., Dereaaz-Greeven, C., Hertzog, W., & Nikendei, C. (2019). Secondary traumatisation in first responders: A systematic review. *European Journal of Psychotraumatology, 10*, 1562840.

Harden, L., Jones, N., Whelan, C., Phillips, A., Simms, A., & Greenberg, N. (2021). A systematic review of psychological training or interventions given to UK military personnel prior to deployment. *BMJ Mil Health, 167*(1), 63–69.

Health and Safety Executive. (2023). *Stress and mental health at work.* https://www.hse.gov.uk/stress/index.htm

Huang, G., Chu, H., Chen, R., Liu, D., Banda, K. J., O'Brien, A. P., Jen, H.-J., Chiang, K.-J., Chiou, J.-F., & Chou, K. R. (2022). Prevalence of depression, anxiety, and stress among first responders for medical emergencies during COVID-19 pandemic: A meta-analysis. *Journal of Global Health, 12*, 05028.

Jameton, A. (1984). *Nursing practice: The ethical issues.* Prentice-Hall.

Kessler, R. C., Aguilar-Gaxiola, S., Alonso, J., Benjet, C., Bromet, E. J., Cardoso, G., Degenhardt, L., Girolamo, G. de, Dinolova, R. V., Ferry, F., Florescu, S., Gureje, O., Haro, J. M., Huang, Y., Karam, E. G., Kawakami, N., Lee, S., Lepine, J.-P., Levinson, D., ... Koenen, K. C. (2017). Trauma and PTSD in the WHO world mental health surveys. *European Journal of Psychotraumatology, 8*(sup5), 1353383.

Koenen, K. C., Ratanatharathorn, A., Ng, L., McLaughlin, K. A., Bromet, E. J., Stein, D. J., Karam, E. G., Meron Ruscio, A., Benjet, C., Scott, K., Atwoli, L., Petukhova, M., Lim, C. C. W., Aguilar-Gaxiola, S., Al-Hamzawi, A., Alonso, J., Bunting, B., Ciutan, M., Girolamo, G. de, Degenhardt, L., ... Kessler, R. (2017). Posttraumatic stress disorder in the world mental health surveys. *Psychological Medicine, 47*(13), 2260–2274.

Lambert, S. F., & Lawson, G. (2013). Resilience of professional counsellors following hurricanes Katrina and Rita. *Journal of Counselling & Development, 91*(3), 261–268.

Layne, C. M., Warren, J. S., Watson, P. J., & Shalev, A. Y. (2007). Risk, vulnerability, resistance, and resilience: Toward an integrative conceptualization of posttraumatic adaptation. In M. J. Friedman, T. M. Keane, & P. A. Resnick (Eds.), Handbook of PTSD: Science and practice (pp. 497–520). Guilford.

Lee, W., Lee, Y. R., Yoon, J. H., Lee, H. J., & Kang, M. Y. (2020). Occupational post-traumatic stress disorder: an updated systematic review. *BMC Public Health, 20*(1), 1–12.

Litz, B. T., Stein, N., Delaney, E., Lebowitz, L., Nash, W. P., Silva, C., & Maguen, S. (2009). Moral injury and moral repair in war veterans: A preliminary model and intervention strategy. *Clinical Psychology Review, 29*(8), 695–706.

Macaron, M. M., Segun-Omosehin, O. A., Matar, R. H., Beran, A., Nakanishi, H., Than, C. A., & Abulseoud, O. A. (2023). A systematic review and meta analysis on burnout in physicians during the COVID-19 pandemic: A hidden healthcare crisis. *Frontiers in Psychiatry, 13*, 1071397.

MacDonald, J. B., Hodgins, G., Saliba, A. J., & Metcalf, D. A. (2023). Journalists and depressive symptoms: A systematic literature review. *Trauma, Violence, & Abuse, 24*(1), 86–96.

Mark, K. M., Stevelink, S. A., Choi, J., & Fear, N. T. (2018). Post-traumatic growth in the military: A systematic review. *Occupational and Environmental Medicine, 75*(12), 904–915.

Marshall, R. E., Milligan-Saville, J. S., Steel, Z., Bryant, R. A., Mitchell, P. B., & Harvey, S. B. (2020). A prospective study of pre-employment psychological testing amongst police recruits. *Occupational Medicine, 70*(3), 162–168.

Marvaldi, M., Mallet, J., Dubertret, C., Moro, M. R., & Guessoum, S. B. (2021). Anxiety, depression, trauma-related, and sleep disorders among healthcare workers during the COVID-19 pandemic: A systematic review and meta-analysis. *Neuroscience & Biobehavioral Reviews, 126*, 252–264.

McCanlies, E. C., Gu, J. K., Andrew, M. E., & Violanti, J. M. (2018). The effect of social support, gratitude, resilience and satisfaction with life on depressive symptoms among police officers following Hurricane Katrina. *International Journal of Social Psychiatry, 64*(1), 63–72.

McCann, I., & Pearlman, L. (1990). Vicarious traumatization: A framework for understanding the psychological effects of working with victims. *Journal of Traumatic Stress, 3*(1), 131–149.

McManus, S., Bebbington, P. E., Jenkins, R., & Brugha, T. (2016). *Mental health and wellbeing in England: The Adult Psychiatric Morbidity Survey 2014*. NHS Digital.

Melinte, B. M., Turliuc, M. N., & Măirean, C. (2023). Secondary traumatic stress and vicarious posttraumatic growth in healthcare professionals: A meta-analysis. Clinical Psychology: Science and Practice, 30(3), 337–351.

Mind. (2021). *The consequences of Coronavirus for mental health: Final report.* https://the-consequences-of-coronavirus-for-mental-health-final-report.pdf

Murphy, D., Karatzias, T., Busuttil, W., Greenberg, N., & Shevlin, M. (2021). ICD-11 posttraumatic stress disorder (PTSD) and complex PTSD (CPTSD) in treatment seeking veterans: Risk factors and comorbidity. *Social Psychiatry and Psychiatric Epidemiology, 56*, 1289–1298.

Murphy, D., Palmer, E., Hill, K., Ashwick, R., & Busuttil, W. (2017). Living alongside military PTSD: A qualitative study of female partners' experiences with UK veterans. *Journal of Military, Veteran and Family Health, 3*(1), 52–61.

Murphy, D., Shevlin, M., Pearson, E., Greenberg, N., Wessely, S., Busuttil, W., & Karatzias, T. (2020). A validation study of the International Trauma Questionnaire to assess post-traumatic stress disorder in treatment-seeking veterans. *The British Journal of Psychiatry, 216*(3), 132–137.

Murray, H., & Ehlers, A. (2021). Cognitive therapy for moral injury in post-traumatic stress disorder. *The Cognitive Behaviour Therapist, 14*, e8.

National Institute for Health and Care Excellence. (2018). *Post-traumatic stress disorder (NICE Guideline NG116)*. https://www.nice.org.uk/guidance/ng116

National Institute of Clinical Excellence. (2005). *Clinical Guideline 26: Post-traumatic stress disorder: The management of PTSD in adults and children in primary and secondary care*. http://guidance.nice.org/CG2

Newman, A., Donohue, R., & Eva, N. (2017). Psychological safety: A systematic review of the literature. *Human Resource Management Review, 27*(3), 521–535.

O'Donovan, R., & Burke, J. (2022). Factors associated with post-traumatic growth in healthcare professionals: A systematic review of the literature. *Healthcare, 10*(12), 2524.

O'Donovan, R., & McAuliffe, E. (2020). A systematic review of factors that enable psychological safety in healthcare teams. *International Journal for Quality in Health Care, 32*(4), 240–250.

Office for National Statistics. (2021). *Suicide by occupation, England and Wales, 2011 to 2020 registrations*. https://www.ons.gov.uk/peoplepopulationandcommunity/

birth sdeathsand marriages/ deaths/ adhocs/ 13 674suicide byoccupati onenglanda ndwales2011to2020registrations

Opie, E., Brooks, S., Greenberg, N., & Rubin, G. J. (2020). The usefulness of pre-employment and pre-deployment psychological screening for disaster relief workers: A systematic review. *BMC Psychiatry*, *20*(1), 1–13.

Ozer, E. J., Best, S. R., Lipsey, T. L., & Weiss, D. S. (2003). Predictors of posttraumatic stress disorder and symptoms in adults: A meta-analysis. *Psychological Bulletin*, *129*(1), 52.

Papazoglou, K., & Chopko, B. (2017). The role of moral suffering (moral distress and moral injury) in police compassion fatigue and PTSD: An unexplored topic. Frontiers in Psychology, 8, 1999.

Pappa, S., Ntella, V., Giannakas, T., Giannakoulis, V. G., Papoutsi, E., & Katsaounou, P. (2020). Prevalence of depression, anxiety, and insomnia among healthcare workers during the COVID-19 pandemic: A systematic review and meta-analysis. *Brain, Behavior, and Immunity*, *88*, 901–907.

Petrie, K., Milligan-Saville, J., Gayed, A., Deady, M., Phelps, A., Dell, L., Forbes, D., Bryant, R. A., Calvo, R. A., Glozier, N., & Harvey, S. B. (2018). Prevalence of PTSD and common mental disorders amongst ambulance personnel: A systematic review and meta-analysis. *Social Psychiatry and Psychiatric Epidemiology*, *53*, 897–909.

Phoenix Australia. (2021). *Australian guidelines for the prevention and treatment of acute stress disorder, posttraumatic stress disorder, and complex posttraumatic stress disorder*.

Rabow, M. W., Huang, C. H. S., White-Hammond, G. E., & Tucker, R. O. (2021). Witnesses and victims both: Healthcare workers and grief in the time of COVID-19. *Journal of Pain and Symptom Management*, *62*(3), 647–656.

Rose, S., Bisson, J., & Wessely, S. (2003). A systematic review of single-session psychological interventions ("debriefing") following trauma. *Psychotherapy and Psychosomatics*, *72*(4), 176–184.

Santomauro, D. F., Herrera, A. M. M., Shadid, J., Zheng, P., Ashbaugh, C., Pigott, D. M., Abbafati, C., Adolph, C., Amlag, J. O., Aravkin, A. Y., Bang-Jensen, B. L., Bertolacci, G. J., Bloom, S. S., Castellano, R., Castro, E., Chakrabarti, S., Chattopadhyay, J., Cogen, R. M., Collins, J. K., ... Ferrari, A. J. (2021). Global prevalence and burden of depressive and anxiety disorders in 204 countries and territories in 2020 due to the COVID-19 pandemic. *The Lancet*, *398*(10312), 1700–1712.

Scott, H. R., Stevelink, S. A., Gafoor, R., Lamb, D., Carr, E., Bakolis, I., Bhundia, R., Docherty, M. J., Dorrington, S., Gnanapragasam, S., Hegarty, S., Hotopf, M., Madan, I., McManus, S., Moran, P., Souliou, E., Raine, R., Razavi, R., Weston, D., Greenberg, N., & Wessely, S. (2023). Prevalence of post-traumatic stress disorder and common mental disorders in health-care workers in England during the COVID-19 pandemic: A two-phase cross-sectional study. *The Lancet Psychiatry*, *10*(1), 40–49.

Shay, J. (1994). *Achilles in Vietnam: Combat trauma and the undoing of character.* Atheneum.

Sodeke-Gregson, E. A., Holttum, S., & Billings, J. (2013). Compassion satisfaction, burnout, and secondary traumatic stress in UK therapists who work with adult trauma clients. *European Journal of Psychotraumatology*, *4*(1), 21869.

Stamm, B. H. (Ed.). (1995). *Secondary traumatic stress: Self-care issues for clinicians, researchers, and educators.* Sidran Press.

Stamm, B. H. (2005). *The Pro-QOL manual.* Sidran Press.

Steel, C., Tehrani, N., Lewis, G., & Billings, J. (2021). Risk factors for complex posttraumatic stress disorder in UK police. *Occupational Medicine*, *71*(8), 351–357.

Stevenson, D. (2017). *Thriving at work: The Stevenson/Farmer review of mental health and employers*. Department for Work and Pensions and Department of Health.

Sutton, L., Rowe, S., Hammerton, G., & Billings, J. (2022). The contribution of organisational factors to vicarious trauma in mental health professionals: A systematic review and narrative synthesis. *European Journal of Psychotraumatology*, *13*(1), 2022278.

Syed, S., Ashwick, R., Schlosser, M., Jones, R., Rowe, S., & Billings, J. (2020). Global prevalence and risk factors for mental health problems in police personnel: A systematic review and meta-analysis. *Occupational and Environmental Medicine*, *77*(11), 737–747.

Tedeschi, R. G., & Calhoun, L. G. (1996). The Posttraumatic Growth Inventory: Measuring the positive legacy of trauma. *Journal of Traumatic Stress*, *9*, 455–471.

Tedeschi, R. G., & Calhoun, L. G. (2004). Posttraumatic growth: Conceptual foundations and empirical evidence. *Psychological Inquiry*, *15*(1), 1–18.

Tehrani, N., & Hesketh, I. (2019). The role of psychological screening for emergency service responders. *International Journal of Emergency Services*, *8*(1), 4–19.

Tekin, S., Glover, N., Greene, T., Lamb, D., Murphy, D., & Billings, J. (2022). Experiences and views of frontline healthcare workers' family members in the UK during the COVID-19 pandemic: A qualitative study. *European Journal of Psychotraumatology*, *13*(1), 2057166.

Terr, L.C. (1991). Childhood trauma: An outline and overview. *The American Journal of Psychiatry*, *148*(1), 10–20.

Tracy, D. K., Tarn, M., Eldridge, R., Cooke, J., Calder, J. D., & Greenberg, N. (2020). What should be done to support the mental health of healthcare staff treating COVID-19 patients? *The British Journal of Psychiatry*, *217*(4), 537–539.

Wang, Y. R., Ford, M. T., Credé, M., Harms, P. D., & Lester, P. B. (2022). A meta-analysis on the crossover of workplace traumatic stress symptoms between partners. *Journal of Applied Psychology*, *108*(7), 1157–1189.

Wild, J., Greenberg, N., Moulds, M. L., Sharp, M. L., Fear, N., Harvey, S., Wessely, S., & Bryant, R. A. (2020). Pre-incident training to build resilience in first responders: Recommendations on what to and what not to do. *Psychiatry*, *83*(2), 128–142.

Wild, J., McKinnon, A., Wilkins, A., & Browne, H. (2022). Post-traumatic stress disorder and major depression among frontline healthcare staff working during the COVID-19 pandemic. *British Journal of Clinical Psychology*, *61*(3), 859–866.

Williamson, V., Lamb, D., Hotopf, M., Raine, R., Stevelink, S., Wessely, S., Docherty, M., Madan, I., Murphy, D., & Greenberg, N. (2023a). Moral injury and psychological wellbeing in UK healthcare staff. *Journal of Mental Health*, *32*(5), 890–898.

Williamson, V., Murphy, D., Aldridge, V., Bonson, A., Seforti, D., & Greenberg, N. (2022a). Development of an intervention for moral injury-related mental health difficulties in UK military veterans: A feasibility pilot study protocol. *European Journal of Psychotraumatology*, *13*(2), 2138059.

Williamson, V., Murphy, D., & Greenberg, N. (2022b). Experiences and impact of moral injury in UK veterinary professional wellbeing. *European Journal of Psychotraumatology*, *13*(1), 2051351.

Williamson, V., Murphy, D., & Greenberg, N. (2023b). Veterinary professionals' experiences of moral injury: A qualitative study. *Veterinary Record*, *192*(2), e2181.

Williamson, V., Murphy, D., Stevelink, S. A., Jones, E., Allen, S., & Greenberg, N. (2023c). Family and occupational functioning following military trauma exposure and moral injury. *BMJ Mil Health, 169*(3), 205–211.

Williamson, V., Stevelink, S. A., & Greenberg, N. (2018). Occupational moral injury and mental health: Systematic review and meta-analysis. *The British Journal of Psychiatry, 212*(6), 339–346.

World Health Organization. (2018). *International classification of diseases for mortality and morbidity statistics* (11th revision).

World Health Organization. (2022). *Mental health and COVID-19: Early evidence of the pandemic's impact – Scientific brief, 2 March 2022* (No. WHO/2019-nCoV/ Sci_Brief/Mental_health/2022.1).

4. Work and non-work boundary management including remote and hybrid working

Xi Wen (Carys) Chan and Gail Kinman

INTRODUCTION

When attempting to manage multiple roles and their associated demands more effectively, workers create, maintain, and adapt role boundaries in various ways. They may use *temporal* strategies (e.g., demarcating the working day via 'fixed' working hours), *spatial* strategies (e.g., separating the office from the home environment), and *psychological* strategies (e.g., avoiding thinking about work after office hours; Cho, 2020). As the COVID-19 pandemic unfolded, the sweeping transition to remote working for many employees (Caringal-Go et al., 2022) meant that these boundaries often became blurred, or eroded entirely (Chan et al., 2023b). There are some advantages to flexible temporal, spatial, and psychological boundaries, such as increased autonomy, and the ability to switch between work and non-work responsibilities promptly (Adekoya et al., 2022). Nonetheless, there is evidence that the move to full-time remote working, with its greater reliance on information and communication technology (ICT; Chandra et al., 2020), has eroded boundaries between roles, and increased the potential for emotional, psychological, cognitive, and physical strain (Pang, 2021). The blurred or eroded boundaries resulting from homeworking have also heightened pressure on many workers, especially in regard to the effective management of their work and non-work demands and commitments (Chan et al., 2023b). For many, boundary management strategies that may have been previously effective needed to be adjusted to accommodate the new working styles, requiring additional effort (Haun et al., 2022; Shirmohammadi et al., 2023).

Against the backdrop of blurred boundaries during the pandemic, research findings suggested that *segmentation preference* (i.e., an individual's preference to keep work and home domains separate through the creation and maintenance of work–home boundaries; Kreiner, 2006) enhanced the positive effects of boundary management tactics (e.g., temporal, spatial, psychological) on detachment and control, enabling homeworkers to be productive and remain well over time (Haun et al., 2022). Nonetheless, higher segmentation preferences are not universally beneficial, as maintaining more rigid boundaries between work and non-work domains can restrict the potential for work–life enrichment and facilitation (Astakhova et al., 2023; Kossek & Lautsch, 2012; McNall et al., 2015). A study of social workers conducted by Chan et al. (2023a), for example, found that many workers struggled to detach themselves psychologically and emotionally from work, with their unmet expectations of work–home segmentation becoming an *additional* source of stress. The other end of the continuum to segmentation is *integration preference*, which reflects the extent to which an individual favours merging their work and non-work (i.e., home) roles (Kreiner, 2006), with higher integration preferences typically resulting in more flexible and permeable boundaries (Astakhova et al., 2023). The literature is consistent in showing that, while integration preference can enhance workers' job outcomes (e.g., work performance, work goal attainment), it tends to impair employee wellbeing, often leading to emotional exhaustion and work–life conflict, as workers frequently manage their work-related issues within their non-work time (Adkins & Premeaux, 2014; Xie et al., 2018).

As COVID-19 lockdowns lifted across the world, many workers moved from full-time remote working to hybrid working, where working time is divided between the home and the office (Bloom et al., 2022). While a hybrid model is favoured by many employees (Bloom, 2021), there is considerable variation in the ability to work from home. For example, statistics from the United Kingdom show that working from home is most common among employees who: (1) are in the age group 35–54; (2) are self-employed or working in the private sector; (3) work in the information and communication, professional, technical, and administrative industries; (4) are managers and supervisors; and (5) have higher qualifications (Mutebi & Hobbs, 2022). While hybrid working arrangements are undoubtedly popular, little is yet known about their implications for boundary management, with the research that is available not being adequately drawn upon to inform organizational policies and practices (Kossek et al., 2022). Kossek and colleagues (2022) argued that hybrid working may harm workers if they have little choice and flexibility over their working patterns. This reflects previous research findings (e.g., Bond & Flaxman, 2006; Grönlund, 2007), where a combination of job control, and job or psychological flexibility, can help workers thrive in different life domains, even in the face of high job demands. Yet, flexibility policies across organizations, and their availability, implementation, use, and impact, have not been examined in detail (Kossek et al., 2022). Given these theoretical and empirical gaps, this chapter reviews the research conducted on work and non-work boundary management to date, and proposes future areas of research to advance scholarship, and provide guidance to support best practice in the post-pandemic workplace.

WORK AND NON-WORK BOUNDARY MANAGEMENT: POPULAR CONCEPTUALIZATIONS AND OPERATIONALIZATIONS OF BOUNDARY MANAGEMENT

Work and non-work boundary management refers to the approach an individual uses to demarcate boundaries and regulate their attendance to work and non-work roles (Kossek & Lautsch, 2012). The two predominant boundary management styles, segmentation and integration preferences, were discussed above; however, Kossek and Lautsch (2012) proposed a novel approach – *alternating* boundary management preference – reflecting a tendency for individuals to favor clear periods of defined segmentation and defined integration. The strength of the boundaries between roles is determined by variations in their flexibility and permeability (Bulger et al., 2007). *Boundary flexibility* refers to the extent to which individuals are able and willing to modify the temporal and physical restrictions of their work or home environment, while *boundary permeability* describes the extent to which individuals experience physical or psychological transitions (or interruptions) between their work and home roles (Matthews et al., 2010). For example, workers who can attend to their family or personal needs during working hours have high temporal boundary flexibility-ability, but those who prefer to work a standard 9-to-5 schedule have low temporal boundary flexibility-willingness. Also, workers who have had a difficult day at work may experience frequent psychological interruptions (via rumination) at home after office hours, thereby increasing the permeability of their work and non-work boundaries. People who regularly encounter emotional and/or dangerous work are particularly vulnerable to rumination after the working day, which can threaten their recovery processes and wellbeing (Kinman & Clements, 2022).

Individuals may be further classified based on their boundary control, role identity centrality, and cross-role interruption behaviors (Allen et al., 2014). *Boundary control* refers to an individual's perceived ability to manage the boundaries between their work and personal life (Kossek & Lautsch, 2012), while *role identity centrality* reflects the relative value the individual places on his or her different identities (Allen et al., 2014). For example, some people are *family-centric* (placing greater importance on their family role or tasks), *career-centric* (placing greater importance on their career role), or *work-centric* (prioritizing their work role or tasks over other roles). It is acknowledged, however, that these preferences are rarely stable, and change over time according to role salience (Kalliath & Brough, 2008). Also, while a high level of involvement and commitment to the work role can enhance job performance and satisfaction, it can also threaten work–life balance and wellbeing (Kinman, 2016; Kinman & Jones, 2008).

Cross-role interruption behaviors refer to the degree to which individuals allow interruptions from one role to the other (Kossek & Lautsch, 2012). Examples are attending to non-work matters (e.g., doing laundry, caring for children, paying bills) during work hours while working remotely; or attending to work issues (e.g., dealing with email, problem-solving) during formal non-work time. Such interruptions may not necessarily be preferred or welcomed and can obviously be a source of distraction, but they may be allowed by the individual. *Symmetrical interruptions* occur when individuals allow work to disturb their non-working life, and non-work to interrupt their working life equally, while *asymmetrical interruptions* occur when one domain (e.g., work) tends to interrupt the other (e.g., family) more often (Gardner et al., 2021).

Popular Theories Underpinning Work and Non-Work Boundary Management

Several theories have informed research on work and non-work boundary management, with boundary theory (Zerubavel, 1991, 1996) and border theory (Clark, 2000) being particularly prominent. *Boundary theory* is a general cognitive theory of social classification that focuses on outcomes such as the meanings individuals assign to work and home (Nippert-Eng, 1996), and the ease and frequency of transitioning between different roles (Ashforth et al., 2000). As applied to the interface between work and personal life, boundary theory concerns the cognitive, physical, and/or behavioral boundaries existing between individuals' work and non-work roles that make the two domains distinct from one another (Ashforth et al., 2000; Nippert-Eng, 1996). Boundaries range from *thick* (i.e., keeping work and non-work separate, or *segmentation*) to *thin* (i.e., blending work and non-work, or *integration*; Allen et al., 2014).

Border theory is specific to the work–home interface and suggests that people cross temporal, spatial, and psychological borders daily, as they move between their work and home (Clark, 2000). For border theory, the outcome of interest is work–life balance, which Clark (2000, p. 751) defined as the 'satisfaction and good functioning at work and at home, with a minimum of role conflict'. In light of evolving gender roles, family systems, life preferences, and personal circumstances, work–life scholars have more recently gone beyond work and traditional domestic or family responsibilities to encompass other life domains. For example, Kalliath and Brough (2008) defined work–life balance as 'the individual perception that work and non-work activities are compatible and promote growth in accordance with an individual's current life priorities' (p. 326), providing a more individualized yet comprehensive approach to assessing work–life balance.

According to border theory, domain members (e.g., co-workers or family members), referred to as *border keepers*, also play a role in boundary management. Supervisors act as border keepers in the work domain, spouses act as border keepers in the home domain, and extended family or friends act as border keepers in the community or social domain. For example, some workplaces may not permit personal calls at work, thus preventing personal life from intruding into the work domain. Similarly, the focal employee's spouse may require that they 'switch off' from work after office hours and dedicate their non-work time to family. Border keepers are involved in the negotiation of what constitutes a domain, and where the borders between these domains occur (Clark, 2000). They may have their own views about what constitutes work and non-work, and offer differing degrees of flexibility that impact the ease with which individuals can cross borders to deal with competing work and non-work demands.

Researchers have used various theoretical frameworks to examine the management of boundaries between work and non-work, but resource-based theories are widely used. The most common resource-based theory is the Conservation of Resources (COR) theory (Hobfoll, 1989). COR theory suggests that individuals have limited resources (e.g., time, energy, focus, money, skills, social support), and managing work and non-work boundaries effectively can help to conserve these resources. For example, segmenting work and home is a particularly useful resource for helping social workers to mentally 'switch off' from work concerns and recover their energies after office hours, enhancing their job performance and supporting their wellbeing (Kalliath et al., 2022). Another resource-based theory that is often used by scholars when examining work and non-work boundary management is the job demands-resources (JD-R) model (Demerouti et al., 2001). This suggests that job demands (e.g., workload, deadlines) and job resources (e.g., job autonomy, co-worker support) impact an individual's ability to manage work and non-work boundaries. Drawing on the JD-R model, studies (e.g., Kubicek & Tement, 2016) have conceptualized boundary management preferences, such as work–home segmentation, as a job resource (i.e., an organizational practice) or a personal resource (i.e., an individual boundary management strategy) that offers protection against demanding work situations, specifically by buffering the negative effects of job demands on wellbeing when job demands are high (Bakker et al., 2007).

The JD-R model has also been extended to include other personal resources such as psychological capital, conscientiousness, and emotion regulation (Grover et al., 2018; Wu et al., 2019), with some evidence that these can attenuate the negative impact of negative workplace experiences, such as burnout, on work–life balance. Some researchers (e.g., Grawitch et al., 2010) have also drawn on these resource-based theories to develop frameworks (e.g., personal resource allocation, or PRA) that inform individual- and organizational-level intervention strategies. For example, at the individual level, the PRA framework accounts for when, where, and how individuals allocate their resources to best fit their personal needs. At the organizational level, the PRA framework guides the development of interventions focused on increasing employees' pool of available resources, moderating the demands that they face and providing support for effective resource allocation. Clearly, frameworks such as the PRA have considerable potential for informing and developing work–life interventions and strategies.

Another theory that has helped to inform boundary management research is the spillover-crossover model (Bakker & Demerouti, 2013), which recognizes the potential for employees' experiences at work (e.g., high work demands, or a poor relationship with a line manager) to 'spill over' to the home environment (e.g., in the form of negative strain). This not only influences their own wellbeing and behaviors at home, but also 'crosses over' to impair their family members' wellbeing (e.g., via negative emotions and lack of recovery; Brough & Westman, 2018). Several mechanisms have been proposed to explain these crossover effects, such as sympathy or empathy between family members, and the discussion of work-related problems (Crossfield et al., 2005). There is also evidence that an individual's positive work-related mood and resources can be beneficial for their family members (Lawson et al., 2014; Li et al., 2021). Moreover, a study of dual-earner couples conducted during the pandemic found evidence that homeworking can enhance these employees' family task completion, but can lead to withdrawal from work for both spouses (Hu et al., 2022). Both positive and negative crossover effects have also been found from supervisors and teams to wellbeing and work–life outcomes at the individual level (Bakker et al., 2008; Chan et al., 2021b; Van Emmerik & Peeters, 2009).

Implications of Work and Non-Work Boundary Management

A significant body of research has established that the way individuals manage their work and non-work boundaries has important implications for their work and personal lives, including their wellbeing. The permeability of work and non-work boundaries makes boundary management a key skill that enables individuals to balance their work and non-work lives effectively (Ollier-Malaterre et al., 2019). Work and non-work boundary management styles and preferences are also consequential because they are strongly linked to work outcomes (e.g., job satisfaction, organizational commitment, and job performance), work–family outcomes (e.g., work–family conflict and work–life balance) and non-work outcomes (e.g., family satisfaction, life satisfaction, and family engagement; Allen et al., 2014; Carlson et al., 2016; Kalliath et al., 2022).

Further, individuals who practise work–home segmentation (i.e., by detaching themselves from work psychologically) report higher levels of psychological wellbeing, positive affect, sleep quality, and job performance than those who remain more psychologically attached to work after office hours (Sonnentag, 2012). Nonetheless, while some separation between domains seems crucial for recovery, whether work and personal life are integrated or separated seems less important than the 'fit' between an individual's current and ideal circumstances and values, and the extent to which they feel in control over their boundary management (Kossek & Lautsch, 2008). The ability to manage role boundaries according to personal needs and preferences is likely to be particularly important for remote workers, to help protect their wellbeing and optimize their productivity.

Researchers have identified several factors that can influence an individual's ability to manage their work and non-work boundaries effectively, including organizational policies (see Chan & Tay, 2022; Mueller & Kempen, 2022), organizational climate and culture (see Fenner & Renn, 2010; Kossek & Lautsch, 2012; Nsair & Piszczek, 2021), supervisor boundary management behavior (see Koch & Binnewies, 2015; McCartney et al., 2023), gender (see Choroszewicz & Kay, 2020; Nsair & Piszczek, 2021; Russo et al., 2018), personality (see Gardner et al., 2021), coping strategy (see McCartney et al., 2023), and support (see Nsair & Piszczek, 2021). Insight into these issues can help inform individual- and organizational-level interventions to minimize work–life conflict and improve balance.

Increasingly, studies are also contextualizing work and non-work boundary management to specific national cultures. For example, Choroszewicz and Kay (2020) explored the use of mobile technologies and work–family boundary management styles among male lawyers in Quebec (French Canada) and in Finland, finding different segmentation and integration preferences. All the lawyers were married or cohabiting with their partners, but not all of them were fathers. The high gender egalitarianism in Nordic countries tends to promote involved fatherhood, and a greater separation of work and family lives, such that only a few male lawyers in the Finnish sample reported working from home as a substitute for office hours, rather than as an extension of their office-based work. On the other hand, while flexible work arrangements are popular in Finnish law firms, they are still relatively new in Canada. Hence, the male lawyers in the Canadian sample were more skeptical about their ability to manage their work and non-work boundaries while teleworking, and those who were parents were less likely to be involved in childcare right from their children's birth. The study also found that senior lawyers who lived in a more 'traditional' family model were more likely to engage in integrating behaviors such as using technology to work outside office hours. Choroszewicz and Kay (2020) recognized that such behavior may be perceived by these lawyers as necessary for career advancement, since 'switching off' from work or being family-focused may lead to a 'flexibility penalty' for men, as they may be seen as less ambitious and less worthy of promotion (Brough et al., 2021; McDowall & Kinman, 2020). There is evidence, however, that requests for flexible working tend to be less stigmatized, and attract fewer career penalties, in female-dominated industries (Krstic & Hideg, 2019).

Taken together, empirical research conducted on work and non-work boundary management demonstrates that *effective* work and non-work boundary management does not merely require individual effort, but action at multiple levels encompassing national legislation, organizational cultures and policies, managerial interventions, and co-worker or team support structures; as well as how aspects of the non-working environment, such as family support, can help individuals to function effectively in different life domains. It should also be acknowledged that individuals' preferences for managing work and non-work boundary management, and the strategies that they find effective, are often vulnerable to organizational pressures and managerial behavior. This can encourage individuals to become more work-centric, thereby enforcing work boundaries while relaxing non-work boundaries, and increasing the potential for work-to-home interference and decreased wellbeing. Workplace cultures that expect and reward long working hours and a high level of commitment are also major risk factors for work–life balance, increasing the potential for time- and strain-based conflict, and reducing opportunities for detachment (Kinman, 2024).

Despite these established relationships, one of the major oversights in the extant literature on work and non-work boundary management is the lack of rigorous multi-level research that examines the combined individual, team/ organizational, and societal/governmental factors that influence work and non-work boundary management. Such insights are crucial to inform interventions that maximize the benefits of remote/hybrid working for individuals and organizations in the post-pandemic workplace. Most studies continue to examine dyadic relationships (e.g., supervisor–subordinate, employee–spouse; see McCartney et al., 2023; Shirmohammadi et al., 2023) – specifically, how the focal employee's work and non-work boundary management preferences and behavior are influenced by their supervisor's work and non-work boundary management preferences and behavior; or how the focal employee's work and non-work boundary management preferences and behavior influence their spouse's wellbeing, attitudes and behavior. Moreover, most studies continue to be cross-sectional, and the workers' cognitive appraisals of boundary management and its associated outcomes are typically examined at the individual level, with the associated risk of sampling bias, and inability to establish causality and direction of the relationships found.

In a limited number of studies (see Hoobler & Brass, 2006; Hoobler & Hu, 2013; Kiewitz et al., 2012; Lagios et al., 2023), work–life scholars have examined the 'trickle-down' effects of supervisors' work and non-work preferences, attitudes, and behavior on focal employees' work and non-work preferences, attitudes, and behavior, and, subsequently, the effects on focal employees' spouses' work and non-work preferences, attitudes, and behavior (i.e., supervisor/co-worker $\tilde{a}$ employee $\tilde{a}$ spouse/family member), or vice versa (i.e., spouse/family member $\tilde{a}$ employee $\tilde{a}$ supervisor/co-worker), as well as other triadic combinations (e.g., father × mother × child/adolescent) (Feldman et al., 2001; Li et al., 2023; Shirmohammadi et al., 2023). Most of these studies have drawn upon displaced aggression (Marcus-Newhall et al., 2000; Tedeschi & Norman, 1985) and work–family conflict theory (Greenhaus & Beutell, 1985) to examine the negative effects of leaders' abusive supervision on their employees, and the subsequent impact on employees' negative conflict with their family members, against the contextual backdrop of work–home boundaries.

Only one of these studies (i.e., Shirmohammadi et al., 2023) has used family systems theory to examine how family units as a collective (i.e., dual-income households with school-age children) adopted and applied boundaries to ensure the entire family continued to function during the pandemic. Specifically, the authors identified four strategies to define boundaries within the collective: repurposing the home space, revisiting family members' responsibilities, aligning family members' schedules, and distributing technology access and use. The authors also identified five strategies to apply boundaries to accommodate the collective: designating an informal boundary governor, maintaining live boundary agreements, increasing family communication, incentivizing/ punishing boundary respect/violation, and outsourcing (Shirmohammadi et al., 2023). These findings assist in shaping more relevant and acceptable boundary management strategies at the holistic level, and minimize the risk of conflict between role domains.

Theoretical Gaps and Future Areas of Research

Although research on work and non-work boundary management has advanced significantly over the past three decades, scholars have highlighted priorities for future research using quantitative, qualitative, or mixed methods. Insight into these issues is particularly important to inform organizational- and individual-level strategies to enhance wellbeing and functioning among hybrid/remote workers in what is likely to remain an uncertain climate.

First, despite the emerging studies that have examined supervisor–subordinate dyads in the extant work–life literature, as well as research that focuses on work and non-work boundary management, there remains a noticeable gap between leadership research and work–life balance research (Kossek et al., 2023). For example, it is expected that empathetic leadership (i.e., leadership characterized by an understanding of another's situation and the willingness to care about their situation) would influence the work and non-work boundary management dynamics between leaders and employees, which in turn is expected to affect how employees interact with their family members. However, Kossek et al. (2023) noted that both leadership and work–life scholars have not linked leadership styles to work–life outcomes explicitly. They call upon work–life scholars to broaden their focus to encompass leadership and the work domain, and leadership scholars to examine work–life supportive leadership (where leaders provide active, evidence-informed support to help employees' meet their individual needs and preferences for managing work, family and personal life) and establish its influence on subordinates' engagement, satisfaction, job performance, and retention, as well as on non-work outcomes such as wellbeing and life satisfaction.

Further, the strong growth in research integrating the use of ICTs and work and non-work boundary management in the past decade (see Park & Jex, 2011; Yang et al., 2019) was accelerated by the shift en masse to remote/hybrid working during the COVID-19 pandemic (see Sun et al., 2023). While technology facilitates flexible working – which has the potential to enhance boundary management, wellbeing, and productivity – it can be a demand as well as a resource, eroding boundaries between work and personal life and *increasing* the risk of conflict. Insight is therefore needed into the organizational- and individual-level strategies that can help reduce the risks, and maximize the benefits of ICT use. Moreover, an important question that has largely been overlooked is the inclusion of the 'softer' aspect of communication dynamics, as opposed to the 'hardware' (that is, ICTs). Softer aspects include, for example, informal work–life conversations a leader initiates with their subordinates (e.g., asking employees about their families, or their personal life; Chan et al., 2023b), or how work-related news is communicated during work or non-work hours, with or without empathy (Kossek et al., 2022). This opens up new avenues of qualitative inquiry for research on work and non-work boundary management, and the possibility of informing targeted managerial interventions (e.g., through more empathetic or inclusive communication) that could assist managers in helping their employees manage boundaries between work and non-work more effectively.

The extant work–life literature has also largely overlooked how the macro-level cultural values and institutional context influence work and non-work boundary management issues (Shang et al., 2021). For example, in the Confucian Chinese culture, valuing work is considered a familial responsibility, so valuing work *and* life (such as by enforcing strict work and non-work boundaries) may not come naturally to employees, particularly managers who are expected to lead by example. Another macro-level factor that should be considered is the institutional context, particularly how institutional policies are enacted to influence work and non-work boundary management conditions and practices. Insight is also needed into how the characteristics of some jobs can destabilize work–life balance and recovery. For example, the emotional demands experienced by workers in sectors such as health and social care, and the emergency and security services, can increase the risk of affective rumination, and impair their wellbeing, sleep, and recovery (Chan et al., 2021a; Kinman & Clements, 2022). Finally, as mentioned above, research from a multi-level perspective, from public policy to individual boundary management preferences and practices, is needed to identify the factors that promote positive and sustainable work, non-work, and wellbeing outcomes.

COVID-19 AND WORK AND NON-WORK BOUNDARY MANAGEMENT RESEARCH

Hybrid/Remote Working

The results of a survey conducted by Adaptavist (2022) involving 3,439 workers across the United States, United Kingdom, Canada, and Australia indicated that nearly two-thirds of respondents preferred to choose where they work, with 59 per cent preferring either a hybrid or full-time remote working arrangement. However, only 44 per cent of those surveyed worked for an employer that allowed hybrid or remote work, and 25 per cent of this group had been obliged to return to the office on a full-time basis after restrictions were lifted (Adaptavist, 2022). Providing opportunities for flexible, hybrid working is increasingly considered crucial for retaining valued employees and avoiding talent loss (CIPD, 2022). More insights are therefore required into the implications of hybrid working for work–life balance and wellbeing, as well as outcomes such as retention.

Most studies (e.g., Appel-Meulenbroek et al., 2022; Bloom et al., 2022) find that hybrid working is highly valued by employees, with benefits for job satisfaction. Nonetheless, Bloom and colleagues (2022) also found that hybrid working had negative as well as positive implications for work–life balance, leading to a pattern of reduced working hours on work-from-home days, and longer working hours on office days and weekends; as well as increased messaging and video calls, even if employees were in the office. There was also found to be a marked contrast between the uptake of hybrid working arrangements between managers, who were less likely to work from home on eligible days, and employees, who were more likely to work from home on eligible days. More research is needed to identify why managers may be reluctant to adopt opportunities for hybrid working, the individual and contextual factors that underpin such attitudes, and their implications for employees' choice of working patterns and outcomes in the work and personal domains.

Appel-Meulenbroek and colleagues (2022) observed that research on hybrid working typically focuses on the positive aspects only, with many studies highlighting *boundary flexing* (i.e., the ability to navigate and manage the interplay between work and non-work responsibilities and commitments) as a major benefit for employees' functioning and wellbeing, while overlooking key issues such as variation in the availability and quality of a home-based or office workspace, and the impact of caring responsibilities and interruptions in the home domain. Greater insight is also needed into how the type of tasks planned for the day (e.g., deep work requiring focus and concentration, or stakeholder engagement involving communication via meetings), and the working patterns of co-workers, influence individual hybrid working preferences, uptake, and effectiveness.

In the post-pandemic environment, Kossek and Kelliher (2023) suggested that hybrid working is not necessarily flexible, and may be implemented in ways that increase inequality, such as where employees are required to come into the office on certain days and work from home on other days, which may not be congruent with their work and non-work boundary management needs and preferences. Female workers are more likely to use flexibility practices (e.g., engaging in boundary flexing practices to care for children; Brough et al., 2021), whereas many male workers still face career penalties when working flexibly, as was discussed above. Most organizations continue to reward workers who work more frequently in the office, or those who are more likely to integrate work into personal life than vice versa, thereby increasing the risk of negative work-to-non-work conflict and impairing family performance and wellbeing (cf. Chan et al., 2021b). To minimize such disparities, many work–life scholars (e.g., Chan et al., 2023b; Kossek & Kelliher, 2023) have highlighted the potential benefits of enabling workers – as a collective – to collaborate with their employers to customize their work schedule, workplace, workload, work and non-work boundaries, during- and after-hours work connectivity, and employment arrangements. Clearly, however, this would involve a major shift in mindsets and cultural norms for organizations and employees, and the provision of equitable, evidence-informed support structures.

Boundary Management During Turbulent Times

To minimize work–life conflict, scholars typically recommend that homeworkers use boundaries to segment domains. During turbulent times such as the COVID-19 pandemic (or in other emergency situations such as family crises), boundaries for many workers can become increasingly blurred as individuals react to multi-faceted situational demands (Chan et al., 2023b; Sun et al., 2023). Due to the widespread uncertainty and job insecurity felt during the pandemic, and the perceived need to respond rapidly to work issues, many employees prioritized work over family, regardless of any individual preference they had for strict work–home boundaries (Allen et al., 2021; Vaziri et al., 2020). Moreover, boundary violations commonly occurred from home to work, such as meetings interrupted by children or pets (causing family-to-work conflict), as physical boundaries between the domains were often non-existent (Carvalho et al., 2021).

Other research also found that work–home integration significantly increased work–family conflict among working parents during the pandemic (Schieman et al., 2021). There is evidence that minority employees experienced anxiety over revealing their non-work lives to colleagues during video calls when working from home, as the erosion of physical and spatial boundaries was believed to undermine their ability to exercise agency and control over how they presented their identities (Roberts & McCluney, 2020). The homeworking challenges experienced by people working in sensitive and often disturbing areas (such as child-protection police officers) have been identified, as they may no longer see their home as a place of refuge, comfort, and relaxation; and their family members may be at increased risk of secondary trauma (Tehrani et al., 2020). Research conducted during the pandemic is consistent with the extant literature on work and non-work boundary management during times of crisis, in that: (1) the key challenges faced by many employees when managing the work and non-work domains are caused by blurred boundaries or role conflict, (2) social support (organizational, supervisor, co-worker, and family) in both life domains contributes to effective boundary management, and (3) the variance in employee boundary management preferences suggests there is no 'one size fits all' solution, so organizational leaders and managers are encouraged to respect and embrace individual preferences wherever possible (Kossek et al., 2021).

At the individual level, drawing on recent research examining how frontline workers navigate their work and non-work boundaries amidst intense workloads, client emergencies, and the COVID-19 pandemic, this research suggests that creating 'safe third spaces', or buffer zones, can facilitate virtual commuting (i.e., routines that separate work time and family/leisure time), and can help workers transition between roles (Chan et al., 2021a). For homeworkers in particular, these seemingly banal activities (e.g., going for a walk, changing clothes, or listening to music or podcasts) create a ritual to facilitate transitions between their work and non-work roles, enhancing detachment and recovery and reducing anxiety, stress, and frustration (Kossek, 2016).

It is also important to provide line managers with guidance about how best to support the wellbeing of frontline workers remotely, helping them reduce rumination and encourage detachment (Kinman, 2021). Interestingly, since the onset of the COVID-19 pandemic, virtual communication tools such as Microsoft Viva Insights (embedded within Microsoft Teams) now provide wellbeing features such as the 'virtual commute'. Features include 'Begin your commute' (i.e., signaling the start of a virtual commute), 'Meetings' (i.e., reviewing tomorrow's events), 'Tasks' (i.e., reviewing open tasks), 'Wind down' (i.e., activities that help to conclude the workday mindfully and disconnect from work; Microsoft, 2023). To date, little is known about the effectiveness of such technological tools, or if they help or hinder employees' work and non-work boundary management (see, for example, the chapter by Russell and Grant in this collection). This is likely to be a fruitful area for future research.

CONCLUSION

In the context of the COVID-19 pandemic and the widespread shift to remote and hybrid work arrangements, effectively managing boundaries between work and personal life has become vital. Blurring these boundaries can lead to strain and affect work performance. Employees' preferences for separating or integrating work and home roles influence how the boundary management strategies used impact psychological detachment and control. Segmentation preference appears to benefit productivity and wellbeing, while integration preference can harm wellbeing, causing exhaustion and work–life conflict. More research is needed that examines effective hybrid work transitions, focusing on boundary management policies and practices that consider the work context. Job control and flexibility aid worker thriving, but the consequences of organizational flexibility policies require more examination. Other factors, such as organizational culture, supervisor behavior, and support networks, also affect boundary management effectiveness. The lack of rigorous multi-level research to identify the nature and impact of these factors is a major gap in the current literature. Future studies should examine the combined effects of individual, team/organizational, and societal/governmental factors on work and non-work boundary management. By understanding the complex dynamics and interactions between these factors, organizations can develop comprehensive strategies to support employees in managing their work and non-work boundaries, whether they work entirely at the office, at home, or somewhere in between, leading to improved wellbeing and positive work and non-work outcomes.

REFERENCES

Adaptavist. (2022, September). *Digital etiquette: Reinventing work report.* https://
static.adaptavistassets.com/downloads/Adaptavist_Digital_Etiquette-Reinventing
_Work_Report.pdf

Adekoya, O. D., Adisa, T. A., & Aiyenitaju, O. (2022). Going forward: Remote
working in the post-COVID-19 era. *Employee Relations: The International Journal,
44*(6), 1410–1427.

Adkins, C. L., & Premeaux, S. A. (2014). The use of communication technology to
manage work-home boundaries. *Journal of Behavioral and Applied Management,
15*(2), 82–100.

Allen, T. D., Cho, E., & Meier, L. L. (2014). Work–family boundary dynamics. *Annual
Review of Organizational Psychology and Organizational Behavior, 1*(1), 99–121.

Allen, T. D., Merlo, K., Lawrence, R. C., Slutsky, J., & Gray, C. E. (2021). Boundary
management and work-nonwork balance while working from home. *Applied
Psychology, 70*(1), 60–84.

Appel-Meulenbroek, R., Kemperman, A., Van de Water, A., Weijs-Perrée, M., &
Verhaegh, J. (2022). How to attract employees back to the office? A stated choice
study on hybrid working preferences. *Journal of Environmental Psychology, 81*,
101784.

Ashforth, B. E., Kreiner, G. E., & Fugate, M. (2000). All in a day's work: Boundaries
and micro role transitions. *Academy of Management Review, 25*(3), 472–491.

Astakhova, M. N., Ho, V. T., & McKay, A. S. (2023). Passion amid the pandemic:
Applying a person-centered approach to examine cross-domain multi-passion pro-
files during a crisis. *Journal of Management Studies.* Advance online publication.
https://doi.org/10.1111/joms.12929

Bakker, A. B., & Demerouti, E. (2013). The spillover-crossover model. In J. G.
Grzywacz & E. Demerouti (Eds.), *New frontiers in work and family research*
(pp. 54–70). Psychology Press.

Bakker, A. B., Demerouti, E., & Dollard, M. F. (2008). How job demands affect
partners' experience of exhaustion: Integrating work-family conflict and crossover
theory. *Journal of Applied Psychology, 93*(4), 901–911.

Bakker, A. B., Hakanen, J. J., Demerouti, E., & Xanthopoulou, D. (2007). Job resources
boost work engagement, particularly when job demands are high. *Journal of
Educational Psychology, 99*(2), 274–284.

Bloom, N. (2021). *Hybrid is the future of work.* Stanford Institute for Economic Policy
Research (SIEPR). https://siepr.stanford.edu/publications/policy-brief/hybrid-future
-work

Bloom, N., Han, R., & Liang, J. (2022). *How hybrid working from home works out* (No.
w30292). National Bureau of Economic Research. https://www.nber.org/papers/
w30292

Bond, F. W., & Flaxman, P. E. (2006). The ability of psychological flexibility and
job control to predict learning, job performance, and mental health. *Journal of
Organizational Behavior Management, 26*(1–2), 113–130.

Brough, P., Kinman, G., McDowall, A., & Chan, X. W. (2021). "#MeToo" for
work-life balance. *Work-Life Balance Bulletin: A DOP Publication, 5*(1), 4–8.

Brough, P., & Westman, M. (2018). Crossover, culture, and dual-earner couples. In K.
M. Shockley, W. Shen, & R. C. Johnson (Eds.), *The Cambridge handbook of the
global work–family interface* (pp. 629–645). Cambridge University Press.

Bulger, C. A., Matthews, R. A., & Hoffman, M. E. (2007). Work and personal life boundary management: Boundary strength, work/personal life balance, and the segmentation–integration continuum. *Journal of Occupational Health Psychology*, *12*(4), 365–375.

Caringal-Go, J. F., Teng-Calleja, M., Bertulfo, D. J., & Manaois, J. O. (2022). Work-life balance crafting during COVID-19: Exploring strategies of telecommuting employees in the Philippines. *Community, Work & Family*, *25*(1), 112–131.

Carlson, D. S., Ferguson, M., & Kacmar, K. M. (2016). Boundary management tactics: An examination of the alignment with preferences in the work and family domains. *Journal of Behavioral and Applied Management*, *16*(2), 51–70.

Carvalho, V. S., Santos, A., Ribeiro, M. T., & Chambel, M. J. (2021). Please, do not interrupt me: Work–family balance and segmentation behavior as mediators of boundary violations and teleworkers' burnout and flourishing. *Sustainability*, *13*(13), 7339.

Chan, X. W., Fan, S. X., & Snell, D. (2021a). Managing intense work demands: How child protection workers navigate their professional and personal lives. *Community, Work & Family*, *24*(2), 208–225.

Chan, X. W., Kalliath, T., & Cheng, D. (2021b). When the boss is blue: Examining the effects of supervisors' negative emotions on subordinates' cognitive work engagement and family undermining. *Personnel Review*, *50*(2), 575–595.

Chan, X. W., Kalliath, P., Fan, S. X., & Kalliath, T. (2023a). Examining work–home segmentation as a coping strategy for frontline workers: A mixed method study of social workers across Australia. *The International Journal of Human Resource Management*, *34*(4), 693–715.

Chan, X. W., Shang, S., Brough, P., Wilkinson, A., & Lu, C. Q. (2023b). Work, life and COVID-19: A rapid review and practical recommendations for the post-pandemic workplace. *Asia Pacific Journal of Human Resources*, *61*(2), 257–276.

Chan, X. W., & Tay, S. (2022). Extending work-life balance initiatives. In P. Brough, E. Gardiner, & K. Daniels (Eds.), *Handbook on management and employment practices* (pp. 711–726). Springer.

Chandra, S., Shirish, A., & Srivastava, S. C. (2020). Theorizing technological spatial intrusion for ICT enabled employee innovation: The mediating role of perceived usefulness. *Technological Forecasting and Social Change*, *161*, 120320.

Cho, E. (2020). Examining boundaries to understand the impact of COVID-19 on vocational behaviors. *Journal of Vocational Behavior*, *119*, 103437.

Choroszewicz, M., & Kay, F. (2020). The use of mobile technologies for work-to-family boundary permeability: The case of Finnish and Canadian male lawyers. *Human Relations*, *73*(10), 1388–1414.

CIPD. (2022). *An update on flexible and hybrid working practices*. https:// www .cipd .org/ globalassets/ media/ knowledge/ knowledge -hub/ reports/ flexible -hybrid -working-practices-report_tcm18-108941.pdf

Clark, S. C. (2000). Work/family border theory: A new theory of work/family balance. *Human Relations*, *53*(6), 747–770.

Crossfield, S., Kinman, G., & Jones, F. (2005). Crossover of occupational stress in dual-career couples: The role of work demands and supports, job commitment and marital communication. *Community, Work and Family*, *8*(2), 211–232.

Demerouti, E., Bakker, A. B., Nachreiner, F., & Schaufeli, W. B. (2001). The job demands-resources model of burnout. *Journal of Applied Psychology*, *86*(3), 499–512.

Feldman, R., Masalha, S., & Nadam, R. (2001). Cultural perspective on work and family: Dual-earner Israeli Jewish and Arab families at the transition to parenthood. *Journal of Family Psychology*, *15*(3), 492–509.

Fenner, G. H., & Renn, R. W. (2010). Technology-assisted supplemental work and work-to-family conflict: The role of instrumentality beliefs, organizational expectations and time management. *Human Relations*, *63*(1), 63–82.

Gardner, D. M., Lauricella, T., Ryan, A. M., Wadlington, P., & Elizondo, F. (2021). Managing boundaries between work and non-work domains: Personality and job characteristics and adopted style. *Journal of Occupational and Organizational Psychology*, *94*(1), 132–159.

Grawitch, M. J., Barber, L. K., & Justice, L. (2010). Rethinking the work–life interface: It's not about balance, it's about resource allocation. *Applied Psychology: Health and Well-Being*, *2*(2), 127–159.

Greenhaus, J. H., & Beutell, N. J. (1985). Sources of conflict between work and family roles. *Academy of Management Review*, *10*(1), 76–88.

Grönlund, A. (2007). Employee control in the era of flexibility: A stress buffer or a stress amplifier? *European Societies*, *9*(3), 409–428.

Grover, S. L., Teo, S. T., Pick, D., Roche, M., & Newton, C. J. (2018). Psychological capital as a personal resource in the JD-R model. *Personnel Review*, *47*(4), 968–984.

Haun, V. C., Remmel, C., & Haun, S. (2022). Boundary management and recovery when working from home: The moderating roles of segmentation preference and availability demands. *German Journal of Human Resource Management*, *36*(3), 270–299.

Hobfoll, S. E. (1989). Conservation of resources: A new attempt at conceptualizing stress. *American Psychologist*, *44*(3), 513–524.

Hoobler, J. M., & Brass, D. J. (2006). Abusive supervision and family undermining as displaced aggression. *Journal of Applied Psychology*, *91*(5), 1125–1133.

Hoobler, J. M., & Hu, J. (2013). A model of injustice, abusive supervision, and negative affect. *The Leadership Quarterly*, *24*(1), 256–269.

Hu, J., Chiang, J. T. J., Liu, Y., Wang, Z., & Gao, Y. (2023). Double challenges: How working from home affects dual-earner couples' work–family experiences. *Personnel Psychology*, *76*(1), 141–179.

Kalliath, T., & Brough, P. (2008). Work–life balance: A review of the meaning of the balance construct. *Journal of Management & Organization*, *14*(3), 323–327.

Kalliath, P., Chan, X. W., & Kalliath, T. (2022). Keeping work and family separate: A serial mediation analysis of social workers' work–family segmentation, work–family enrichment and job performance in Australia. *The British Journal of Social Work*, *52*(1), 236–255.

Kiewitz, C., Restubog, S. L. D., Zagenczyk, T. J., Scott, K. D., Garcia, P. R. J. M., & Tang, R. L. (2012). Sins of the parents: Self-control as a buffer between supervisors' previous experience of family undermining and subordinates' perceptions of abusive supervision. *The Leadership Quarterly*, *23*(5), 869–882.

Kinman, G. (2016). Effort–reward imbalance and overcommitment in UK academics: Implications for mental health, satisfaction and retention. *Journal of Higher Education Policy and Management*, *38*(5), 504–518.

Kinman, G. (2021). *Supporting wellbeing remotely*. Leaders' Briefings. Research in Practice. https:// www .researchinpractice .org .uk/ media/ hd1isj2j/ supporting _wellbeing_remotely_lb_web.pdf

Kinman, G. (2024, in press). Work-life balance and wellbeing in academic employees. In M. Edwards, A. Martin, & N. Ashkanasy (Eds.), *Handbook of academic mental health*. Edward Elgar Publishing.

Kinman, G., & Clements, A. J. (2022). Prison officers' experiences of aggression: Implications for sleep and recovery. *Occupational Medicine, 72*(9), 604–608.

Kinman, G., & Jones, F. (2008). A life beyond work? Job demands, work-life balance, and wellbeing in UK academics. *Journal of Human Behavior in the Social Environment, 17*(1–2), 41–60.

Koch, A. R., & Binnewies, C. (2015). Setting a good example: Supervisors as work-life-friendly role models within the context of boundary management. *Journal of Occupational Health Psychology, 20*(1), 82–92.

Kossek, E. E. (2016). Managing work–life boundaries in the digital age. *Organizational Dynamics, 45*(3), 258–270.

Kossek, E. E., Dumas, T. L., Piszczek, M. M., & Allen, T. D. (2021). Pushing the boundaries: A qualitative study of how stem women adapted to disrupted work–nonwork boundaries during the COVID-19 pandemic. *Journal of Applied Psychology, 106*(11), 1615–1629.

Kossek, E. E., & Kelliher, C. (2023). Making flexibility more i-deal: Advancing work-life equality collectively. *Group & Organization Management, 48*(1), 317–349.

Kossek, E. E., & Lautsch, B. A. (2008). *CEO of me: Creating a life that works in the flexible job age*. Pearson Prentice Hall.

Kossek, E. E., & Lautsch, B. A. (2012). Work–family boundary management styles in organizations: A cross-level model. *Organizational Psychology Review, 2*(2), 152-171.

Kossek, E. E., Perrigino, M. B., & Lautsch, B. A. (2022). Work-life flexibility policies from a boundary control and implementation perspective: A review and research framework. *Journal of Management*. Advance online publication. https://doi.org/10.1177/01492063221140354

Kossek, E. E., Perrigino, M. B., Russo, M., & Morandin, G. (2023). Missed connections between the leadership and work-life fields: Work-life supportive leadership for a dual agenda. *Academy of Management Annals, 17*(1), 181–217.

Kreiner, G. E. (2006). Consequences of work-home segmentation or integration: A person-environment fit perspective. *Journal of Organizational Behavior, 27*(4), 485–507.

Krstic, A., & Hideg, I. (2019). The effect of taking a paternity leave on men's career outcomes: The role of communality perceptions. *Academy of Management Proceedings, 2019*(1), 13912.

Kubicek, B., & Tement, S. (2016). Work intensification and the work-home interface. *Journal of Personnel Psychology, 15*(2), 76–89.

Lagios, C., Restubog, S. L. D., Garcia, P. R. J. M., He, Y., & Caesens, G. (2023). A trickle-out model of organizational dehumanization and displaced aggression. *Journal of Vocational Behavior, 141*, 103826.

Lawson, K. M., Davis, K. D., McHale, S. M., Hammer, L. B., & Buxton, O. M. (2014). Daily positive spillover and crossover from mothers' work to youth health. *Journal of Family Psychology, 28*(6), 897–907.

Li, A., Cropanzano, R., Butler, A., Shao, P., & Westman, M. (2021). Work–family crossover: A meta-analytic review. *International Journal of Stress Management, 28*(2), 89–104.

Li, A., Zhou, Z. E., Shao, P. T., & Lin, Q. (2023). The father's and the mother's intrinsic work motivation and their work-to-family conflict perceived by the adolescent: Dyadic and triadic analyses. *Journal of Organizational Behavior, 44*(3), 441–457.

Marcus-Newhall, A., Pedersen, W. C., Carlson, M., & Miller, N. (2000). Displaced aggression is alive and well: A meta-analytic review. *Journal of Personality and Social Psychology, 78*(4), 670–689.

Matthews, R. A., Barnes-Farrell, J. L. & Bulger, C. A. (2010). Advancing measurement of work and family domain boundary characteristics. *Journal of Vocational Behavior, 77*(3), 447–460.

McCartney, J., Franczak, J., Gonzalez, K., Hall, A. T., Hochwarter, W. A., Jordan, S. L., Wikhamn, W., Khan, A. K., & Babalola, M. T. (2023). Supervisor off-work boundary infringements: Perspective-taking as a resource for after-hours intrusions. *Work & Stress.* Advance online publication. https://doi.org/10.1080/02678373.2023 .2176945

McDowall, A., & Kinman, G. (2021). Work-life balance and gender: Challenging assumptions and unravelling complexity. In J. Hassard & L. D. Torres (Eds.), *Aligning perspectives in gender mainstreaming: Gender, health, safety, and wellbeing* (pp. 37–60). Springer.

McNall, L. A., Scott, L. D., & Nicklin, J. M. (2015). Do positive affectivity and boundary preferences matter for work–family enrichment? A study of human service workers. *Journal of Occupational Health Psychology, 20*(1), 93–104.

Microsoft. (2023). *Virtual commute in Viva Insights – Wellbeing.* https:// support .microsoft.com/en-us/topic/virtual-commute-in-viva-insights-8be83785-f5ec-4e84 -8cff-f0abb117f876

Mueller, N., & Kempen, R. (2022). The influence of boundary management preference on work–nonwork policy effectiveness: Is "turning off" the solution? *European Journal of Work and Organizational Psychology, 32*, 402–417.

Mutebi, N., & Hobbs, A. (2022, October 17). The impact of remote and hybrid working on workers and organisations. *UK Parliament POST Research Briefing (POSTbrief) 49.* https://post.parliament.uk/research-briefings/post-pb-0049/

Nippert-Eng, C. (1996). *Home and work.* University of Chicago Press.

Nsair, V., & Piszczek, M. (2021). Gender matters: The effects of gender and segmentation preferences on work-to-family conflict in family sacrifice climates. *Journal of Occupational and Organizational Psychology, 94*(3), 509–530.

Ollier-Malaterre, A., Jacobs, J. A., & Rothbard, N. P. (2019). Technology, work, and family: Digital cultural capital and boundary management. *Annual Review of Sociology, 45*, 425–447.

Pang, H. (2021). How compulsive WeChat use and information overload affect social media fatigue and well-being during the COVID-19 pandemic? A stressor-strain-outcome perspective. *Telematics and Informatics, 64*, 101690.

Park, Y., & Jex, S. M. (2011). Work-home boundary management using communication and information technology. *International Journal of Stress Management, 18*(2), 133–152.

Roberts, L. M., & McCluney, C. L. (2020, June 17). Working from home while black. *Harvard Business Review.* https://hbr.org/2020/06/workingfrom-home-while-black

Russo, M., Ollier-Malaterre, A., Kossek, E. E., & Ohana, M. (2018). Boundary management permeability and relationship satisfaction in dual-earner couples: The asymmetrical gender effect. *Frontiers in Psychology, 9*, 1723.

Schieman, S., Badawy, P. J., A. Milkie, M., & Bierman, A. (2021). Work-life conflict during the COVID-19 pandemic. *Socius, 7*, 1–19.

Shang, S., Chan, X. W., & Liu, X. (2021). Work–life conflict in China: A Confucian cultural perspective. In T. A. Adisa & G. Gbadamosi (Eds.), *Work–life interface: Non-Western perspectives* (pp. 249–284). Palgrave Macmillan.

Shirmohammadi, M., Beigi, M., Au, W. C., & Tochia, C. (2023). Who moved my boundary? Strategies adopted by families working from home. *Journal of Vocational Behavior, 143*, 103866.

Sonnentag, S. (2012). Psychological detachment from work during leisure time: The benefits of mentally disengaging from work. *Current Directions in Psychological Science, 21*(2), 114–118.

Sun, L., Liu, T., & Wang, W. (2023). Working from home in Urban China during the COVID-19 pandemic: Assemblages of work-family interference. *Work, Employment and Society, 37*(1), 157–175.

Tedeschi, J. T., & Norman, N. M. (1985). A social psychological interpretation of displaced aggression. *Advances in Group Processes, 2*, 29–56.

Tehrani, N., Colville, T., Fraser, J., Breslin, G., Waites, B., & Kinman, G. (2020). *Taking trauma related work home: Advice for reducing the likelihood of secondary trauma.* British Psychological Society.

Van Emmerik, I. J. H., & Peeters, M. C. (2009). Crossover specificity of team-level work-family conflict to individual-level work-family conflict. *Journal of Managerial Psychology, 24*(3), 254–268.

Vaziri, H., Casper, W. J., Wayne, J. H., & Matthews, R. A. (2020). Changes to the work-family interface during the COVID-19 pandemic: Examining predictors and implications using latent transition analysis. *Journal of Applied Psychology, 105*(10), 1073–1087.

Wu, T. J., Yuan, K. S., Yen, D. C., & Xu, T. (2019). Building up resources in the relationship between work–family conflict and burnout among firefighters: Moderators of guanxi and emotion regulation strategies. *European Journal of Work and Organizational Psychology, 28*(3), 430–441.

Xie, J., Ma, H., Zhou, Z. E., & Tang, H. (2018). Work-related use of information and communication technologies after hours (W_ICTs) and emotional exhaustion: A mediated moderation model. *Computers in Human Behavior, 79*, 94–104.

Yang, J., Zhang, Y., Shen, C., Liu, S., & Zhang, S. (2019). Work-family segmentation preferences and work-family conflict: Mediating effect of work-related ICT use at home and the multilevel moderating effect of group segmentation norms. *Frontiers in Psychology, 10*, 834.

Zerubavel, E. (1991). *The fine line.* Free Press.

Zerubavel, E. (1996). Lumping and splitting: Notes on social classification. *Sociological Forum, 11*(3), 421–423.

5. Supporting diversity and intersectionality at work: implications for wellbeing

Almuth McDowall

DIVERSITY AND INTERSECTIONALITY: THE RELEVANCE TO WELLBEING AT WORK

The global pandemic has undoubtedly influenced how we experience wellbeing at work. An international study (AXA Health, 2023), which surveyed 30,000 workers across 16 countries after the pandemic, reported wellbeing differences by country, sex, and age. Overall, self-reported levels of functioning were low, with the majority either 'getting by' or 'languishing'; only around a fifth of participants indicated that they were flourishing. Those flourishing were more likely to feel productive in their jobs. The findings also confirm the business case for supporting worker wellbeing, as self-reported wellbeing was three times higher in workplaces with access to mental health support. The percentage of people reporting that their employer offered good 'mind health support' varied considerably by country, from 56 per cent in China to 40 per cent in the UK, 34 per cent in Germany, 31 per cent in Hong Kong, and only 20 per cent in Japan.

The wellbeing domain at work is multifaceted (see also the section below on conceptual models of wellbeing at work), and shaped by people's views of their careers and prospects. The percentage of people uncertain of their career prospects varied considerably, from 46 per cent in Spain, a country arguably hard hit by the global recession at the end of the 2000s, to Germany at 27 per cent, where the economy has remained more stable to date. The study further found that women typically reported that they flourished less and struggled more, which was linked to unwanted comments about their gender, and having their abilities questioned at work. Young people in the 18–24 age group were more likely to report that they were struggling, with only one in 12 claiming that they were flourishing. Many respondents in this age group cited high technology use as a key factor in their struggles. Such findings provide guidance for organizations when formulating policies and targeting support for employee wellbeing.

Any study of wellbeing and diversity at work should refer to health in(equalities), because workplace experiences are contextualized. The World Health Organization (WHO, n.d., a) asserts that health is a fundamental human right, and a resource for everyone regardless of their race, religion, political belief, or economic or social condition; physical, mental, and social wellbeing should be considered holistically.

Certain differences occur naturally – for example, older adults are more likely to die than younger adults (McCartney et al., 2019). Other differences, however, are avoidable, and the product of social inequalities. Global trends in health outcomes are complex, because although overall life expectancy (LE), a common proxy measure for health inequalities, has increased, healthy life expectancy (HALE – the number of years that people experience 'good' health) has not increased at the same rate (WHO, n.d., b). Although LE and HALE will probably continue to increase due to advances in medicine and healthcare, both are influenced by international and regional circumstances. Both LE and HALE are, for example, higher in America, Australia, North America, and Europe, but lower in Africa (WHO, n.d., b). Wellbeing experiences are also commonly influenced by membership of more than one demographic group ('intersectionality').

'Intersectionality' holds that a person can have more than one marginalizing identity or 'occupy multiple disadvantage statuses' (Brown & Moloney, p. 94), and offers a lens for understanding workplace wellbeing. The concept originates from Crenshaw's (1989) work which documented the specific hardships of Black women's work experiences, and found that the intersection of sex and race held more explanatory power than the effects of each independent characteristic. The term 'intersectionality' has since taken on a wider meaning, to also encompass other social and demographic characteristics such as age, ethnicity, nationality, sexual orientation, religious belief, and disability (see, for example, Bauer et al., 2021). Such characteristics are subject to lcoal law in many countries, including the UK, where the Equality Act (2010) legally protects individuals from discrimination at work and in society[1] on the grounds of nine protected characteristics, including pregnancy and parental leave. Equally, legislation and directives exist in many geographical contexts to protect the wellbeing of workers and societies – yet inequality, stigma, and prejudice persist. For example, in the mental health field, a UK-based study of depression found that older people are less likely to be referred for specialist treatment (Walters et al., 2017). This is concerning, given the likelihood that many of us will need to work for longer, due to diminished pension incomes and ageing populations. Comparative lack of access to appropriate treatment may make older workers more vulnerable if they present with depressive symptoms, indicating a potential need for targeted support.

Turning to intersectionality, experiencing prejudice or stigma due to multiple personal characteristics is associated with poor wellbeing (e.g., Cruwys & Gunaseelan, 2016). This is not only due to differences regarding diagnosis and treatment, but also relates to how workers may be treated by colleagues and managers. Intersectionality effects can occur with regard to the following indicative marginalized identities.

Age, Health and Workability

The concepts of age and ageing are rooted in the observation that all organisms undergo changes over time, and that ageing is influenced by physiological, psychological, and social changes (see Balcom & Sinclair, 2001, for an overview). A distinction between chronological (calendar) and functional age is often employed, the latter measured by a range of health indicators (Koolhaas et al., 2012). A recent rapid review found age differences in perceptions of work characteristics, such as the level of occupational risk, and use of remote working in the wake of the COVID-19 pandemic (Bellotti et al., 2021). A public health study of nearly 3,000 participants in the Netherlands across four different industry sectors (health care, education, government, and industry) considered self-reports of health and disease, and work ability, for workers 45 years and older (Koolhaas et al., 2012), finding a strong negative link between having a chronic health condition and work ability. Perhaps surprisingly, workers over 60 years old self-reported better health then those aged 45–59 years. Nonetheless, participants cited challenges, with declining energy, muscle function, concentration, and memory, where support from colleagues, and (positive) relationships at work and with their supervisor, were identified to be facilitators to wellbeing.

In a global context, several societies are ageing (fewer children being born and people on average living longer; for example, Japan[2]) and some of these societies have extended their retirement age (for example, France and the UK). Curiously, a Czech study by Rašticová et al. (2019) showed that economically active Czechs aged between 50 and 59 years reported *worse* health than those who were economically inactive. While the study does not allow inferences of cause and effect, it is plausible that working conditions might have accounted for this effect, which indicates that active age management is important at work. Thus, it is important to upskill and support line managers; for example, a qualitative Australian study with 58 human resources (HR) managers pointed to a gap between policy and practice for the management of ageing workers (Earl & Taylor, 2015).

Disability

Disability is complex to define, the concept evokes strong views, and is shaped by local legislation and policies. Medical or clinical models of disability focus on pathology (i.e., what does not work), while the social model emphasizes that it is usually the environment which is disabling (for an overview, see Altman, 2001). The WHO (n.d., c) currently states that an experience of disability results from the interaction between individuals with a health condition and a range of personal and environmental factors. Workplace disability research is dispersed and is often condition-specific. For example, a qualitative study of cancer survivors, health care providers, and employer representatives indicated that stigma and workplace discrimination are a significant concern due to 'myths' regarding work ability and productivity (Stergiou-Kita et al., 2016). The authors make valid points about the need to educate workplaces and readjust these perceptions.

Brown and Moloney (2019) offered a thoughtful exemplar adopting an intersectional lens with US data on disabled women workers, who are a rarely studied and, therefore, poorly understood population. The authors used a two-wave community survey of working adults in Florida to assess the impact of physical disability and gender on six different aspects of work experiences, including workplace stress exposure, occupational prestige, job autonomy, and creativity. The findings showed that gender and disability have indirect but significant effects, because they are linked to employment factors such as income and exposure to work stress. Their analyses found that women and disabled people are overrepresented in lower-paid, less prestigious, and less engaging work, and that consequently disabled women experience more negative work experiences because they earn less, are exposed to more workplace stress, and are less likely to have autonomy at work.

Gender Identity and Sexual Orientation

'Gender identity' refers to how someone self-identifies their gender; they may refer to their birth-assigned gender, or to a different gender, or as non-binary. Many psychological and biological factors influence gender identity, or gender dysphoria – a mismatch between biological sex and identity (see Steensma et al., 2013, for an introduction). Academic research on non-binary[3] work inclusion is sparse. In the UK, for example, the Chartered Institute of Personnel and Development (CIPD) has published guidance on the issue, making a case for safe and equal work cultures, leave provisions, ensuring inclusion through the employment lifecycle from hiring to career progression, and the management of different opinions, while supporting individual employee gender transitions (Fletcher & Marvell, 2023).

'Sexual orientation' refers to people's relative sexual attraction to men, women, or both, with heteronormativity (relationships between women and men) still considered the norm; indeed the deviation from this norm remains illegal in some countries. There has been a strong movement to improve the political rights of lesbian, gay, bisexual, transgender, queer, questioning, inter-sex, or asexual people (LGBTQIA+), but with very different trajectories across the world (for a review, see Bailey et al., 2016). An insightful study (Fletcher & Everly, 2022) considered the psychological mechanisms underpinning identity disclosure for people who identify as lesbian, gay, bisexual, and transgender. Disclosure and authenticity are interrelated, and in turn, authenticity mediates the link between perceived LGBT support practices and life satisfaction. The implication is that a stable sense of identity is particularly important for life satisfaction, an important aspect of workplace wellbeing.

A small scale, in-depth, and sobering qualitative study from Canada asked 35 LGBTQ (lesbian, gay, bisexual, transgender, and queer) academics about their everyday work experiences (Beagan et al., 2021). The participants reported frequent micro-aggressions, which can be a profound stressor (Lui & Quezada, 2019). These workers felt isolated, and either invisible or hyper-visible regard-ing their sexual identity. They perceived a lack of institutional support and, in some cases, were even dismissed. While this is, of course, only one study in a specific context, it highlights that frequent micro-aggressions in a heter-onormative context are difficult to address, as they usually fall outside formal discrimination and equality policies.

Racial Identity

There is a spectrum of biological and social definitions and constructions of race, where terminology remains open to debate and change. Ethnic, racial, and indigenous identities interlink. The Organization for Economic Co-operation and Development (OECD, 2018) defines race as shaped by phenotype, appearance, and ancestry; ethnicity is the shared culture in terms of practices, values, and beliefs. Indigenous identity refers to tribal people with distinct conditions and traditions. Although there is much workplace research and several reviews on the topic, there is comparatively less on the direct link between employee race and wellbeing outcomes. For example, Oerlemans et al. (2009) highlighted the detrimental effects of belonging to an ethnic minor-ity on wellbeing at work.

A critical diversity study conducted with Italian hotel workers (Alberti & Ianuzzi, 2020) examined how hotel management allocated workers for reception work, the kitchen, or 'back-of-house' work, according to the perceived desirability of their embodied characteristics. The data show that some workers internalized stereotypical assumptions, such as some ethnic groups being 'slower', or being particularly service-orientated. Additionally, housekeeping skills were considered a feminine attribute and a source of pride. The authors proposed the idea of 'intersectional management' to pay greater attention to notions of relative advantage and disadvantage across and within different groups. The analysis further highlighted persistent inequalities, where migrant women workers were overly represented in the lowest and most precarious employment positions. Such a nuanced analysis is different from traditional perspectives on diversity management, which have focused on organizational performance and efficiency, arguing that diversity benefits the business (e.g., Robinson & Dechant, 1997). Köllen (2021), in a review of diversity management, concluded that given falling birthrates in industrialized countries, shrinking 'pools of potential domestic manpower [*sic*]' (p. 23) serve as an incentive to increase focus on facilitating diversity with a holistic perspective. However, employee wellbeing has been neglected as a core concern of diversity initiatives, which often focus on more equal representation of groups, and/or training workers to recognize and manage both overt and subconscious biases.

Neurodiversity

Neurodiversity is increasingly prominent in work and society, and refers to the breadth of human functioning and neurocognition. It includes, but is not limited to, neurodevelopmental conditions such as autism, attention deficit hyperactivity disorder, or dyslexia (see Doyle & McDowall, 2021). Recently, much research has focused on autism, a neurodevelopmental spectrum condition marked by differential preferences in social functioning that affect how people communicate, learn, and interact. Differences by biological sex in autism rates are debated, given that men are diagnosed more frequently. However, the masking of autism is common in women, meaning that they are more likely to suppress behaviours such as *stimming* (e.g., rocking to self-stimulate) to match neuronormative stereotypes. A thematic in-depth meta-synthesis of 12 papers concerned with the intersection of autism and gender revealed that identities and discourses are complex and intertwined (Moore et al., 2022). Prevalent autism discourses influence and restrict (women's) gender identities, and gendered autistic identities are perceived as 'othered'. Moore et al. (2022) also offered valuable implications for professionals to reflect on their own positioning regarding autism and gender, and the implications this might have for their practice, offering active support to minimize self-blaming and shame.

As with disability research, workplace (non-)disclosure of autism is also important to consider. Johnson and Joshi (2016) investigated the age relationship of autism diagnosis, whether or not individuals disclosed at work, social demands at work, and organizational support policies for autism. The results showed that people who were diagnosed earlier have greater self-esteem, lower perceived discrimination, had jobs with fewer social demands, and were more likely to be in work with supportive policies. Similarly, Doyle et al. (2022) investigated intersectional stigma for autistic people, and participation in autism-specific work schemes, which are employment schemes aimed at recruiting autistic people into specific job roles; for example, in the high-tech sector or in computer programming. These authors found that autistic employment participation varied between international contexts, and that people who identified as women or non-binary people had lower perceptions of inclusion and belonging at work.

To better understand organizational practice, we undertook a co-produced survey of nearly 130 UK employer representatives (e.g., HR professionals) and over 990 employees funded by a UK charity (McDowall et al., 2023). We asked workers who identified as 'neurodivergent' (ND) (a debated term – see below[4]) about their experiences, the strengths they bring, and if there was any gap between demand (what people need) and supply (what employers offer), and a range of other variables.[5] Gender and sexual orientation were included because LGBTQIA+ has a high prevalence in the ND community, although reasons for this intersection are not well understood (see Doyle & McDowall, 2023). Overall, very low levels of wellbeing were reported by the respondents, signposting a need for urgent attention. Interestingly, employers and employees converged in the reporting of neurodivergent strengths and challenges, although the study also observed that strengths were remarkably consistent across conditions, yet the challenges varied. We also asked about the provision of accommodations; that is, what employers provided to help people do their best work. Again, employers and employees broadly concurred that assistive technology, environmental adaptations, and coaching are each useful. Our results showed that respondents' perceptions of opportunities for career progression, and psychological safety, were associated with their positive wellbeing. Neither staff support, company knowledge of neurodivergency, the tailoring of adjustments, nor managers' support were important correlates of workers' wellbeing in this sample.

We also found differences by condition with, for example, those with a mental health or a tic condition (such as Tourette's, marked by involuntary, repeated, and sudden twitches, movements, and sounds) reporting lower levels of wellbeing than respondents with other conditions. Employees who identified as non-binary, or as women, reported significantly lower wellbeing than men. A sizeable number of employees also reported that a fear of stigma and prejudice occurring from their managers (64.7 per cent) and colleagues (55 per cent) prevented them from disclosing their condition.

From the employers' perspective, we asked about any challenges they experienced in implementing adjustments for these neurodiverse workers. Nearly three-quarters (69 per cent) of employers who were sampled reported that a key barrier is a lack of disclosure by employees; 65 per cent reported a lack of understanding of their needs, yet only 25 per cent identified costs as a barrier. These results point to an urgent necessity to address fear of stigma and prejudice when disclosing neurodiverse conditions, paired with a need to upskill managers and decision-makers who work with neurodiverse employees.

Other Influences on Wellbeing: Societal and Work Context and Individual Differences

The discussions above provide some illustration of how marginalized identities can intersect, and the experiences of work-related wellbeing. The wider context has come to the forefront since the global COVID-19 pandemic, and given rising levels of migration, where 281 million people were migrants in 2020 – 3.6 per cent of the global population (IOM, 2022). It is strongly apparent that more research is needed to better understand work and wellbeing issues amongst migrant workers. For example, a qualitative interpretative pre-pandemic review of wellbeing in Asian Labour migrants documented that poor working conditions, low access to public services, and lack of legal (including employment) rights impact negatively on their levels of wellbeing (Reza et al., 2019). Legislative local context is crucial for affording workers' rights and protection.

Where and how people work also affects their wellbeing. A much-cited study (Johnson et al., 2005) compared 26 different occupations, and found that workers from six occupational contexts (namely, ambulance workers, teachers, customer services, call centres, prison officers, and police) had, on average, a higher risk of occupational stress experiences than other occupational groups. The authors noted the probability that these occupations each rely on high levels of emotional labour (defined as the display of emotions considered important for a given job) as an influence on poor wellbeing and high levels of occupational stress commonly reported by these workers (see, for example, Chapter 7 in this book by Troth, Jordan, and Rafferty).

So far, I have considered the intersection of different marginalized identities as a key concern for wellbeing at work, as well as the associated influence of societal/legal and organizational environments. I now turn to several examples of theoretical work wellbeing models.

THEORETICAL MODELS OF WORK WELLBEING

Warr's Vitamin model (1994, 2007) describes 12 job features, including job autonomy, variety, and pay level, and their link to wellbeing outcomes. Importantly, relationships between the different aspects of work and wellbeing are hypothesized as non-linear (the effect of 'vitamins' can level off). A German study tested this model with a sample of horticulture workers and found broad support for the model's non-linear associations (Meyerding, 2015; Stiglbauer & Kovacs, 2018).

A Spanish study (Sanclemente et al., 2022) combined the job demands-resources (JD-R) model – which broadly conceptualizes a range of work and individual characteristics which protect or affect engagement and burnout (Bakker & Demerouti, 2007) – and the Vitamin model. The authors studied workers from five Spanish service industries, and found that relationships between job demands, resources, and physical and psychological symptoms were linear or non-linear depending on the specific work sector. In general, job autonomy buffered health; and the effects of task complexity, time pressure, and contact with users were curvilinear, which means a cumulative negative effect on health. Older workers employed in the education and commerce sectors generally reported a greater negative impact of their work upon their mental health. Similarly, female workers reported more ill health symptoms than male workers. The authors noted complex factors could account for such observations, including the higher prevalence of women in some sectors, combined with social expectations for women to juggle family and work demands.

Sorensen et al. (2021) offered a systemic conceptual model for future research on work, safety, health, and wellbeing which combined macro-level influences, including the social and political environment, employment patterns, working conditions (physical and psychosocial), and individual worker characteristics. From a psychological perspective however, the model is missing individual differences as an important element for understanding wellbeing (Warr, 2017). Relevant influences include personality, a relatively stable characteristic; as well as more malleable beliefs such as self-efficacy – the belief in one's capabilities – and personal salience. Warr (2017, p. 89) posits that such individual differences moderate experiences of wellbeing at work and can also influence 'lower or higher tipping points'. For example, those with high degrees of perfectionism may react to work pressure differently, which might be heightened under certain conditions; for example, where jobs are scarce, and legislative protection is lacking or not enforced. What does this mean, given earlier emphasis on intersectionality? This observation means that researchers and practitioners need a nuanced understanding of wellbeing that takes into consideration that wellbeing experiences are likely to differ between people, and depend on the work they do, as well as potential intersections between marginalized identities.

A CONCEPTUAL MODEL FOR INTERSECTIONALITY AND WELLBEING

To advance work in this area, I combine aspects of Sorensen's model (2021) with Warr's consideration of individual differences (Warr, 1994, 2017) in a conceptual model (Figure 5.1), with the likely influence of intersectionality and the wider societal context, as discussed in this chapter.

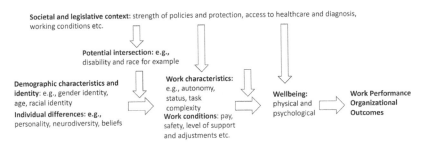

Figure 5.1   *A conceptual model for multi-level influences on wellbeing, including intersectionality*

The model is simplified for illustration purposes – it is equally plausible, for example, that reciprocal relationships exist between some constructs. The greater their wellbeing, the more likely workers might negotiate jobs with higher autonomy or more favourable work conditions; individual and social characteristics thus influence workplace experiences. Links between the various components of the model are likely; for example, where disabled women have jobs with less variety and autonomy, or are more likely to be exposed to work pressures. Working conditions and particular characteristics of work settings are also likely to be linked. For example, better paid jobs, or more senior jobs, may offer more autonomy and variety. Such issues directly impact employee wellbeing, and positive wellbeing is, in turn, associated with improved individual performance and organizational outcomes (e.g., productivity and effectiveness).

Of course, individual and social characteristics could also have a direct link to wellbeing, as might the wider social and legal context. The model therefore shows organizations how they might navigate times of uncertainty, and where to direct efforts. There are aspects which are under organizational control, such as the working conditions and the work itself. There is a need to monitor levels of wellbeing, and put into place appropriate support, which is even more important in times of external upheaval and change. For example, initiatives to foster and further equality/equity, diversity, and inclusion have gained traction in organizational practice as evidenced by a number of practice and policy initiatives; but these need to accompany efforts to support individual and collective wellbeing.

DIRECTIONS FOR FUTURE RESEARCH

Much research has considered wellbeing at work from a range of conceptual and theoretical perspectives; likewise, there is a substantial body of research concerned with diversity and intersectionality. Regarding the latter, however, it is less clear 'what works'. Alhejji and colleagues (2016) synthesized existing research on diversity training and found this research to be 'fragmented and diverse', and overly focused on business and learning outcomes, with far less evidence about social justice. Unfortunately, the topics of wellbeing and identity were outside the scope of their work. Given current geopolitical contexts, worker diversity is likely to continue to change through trends such as increased migration, changing birthrates, policy changes regarding retirement ages, and increased use of information and communication technologies; paired with increased focus on more understandings of nuanced identities (e.g., beyond a binary gender distinction). There is, therefore, a clear need to bring these strands of research together.

This is a complex task, as no accepted methods for researching diversity or intersectionality analysis exist. Numbers will be small for minoritized groups, particularly for quantitative studies, making it hard to detect any effects. Minoritized groups will also be less likely to participate in research. Taking the example of our autism-at-work study (Doyle et al., 2022), we relatively quickly had a reasonable response, but all these responses were only from white respondents. Informal feedback through social media channels told us that our study was considered irrelevant to some marginalized communities. We therefore had to direct specific calls to engage (for example) workers from the Black and Brown communities.

Another issue is that many studies do not report findings by demographic group so, although differences exist, we may be unaware of these. Efforts are being made to change this as many journals (e.g., the *Journal of Occupational Health Psychology*[6]) now make it a submission requirement to report on sample characteristics such as racial identity, ethnicity, immigration history, or socioeconomic status. For qualitative studies, there is the challenge of ensuring that marginalized voices are heard, versus the need to protect anonymity and safeguard participants (who might fear reprisal from employers), as documented by the Italian study (Alberti & Ianuzzi, 2020) discussed above.

Another noteworthy aspect is the influence of leadership and supervision. Inceoglu and colleagues (2018) clearly summarized the research evidence on different types of leadership and a range of health outcomes. Future research is recommended to build on this, by investigating how leadership could be developed and strengthened, with particular reference to wellbeing across the entire organization. A 2017 meta-analysis documented that leadership behaviour was linked to follower wellbeing, which impacted leader wellbeing in turn, with change-orientated and relational leadership styles having positive effects, and active destructive behaviour being worse than laissez-faire styles (Kaluza et al., 2020). This demonstrates that leadership development should consider workers' intersectional characteristics, given leaders' impact on workers, teams, and organizations; paired with organizational health interventions directed at the leaders, and potentially some reflective elements to facilitate focus on their position of privilege. Dang and colleagues (2023), for example, found across two experimental studies that leaders who acknowledge people's racial/ethnic identities are considered more ethical by their followers, who were accordingly more proactive at work. A next step would be to also research links to wellbeing outcomes – do followers feel psychologically safer with better physical and mental wellbeing, for example?

Leadership and management can have a detrimental impact on subordinates, one example being abusive supervision, or displays of overt hostility (Tepper et al., 2017). Role models and cultural/organizational norms play a significant role in leadership practices, with research documenting that abusive supervision is more likely in certain contexts (Mackey et al., 2017). Subtle slights including micro-aggressions, everyday discrimination, and workplace incivilities are also significant, which to date has been found in largely US-centric research and focused on race (see Smith & Griffiths, 2022, for an excellent overview). Smith and Griffiths (2022) appeal for more systems-focused research to further understand why and how such subtle slights are more likely to take place.

In summary, I posit that priorities for future research assessing intersectionality and workers' wellbeing are:

1. Robust longitudinal studies which track interventions aimed at a diversity- and an intersectionality-sensitive approach to wellbeing at work over time.
2. Culturally sensitive studies which attend to wellbeing initiatives in international work contexts, where legislation, worker demographics, and other aspects may vary considerably, even within the organization.
3. Research focused on leaders and supervisors regarding wellbeing, and intersectionality or diversity.
4. Qualitative research focused on lived experience, and bringing together diverse voices; for example, using focus groups.
5. Research on understudied populations such as migrants.

6. Research which helps to build the business case for focusing on diversity and wellbeing jointly.

IMPLICATIONS FOR PRACTICE

This chapter highlights the complexities inherent in issues surrounding diversity, intersectionality, and wellbeing at work, in global, changing societies; there are no easy solutions. Yet we are increasingly relying on diverse workforces who need to be well to do their best work and to navigate changing workplaces amid growing uncertainty. To do so, I suggest a stepwise and cyclical approach:

1. Collection and monitoring of robust wellbeing data and process-focused evaluation
2. Leadership accountability and representation of diverse worker groups in any activities and solutions which is diversity- and intersectionality-sensitive
3. Supporting the individual worker through adjustments and coaching

I now address each of these three aspects in turn.

Collection and Monitoring of Wellbeing Data

Organizations can use many sources to inform priorities, by analysing and monitoring wellbeing data which is diversity-relevant, and compliant with legislation and norms. Monitoring of relevant data should start when individuals apply for a particular work role, so that any adjustments or accommodations can be made. In the UK, for example, employers are obliged to proactively ask about any special requirements, rather than waiting for applicants to tell them. In a previous paper, we outlined 'universal design' as a framework to underpin good practice across the employee lifecycle (Doyle & McDowall, 2021).

Good job design and working conditions are important. It is vital that work characteristics, including the degree of autonomy, variety, level of pressure, and opportunity to find meaning; and the working conditions, such as remuneration, or exposure to hazards, are monitored within and between groups to detect any differences. It is likely ineffective to introduce training or other wellbeing interventions if the job itself is making individuals or groups unwell. Where possible, and contextually relevant, organizations should refer to policy and other guidance; for example, in the UK there are Stress Management Standards.[7]

It is crucial to monitor retention. Are any particular groups more likely to leave, be sick, be absent, or report discrimination? Can anything be learned about issues related to wellbeing? Other opportunities for data collection are performance appraisals and development reviews, as well as regular staff surveys. Many organizations now undertake regular 'employee engagement' surveys, which usually include some kind of wellbeing-related questions. Ideally, the questions and format used should be appropriately benchmarked against other organizations in this sector, and compare different groups in the organization, going beyond one characteristic at a time. Wellbeing, and equality, diversity, inclusion, and belonging (EDIB), are time-critical issues. Lack of action, or misguided action, can potentially land employers in the court-room. I have mapped suggestions and reflective questions onto Kirkpatrick's model of programme evaluation, which has been widely applied in the EDIB field (Kirkpatrick Partners, n.d.). As these levels do not necessarily follow on neatly in practice, it is best to address all four levels from the design stage of any activity:

- Level 1 – reaction: to what extent do workers find any wellbeing initiatives relevant and engaging? Are there differences between groups? If so, how can any differences be addressed (for example, by adjusting language and framing, or indeed substantive content)?
- Level 2 – learning: what have people learned from wellbeing training or other initiatives? To what extent does learning reflect intended outcomes? If not, is there scope to revisit objectives, and/or ensure that these are equally relevant to all groups in the organization?
- Level 3 – behaviour: how is any learning applied on the job? Crucially, are there potential barriers due to prejudice/stigma against certain groups of people, or lack of knowledge? What can be done to encourage uptake and counteract stigma and prejudice (where relevant)?
- Level 4 – results: to what extent have wellbeing initiatives reaped intended benefits such as reductions in staff turnover and sickness absence? Are there differences between groups? If so, what are the patterns and what are priorities for action?

Both quantitative and qualitative methods of data collection are essential. Senior managers often respond better to numbers. But it is hard to illuminate lived experience without the rich detail gathered in personal conversations or focus groups.

Leadership Accountability and Representation of Diverse Worker Groups in Any Activities and Solutions

Wellbeing needs to be embedded into corporate strategy through responsibility and accountability at senior levels to facilitate diversity, as is documented by research on diversity management (Thomas, 2016). But top-down accountability is insufficient on its own; and representative, diverse worker voices should be involved in the crafting of solutions and any activities. There are frameworks and concepts from healthcare which can be adopted, such as co-production (National Institute for Health and Care Research, 2021), to ensure that local need is met, language and framing resonate, and continued dialogue and reflection is embedded into any process, and so that business requirements are balanced with a duty of care for the workforce.

Reasonable Adjustments and Coaching to Support Wellbeing and Diversity

The activities and processes referenced above largely occur at an organizational level, but need to be paired with appropriate support and action at an individual level. For example, in the UK a disability is defined by whether an impairment has a 'substantial' and 'long-term' negative effect on a person's daily activities. This definition applies regardless of whether or not someone has a diagnosis. Some conditions automatically qualify, and others are exempt (such as addiction to non-prescribed drugs). It is very important that any conversations about reasonable adjustments are therefore undertaken with due regard for diversity. Adjustments should be tailored, and can draw on a range of supports and activities. These might include training in and use of technology assistance, choice in where and how to work, or psychosocial support through mentoring and coaching. Employees' fear of disclosure due to stigma and prejudice is real (Brohan & Thornicroft, 2010), highlighting the key role of employer attitudes and behaviour (van Beukering et al., 2021).

A positive approach to empowering workers to help themselves is through targeted and tailored work coaching, which supports wellbeing and is diversity-sensitive. Coaching helps people to boost their resources, and better negotiate ways of working which support individual effectiveness and health. Our previous research has found that an integrative coaching approach, bringing together a wide-ranging toolkit across a range of approaches, appears particularly effective (Wang et al., 2021).

CONCLUSION

This chapter has made a case to adopt an intersectional lens to understand the link between workers' diversity and their work-related wellbeing. Research documents that the influence of marginalized identities is complex as, for example, the influences of gender and race intersect; and more recent research also acknowledges that differences in neurocognition also need to be addressed and supported. I have offered a conceptual model which highlights the need to holistically address social and individual characteristics and how these might intersect, as well as work design and conditions, in an ever-changing global and legal context. Priorities for research include addressing the lack of longitudinal work which documents 'what works', and advocating for consistent reporting of diversity characteristics. The section on implications for practice offers a simple framework for a stepwise approach to collecting and monitoring data, and highlights the need to involve all stakeholders, including leaders, and diverse worker representation. Such approaches need to run alongside tailored support for individual workers, such as coaching. Supporting workplace wellbeing through an intersectional lens is no easy task, but a 'must', to ensure that our global and diverse workforces can navigate future challenges and, in turn, organizations can continue to thrive as good places to work.

NOTES

1. https://www.gov.uk/guidance/equality-act-2010-guidance
2. https://www.ilo.org/global/WCM_041965/lang--en/index.htm
3. A gender identity which does not conform to traditional binary male or female.
4. We agreed that this term best reflected a range of different conditions such as autism, attention deficit hyperactivity disorder, dyslexia, dyspraxia, and mental health conditions.
5. For example, wellbeing, psychological safety that they are accepted, that it is OK to make mistakes, and career satisfaction, as well as other demographic questions.
6. https://www.apa.org/pubs/journals/ocp?tab=1#tabs
7. https://www.hse.gov.uk/stress/standards/

REFERENCES

Alberti, G., & Iannuzzi, F. E. (2020). Embodied intersectionality and the intersectional management of hotel labour: The everyday experiences of social differentiation in customer-oriented work. *Gender, Work & Organization, 27*(6), 1165–1180.

Alhejji, H., Garavan, T., Carbery, R., O'Brien, F., & McGuire, D. (2016). Diversity training programme outcomes: A systematic review. *Human Resource Development Quarterly, 27*(1), 95–149.

Altman, B. M. (2001). Disability definitions, models, classification schemes, and applications. In G. L. Albrecht, K. Seelman, & M. Bury (Eds.), *Handbook of disability studies* (pp. 97–122). SAGE.

AXA Health. (2023). *Global Workplace Mind Health Report.* https://www.axahealth.co.uk/microsites-new/mindhealth/download-the-report2/

Bailey, J. M., Vasey, P. L., Diamond, L. M., Breedlove, S. M., Vilain, E., & Epprecht, M. (2016). Sexual orientation, controversy, and science. *Psychological Science in the Public Interest, 17*(2), 45–101.

Bakker, A. B., & Demerouti, E. (2007). The job demands-resources model: State of the art. *Journal of Managerial Psychology, 22*(3), 309–328.

Bauer, G. R., Churchill, S. M., Mahendran, M., Walwyn, C., Lizotte, D., & Villa-Rueda, A. A. (2021). Intersectionality in quantitative research: A systematic review of its emergence and applications of theory and methods. *SSM – Population Health, 14*, 100798.

Beagan, B. L., Mohamed, T., Brooks, K., Waterfield, B., & Weinberg, M. (2021). Microaggressions experienced by LGBTQ academics in Canada: "Just not fitting in … it does take a toll". *International Journal of Qualitative Studies in Education, 34*(3), 197–212.

Bellotti, L., Zaniboni, S., Balducci, C., & Grote, G. (2021). Rapid review on COVID-19, work-related aspects, and age differences. *International Journal of Environmental Research and Public Health, 18*(10), 5166.

Brohan, E., & Thornicroft, G. (2010). Stigma and discrimination of mental health problems: Workplace implications. *Occupational Medicine, 60*(6), 414–415.

Brown, R. L., & Moloney, M. E. (2019). Intersectionality, work, and well-being: The effects of gender and disability. *Gender & Society, 33*(1), 94–122.

Crenshaw, K. (1989). Demarginalizing the intersection of race and sex: A black feminist critique of antidiscrimination doctrine, feminist theory and antiracist politics. *University of Chicago Legal Forum 1998* (1), 139–167.

Cruwys, T., & Gunaseelan, S. (2016). "Depression is who I am": Mental illness identity, stigma and wellbeing. *Journal of Affective Disorders, 189*, 36–42.

Dang, C. T., Volpone, S. D., & Umphress, E. E. (2023). The ethics of diversity ideology: Consequences of leader diversity ideology on ethical leadership perception and organizational citizenship behavior. *Journal of Applied Psychology, 108*(2), 307–329.

Doyle, N., & McDowall, A. (2021). Diamond in the rough? An "empty review" of research into "neurodiversity" and a road map for developing the inclusion agenda. *Equality, Diversity and Inclusion: An International Journal, 41*(3), 352–382.

Doyle, N., & McDowall, A. (2023). Introduction to Neurodiversity. In N. Doyle & A. McDowall, *Neurodiversity coaching* (pp. 15–41). Routledge.

Doyle, N., McDowall, A., & Waseem, U. (2022). Intersectional stigma for autistic people at work: A compound adverse impact effect on labor force participation and experiences of belonging. *Autism in Adulthood, 4*(4), 340–356.

Earl, C., & Taylor, P. (2015). Is workplace flexibility good policy? Evaluating the efficacy of age management strategies for older women workers. *Work, Aging and Retirement, 1*(2), 214–226.

Fletcher, L., & Everly, B. A. (2021). Perceived lesbian, gay, bisexual, and transgender (LGBT) supportive practices and the life satisfaction of LGBT employees: The roles of disclosure, authenticity at work, and identity centrality. *Journal of Occupational and Organizational Psychology, 94*(3), 485–508.

Fletcher, L., & Marvell, R. (2023). *Transgender and non-binary inclusion at work.* CIPD guide. https://www.cipd.org/globalassets/media/knowledge/knowledge-hub/guides/2023-pdfs/transgender-non-binary-edi-in-the-workplace-guide-2023.pdf

Inceoglu, I., Thomas, G., Chu, C., Plans, D., & Gerbasi, A. (2018). Leadership behavior and employee well-being: An integrated review and a future research agenda. *The Leadership Quarterly, 29*(1), 179–202.

IOM (UN Migration). (2022). *World migration report.* https://worldmigrationreport.iom.int/wmr-2022-interactive/

Johnson, S., Cooper, C., Cartwright, S., Donald, I., Taylor, P., & Millet, C. (2005). The experience of work-related stress across occupations. *Journal of Managerial Psychology, 20*(2), 178–187.

Johnson, T. D., & Joshi, A. (2016). Dark clouds or silver linings? A stigma threat perspective on the implications of an autism diagnosis for workplace well-being. *Journal of Applied Psychology, 101*(3), 430.

Kaluza, A. J., Boer, D., Buengeler, C., & Van Dick, R. (2020). Leadership behaviour and leader self-reported well-being: A review, integration and meta-analytic examination. *Work & Stress, 34*(1), 34–56.

Kirkpatrick Partners. (n.d.). *The Kirkpatrick Model*. https://www.kirkpatrickpartners.com/the-kirkpatrick-model/

Köllen, T. (2021). Diversity management: A critical review and agenda for the future. *Journal of Management Inquiry, 30*(3), 259–272.

Koolhaas, W., Van der Klink, J. J., Groothoff, J. W., & Brouwer, S. (2012). Towards a sustainable healthy working life: Associations between chronological age, functional age and work outcomes. *The European Journal of Public Health, 22*(3), 424–429.

Lui, P. P., & Quezada, L. (2019). Associations between microaggression and adjustment outcomes: A meta-analytic and narrative review. *Psychological Bulletin, 145*(1), 45–78.

Mackey, J. D., Frieder, R. E., Brees, J. R., & Martinko, M. J. (2017). Abusive supervision: A meta-analysis and empirical review. *Journal of Management, 43*(6), 1940–1965.

McCartney, G., Popham, F., McMaster, R., & Cumbers, A. (2019). Defining health and health inequalities. *Public Health, 172*, 22–30.

McDowall, A., Doyle, N., & Kiseleva, M. (2023). *Neurodiversity at work 2023: Demand, supply and a gap analysis*. https://www.researchgate.net/analysis.publication/369474902_Neurodiversity_at_Work_2023

Meyerding, S. G. (2015). Job characteristics and job satisfaction: A test of Warr's vitamin model in German horticulture. *The Psychologist-Manager Journal, 18*(2), 86.

Moore, I., Morgan, G., Welham, A., & Russell, G. (2022). The intersection of autism and gender in the negotiation of identity: A systematic review and metasynthesis. *Feminism & Psychology, 32*(4), 421–442.

National Institute for Health and Care Research. (2021). *Guidance on co-producing a research project*. https://www.learningforinvolvement.org.uk/content/resource/nihr-guidance-on-co-producing-a-research-project/?

Oerlemans, W. G. M., Peeters, M. C. W. and Schaufeli, W. B. (2009). Ethnic diversity at work: An overview of theories and research. In K. Näswall, J. Hellgren, & M. Sverke (Eds.), *The individual in the changing working life* (pp. 211–232). Cambridge University Press.

Organization for Economic Co-operation and Development. (2018). *Diversity statistics in the OECD*. SDD working paper No. 96, Accessed https://one.oecd.org/document/SDD/DOC(2018)9/En/pdf

Rašticová, M., Birčiaková, N., Bédiová, M., & Mikušová, J. (2019). Older workers economic activity and the health status: The implication of age management. *Polish Journal of Management Studies, 19*, 322–337.

Reza, M. M., Subramaniam, T., & Islam, M. R. (2019). Economic and social well-being of Asian labour migrants: A literature review. *Social Indicators Research, 141*, 1245–1264.

Robinson, G., & Dechant, K. (1997). Building a business case for diversity. *The Academy of Management Executive, 11*(3), 21–31.

Sanclemente, F. J., Gamero, N., Arenas, A., & Medina, F. J. (2022). Linear and non-linear relationships between job demands-resources and psychological and physical symptoms of service sector employees. When is the midpoint a good choice? *Frontiers in Psychology*, *13*, 950908.

Smith, I. A., & Griffiths, A. (2022). Microaggressions, everyday discrimination, workplace incivilities, and other subtle slights at work: A meta-synthesis. *Human Resource Development Review*, *21*(3), 275–299.

Sorensen, G., Dennerlein, J. T., Peters, S. E., Sabbath, E. L., Kelly, E. L., & Wagner, G. R. (2021). The future of research on work, safety, health and wellbeing: A guiding conceptual framework. *Social Science & Medicine*, *269*, 113593.

Steensma, T. D., Kreukels, B. P., de Vries, A. L., & Cohen-Kettenis, P. T. (2013). Gender identity development in adolescence. *Hormones and Behavior*, *64*(2), 288–297.

Stergiou-Kita, M., Pritlove, C., & Kirsh, B. (2016). The "Big C": Stigma, cancer, and workplace discrimination. *Journal of Cancer Survivorship*, *10*, 1035–1050.

Stiglbauer, B., & Kovacs, C. (2018). The more, the better? Curvilinear effects of job autonomy on well-being from vitamin model and PE-fit theory perspectives. *Journal of Occupational Health Psychology*, *23*(4), 520.

Tepper, B. J., Simon, L., & Park, H. M. (2017). Abusive supervision. *Annual Review of Organizational Psychology and Organizational Behavior*, *4*, 123–152.

Thomas, D. A. (2016). Diversity as strategy. In S. B. Reiche, G. K. Stahl, M. E. Mendenhall, & G. R. Oddou (Eds.), *Readings and cases in international human resource management* (pp. 105–118). Routledge.

Van Beukering, I. E., Smits, S. J. C., Janssens, K. M. E., Bogaers, R. I., Joosen, M. C. W., Bakker, M., & Brouwers, E. P. M. (2021). In what ways does health related stigma affect sustainable employment and well-being at work? A systematic review. *Journal of Occupational Rehabilitation*, *32*(3), 365–379.

Walters, K., Falcaro, M., Freemantle, N., King, M., & Ben-Shlomo, Y. (2017). Sociodemographic inequalities in the management of depression in adults aged 55 and over: An analysis of English primary care data. *Psychological Medicine*, *48*(9), 1504–1513.

Wang, Q., Lai, Y. L., Xu, X., & McDowall, A. (2021). The effectiveness of workplace coaching: A meta-analysis of contemporary psychologically informed coaching approaches. *Journal of Work-Applied Management*, *14*(1), 77–101.

Warr, P. (1994). A conceptual framework for the study of work and mental health. *Work & Stress*, *8*(2), 84–97.

Warr, P. (2017). Happiness and mental health: A framework of vitamins in the environment and mental processes in the person. In J. C. Quick & C. L. Cooper (Eds.), *The handbook of stress and health: A guide to research and practice* (pp. 57–74). Wiley.

World Health Organization. (n.d., a). *Constitution*. https:// www .who .int/ about/ governance/constitution

World Health Organization. (n.d., b). *The Global Health Observatory: Life expectancy and healthy life expectancy*. https:// www .who .int/ data/ gho/ data/ themes/ mortality -and-global-health-estimates/ghe-life-expectancy-and-healthy-life-expectancy

World Health Organization. (n.d., c). *Disability*. https:// www .who .int/ health -topics/ disability#tab=tab_1

6. The interplay between uncertainty and insecurity and employee wellbeing during planned and emergent changes

Phong T. Nguyen, Alannah E. Rafferty, and Matthew J. Xerri

INTRODUCTION

Organizations regularly implement planned changes to enhance competitive advantage as they seek to respond to technological advances and a dynamic market environment (Allen et al., 2007; Carter et al., 2013). Levy (1986) and Lippitt et al. (1958) suggest that planned change originates with a decision by top-level management to deliberately improve the functioning of the organization, and typically involves the use of outside expertise and resources. Recently, many organizations have transformed their work routines and practices due to the COVID-19 global pandemic (Andrulli & Gerards, 2023; Sanders et al., 2020). As a result, organizations were required to engage in emergent change, which occurs when planning for change converges with the implementation of change (Weingart, 1992), so that improvisation is required as the composition and execution of action converge over time (Moorman & Miner, 1998). While these emergent change efforts are crucial for organizational survival in highly turbulent global environments, they may result in a range of negative consequences for employee health and wellbeing.

Researchers argue that planned organizational change models may not be completely adequate during the COVID-19 pandemic (Choflet et al., 2021). Hite and McDonald (2020) argued that the COVID-19 pandemic was unpredictable and outside the control of individuals. As such, organizations responded by implementing a wide range of fundamental changes to work practices, including implementing mandated social distancing and the use of remote and flexible work arrangements (Vyas, 2022). Importantly, those changes have carried over so that organizations have embraced a "new normal" where, for instance, the work arrangements have shifted to emphasize a remote model (Franken et al., 2021), while others focus on a mixture of remote (i.e., work from home) and non-remote (i.e., work completed outside of the home) work.

In this chapter, we present a model (see Figure 6.1) that identifies change event characteristics, which capture how change recipients experience change on key dimensions, including change management processes, the internal change context, and the content of change (Armenakis & Bedeian, 1999; Oreg et al., 2011; Rafferty et al., 2013), as drivers of uncertainty and insecurity, which in turn influence employee wellbeing. While our model has applicability for both planned and emergent organizational changes induced by crises such as the COVID-19 pandemic, we argue that during emergent change, the relationships between change event characteristics, and uncertainty and insecurity, are heightened. We draw on Danna and Griffin's (1999) conceptualization of employee wellbeing, which encompasses physiological and psychological health, and incorporates context-free measures of life experiences such as life satisfaction and happiness, and generalized job-related experiences, including job satisfaction and attachment (Danna & Griffin, 1999).

We contribute to the change field in three ways. First, while most research

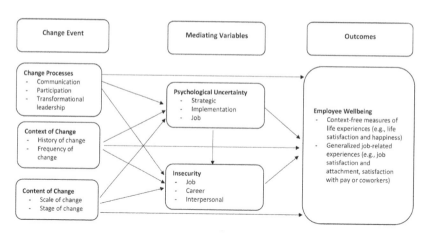

Figure 6.1   *The impact of change event characteristics on employee wellbeing*

has concentrated on stressors during planned change efforts, it is likely that uncertainty and insecurity will be heightened during emergent change, and so we consider the role of these stressors during planned and emergent change. Second, our focus on uncertainty and insecurity as mediators allows us to identify additional psychological pathways through which change event characteristics influence employee wellbeing. Finally, we argue that a serial mediation relationship occurs between uncertainty about change and insecurity, such that the three types of uncertainty influence the three types of insecurity, which in turn influence employee wellbeing.

THEORETICAL BACKGROUND: ORGANIZATIONAL CHANGE AND UNCERTAINTY AND INSECURITY ABOUT CHANGE

When asked to engage in planned organizational change, employees experience high levels of psychological uncertainty (Rafferty & Griffin, 2006), which refers to "the psychological state of doubt about what an event signifies or portends" (DiFonzo & Bordia, 1998, p. 296). Allen et al. (2007) identified three types of uncertainty that emerge during change: strategic, implementation, and job-related (see also Bordia et al., 2004a; Bordia et al., 2004b). *Strategic uncertainty* refers to a sense of psychological doubt about the reasons, vision, and future directions, of the change and organization. During COVID-19, as changes were often implemented "on the run", and action and planning occurred together, it is likely that strategic uncertainty was heightened throughout an organization. In a post-COVID-19 environment, with more time being available to devote to careful planning and consideration of change, we expect that strategic uncertainty will decline as planned change becomes more common, with expected improvements in wellbeing.

Allen and colleagues (2007, p. 195) defined *implementation uncertainty* as the extent to which employees are unclear about issues related to the implementation of the proposed change, including how change will impact key aspects of organization including the culture and structure (see also Kramer et al., 2004). We suggest that this type of uncertainty is closely related to the structural uncertainty identified by Bordia et al. (2004a, p. 510), which refers to "uncertainty arising from changes to the inner workings of the organization, such as reporting structures and functions of different work-units". During COVID-19, the introduction of emergent change is likely to have heightened implementation uncertainty as managers rushed to introduce changes in a rapidly changing environment. In a post-COVID-19 environment, as planned change becomes more common, we expect that implementation uncertainty will decline as more time and resources are available to design and execute changes, which as a result positively influences wellbeing.

Finally, *job-related uncertainty* captures employees' concerns about their workload, job roles, and promotion opportunities (Allen et al., 2007; Bordia et al., 2004a). Although Allen and colleagues include job insecurity in their uncertainty definition, we argue that uncertainty and insecurity are distinct concepts. Thus, we exclude job insecurity when discussing job-related uncertainty. We argue that job-related uncertainty also involves the extent to which employees are unsure about the skills and training needed to handle new tasks and responsibilities resulting from the change (Olsen & Stensaker, 2014; Schweiger & DeNisi, 1991). Job-related uncertainty is among the most prevalent types of uncertainty that develop during planned organizational change (e.g., Allen et al., 2007). We expect that the rise in emergent changes that occurred in response to COVID-19 was matched by the growth in job-related uncertainty, and subsequently poorer wellbeing. As planned changes become more common post-COVID-19, we would expect that this type of uncertainty will fall.

Insecurity about one's job is the most studied aspect of insecurity in a planned change context (e.g., Baillien & De Witte, 2009; Çalışkan & Özkoç, 2020; Mauno et al., 2001; Schumacher et al., 2016; Smet et al., 2016; Spagnoli & Balducci, 2017). However, based on existing theory and research, we identify that career and interpersonal insecurity are also important during planned and emergent change. Spurk et al. (2022) identifies three ways that the job and career insecurity constructs differ. First, *job insecurity* largely focuses on short-term or near-future job insecurities. In contrast, *career insecurity* "spans the entire career and thus focuses on short-term, mid-term, and long-term thoughts and worries" (Spurk et al., 2022, p. 257). Second, job insecurity typically captures the insecurities related to an individual's current job in the organization. Meanwhile, career insecurity focuses on an individual's career path and is not necessarily restricted to a single organization. Third, individual perceptions of career insecurity do not involve job characteristics, but broader career development aspects such as unemployment and career opportunities.

We also argue that interpersonal insecurity is distinct from job and career insecurity. Building on Lu et al. (2018), we define *interpersonal insecurity* as the extent to which employees worry about being rejected or getting hurt by others due to implementing an organizational change. Unlike career insecurity, we suggest that job and interpersonal insecurity focus on short-term and near-future insecurities; and that interpersonal insecurity mainly captures insecurities within teams and organizations. In an emergent change context, all three forms of insecurity will be heightened compared to a planned change context, as employees have less time, and likely have access to considerably less information, than in a planned change context. As a result, fears about one's job career and interpersonal relationships will be heightened, which will negatively influence wellbeing.

Many scholars have argued that even a planned organizational change is associated with a high level of job insecurity. Change threatens employees' feeling of control, and enhances the possibility of breaking the social exchange and the implicit promises between employee and employer, which results in job insecurity (Kalyal et al., 2010; Keim et al., 2014; Lingmont & Alexiou, 2020; Smet et al., 2016). Job insecurity resulting from planned change has consistently been found to be negatively related to individual health and wellbeing (e.g., Hellgren & Sverke, 2003; Hellgren et al., 1999; Sverke et al., 2002). In the context of a large-scale downsizing, Hellgren and Sverke (2003) documented a cross-lagged effect of job insecurity on employee mental health complaints. We suggest that these effects will be heightened in a context in which high levels of emergent change are occurring. In a post-COVID-19 context, we expect that the introduction of planned change, rather than emergent change, will result in less job insecurity, which will have positive consequences for wellbeing.

Only a few studies have discussed the negative implications of planned organizational change on career insecurity (Goffee & Scase, 1992; Lips-Wiersma & Hall, 2007; Simpson, 1998). Changes such as delayering an organization to increase adaptability and flexibility generally harm employees' career progress (Lips-Wiersma & Hall, 2007). Goffee and Scase (1992) noted that a marked decline in career opportunities, such as promotion for managers, due to restructuring efforts resulted in individuals withdrawing from work by performing the minimum to "get by", and reducing their dependency on the organization. This latter strategy may involve frequently moving between organizations, opting for early retirement, self-employment, or redirecting efforts to focus on personal and family life. Simpson (1998) found that organizational restructuring can produce negative career outcomes, including "competitive presenteeism", which occurs when managers compete over who stays longest in the office. This outcome had negative implications for women, who had difficulty competing in this regard due to their family commitments.

During COVID-19, with reduced career opportunities due to restricted career mobility, lower economic activity, and more emergent changes, it is likely that career insecurity was very high, and that career dependency was also high. Recent research findings indicate complexities in the post-COVID environment in relation to career implications. Brough et al. (2021) outlined evidence that accessing work–life balance leave might generate "a permanent negative mark" on employee's record that would hinder their future career advancement in a post-COVID environment. Additionally, employees (especially male employees) who request work–life balance leave are likely to be perceived as "less dominant and ambitious and less worthy of promotion" (Brough et al., 2021, p. 2). Overall, these findings suggest that career insecurity may have differentially impacted different groups during and after COVID-19, suggesting a need to further explore these issues.

Planned organizational change may also negatively influence social relationships in the workplace (e.g., Baillien & De Witte, 2009; Bala et al., 2021). Bala et al. (2021) explored the impact of an enterprise system change and reported that aspects of the change process, such as process complexity, rigidity, and radicalness, significantly explained the decline of co-worker relationship quality during the initial introduction of an enterprise system. The decreasing trajectory of change in the quality of relationships with co-workers led to declining job performance and job satisfaction. In addition, planned organizational change has been associated with workplace aggression, violence, and harassment toward others (e.g., Baron & Neuman, 1996; De Vries & Balazs, 1997). In their analysis of 1260 employees in 10 private organizations, Baillien and De Witte (2009) documented a positive association between experiencing change and workplace bullying, as reflected in gossiping, insulting teasing, verbal abuse, and social exclusion from co-workers (see Einarsen & Raknes, 1997). Further, the authors found that one possible reason for this association was because of the role conflict that results from experiencing planned change implementation. Overall, we argue that change recipients may experience interpersonal insecurity, as organizational change threatens recipients with rejection and being hurt by colleagues. Additionally, we expect emergent change will be associated with stronger negative interpersonal impacts than planned organizational change. When emergent changes are implemented, individuals have less time and resources to consider and respond to changes in their relationships in the workplace, with costs for wellbeing. In a post-COVID-19 setting, with the growth in planned change efforts, we expect that interpersonal insecurity will fall, with positive consequences for wellbeing over time.

PROPOSITION DEVELOPMENT

Change Management Processes

The first change event characteristic that influences change success involves the processes – the specific actions and methods undertaken by management – used to implement change (Armenakis & Bedeian, 1999). Key change processes include communication efforts, the extent of participation in decision-making about change, and the utilization of leadership behaviors, such as those encompassed by transformational leadership (Rafferty et al., 2013).

Change communication typically involves the delivery of change-related information from managers to work groups. High-quality change communication should convey a clear vision regarding the need for change, and deliver instructions, feedback, and social support during change (Lewis, 1999; Russ, 2008). Research supports the link between high communication quality and positive employee responses to change (e.g., Allen et al., 2007; Bordia et al., 2004b; McKay et al., 2013; Miller et al., 1994; Rafferty & Restubog, 2010; Wanberg & Banas, 2000). Specifically, high communication quality has been associated with favorable responses including commitment to change (e.g., Rafferty & Restubog, 2010), reduced cynicism, and reduced resistance to change (e.g., McKay et al., 2013; Qian & Daniels, 2008). High change communication quality also has been associated with lower uncertainty (Allen et al., 2007; Bordia et al., 2004a; Bordia et al., 2004b; Schweiger & DeNisi, 1991) and change anxiety (Rafferty & Restubog, 2010).

Research during the COVID-19 pandemic supports previous research on planned change. Sun et al. (2021) found that high-quality change communication was important when implementing changes induced by the COVID-19 pandemic. In particular, this research revealed that high-quality communication translated into enhanced perceptions of organizational support, and positive employee emotions about the company's responses to the pandemic (Sun et al., 2021). Additionally, Sanders et al. (2020) argued that during crises (e.g., COVID-19), organizational members often turn to their managers for relevant information, placing high demands on these individuals for clear and effective communication of critical decisions. In this respect, the authors suggest that to ensure employees clearly understand manager communication and interpret its messages as intended, such communication should be delivered in a way that draws employees' attention to the communication, and delivers consistent messages over time and across departments.

Participation in decision-making about change refers to the extent to which employees are provided with opportunities to have input regarding change (Wanberg & Banas, 2000). Change scholars argue that an organizational climate that facilitates open communication and participation in decision-making is positively related to positive organizational change implementation, through encouraging idea exchange without fear of retribution, which contributes to greater employee confidence in their ability to adapt to the changes (Yean et al., 2022). During planned change efforts, researchers find that participation is positively associated with favorable employee responses to change (e.g., Bartunek et al., 2006; Eby et al., 2000; Helpap, 2016; Wanberg & Banas, 2000). Employees who report high levels of participation in change-related decision-making tend to report favorable attitudes like readiness, commitment, and openness to change (e.g., Eby et al., 2000; Van der Voet, 2016; Wanberg & Banas, 2000), and lower uncertainty about change (Bordia et al., 2004a), when compared with individuals who report low levels of participation. When emergent changes are implemented, and planning and implementation converge in time – which was prevalent during the COVID-19 pandemic – there are likely to be fewer opportunities to utilize participation in change decision-making to manage uncertainty and insecurity. However, research has also documented evidence for the role of participation in ensuring employee favorable responses during emergent changes that were implemented in response to the COVID-19 pandemic. Sun and colleagues (2021) found that during the COVID-19 outbreak, employees who perceived that the organization encouraged them to express ideas, and considered and incorporated their opinions and feedback, also reported high levels of perceived organizational support and positive emotions, which in turn shaped their organizational identification.

Transformational leadership refers to the extent to which a leader moves followers "beyond immediate self-interests through idealized influence (charisma), inspiration, intellectual stimulation, or individualized consideration" (Bass, 1999, p. 11). Transformational leaders convey a sense of optimism about change, enable their followers to see the necessity and feasibility of change as well as challenge existing approaches, and guide followers through change (Carter et al., 2013; DeCelles et al., 2013). Kim et al. (2021) argued that transformational leadership becomes a social resource during a crisis like COVID-19, as these leaders may help employees cope with stress by inspiring and reframing a stressful situation into an opportunity.

Building on previous research, we expect that positive change management processes that involve a high level of change communication quality, employee participation and involvement in change-related decision-making, and/or transformational leadership, will provide employees with relevant information that alleviates their concerns about change as well as its implications for their job, career, and interpersonal relationships at work, which in turn results in enhanced wellbeing. We also expect that these effects are likely to be heightened when emergent changes occur, compared to when planned change efforts are introduced. Thus, we offer the following propositions:

Proposition 1: For both planned and emergent changes, positive change management processes will be negatively associated with strategic uncertainty, implementation uncertainty, and job-related uncertainty.

Proposition 2: For both planned and emergent changes, positive change management processes will be negatively associated with job insecurity, career insecurity, and interpersonal insecurity.

We also argue that there are indirect relationships between positive change management processes and employee wellbeing, via psychological uncertainty and insecurity about change, for both planned and emergent change. We propose these relationships as follows:

Proposition 3: For planned and emergent changes, there is an indirect positive relationship between positive change management processes and employee wellbeing via strategic uncertainty, implementation uncertainty, and job-related uncertainty.

Proposition 4: For planned and emergent changes, there is an indirect positive relationship between positive change management processes and employee wellbeing via job insecurity, career insecurity, and interpersonal insecurity.

Internal Change Context

The internal change context is the second change event characteristic that we identify as a key influence on individuals' responses to change. Johns (2006) defined context as the "situational opportunities and constraints that affect the occurrence and meaning of organizational behavior as well as functional relationships between variables" (p. 386). Researchers have identified an organization's change history (Bordia et al., 2011; Rafferty & Restubog, 2010; Van der Smissen et al., 2013), and the frequency with which change occurs in an organization (Carter et al., 2013; Rafferty & Griffin, 2006; Rafferty & Jimmieson, 2017), as key aspects of the internal change context. An organization's change history refers to employee perceptions of how well the company has managed change in the past (Rafferty & Restubog, 2010).

The frequency of change concerns "individuals' perceptions regarding how often change has occurred" (Rafferty & Griffin, 2006, p. 1154). A high frequency of change involves a sense that an individual is operating in a turbulent environment where people are constantly required to engage in change (Rafferty & Jimmieson, 2017), which disrupts work routines (Carter et al., 2013). Empirical research of planned organizational changes suggests that frequent change is associated with low job satisfaction, as well as high stress, fatigue, psychological uncertainty, and turnover intentions (see Rafferty & Jimmieson, 2017). When responding to a crisis such as COVID-19, which required the rapid introduction of emergent organizational changes, it is likely that, as the frequency of changes increases, employee wellbeing will deteriorate, as people struggle to adapt due to lack of opportunity to prepare for change and to engage in anticipatory coping efforts to ameliorate the impact of these changes.

Overall, previous research has implied that the internal change context, as reflected in an organization's change history and the frequency of change, provides information that employees use to make sense of current change events (e.g., Rafferty & Restubog, 2010; Rafferty & Griffin, 2006). In organizations with a poor history of change management and/or a high frequency of change, employee concerns about a change event will be amplified, enhancing uncertainty and insecurity about change. These effects will be heightened when an organization implements emergent changes, where there is little planning or deliberation to manage employee concerns. In contrast, we argue that an organization with a successful change management history and/or a relatively stable environment with a low perceived change frequency will more easily allow employees to gather and interpret information to alleviate their concerns about change. In these environments, it is also less likely that emergent change will be required. In such environments, employees will likely report lower uncertainty and insecurity. Thus, we propose:

Proposition 5: For planned and emergent changes, there is an indirect positive relationship between a positive internal change context (i.e., positive change management history, low frequency of change) and employee wellbeing via strategic, implementation, and job-related uncertainty.
Proposition 6: For planned and emergent changes, there is an indirect positive relationship between a positive internal change context (i.e., positive change management history, low frequency of change) and employee wellbeing via job insecurity, career insecurity, and interpersonal insecurity.

Content of Change

The third change event characteristic is the content of change, which refers to the nature of the change being experienced. In this chapter, we consider the scale and stage of change as key aspects of the content of change (Rafferty & Griffin, 2006). In terms of the scale of change, large-scale (or transformational) planned changes tend to be associated with less favorable change responses from employees compared to smaller-scale changes. Rafferty and Simons (2006, p. 330), suggested "transformational changes generally have a detrimental effect on individuals as they involve a great deal of conflict and often bring to the fore personality issues and other differences that have previously been sublimated, adding to the confusion and uncertainty within the organization". Individuals who experienced smaller-scale planned changes reported a higher level of change readiness than those who experienced transformational change (Rafferty & Simons, 2006). In addition, large-scale planned changes such as restructuring, mergers and acquisitions, and downsizing often result in high levels of employee uncertainty and insecurity, and thereby negatively influence employee wellbeing (Belschak et al., 2020; Bordia et al., 2004a; Schweiger & DeNisi, 1991; Schweiger & Weber, 1992).

Interestingly, Andrulli and Gerards (2023) found that new ways of working induced by the COVID-19 pandemic resulted in enhanced job-related affective wellbeing through influencing employee's technostress, need for recovery, and work engagement. It is not clear though whether new ways of working were experienced as incremental or transformational changes. Sudo (2022) observed that the impact of COVID-19 on subjective wellbeing differed between socially advantaged and disadvantaged individuals, such that only the former groups experienced positive effects of the pandemic on their wellbeing. Those studies suggest potential contextual factors, such as the role of access to resources and support inside and outside the workplace, may explain relationships between the scale of change and employee outcomes, during emergent changes implemented in response to a crisis. We encourage future research to examine these factors and mechanisms.

Research suggests that the stage of change is also associated with different responses to change. Empirical studies (e.g., Bastien, 1987; Fugate et al., 2002; Schweiger & DeNisi, 1991) indicate that employee reactions vary as a function of the stage of planned change. Without an appropriate organizational communication plan (e.g., a realistic merger preview program), Schweiger and DeNisi observed that employees' job satisfaction, uncertainty about change, and perceptions of their organization became more negative in the later stages of a merger. Bordia et al. (2004a) suggest that in the earlier stages of change, employees first experience strategic uncertainty, leading to implementation or structural uncertainty and, subsequently, job-related uncertainty. Fugate et al. (2002) found that employees had the lowest level of perceived control at the early stage of a merger, while control increased in the later stages as employees learnt how the change event would affect them. In the case of emergent changes implemented in response to the COVID-19 pandemic, it is likely that the discussion and planning stages of change were highly truncated with the focus being on the implementation of change. The lack of planning and discussion is likely to have reduced the time for both managers and employees to engage in anticipatory coping and, therefore, heightened distress and reduced wellbeing.

We expect that a favorable change content, which encompasses smaller-scale and/or a later stage of change, is likely to be associated with less employee uncertainty and insecurity about change. We suggest that emergent changes are likely to be perceived as more transformational because of the lack of prior preparation and planning associated with these changes. Employees are likely to perceive them as more transformational simply due to the element of "surprise" associated with these changes, which will then be associated with higher uncertainty and insecurity, and therefore lower wellbeing.

We also expect employees to experience higher levels of uncertainty and insecurity at the onset of planned change efforts compared to later in the change. At the early stage of change, employees do not have sufficient time and resources to assess the change situation carefully (Schumacher et al., 2016), and to understand its implications for the organization's strategic direction, key organizational systems and processes, or their job and promotion opportunities. We suggest that as employees get involved in change, and managers are provided more information that they can then share with their direct reports, uncertainty about change and insecurity will generally decrease over time. In relation to emergent changes, due to the lack of prior planning and preparation associated with these changes, we expect that there will be greater uncertainty and insecurity during all stages of the change process compared to a planned change process. Overall, we propose:

Proposition 7: For planned and emergent change, there is an indirect positive relationship between a favorable content of change (i.e., smaller-scale and a later stage of change) and employee wellbeing via strategic, implementation, and job-related uncertainty.

Proposition 8: For planned and emergent change, there is an indirect positive relationship between a favorable content of change (i.e., smaller-scale and a later stage of change) and employee wellbeing via job, career, and interpersonal insecurity.

Interplay Between Types of Uncertainty and Insecurity About Change

Limited studies have simultaneously incorporated uncertainty and insecurity measures in a change setting (e.g., De Cuyper et al., 2010; Li & Griffin, 2022; Priyadarshi & Premchandran, 2022). Li and Griffin (2022) documented that job insecurity was associated with reduced job satisfaction via enhancing the psychological uncertainty about COVID-19. In contrast, Priyadarshi and Premchandran found that psychological uncertainty about change resulted in job insecurity and influenced employee intentions to quit the organization. These studies suggest contrasting results in terms of whether uncertainty precedes insecurity or vice versa. However, based on the initial evidence, we argue that the types of uncertainty heighten insecurity in an individual's job, career, and interpersonal relationships. When employees are uncertain or unable to predict how a change will unfold, they will experience perceived threats to their job roles, career development, and interpersonal relationships (Fugate et al., 2002; Priyadarshi & Premchandran, 2022). With this link between uncertainty and insecurity, we propose the following serial mediation:

Proposition 9: For planned and emergent changes, there is a serial mediation relationship between the characteristics of change events and employee wellbeing via strategic uncertainty, implementation uncertainty, and job-related uncertainty, which in turn are positively associated with job insecurity, career insecurity, and interpersonal insecurity, which in turn influence employee wellbeing.

CONCLUDING REMARKS

Organizations transformed their work routines and practices due to the COVID-19 global pandemic (Andrulli & Gerards, 2023; Sanders et al., 2020). These changes were often emergent in that planning for the change converged with change implementation (Weingart, 1992). In this chapter, we considered planned and emergent organizational change, arguing that heightened levels of uncertainty and insecurity will be experienced during emergent change implementation, which will have a greater negative influence on employee wellbeing compared to planned change efforts. We also argued that negative change event characteristics (e.g., poor prior change history, very frequent change, low levels of participation or a lack of a participatory climate) will be more common and more impactful during emergent change compared to planned change implementation. Our work offers a conceptual model that enables future research to unpack the psychological pathways between change event characteristics and employee wellbeing. We also provide practical implications for ensuring employee health and wellbeing during (and after) turbulent times that require the implementation of emergent rather than planned organizational changes.

We argue that during planned and emergent changes, change leaders need to develop positive change processes including high-quality communication, high levels of employee participation and involvement, and effective utilization of transformational leadership. In addition, the change context – including change frequency in the organization and a history of successful change management, and the content of change – including the scale of change and the influence of the stage of the proposed change, are critical to employee perceptions of uncertainty and insecurity. When these three change event characteristics (i.e., process, context, and content) are monitored and managed effectively, managers are best equipped to address uncertainty and insecurity about change. In this respect, employees' health and wellbeing are likely to be ensured and, thereby, the proposed changes are likely to be well implemented and sustained.

In conclusion, considering planned and emergent organizational changes, we have identified three types of uncertainty and of insecurity as key psychological processes through which change event characteristics translate into employee wellbeing. These types of uncertainty and insecurity need to be managed appropriately during planned and emergent changes so that organizations can change more successfully and sustainably.

REFERENCES

Allen, J., Jimmieson, N. L., Bordia, P., & Irmer, B. E. (2007). Uncertainty during organizational change: Managing perceptions through communication. *Journal of Change Management*, *7*(2), 187–210. https://doi.org/10.1080/14697010701563379

Andrulli, R., & Gerards, R. (2023). How new ways of working during COVID-19 affect employee well-being via technostress, need for recovery, and work engagement. *Computers in Human Behavior*, *139*, 107560. https://doi.org/10.1016/j.chb.2022.107560

Armenakis, A. A., & Bedeian, A. G. (1999). Organizational change: A review of theory and research in the 1990s. *Journal of Management*, *25*(3), 293–315.

Baillien, E., & De Witte, H. (2009). Why is organizational change related to workplace bullying? Role conflict and job insecurity as mediators. *Economic and Industrial Democracy*, *30*(3), 348–371.

Bala, H., Venkatesh, V., Ganster, D. C., & Rai, A. (2021). How does an enterprise system implementation change interpersonal relationships in organizations. *Industrial Management & Data Systems*, *121*(8), 1824–1847. https://doi.org/10.1108/IMDS-06-2020-0380

Baron, R. A., & Neuman, J. H. (1996). Workplace violence and workplace aggression: Evidence on their relative frequency and potential causes. *Aggressive Behavior*, *22*, 161–173. https://doi.org/10.1002/(SICI)1098-2337(1996)22:3<161::AID-AB1>3.0.CO;2-Q

Bartunek, J. M., Rousseau, D. M., Rudolph, J. W., & DePalma, J. A. (2006). On the receiving end: Sensemaking, emotion, and assessments of an organizational change initiated by others. *Journal of Applied Behavioral Science*, *42*(2), 182–206. https://doi.org/10.1177/0021886305285455

Bass, B. M. (1999). Two decades of research and development in transformational leadership. *European Journal of Work and Organizational Psychology*, *8*(1), 9–32. https://doi.org/10.1080/135943299398410

Bastien, D. T. (1987). Common patterns of behavior and communication in corporate mergers and acquisitions. *Human Resource Management*, *26*(1), 17–33.

Belschak, F. D., Jacobs, G., Giessner, S. R., Horton, K. E., & Bayerl, P. S. (2020). When the going gets tough: Employee reactions to large-scale organizational change and the role of employee Machiavellianism. *Journal of Organizational Behavior*, *41*(9), 830–850. https://doi.org/10.1002/job.2478

Bordia, P., Hobman, E., Jones, E., Gallois, C., & Callan, V. J. (2004a). Uncertainty during organizational change: Types, consequences, and management strategies. *Journal of Business and Psychology*, *18*(4), 507–532. https://doi.org/10.1023/B:JOBU.0000028449.99127.f7

Bordia, P., Hunt, E., Paulsen, N., Tourish, D., & DiFonzo, N. (2004b). Uncertainty during organizational change: Is it all about control? *European Journal of Work and Organizational Psychology*, *13*(3), 345–365.

Bordia, P., Restubog, S. L. D., Jimmieson, N. L., & Irmer, B. E. (2011). Haunted by the past: Effects of poor change management history on employee attitudes and turnover. *Group & Organization Management*, *36*(2), 191–222.

Brough, P., Kinman, G., McDowall, A., & Chan, X. W. (2021). "#MeToo" for work-life balance. *Bulletin of the British Psychological Society*, *5*, 4–8. https://doi.org/10.53841/bpswlb.2021.1.5.4

Çalışkan, N., & Özkoç, A. G. (2020). Organizational change and job insecurity: The moderating role of employability. *International Journal of Contemporary Hospitality Management, 32*(12), 3971–3990. https://doi.org/10.1108/IJCHM-05-2020-0387

Carter, M. Z., Armenakis, A. A., Feild, H. S., & Mossholder, K. W. (2013). Transformational leadership, relationship quality, and employee performance during continuous incremental organizational change. *Journal of Organizational Behavior, 34*(7), 942–958. https://doi.org/10.1002/job.1824

Choflet, A., Packard, T., & Stashower, K. (2021). Rethinking organizational change in the COVID-19 era. *Journal of Hospital Management and Health Policy, 5.* https://jhmhp.amegroups.org/article/view/6699

Danna, K., & Griffin, R. W. (1999). Health and well-being in the workplace: A review and synthesis of the literature. *Journal of Management, 25*(3), 357–384.

De Cuyper, N., De Witte, H., Vander Elst, T., & Handaja, Y. (2010). Objective threat of unemployment and situational uncertainty during a restructuring: Associations with perceived job insecurity and strain. *Journal of Business and Psychology, 25*(1), 75–85. https://doi.org/10.1007/s10869-009-9128-y

De Vries, M. F. R. K., & Balazs, K. (1997). The downside of downsizing. *Human Relations, 50*(1), 11–50. https://doi.org/10.1023/A:1016901315958

DeCelles, K., Tesluk, P., & Taxman, F. (2013). A field investigation of multilevel cynicism toward change. *Organization Science, 24*, 154–171. https://doi.org/10.2307/23362105

DiFonzo, N., & Bordia, P. (1998). A tale of two corporations: Managing uncertainty during organizational change. *Human Resource Management, 37*(3-4), 295–303. https://doi.org/10.1002/(SICI)1099-050X(199823/24)37:3/4<295::AID-HRM10>3.0.CO;2-3

Eby, L., Adams, D., Russell, J., & Gaby, S. (2000). Perceptions of organizational readiness for change: Factors related to employees' reactions to the implementation of team-based selling. *Human Relations, 53*, 419–442. https://doi.org/10.1177/0018726700533006

Einarsen, S., & Raknes, B. I. (1997). Harassment in the workplace and the victimization of men. *Violence Vict, 12*(3), 247–263.

Franken, E., Bentley, T., Shafaei, A., Farr-Wharton, B., Onnis, L.-a., & Omari, M. (2021). Forced flexibility and remote working: Opportunities and challenges in the new normal. *Journal of Management & Organization, 27*(6), 1131–1149. https://doi.org/10.1017/jmo.2021.40

Fugate, M., Kinicki, A. J., & Scheck, C. L. (2002). Coping with an organizational merger over four stages. *Personnel Psychology, 55*(4), 905–928.

Goffee, R., & Scase, R. (1992). Organizational change and the corporate career: The restructuring of managers' job aspirations. *Human Relations, 45*(4), 363–385. https://doi.org/10.1177/001872679204500404

Hellgren, J., & Sverke, M. (2003). Does job insecurity lead to impaired well-being or vice versa? Estimation of cross-lagged effects using latent variable modelling. *Journal of Organizational Behavior, 24*(2), 215–236. https://doi.org/10.1002/job.184

Hellgren, J., Sverke, M., & Isaksson, K. (1999). A two-dimensional approach to job insecurity: Consequences for employee attitudes and well-being. *European Journal of Work and Organizational Psychology, 8*(2), 179–195. https://doi.org/10.1080/135943299398311

Helpap, S. (2016). The impact of power distance orientation on recipients' reactions to participatory versus programmatic change communication. *Journal of Applied Behavioral Science, 52*(1), 5–34. https://doi.org/10.1177/0021886315617530

Hite, L. M., & McDonald, K. S. (2020). Careers after COVID-19: Challenges and changes. *Human Resource Development International, 23*(4), 427–437.

Johns, G. (2006). The essential impact of context on organizational behavior. *The Academy of Management Review, 31*(2), 386–408. http:// www .jstor .org/ stable/ 20159208

Kalyal, H. J., Berntson, E., Baraldi, S., Näswall, K., & Sverke, M. (2010). The moderating role of employability on the relationship between job insecurity and commitment to change. *Economic and Industrial Democracy, 31*(3), 327–344.

Keim, A. C., Landis, R. S., Pierce, C. A., & Earnest, D. R. (2014). Why do employees worry about their jobs? A meta-analytic review of predictors of job insecurity. *Journal of Occupational Health Psychology, 19*(3), 269.

Kim, H., Im, J., & Shin, Y. H. (2021). The impact of transformational leadership and commitment to change on restaurant employees' quality of work life during a crisis. *Journal of Hospitality and Tourism Management, 48*, 322–330. https://doi.org/10 .1016/j.jhtm.2021.07.010

Kramer, M. W., Dougherty, D. S., & Pierce, T. A. (2004). Managing uncertainty during a corporate acquisition: A longitudinal study of communication during an airline acquisition. *Human Communication Research, 30*(1), 71–101.

Levy, A. (1986). Second-order planned change: Definition and conceptualization. *Organizational Dynamics, 15*(1), 5–23. https://doi.org/10.1016/0090-2616(86)90022 -7

Lewis, L. (1999). Disseminating information and soliciting input during planned organizational change: Implementers' targets, sources, and channels for communicating. *Management Communication Quarterly, 13*(1), 43–75. https://doi.org/10 .1177/0893318999131002

Li, K., & Griffin, M. A. (2022). Safety behaviors and job satisfaction during the pandemic: The mediating roles of uncertainty and managerial commitment. *Journal of Safety Research, 82*, 166–175. https://doi.org/10.1016/j.jsr.2022.05.008

Lingmont, D. N., & Alexiou, A. (2020). The contingent effect of job automating technology awareness on perceived job insecurity: Exploring the moderating role of organizational culture. *Technological Forecasting and Social Change, 161*, 120302.

Lippitt, R., Watson, J., Westley, B., & Spalding, W. B. (1958). *The dynamics of planned change: A comparative study of principles and techniques.* Harcourt, Brace & World.

Lips-Wiersma, M., & Hall, D. T. (2007). Organizational career development is not dead: A case study on managing the new career during organizational change. *Journal of Organizational Behavior, 28*(6), 771–792. https:// doi .org/ 10 .1002/ job .446

Lu, J., Zhang, Y., & Liu, J. (2018). Interpersonal insecurity and risk-taking propensity across domains and around the globe. *Evolutionary Psychology, 16*(3), 1474704918795520. https://doi.org/10.1177/1474704918795520

Mauno, S., Leskinen, E., & Kinnunen, U. (2001). Multi-wave, multi-variable models of job insecurity: Applying different scales in studying the stability of job insecurity. *Journal of Organizational Behavior, 22*(8), 919–937. http:// www .jstor.org/ stable/ 3649579

McKay, K., Kuntz, J. R., & Näswall, K. (2013). The effect of affective commitment, communication and participation on resistance to change: The role of change readiness. *New Zealand Journal of Psychology (Online)*, *42*(2), 29.

Miller, V. D., Johnson, J. R., & Grau, J. (1994). Antecedents to willingness to participate in a planned organizational change. *Journal of Applied Communication Research*, *22*(1), 59–80. https://doi.org/10.1080/00909889409365387

Moorman, C., & Miner, A. S. (1998). Organizational improvisation and organizational memory. *The Academy of Management Review*, *23*(4), 698–723. https://doi.org/10.2307/259058

Olsen, T. H., & Stensaker, I. (2014). A change-recipient perspective on training during organizational change. *International Journal of Training and Development*, *18*(1), 22–36. https://doi.org/10.1111/ijtd.12018

Oreg, S., Vakola, M., & Armenakis, A. (2011). Change recipients' reactions to organizational change: A 60-year review of quantitative studies. *The Journal of Applied Behavioral Science*, *47*(4), 461–524.

Priyadarshi, P., & Premchandran, R. (2022). Insecurity and turnover as robots take charge: Impact of neuroticism and change-related uncertainty. *Personnel Review*, *51*(1), 21–39. https://doi.org/10.1108/PR-06-2019-0310

Qian, Y., & Daniels, T. D. (2008). A communication model of employee cynicism toward organizational change. *Corporate Communications: An International Journal*, *13*(3), 319–332.

Rafferty, A., Jimmieson, N., & Armenakis, A. (2013). Change readiness: A multi-level review. *Journal of Management*, *39*(1), 110–135. https://doi.org/10.1177/0149206312457417

Rafferty, A., & Restubog, S. (2010). The impact of change process and context on change reactions and turnover during a merger. *Journal of Management*, *36*, 1309–1338. https://doi.org/10.1177/0149206309341480

Rafferty, A., & Simons, R. (2006). An examination of the antecedents of readiness for fine-tuning and corporate transformation changes. *Journal of Business and Psychology*, *20*(3), 325. https://doi.org/10.1007/s10869-005-9013-2

Rafferty, A. E., & Griffin, M. A. (2006). Perceptions of organizational change: A stress and coping perspective. *Journal of Applied Psychology*, *91*, 1154–1162. https://doi.org/10.1037/0021-9010.91.5.1154

Rafferty, A. E., & Jimmieson, N. L. (2017). Subjective perceptions of organizational change and employee resistance to change: Direct and mediated relationships with employee well-being. *British Journal of Management*, *28*(2), 248–264. https://doi.org/10.1111/1467-8551.12200

Russ, T. L. (2008). Communicating change: A review and critical analysis of programmatic and participatory implementation approaches. *Journal of Change Management*, *8*(3-4), 199–211. https://doi.org/10.1080/14697010802594604

Sanders, K., Nguyen, P. T., Bouckenooghe, D., Rafferty, A., & Schwarz, G. (2020). Unraveling the what and how of organizational communication to employees during COVID-19 pandemic: Adopting an attributional lens. *The Journal of Applied Behavioral Science*, *56*(3), 289–293.

Schumacher, D., Schreurs, B., Van Emmerik, H., & De Witte, H. (2016). Explaining the relation between job insecurity and employee outcomes during organizational change: A multiple group comparison. *Human Resource Management*, *55*(5), 809–827.

Schweiger, D. M., & DeNisi, A. S. (1991). Communication with employees following a merger: A longitudinal field experiment. *Academy of Management Journal, 34*(1), 110–135. https://doi.org/10.2307/256304

Schweiger, D. M., & Weber, Y. (1992). Strategies for managing human resources during mergers and acquisitions: An empirical investigation. In D. M. Schweiger & K. Papenfuß (Eds.), *Human resource planning: Solutions to key business issues – Selected articles* (pp. 101–118). Gabler Verlag.

Simpson, R. (1998). Presenteeism, power and organizational change: Long hours as a career barrier and the impact on the working lives of women managers. *British Journal of Management, 9*(s1), 37–50. https://doi.org/10.1111/1467-8551.9.s1.5

Smet, K., Vander Elst, T., Griep, Y., & De Witte, H. (2016). The explanatory role of rumours in the reciprocal relationship between organizational change communication and job insecurity: A within-person approach. *European Journal of Work and Organizational Psychology, 25*(5), 631–644. https://doi.org/10.1080/1359432X.2016.1143815

Spagnoli, P., & Balducci, C. (2017). Do high workload and job insecurity predict workplace bullying after organizational change? *International Journal of Workplace Health Management, 10*(1), 2–12.

Spurk, D., Hofer, A., Hirschi, A., De Cuyper, N., & De Witte, H. (2022). Conceptualizing career insecurity: Toward a better understanding and measurement of a multidimensional construct. *Personnel Psychology, 75*(2), 253–294. https://doi.org/10.1111/peps.12493

Sudo, N. (2022). The positive and negative effects of the COVID-19 pandemic on subjective well-being and changes in social inequality: Evidence from prefectures in Japan. *SSM – Population Health, 17,* 101029. https://doi.org/10.1016/j.ssmph.2022.101029

Sun, R., Li, J.-Y. Q., Lee, Y., & Tao, W. (2021). The role of symmetrical internal communication in improving employee experiences and organizational identification during COVID-19 pandemic-induced organizational change. *International Journal of Business Communication, 60*(4), 23294884211050628. https://doi.org/10.1177/23294884211050628

Sverke, M., Hellgren, J., & Näswall, K. (2002). No security: A meta-analysis and review of job insecurity and its consequences. *Journal of Occupational Health Psychology, 7,* 242–264. https://doi.org/10.1037/1076-8998.7.3.242

Van der Smissen, S., Schalk, R., & Freese, C. (2013). Organizational change and the psychological contract. *Journal of Organizational Change Management, 26*(6), 1071–1090. https://doi.org/10.1108/JOCM-08-2012-0118

Van der Voet, J. (2016). Change leadership and public sector organizational change: Examining the interactions of transformational leadership style and red tape. *The American Review of Public Administration, 46*(6), 660–682. https://doi.org/10.1177/0275074015574769

Vyas, L. (2022). "New normal" at work in a post-COVID world: Work–life balance and labor markets. *Policy and Society, 41*(1), 155–167.

Wanberg, C. R., & Banas, J. T. (2000). Predictors and outcomes of openness to changes in a reorganizing workplace. *Journal of Applied Psychology, 85*(1), 132–142. https://doi.org/10.1037/0021-9010.85.1.132

Weingart, L. R. (1992). Impact of group goals, task component complexity, effort, and planning on group performance. *Journal of Applied Psychology, 77*(5), 682–693. https://doi.org/10.1037/0021-9010.77.5.682

Yean, T. F., Tan, F. C., & Nadarajah, D. (2022). Determinants of adaptability and its impact on the change readiness of civil servants. *International Journal of Public Sector Management, 35*(5), 622–639. https://doi.org/10.1108/IJPSM-12-2021-0263

7. Workplace emotions in turbulent environments: implications for workers' wellbeing and performance

Ashlea C. Troth, Peter J. Jordan, and Alannah E. Rafferty

INTRODUCTION

Turbulent environments, defined as environments characterized by unexpected and unpredictable forms of change that is volatile, complex, and ambiguous (Schoemaker & Day, 2021; Van Zoonen et al., 2021) are a phenomenon most employees and managers have dealt with since the COVID-19 pandemic. Turbulent environments are created by factors exogenous and endogenous to organizations (Ansell & Trondal, 2018). This means they may be produced by factors external to organizations, such as cybersecurity breaches, extreme weather events, financial crises, and rapid technological change. They can also emerge within organizations from a range of factors including staff turnover, conflicting rules, internal reforms, and changes to complex operations (Ansell & Trondal, 2018). COVID-19 brought significant changes to our work and family lives that impacted on wellbeing (Zacher & Rudolph, 2021).

One important change in the work domain is a huge upswing in remote and hybrid ways of operating, collaborating, and leading. As Chung (2022) notes, this instability has given rise to a myriad of challenges and concerns that include 'Zoom fatigue,' poor 'digital demarcation,' shifting power balances at work, and declining mental health and safety (see for example, Chapter 10 in this collection, discussing the impact of technology and employee wellbeing). The popular media have created novel terms to capture new phenomena, like the *great resignation* (an ongoing post-COVID-19 trend in which employees voluntarily resign from their jobs en masse), the *great renegotiation* (a trend in which employees renegotiate the relationship with their employer to demand better jobs and conditions, rather than leave the workforce altogether), and *mini commutes* (a term capturing the small distances some employees now travel from the bedroom to their home office). These terms provide insights as to how individuals have reassessed and reimagined their work and non-work lives in this turbulent environment, with consequences for their wellbeing and performance. According to Pazzanese (2021, para. 12) 'the pandemic has jolted the foundation of a workplace model that had been relatively unchanged since the late 1920s.'

In this chapter, we contend that understanding the ways individuals emotionally experience and respond to change caused by turbulent contexts is critical for employees, managers, and human resource practitioners, to enable optimal responses, processes, and policies to support them. There is now a well-established body of research to demonstrate that workplaces are emotionally laden, and emotions are integral to work life (Ashforth & Humphrey, 1995), and that the way they are managed (by employees, supervisors, and the organization) have implications for employee wellbeing and performance (Troth et al., 2021). Thus, we propose that emotions and other affect-related concepts (e.g., emotional intelligence, emotional exhaustion) provide insights to assist us in understanding more fully the experiences and reactions of employees in organizations in turbulent environments.

The literature addressing the nexus between emotions and wellbeing in the context of turbulence and disruption (a break or interruption in the normal course or continuation of some activity or process) is surprisingly scant. Recent examples include Barboza-Wilkes et al.'s (2023) research on emotional labor and burnout in not-for-profit employees working with high-risk youth during COVID-19, and Merlini et al.'s (2023) diary study on the role of affect when employees need to allocate resources to meet multiple goals during disruption. In this chapter, we draw on organizational change literature that examines individuals' change-related emotional responses, to consider how this increases our understanding of workers' wellbeing in turbulent times. We also move beyond large-scale organizational change frameworks to review a selection of recent literature that considers the role of emotions and affective processes in organizations during disruption in its various forms (see Troth et al., 2023b). We conclude this chapter with learnings and future directions that are useful to practitioners, leaders, and organizations.

AFFECT, MOODS, AND EMOTIONS

Given that our chapter deals with emotion phenomena, it is important to have clear construct definitions to understand the nuances between different, but related, concepts. First, *affect* is the umbrella term used by researchers to encompass affective dispositions, moods, and emotions (Kelly & Barsade, 2001), and is generally and inclusively defined as a 'subjective feeling state' (Ashforth & Humphrey, 1995). *Dispositional affect* consists of a person's affective predispostion or tendency towards perceiving the world around them in a positive or negative light (Lazarus, 1991). This is an individual difference variable that captures the characteristic way basic emotions are experienced and expressed, and permeates all of one's experiences. Dispositional affect is typically referred to by an individual's level of trait negative or trait positive affect that pervades their view of the world, and can subsequently impact their wellbeing (De Ridder & Gillebaart, 2017). *Moods* are low-intensity, diffuse feeling states that usually do not have a clear antecedent (Forgas, 1995), and can be caused by dispositional affect and/or emotions, again with implications for wellbeing (Adiyaman & Meier, 2022). In contrast, *emotions* are distinct from dispositional affect and moods, in that they have a clear cause (e.g., an encounter with an angry client) or target (e.g., a colleague, supervisor, work task), are shorter in duration, and are more focused and intense (Fridja, 1993). Examples of discrete emotions include fear, anger, happiness, pride, and sadness, which have been examined in relation to wellbeing at work (Lambert et al., 2019). The terms *dispostional affect, mood, emotion,* and *affect* may all be seen to represent the broader notion of 'affect' in this chapter.

UNDERSTANDING EMOTIONS AND WELLBEING DURING CHANGE-RELATED TURBULENCE

As mentioned previously, some of what we know about emotions in turbulent contexts can be derived from the organizational change literature. While turbulent contexts are typically viewed as unexpected forms of change that can be highly disruptive and associated with uncertainty (Gibson, 2020; Van Zoonen et al., 2021), in this chapter we argue that important knowledge can be gained from the growing, albeit small, body of organizational change research that considers change as an affective phenomenon (see Rafferty & Minbashian, 2019). Specifically, in this section we discuss how two key theories (Transactional Theory of Stress and Coping – Lazarus & Folkman, 1984; Affective Events Theory, or AET – Weiss & Cropanzano, 1996) and a key affective construct (Emotional Intelligence – Mayer & Salovey, 1998) have been used to consider change-related emotional experiences and responses. We also consider ways this knowledge can be applied in more turbulent change contexts.

Appraisal Theories of Emotion

Appraisal theories of emotions (Agote et al., 2016; Fugate et al., 2011) predominantly describe how individuals respond emotionally to change, and the subsequent implications for employees' health and performance. More specifically, the main appraisal theory adopted in the change field is the Transactional Theory of Stress and Coping (Lazarus & Folkman, 1984; see also Rafferty

& Minbashian, 2019). This model assumes that stress occurs because of an interplay between an individual and their environment (Dewe, 1991). The two key processes that capture this person–environment relationship are cognitive appraisal and coping. In essence, this theory proposes that the level of stress experienced by an individual depends on their appraisals of the situation, and their judgment about whether the internal or external demands related to the stressor exceed their own resources and their ability to cope (Lazarus & Folkman, 1984).

Three forms of appraisals identified in the transactional model – challenge, threat, and harm – are identified as leading to emotional responses (Lazarus, 1991), although more recent research has reported a synchronous reciprocal relationship between negative appraisal and negative emotions (Fugate et al., 2011). Challenge appraisals involve an evaluation by the individual that the demands associated with a stressor offer the potential for growth or development. Such appraisals are often followed by positive emotions such as eagerness, excitement, and exhilaration, and favorable wellbeing outcomes (Rafferty & Minbashian, 2019; Rafferty et al., 2023). For instance, during the COVID-19 pandemic, initial turbulent environments resulting from the shift to remote working were appraised favorably by many workers as an opportunity to enhance their job performance, in part due to the flexibility afforded to them to improve their work–life balance (Van Zoonen et al., 2021).

In contrast, threat appraisals involve an appraisal that demands will create obstacles to personal growth, or hinder one's ability to achieve valued goals. Such appraisals have been found to lead to negative emotions, and wellbeing outcomes such as emotional exhaustion (Rodell & Judge, 2009; Searle & Auton, 2015; Searle et al., 2022). For example, during COVID-19, employees expressed concerns about the quality of communication technology, and communication more generally, within organizations, as potential barriers to their adjustment to remote working (Van Zoonen et al., 2021).

Finally, a harm appraisal is an assessment that damage has already occurred because of the situation, and the necessary resources to cope with the situation effectively may not be available. As with threat appraisals, harm appraisals are linked to unfavorable emotional responses and wellbeing outcomes. Again, using the example of COVID-19, employees who perceived greater social isolation during their remote working experiences reported significantly lower levels of adjustment (Van Zoonen et al., 2021).

Other examples of these different forms of appraisals in the face of turbulent contexts can be found in the deterioration of construction workers' (Pirzadeh & Lingard, 2021) and health workers' (Morgan et al., 2022) levels of wellbeing during COVID-19. These wellbeing declines were primarily caused by emotional exhaustion in response to unprecedented workplace demands, including rostering, infection protocols, and patient care. These chronically high work demands significantly outweighed the internal and external resources of these workers, leading to stress and negative wellbeing reactions. Across this research, we suggest that challenge appraisals in turbulent environments promote positive emotions and more favorable psychological functioning, in contrast to threat and harm appraisals that are more likely to lead to negative emotions and poorer health outcomes.

It is important to note, however, that empirical tests of appraisal theories in a change context reveal a more complex set of relationships between appraisals, emotions, and coping than was outlined in the initial formulation of the transactional model (see Rafferty et al., 2023). For instance, while empirical work by Fugate et al. (2008) suggested that emotions are an *outcome* of the appraisal and coping process rather than an antecedent, a later study (Fugate et al., 2011) found a concurrent reciprocal relationship between negative appraisals and negative emotions. These studies suggest that employee's emotions may act as *both* an antecedent and an outcome of appraisals and coping during organizational change and in turbulent environments. Notwithstanding, the literature on stressor appraisals and emotions demonstrates that organizations should be mindful of the way in which change, or turbulent contexts, are appraised by employees. These employee appraisals are likely to be varied, with significant consequences for employees' health, wellbeing, and performance (Rafferty et al., 2023; Van Zoonen et al., 2021). More specifically, these appraisals are dependent on employees' perceived capacity to balance the demands of change (i.e., the perceived magnitude of change, and the organization's change history, which will influence the extent of uncertainty that develops) with the resources available to them (i.e., both organizational and personal resources).

Affective Events Theory

Another theoretical framework that has been used when considering emotions associated with change is AET (Weiss & Cropanzano, 1996). This major theory proposes that a range of daily events at work (e.g., employee and customer interactions, job design changes) act as affective events that give rise to employees' emotional responses which, in turn, influence their attitudinal and behavioral states and subsequent decision-making, and ultimately their levels of wellbeing. In the change field, Rafferty et al. (2023) discussed how researchers have used AET in a restricted way, by arguing that organizational changes are affectively-charged events that influence outcomes. For example, in a program of three studies, Chen et al. (2013) used AET to identify change as an affective event and concluded that greater attributions of leaders' charisma during organizational change was associated with stronger positive emotions among followers, and weaker negative emotions about change. We suggest that this has interesting implications for the role of leaders in turbulent environments, when affectively-charged events are more intense given the heightened demands that face employees in such settings.

In another pertinent study, Paterson and Cary (2002) studied the impact of downsizing – a form of internal organizational turbulence – in an Australian public corporation. They utilized AET to argue that the characteristics of a change implementation process (i.e., communication quality and partici-pation) predicted appraisals about the change that, in turn, predicted cogni-tive (justice) and affective (anxiety) responses. These responses determined employee change outcomes including acceptance of change, morale, and turn-over. More specifically, they found that positive appraisals reduced anxiety about the change both directly and indirectly, by increasing the perceived fairness of the outcomes. Perceptions that the procedures were fair and low levels of anxiety, in turn, increased employees' acceptance of the downsizing event. Moreover, low change anxiety was positively associated with employee morale. These conclusions have largely been reaffirmed by more recent research, including by Oreg et al. (2018) and Kiefer (2005).

While research adopting an AET perspective has viewed change broadly as an affective event, Rafferty et al. (2023) noted that there has been little consideration of what aspects of the event make change affectively important (an exception is Paterson & Cary, 2002, outlined above). This downplays the potential of this theory to understand and manage wellbeing during change. AET proposes that characteristics of the workplace environment influence the occurrence of affectively-laden work events, subsequent affective reac-tions, and work attitudes and behaviors (Weiss & Cropanzano, 1996). It is therefore ideally situated to explain the impact of change on wellbeing. Further, it is likely that other aspects of turbulence will influence the extent to which a change is experienced as an affectively-charged event, including whether other forms of uncertain, unexpected, and ambiguous change have previously been (un)successfully implemented in the organization (Rafferty & Jimmieson, 2017), and the degree of transformation experienced in a turbulent environment (Van Zoonen et al., 2021). Research has found that the intensity of emotional experience has been directly linked to employee wellbeing (Zapf, 2002).

Emotional Intelligence

Mayer and Salovey (1997) defined emotional intelligence (EI) as consisting of four basic abilities: (1) the ability to perceive and to recognize emotions in both self and others, (2) the ability to incorporate emotional information in decision-making and thinking, (3) the ability to understand the effects of emotion in self and others, and (4) the ability to use and to manage emotion in self and others. Significantly, Mayer and Salovey focused on EI as an ability, rather than a trait, and argued that these abilities can be developed by individuals. There is considerable evidence to show that an individual's level of EI is positively associated with their level of workplace wellbeing. Miao, Humphrey, and Qian's (2017) meta-analysis showed that employees with high EI have higher levels of job satisfaction and organizational commitment, and lower turnover intentions. These authors concluded that EI improves job satisfaction by helping employees to reduce negative feelings, by increasing positive feelings, and/or improving job performance. We note that these are desired outcomes in any change process, and that EI may be particularly protective in emotionally demanding jobs such as health and social care.

In their model, Rafferty et al. (2023) noted the importance of employees' EI during change, by identifying it as an individual resource that moderates the relationship between the characteristics of an organizational change event and individuals' emotional and cognitive reactions to change. They also recognized that both leader EI and change-recipient EI may moderate relationships between recipients' emotional and cognitive responses to change and coping behaviors. It is feasible that these competencies will be even more useful in a turbulent environment. In support of this, Chaudhary et al.'s (2022) survey study with 810 information technology (IT) employees during COVID-19 showed that the positive effect of leader e-competencies (e-communication skills, e-change management skills, and e-technological skills) on employee wellbeing was improved (moderated) by the leader's EI.

Researchers have both theoretically (Huy, 1999) and empirically (Neil et al., 2016) explored the role of EI during change. Jordan and Troth (2002) said that EI is likely to be important during organizational change because individuals with high EI prefer to seek collaborative solutions when confronted with conflict. Later, Jordan (2005) argued that individuals who can manage and make sense of their own and others' emotions during organizational change are able to influence social relationship outcomes and positively contribute to the change process. Jordan also argued that high EI individuals will be under less stress during organizational change, because of their awareness of their own emotions and their ability to control them.

Several empirical studies have examined relationships between EI and change outcomes. Vakola, Tsaousis, and Nikolaou (2004) conducted a cross-sectional study of 137 professionals who completed self-report inventories assessing EI, personality traits, and attitudes towards change. Findings showed that the EI dimension of 'use of emotions for problem-solving' was positively associated with a measure of 'attitude to change' above and beyond the effect of personality. Ferres and Connell (2004) examined the relationship between leader EI and employee cynicism about change via a cross-sectional study with Australian public servants, which showed that three aspects of employee-rated leader EI – empathy, social skills, and motivation – were significantly negatively associated with employee cynicism.

Smollan and Parry (2011) conducted interviews with 24 employees from New Zealand organizations experiencing change. These authors found that followers reported more psychological support if they perceived their leaders as genuinely responding to their emotions. This led to a tendency by employees to adopt more positive attitudes towards the change. Conversely, a lack of acknowledgment of their emotions often led change recipients to feel a sense of alienation, which contributed to them deciding to exit the organization. In addition, leaders perceived by their followers as failing to regulate their emotions were considered to have acted inappropriately, with negative consequences for the followers' wellbeing and attitudes to change. Finally, Smollan and Parry concluded that employees who reported their leaders as being unable or unwilling to deal with followers' emotions were also more likely to conceal their emotional responses to change, with more adverse consequences over time for wellbeing. In a similar vein, Seo et al. (2012) found that workgroup managers' transformational leadership shapes employees' affective reactions and commitment in the initial phase of change, and their subsequent behavioral responses to change 12 months later.

In earlier research, Huy (1999) argued that an individual's EI is positively related to the individual's ability to change and adapt personally. Similarly, at the organizational level, an organization's emotional capability is argued to be positively related to its ability to change. The more emotionally capable an organization, the more successful will be its change efforts. At the organizational level, Huy (2005) defined emotional capability as 'the organization's ability to acknowledge, recognize, monitor, discriminate, and attend to emotions at both the individual and the collective levels' (p. 303). This ability is built into the organization's habitual procedures for actions or their routines, which reflect the collective knowledge and skills demonstrated in local contexts to manage emotions related to change.

In summary, in line with Rafferty et al. (2023), we reiterate the importance of employee and leader EI, by identifying EI as moderating relationships between change event characteristics, and individuals' emotional responses and appraisals of change. We also identify employee EI as a moderator of relationships between individuals' emotional responses and appraisals of change, and individuals' coping behaviors in responses to change. These outcomes, in turn, can have an impact on the health and wellbeing of employees experiencing change. In this chapter, we argue that these relationships are likely to be heightened when there is a highly turbulent environment.

FURTHER LEARNINGS AND CHALLENGES FOR ORGANIZATIONS IN A TURBULENT ENVIRONMENT

In this section, guided by the preceding sections, we draw on recent work by Troth et al. (2023a), examining emotions and the disruption that emerges in a highly turbulent environment, to suggest some solutions for optimizing employee health, wellbeing, and performance. Further, based on Troth et al. (2023b), we have arranged these insights into three overarching themes:

1. the heightened salience and complexity of emotions and emotion processes in turbulent environments;
2. the potential benefits of turbulent environments if emotions are managed effectively; and
3. the vital role of leader emotional competencies and responses in a turbulent environment.

We recognize the potential negative (and sometimes catastrophic) effects of major disruptions and ongoing environmental turbulence, such as COVID-19, on employees. In support of Troth et al. (2023b), we contend that favorable outcomes for employees and their organizations can be achieved in difficult situations, if they are managed carefully.

The Salience and Complexity of Emotions and Emotion Processes in Turbulent Environments

We argue that environmental turbulence creates conditions consistent with what Weiss and Cropanzano (1996) categorize as 'affective events.' These events are invariably associated with intense and complex emotions, which lead in turn to a complex array of emotional and cognitive responses. This is demonstrated by Barboza-Wilkes et al. (2023), who collected data from female full- and part-time employees of a Californian non-profit organization who were attempting to adjust to changes in their work environment during the height of the pandemic. Their results showed that the way employees reacted emotionally to these changes depended on a range of different factors, including their employment status. A critical factor that had significant impact on stress and burnout (and therefore had implications for wellbeing) concerned how different worker cohorts (full-time versus part-time) were socialized into their changed organization. The authors reported that managers formally managed the full-time workers' emotions, while the part-time workers were managed informally – the latter with more adverse consequences. This research highlights the necessity of having a formal, and consistently applied, management plan to deal with employees' emotional responses to change (Huy & Zott, 2019).

Sai (2023) conducted a qualitative study detailing the effects of 'emotional ambivalence' on employees working in two English non-profit organizations undergoing major organizational change. They found that emotional ambivalence occurs when employees experience conflicting positive and negative emotions about the changes going on in their workplace. Likewise, Simões et al.'s (2023) research involving a multi-source and multilevel quantitative study of emotion work occurring within the dynamic setting of a hospital demonstrated that the way emotions play out may be much more complex than previously thought (where the prevailing view is that change leads to either positive or negative emotions). Sai concluded that managers need to recognize ambiguity arising from turbulence, and to engage differently with emotionally ambivalent employees and see them as a positive resource. This idea (that emotions are often not simply positive or negative; see Lindebaum & Jordan, 2012) represents a challenge, not only for managers, but also for scholars attempting to understand the complexity of emotional events in turbulent contexts. A central conclusion emerging from these studies is the intensity and complexity of emotions experienced in such situations. Furthermore, ambiguous experiences of emotion in turbulent contexts can result in the need for considered responses by managers.

Research by Parkinson (2023) proposes that improved interpersonal relationships offer one remedy to resolve employees' sense of helplessness, associated with the heightened and complex emotions that occur in turbulent environments. Parkinson found, in a study of British public service organizations during pre-Brexit disruption, that relationships are critical to enabling employees to deal with the emotional stresses and strains they experience while attempting to adapt to a changing environment. In this regard, the formation of close relationships enabled employees to transition from feelings of passive to activated emotions, resulting in higher levels of engagement and psychological safety (which could enhance wellbeing). Parkinson argued for additional research to understand how relationship development can serve as an antidote to the pressures of today's disruptive work environments and contribute to healthier workplaces.

The Potential Benefits of Environmental Turbulence If Emotions Are Managed Effectively

Despite the many downsides to turbulent environments (see Chung, 2022), researchers have also demonstrated how harnessing affect and affective processes during periods of rapid organizational change due to environmental turbulence can promote beneficial outcomes, in the right contexts and with the right skills. This view aligns with Meyer's (1982) assertions that volatile events can be variously interpreted as either organizational opportunities, threats, or crises. Indeed, several recent empirical studies that are reviewed in Troth et al. (2023a) examine a broad range of types of disruptions at the intra-personal (Merlini et al., 2023), individual (Choi et al., 2023), group (Collins et al., 2023), and organizational (Nanayakkara et al., 2023) levels of analysis. These studies demonstrate that such changes can have positive effects on per-formance, and performance-related outcomes including wellbeing, if managed appropriately.

Merlini et al. (2023), for example, suggested that during times of disruption, managers may be able to engage in interpersonal emotion management tech-niques to help employees allocate resources to important goals, by provoking highly activated emotions relevant to the goals, and reducing highly activated emotions irrelevant to the task at hand (see Niven et al., 2019). For instance, managers may help employees to focus on a particular task by encouraging a sense of excitement about that task, but also by reducing anxiety associ-ated with competing tasks. The implications of the findings are particularly salient in the context of environmental turbulence, which results in significant changes in our work and non-work lives that increase the frequency or likeli-hood of high-activation emotions (e.g., fear, excitement). Concurrently, times of environmental turbulence tend to create novel instances of conflicting goals, which force us to reprioritize where we allocate our attention, time, and effort. Thus, we must be particularly aware of the role of affect activation in driving those resource allocation decisions, and be prepared to engage in emotion regulation strategies if we are to reduce (or increase) the extent to which we are pulled in one direction or another, and the subsequent impact on performance and wellbeing.

Choi et al.'s (2023) experimental work also suggests that an individual's capacity to use appropriate emotion regulation strategies is critical to ensuring whether the impact of various forms of interruptions from turbulent environ-ments, and the subsequent organizational changes, produce positive or negative outcomes. Importantly, Choi and his colleagues described the potential 'bright side' to disruptions at work, and called for researchers (and practitioners) to consider how different forms of 'micro' disruptions can be used to break the monotony of work, or how they can result in individuals 'recalibrating' and 'starting afresh,' leading to innovation. The authors' typology of the differen-tial effects of work-enhancing (intervention, recovery) versus work-hindering interruptions (disturbance, mind-wandering) on wellbeing and performance suggests the important role that emotional regulation strategies (e.g., cognitive reappraisal, suppression) have in this process. Such strategies can be adapted to guide approaches to managing effectively in turbulent environments.

In practical terms, Choi et al.'s (2023) research suggests emotional regulation competencies can be developed to help employees manage their emotions associated with different interruptions to increase (or decrease) positive (or negative) outcomes. Their model also provides information for managers about what types of interruptions are likely to be productive, and which will negatively impact on outcomes, in part due to the emotions they generate. For researchers, it is important to note that this area of research is underexplored, and that we need more knowledge about the specific impact of emotion regulation processes on the way workers deal with interruptions (while at the same time recognizing that not all interruptions are qualitatively the same). In turbulent environments, interruptions can exacerbate employees' positive and negative experiences at work, with a 'flow on' effect on both performance and wellbeing.

Troth et al. (2023a) argued that another productive direction for future research is consideration of the moderating role of EI on employees' emotional regulation responses to interruptions and other turbulent contexts. Their recent work demonstrates that frontline managers who report higher task-related negative affect across their working day, and who adopt the emotional regulation strategy of suppression, have significantly higher levels of stress at the end of the day. In contrast, these researchers found managers high on EI are more likely to use reappraisal in response to tasks eliciting negative affect, with no detrimental effects for daily stress. Considering these findings, it may be valuable for scholars to investigate how EI moderates the relationship between different types of organizational change events that may emerge in turbulent contexts and an individual's emotional regulation responses, leading to subsequent performance and wellbeing outcomes.

Finally, Collins et al. (2023) offer further insight regarding the role of emotions on performance and wellbeing outcomes in teams' decision-making in extreme contexts (for example, when under pressure). These researchers showed that the variation in team members' positive affect, and *not* a team's overall level of positive affect, had the biggest impact on team decision-making. That is, teams with similar levels of positive affect (either high or low) make better decisions overall, compared to teams comprising members with discrepant levels of positive affect, suggesting the important role of emotional contagion whereby individuals' emotions within a team converge and represent an affective tone (Collins et al., 2013). While research on the role of affect *dispersion* is still in its infancy, several valuable points emerge from this study for both researchers and practitioners. First, organizational managers and team leaders should pay more attention to the *distribution* of positive affect among team levels, rather than encouraging universally high levels of positive affect – a common practice – in turbulent environments. Further, the affective profile of a team appears to be an important contingency dictating how teams make decisions in crisis situations. These findings also highlight how team process norms beyond the effects of emotion on judgments and decision-making in pressured contexts, which, in turn, can impact on the performance of teams and the wellbeing of team members.

The Vital Role of Leader Emotional Competencies and Responses in a Turbulent Environment

Good leadership is crucial to how organizations handle the two preceding themes. The first theme discussed the heightened salience and complexity of emotions and emotional processes during disruption. According to Humphrey (2002, p. 493), 'a key leadership function is to manage the emotions of group members, especially with regard to feelings related to frustration and optimism.' Change, uncertainty, and disruption often produce intense feelings of frustration. Humphrey argued that it is a leader's responsibility to help employees transform these feelings of frustration into feelings of confidence and optimism. Even apparently entirely negative disruptions, which may include the COVID-19 pandemic, can present some opportunities for positive change, such as employees' re-evaluating their working hours and over-commitment. As we have discussed earlier, many governments across the globe encouraged organizations to allow employees to work from home during COVID-19. Whereas some employees reacted with anxiety at the thought of working at home and away from their colleagues, others discovered that working from home produced some major benefits, such as reduced commuting time and costs, a more comfortable working environment, freedom from continual monitoring, and in some cases the opportunity to live in desirable locations rather than close to work (see, for example, the boundary management discussion in Chapter 4 in this book).

Leaders may help subordinates overcome their anxiety in part by providing necessary resources, such as laptops and appropriate training for working online. Perhaps more importantly, leaders may also role model the appropriate emotional responses to the challenges caused by disruptive events, and express confidence that the employees can handle the challenges successfully if they have the resources required. Research has shown that leaders' emotions are particularly emotionally contagious, especially when they create an empathic bond with their followers (Kellett et al., 2006). To create these empathic bonds or sense of resonance, leaders may have to lead with emotional labor (Humphrey, 2008). Although the early research on emotional labor focuses on service and frontline workers, there is growing recognition that it is frequent among leaders. As Humphrey (2008) explains, in the leadership field most research on emotions has focused on charismatic communication; and most research on charisma recognizes that charismatic leaders use emotions in their communications. Yet this research largely attributes this to rhetorical skills, often described in largely cognitive terms (Humphrey et al., 2016). The stress on leaders that may result from performing emotional labor is overlooked by the charisma literature (Humphrey et al., 2016). To illustrate, Hudson et al.'s (2023) interview study of leaders who were managing organizational change showed leaders who suppress their emotions when communicating with their followers felt additional stress as a result, and thus were more likely to experience burnout. During periods of extreme disruption, it is only natural for leaders to experience the same feelings of anxiety that beset their follow-ers. According to Humphrey et al. (2008, p. 157) 'Leaders have to express optimism even when facing the same confidence-shattering crisis as the other group members.' A potential implication of this, however, is the negative impact on leaders' own wellbeing.

The type of emotional labor used by the managers in Hudson et al.'s (2023) study to suppress their emotions is called *surface acting*, and considerable research shows that this type of emotional labor has deleterious effects upon the actor. However, according to the 'bright side' perspective on emotional labor, employees and leaders who use 'deep acting' emotional labor, and the natural and genuine expression of emotions, can experience positive outcomes (Humphrey et al., 2015), primarily though emotional contagion (Visser et al., 2013).

As previously mentioned, leaders' emotional expressions, as managed through emotional labor processes, can strongly influence whether followers respond to disruptions with feelings of frustration or optimism and, in turn, these feelings can influence performance. In addition, leaders' personality traits can also influence how they lead their followers, and thus influence a wide variety of workplace outcomes. Several meta-analyses have estab-lished the predictive validity of leader EI. In their meta-analysis, Miao et al. (2016), for example, found that leader EI was an important predictor, and had substantial and meaningful impact, on subordinate job satisfaction. Likewise, Miao et al. (2018) established that leader EI also predicted subordinate task performance and subordinate organizational citizenship behaviors. Based on these studies, the importance of managing emotion in turbulent environments is clear, and can have an impact on both the performance and the wellbeing of employees and leaders, with more work required to fully understand these connections.

CONCLUSION

In this chapter, we considered the role of emotions in how employees, leaders, and organizations experience and respond to turbulent environments within and outside the organization, and what this means for employee performance and wellbeing. To begin with, we outlined research and theoretical frame-works used to investigate employees' change-related affective responses. We contend that there is valuable knowledge to be gained in the organizational change literature that can be applied to more unexpected and unpredictable forms of change that are volatile, complex, and ambiguous, and that are likely to arise in highly turbulent environments. This analysis resulted in the identi-fication of three key affective theories/constructs that add value to our under-standing of how we can better support employees in turbulent environments. Next, we considered some recent empirical research and commentary that has examined the role of emotions during disruption – as a break or interruption in the normal course or continuation of some activity or process – in a wide variety of forms.

Three key learnings were highlighted that should be carefully considered by organizations. Specifically, our chapter reveals that turbulent environments heighten the salience and complexity of emotions and emotion processes, which require nuanced support and understanding to optimize employee wellbeing. A second aspect highlighted was the potential *benefits* of turbulent environments if emotions are managed effectively. The third aspect is the critical role of leader emotional competencies and responses in turbulent envi-ronments. These implications all require organizations to consider employees' emotions as a legitimate concern, requiring active consideration and man-agement at multiple organizational levels, in order to enhance individual and organizational wellbeing and performance.

REFERENCES

Adiyaman, D., & Meier, L. L. (2022). Short-term effects of experienced and observed incivility on mood and self-esteem. *Work & Stress, 36*(2), 133–146.

Agote, L., Aramburu, N., & Lines, R. (2016). Authentic leadership perception, trust in the leader, and followers' emotions in organizational change processes. *The Journal of Applied Behavioral Science, 52*(1), 35–63.

Ansell, C., & Trondal, J. (2018). Governing turbulence: An organizational-institutional agenda. *Perspectives on Public Management and Governance, 1*(1), 43–57. https://doi.org/10.1093/ppmgov/gvx013

Ashforth, B. E., & Humphrey, R. H. (1995). Emotion in the workplace: A reappraisal. *Human Relations, 48*(2), 97–125.

Barboza-Wilkes, C., Le, T. V., & Turesky, M. (2023). Emotional socialization in times of disruption: A mixed-methods case study of emotional labor among nonprofit employees during Covid-19. In A. C. Troth, N. M. Ashkanasy, & R. H. Humphrey (Eds.), *Emotions during times of disruption* (Vol. 18, pp. 15–38). Emerald. https://doi.org/10.1108/S1746-979120220000018002

Chaudhary, P., Rohtagi, M., Singh, R. K., & Arora, S. (2022). Impact of lead-er's e-competencies on employees' wellbeing in global virtual teams during COVID-19: The moderating role of emotional intelligence. *Employee Relations, 44*(5), 1048–1063. https://doi.org/10.1108/ER-06-2021-0236

Chen, C. C., Belkin, L. Y., McNamee, R., & Kurtzberg, T. R. (2013). Charisma attribution during organizational change: The importance of followers' emotions and concern for well-being. *Journal of Applied Social Psychology, 43*(6), 1136–1158. https://doi.org/10.1111/jasp.12078

Choi, M. K., Jordan, P. J., & Troth, A. C. (2023). Workplace interruptions and emotional regulation. In A. C. Troth, N. M. Ashkanasy, & R. H. Humphrey (Eds.), *Emotions during times of disruption* (Vol. 18, pp. 121–142). Emerald. https://doi.org/10.1108/S1746-979120220000018007

Chung, H. (2022). Variable work schedules, unit-level turnover, and performance before and during the COVID-19 pandemic. *Journal of Applied Psychology, 107*(4), 515–532. https://doi.org/10.1037/apl0001006

Collins, A. L., Lawrence, S. A., Troth, A. C., & Jordan, P. J. (2013). Group affective tone: A review and future research directions. *Journal of Organizational Behavior, 34*(S1), S43–S62. http://dx.doi.org/10.1002%2Fjob.1887

Collins, B. J., Munyon, T. P., Ashkanasy, N. M., Gallagher, E., Lawrence, S. A., O'Connor, J., & Kessler, S. (2023). Team decision-making in crisis: How affect asymmetry and team process norms affect decision-making. In A. C. Troth, N. M. Ashkanasy, & R. H. Humphrey (Eds.), *Emotions during times of disruption* (Vol. 18, pp. 169–194). Emerald. https://doi.org/10.1108/S1746-979120220000018014

De Ridder, D., & Gillebaart, M. (2017). Lessons learned from trait self-control in well-being: Making the case for routines and initiation as important components of trait self-control. *Health Psychology Review, 11*(1), 89–99. https://doi.org/10.1080/17437199.2016.1266275

Dewe, P. J. (1991). Primary appraisal, secondary appraisal and coping: Their role in stressful work encounters. *Journal of Occupational Psychology, 64*, 331–351.

Ferres, N., & Connell, J. (2004). Emotional intelligence in leaders: An antidote for cynicism towards change? *Strategic Change, 13*(2), 61–71.

Forgas, J. (1995). Mood and judgment: the affect infusion model (AIM). *Psychological Bulletin, 117*(1), 39–66.

Frijda, N. H. (1993). Moods, emotion episodes, and emotions. In M. Lewis & J. M. Haviland (Eds.), *Handbook of emotions* (pp. 381–403). Guilford Press.

Fugate, M., Harrison, S., & Kinicki, A. J. (2011). Thoughts and feelings about organizational change: A field test of appraisal theory. *Journal of Leadership & Organizational Studies, 18*, 421–437.

Fugate, M., Kinicki, A. J., & Prussia, G. E. (2008). Employee coping with organizational change: An examination of alternative theoretical perspectives. *Personnel Psychology, 61*, 1–36.

Gibson, C. (2020). From "social distancing" to "care in connecting": An emerging organizational research agenda for turbulent times. *Academy of Management Discoveries, 6*(2), 165–169. https://doi.org/10.5465/amd.2020.0062

Hudson, A. J., Jordan, P. J., & Troth, A. C. (2023). How leaders regulate emotions experienced during organization change events. In A. C. Troth, N. M. Ashkanasy, & R. H. Humphrey (Eds.), *Emotions during times of disruption* (Vol. 18, pp. 239–260). Emerald. https://doi.org/10.1108/S1746-979120220000018011

Humphrey, R. H. (2002). The many faces of emotional leadership. *The Leadership Quarterly, 13*(5), 493–504. https://doi.org/10.1016/S1048-9843(02)00140-6

Humphrey, R. H. (2008). The right way to lead with emotional labor. In R. H. Humphrey (Ed.), *Affect and emotion: New directions in management theory and research* (pp. 1–17). Information Age Publishing.

Humphrey, R. H., Ashforth, B. E., & Diefendorff, J. M. (2015). The bright side of emotional labor. *Journal of Organizational Behavior, 36*(6), 749–769. https://doi.org/10.1002/job.2019

Humphrey, R. H., Burch, G. F., & Adams, L. L. (2016). The benefits of merging leadership research and emotions research. *Frontiers in Psychology, 7*, 1022. https://doi.org/10.3389/fpsyg.2016.01022

Humphrey, R. H., Pollack, J. M., & Hawver, T. (2008). Leading with emotional labor. *Journal of Managerial Psychology, 23*(2), 151–168. https://doi.org/10.1108/02683940810850790

Huy, Q., & Zott, C. (2019). Exploring the affective underpinnings of dynamic managerial capabilities: How managers' emotion regulation behaviors mobilize resources for their firms. *Strategic Management Journal, 40*(1), 28–54.

Huy, Q. N. (1999). Emotional capability, emotional intelligence, and radical change. *Academy of Management Review, 24*(2), 325–345. https://doi.org/10.5465/amr.1999.1893939

Huy, Q. N. (2005). Emotion management to facilitate strategic change and innovation: How emotional balancing and emotional capability work together. In C. Hartel, N. M. Ashkanasy, & W. Zerbe (Eds.), *Emotions in organizational behavior* (pp. 295–316). Psychology Press. https://doi.org/10.4324/9781410611895

Jordan, P. (2005). Dealing with organizational change: Can emotional intelligence enhance organizational learning. *International Journal of Organizational Behaviour, 8*(1), 456–471.

Jordan, P. J., & Troth, A. C. (2002). Emotional intelligence and conflict resolution: Implications for human resource development. *Advances in Developing Human Resources, 4*(1), 62–79.

Kellett, J. B., Humphrey, R. H., & Sleeth, R. G. (2006). Empathy and the emergence of task and relations leaders. *The Leadership Quarterly, 17*(2), 146–162. https://doi.org/10.1016/j.leaqua.2005.12.003

Kelly, J. R., & Barsade, S. G. (2001). Mood and emotions in small groups and work teams. *Organizational Behavior and Human Decision Processes, 86*(1), 99–130.

Kiefer, T. (2005). Feeling bad: Antecedents and consequences of negative emotions in ongoing change. *Journal of Organizational Behavior, 26*(8), 875–897. https://doi.org/10.1002/job.339

Lambert, L., Passmore, H. A., & Joshanloo, M. (2019). A positive psychology intervention program in a culturally-diverse university: Boosting happiness and reducing fear. *Journal of Happiness Studies*, 20, 1141–1162.

Lazarus, R. S. (1991). Progress on a cognitive-motivational-relational theory of emotion. *American Psychologist, 46*(8), 819–834.

Lazarus, R. S., & Folkman, S. (1984). *Stress, appraisal, and coping.* Springer.

Lindebaum, D., & Jordan, P. J. (2012). Positive emotions, negative emotions, or utility of discrete emotions? *Journal of Organizational Behavior, 33*(7), 1027–1030.

Mayer, J. D., & Salovey, P. (1997). What is emotional intelligence. In P. Salovey & D. J. Sluyter (Eds.), *Emotional development and emotional intelligence: Educational implications* (pp. 3–31). Basic Books.

Merlini, K. P., Converse, P. D., Richard, E., & Belluccia, A. (2023). Pulled in two directions: How affect activation predicts resource allocation among multiple goals. In A. C. Troth, N. M. Ashkanasy, & R. H. Humphrey (Eds.), *Emotions during times of disruption* (Vol. 18, pp. 143–167). Emerald. https://doi.org/10.1108/S1746-979120220000018008

Meyer, A. D. (1982). Adapting to environmental jolts. *Administrative Science Quarterly, 27*(4), 515–537.

Miao, C., Humphrey, R. H., & Qian, S. (2016). Leader emotional intelligence and subordinate job satisfaction: A meta-analysis of main, mediator, and moderator effects. *Personality and Individual Differences, 102,* 13–24. https://doi.org/10.1016/j.paid.2016.06.056

Miao, C., Humphrey, R. H., & Qian, S. (2017). A meta-analysis of emotional intelligence and work attitudes *Journal of Occupational and Organizational Psychology, 90*(2), 177–202. https://doi.org/10.1111/joop.12167

Miao, C., Humphrey, R. H., & Qian, S. (2018). A cross-cultural meta-analysis of how leader emotional intelligence influences subordinate task performance and organizational citizenship behavior. *Journal of World Business, 53*(4), 463–474. https://doi.org/10.1016/j.jwb.2018.01.003

Morgan, R., Tan, H.-L., Oveisi, N., Memmott, C., Korzuchowski, A., Hawkins, K., & Smith, J. (2022). Women healthcare workers' experiences during COVID-19 and other crises: A scoping review. *International Journal of Nursing Studies Advances, 4,* 100066. https://doi.org/10. 1016/j.ijnsa.2022.100066

Nanayakkara, S., Wickramasinghe, V., & Samarasinghe, D. (2023). Effect of emotional intelligence and strategic management of technology on organizational performance. In A. C. Troth, N. M. Ashkanasy, & R. H. Humphrey (Eds.), *Emotions during times of disruption* (Vol. 18, pp. 195–214). Emerald. https://doi.org/10.1108/S1746-979120220000018009

Neil, R., Wagstaff, C. R., Weller, E., & Lewis, R. (2016). Leader behaviour, emotional intelligence, and team performance at a UK government executive agency during organizational change. *Journal of Change Management, 16*(2), 97–122. https://doi.org/10.1080/14697017.2015.1134624

Niven, K., Troth, A. C., & Holman, D. (2019). Do the effects of interpersonal emotion regulation depend on people's underlying motives? *Journal of Occupational and Organizational Psychology, 92*(4), 1020–1026. https://doi.org/10.1111/joop.12257

Oreg, S., Bartunek, J. M., Lee, G., & Do, B. (2018). An affect-based model of recipients' responses to organizational change events. *Academy of Management Review, 43*(1), 65–86. https://doi.org/10.5465/amr.2014.0335

Parkinson, A. (2023). Releasing the pressure valve: Workplace relationships and engagement in a context of disruption. In A. C. Troth, N. M. Ashkanasy, & R. H. Humphrey (Eds.), *Emotions during times of disruption* (Vol. 18, pp. 61–91). Emerald. https://doi.org/10.1108/S1746-979120220000018005

Paterson, J. M., & Cary, J. (2002). Organizational justice, change anxiety, and acceptance of downsizing: Preliminary tests of an AET-based model. *Motivation and Emotion, 26*(1), 83–103.

Pazzanese, C. (2021). How COVID experiences will reshape the workplace. *The Harvard Gazette.* https:// news .harvard .edu/ gazette/ story/ 2021/ 02/ how -covid -experiences-will-reshape-the-workplace/

Pirzadeh, P., & Lingard, H. (2021). Working from home during the COVID-19 pandemic: Health and well-being of project-based construction workers. *Journal of Construction Engineering and Management, 147*(6), 1–17.

Rafferty, A. E., & Jimmieson, N. L. (2017). Subjective perceptions of organizational change and employee resistance to change: Direct and mediated relationships with employee well-being. *British Journal of Management, 28,* 248–264. https://doi.org/10.1111/1467-8551.12200

Rafferty, A. E., & Minbashian, A. (2019). Cognitive beliefs and positive emotions about change: Relationships with employee change readiness and change-supportive behaviors. *Human Relations*, *72*(10), 1623–1650. https:// doi .org/ 10 .1177 %2F0018726718809154

Rodell, J. B., & Judge, T. A. (2009). Can "good" stressors spark "bad" behaviors? The mediating role of emotions in links of challenge and hindrance stressors with citizenship and counterproductive behaviors. *Journal of Applied Psychology*, *94*(6), 1438–1451.

Sai, L. (2023). Ambivalent feeling about organizational change under NPM. In A. C. Troth, N. M. Ashkanasy, & R. H. Humphrey (Eds.), *Emotions during times of disruption* (Vol. 18, pp. 39–59). Emerald. https://doi.org/ 10.1108/S1746 -979120220000018003

Schoemaker, P. J., & Day, G. (2021). Preparing organizations for greater turbulence. *California Management Review*, *63*(4), 66–88. https:// doi .org/ 10 .1177/ 00081256211022039

Searle, B., Tuckey, M., & Brough, P. (2022). Guest editorial: Are challenges hindering us? The limitations of models that categorize work stressors. *Journal of Managerial Psychology*, *37*(5), 397–403. https://doi.org/10.1108/JMP-07-2022-714

Searle, B. J., & Auton, J.C. (2015). The merits of measuring challenge and hindrance appraisals. *Anxiety, Stress, & Coping*, *28*(2), 121–143.

Seo, M.-G., Taylor, M. S., Hill, N. S., Zhang, X., Tesluk, P. E., & Lorinkova, N. M. (2012). The role of affect and leadership during organizational change. Personnel Psychology, 65(1), 121–165. https://doi.org/10.1111/j.1744-6570.2011.01240.x

Simões, A. C. A., Gondim, S. M. G., & Puente-Palacios, K. E. (2023). Emotional labor in interaction with patients, companions, and coworkers: A multilevel approach in a hospital context. In A. C. Troth, N. M. Ashkanasy, & R. H. Humphrey (Eds.), *Emotions during times of disruption* (Vol. 18, pp. 93–117). Emerald. https://doi.org/ 10.1108/S1746-979120220000018006

Smollan, R. K., & Parry, K. (2011). Follower perceptions of the emotional intelligence of change leaders: A qualitative study. *Leadership*, *7*(4), 435–462.

Troth, A. C., Ashkanasy, N. M., & Humphrey, R. H. (Eds.). (2023a). *Emotions during times of disruption*. Emerald. https://doi.org/10.1108/S1746-9791202318

Troth, A. C., Ashkanasy, N. M., & Humphrey, R. H. (2023b). Learnings and solutions about emotions during disruption. In A. C. Troth, N. M. Ashkanasy, & R. H. Humphrey (Eds.), *Emotions during times of disruption* (Vol. 18, pp. 283–296). Emerald. https://doi.org/10.1108/S1746-979120220000018013

Troth, A. C., Rafferty, A. E., & Jordan, P. J. (2021). Emotions and wellbeing at work: A multilevel perspective. In T. Wall, C. L. Cooper, & P. Brough (Eds.), *The SAGE handbook of organizational wellbeing* (pp. 56–71). SAGE.

Vakola, M., Tsaousis, I., & Nikolaou, I. (2004). The role of emotional intelligence and personality variables on attitudes toward organisational change. *Journal of Managerial Psychology*, *19*(2), 88–110.

Van Zoonen, W., Sivunen, A., Blomqvist, K., Olsson, T., Ropponen, A., Henttonen, K., & Vartiainen, M. (2021). Factors influencing adjustment to remote work: Employees' initial responses to the COVID-19 pandemic. *International Journal of Environmental Research and Public Health*, *18*(13), 6966. https://doi.org/10.3390/ ijerph18136966

Visser, V. A., Van Knippenberg, D., Van Kleef, G. A., & Wisse, B. (2013). How leader displays of happiness and sadness influence follower performance: Emotional contagion and creative versus analytical performance. *The Leadership Quarterly*, *24*(1), 172–188.

Weiss, H. M., & Cropanzano, R. (1996). Affective events theory: A theoretical discussion of the structure, causes and consequences of affective experiences at work. In B. M. Staw & L. L. Cummings (Eds.), *Research in organizational behavior: An annual series of analytical essays and critical reviews* (pp. 1–74). Elsevier Science/JAI Press.

Zacher, H., & Rudolph, C. W. (2021). Individual differences and changes in subjective wellbeing during the early stages of the COVID-19 pandemic. *American Psychologist*, *76*(1), 50. https://psycnet.apa.org/doi/10.1037/amp0000702

Zapf, D. (2002). Emotion work and psychological well-being: A review of the literature and some conceptual considerations. *Human Resource Management Review*, *12*(2), 237–268.

8. Managing sickness absence behaviours in the post-pandemic workplace

Gail Kinman, Andrew J. Clements, and Karen Maher

SICKNESS ABSENCE: ESTIMATING THE PREVALENCE

Sickness absence can be defined as absence from work that is attributed to illness or injury by the employee and accepted as such by their employer (Whitaker, 2021, p. 420). Greater awareness of its 'true' financial burden to organizations makes sickness absence a major cause for concern, particularly in a post-pandemic climate of change and uncertainty (Chartered Institute of Personnel and Development [CIPD], 2023). It is now recognized that the costs of sickness absence far exceed lost wages and sick pay; estimates should include, for example, the recruitment, training, and monitoring of replacement staff, overtime payments for employees who provide cover, and the time spent managing absence by supervisors, and human resources and occupational health personnel (Cooper & Bevan, 2014). Additional costs of absence should also be considered, such as potential reductions in service quality, the health and safety risks of suboptimal staffing levels or inadequately trained replacements, and the impact of covering for sick colleagues on employees' workload and their future wellbeing (Miraglia & Johns, 2021).

Insights into the prevalence and causes of sickness absence in working populations, and any emerging demographic or occupational patterns, are important, particularly in the aftermath of a global pandemic. Data from several countries, including the United Kingdom (UK), Australia, and the United States, documented (unsurprisingly) a substantial increase in absence since the start of the pandemic, particularly in 'front-line' occupations (Bureau of Labor Statistics, 2023; Direct Health Solutions [DHS], 2023; Lyttelton & Zang, 2022; Office for National Statistics [ONS], 2023). Across all sectors in the UK, an estimated 185.6 million working days were taken due to sickness or injury in 2022, with an average of 5.7 days lost per worker – the highest in almost 20 years (ONS, 2023). The prevalence of ill health attributed by employees to their work also rose in this period, with non-fatal injuries, stress, depression or anxiety, and musculoskeletal disorders, as well as cases of COVID-19 (Covid) linked to workplace exposures, together accounting for a total of 36.8 million workdays (Health and Safety Executive [HSE], 2023). Sickness absence among healthcare workers is a particular cause for concern, with the mean number of workdays lost in the UK during the pandemic being four times higher than in the previous five-year period (Appleby, 2021). Post-pandemic statistics suggest that overall work absence has slightly declined in the health-care sector; but, at the time of writing, absence attributed to work-related stress and mental health issues remains high (National Health Service, 2023).

When estimating the prevalence of sickness absence during the pandemic, it should be recognized that steps taken to reduce the risk of transmission, such as furloughing, social distancing, shielding, and the widespread introduction of homeworking, mean that caution is needed when interpreting statistics (ONS, 2023; Palmer & Rolewicz, 2023). This compounds existing difficulties in accurately estimating the scale of absence. Organizational systems are not always fit for purpose, and employees often underestimate the number of days they are absent, especially during long-term absences (Johns & Miraglia, 2015). Moreover, the widespread practice of presenteeism (where employees continue to work while unwell) and leavism (where they use allocated time off, such as annual leave, to recover from illness or childbirth) means that some episodes of sickness will be overlooked.

IDENTIFYING THE CAUSES OF SICKNESS ABSENCE

Data from several countries show that the most common reason for sickness absence is minor illness. More specifically, analysis of data from a represent-ative sample of the UK working population found that minor conditions, such as colds and influenza, musculoskeletal problems, mental health issues, and gastrointestinal conditions, accounted for 34.6 per cent of recorded absences (Bryan et al., 2021). Nonetheless, long-term absence, defined as lasting for at least four weeks (CIPD, 2023), is a particular concern for organizations; although only accounting for around 5 per cent of all absence spells, it is responsible for almost half of the total days lost (Black & Frost, 2011; ONS, 2023). Research across a range of UK organizations found the top five causes of long-term absence included mental ill health (63 per cent), conditions such as cancer or stroke (51 per cent), and musculoskeletal injuries (51 per cent) (CIPD, 2023). Findings that the number of people who are economically inac-tive due to long-term sickness has increased since the pandemic in many coun-tries (ONS, 2022; Organisation for Economic Co-operation and Development,

2023) emphasize the need to manage and support employees with chronic conditions more effectively.

Unsurprisingly, Covid was a major cause of short-term sickness absence during the pandemic. But, although most people recovered quickly, symptoms can be long-lasting for some workers. The term 'long Covid' is commonly used to describe the prolonged and sometimes severe illness experienced following an acute infection (Rayner & Campbell, 2021). A broad spectrum of symptoms has been associated with long Covid, such as fatigue, cognitive impairments, muscle and joint pain, nausea, and depression and anxiety (Davis et al., 2023; ONS, 2023). Symptoms can fluctuate, and the risk of relapse is high in response to, for example, over-exertion, mental activity, and stress (Davis et al., 2023). A review of the prevalence of long Covid (Australian Institute of Health and Welfare, 2022) highlights the wide variation in estimates globally, with studies reporting its occurrence in between 9 per cent and 81 per cent of people previously infected. Such differences have been attributed to the wide range of symptoms linked to long Covid, and inconsistently applied diagnostic criteria across studies (Srikanth et al., 2023). Although any distortion of risk in developing long Covid can engender public anxiety and misdirect healthcare spending, it also has significant implications for individuals, organizations, and economies (Hoeg et al., 2023).

People with long Covid can face a double burden that can delay return to work – obtaining a formal diagnosis and accessing specialist treatment can take some time, and uncertainty about how to manage symptoms and a relapse of illness may engender anxiety (CIPD, 2022; Society of Occupational Medicine [SOM], 2022). Moreover, concerns about sceptical reactions from employers and colleagues, and a lack of support to facilitate return to work, have been identified (Kohn et al., 2022). The implications of long Covid for sickness absence are highlighted in a cohort study with respondents from 56 countries who had experienced symptoms for at least 28 days, where 22 per cent of the sample remained off sick seven months after infection, and almost half (45 per cent) had failed to return to their former working capacity after six months (Davis et al., 2021).

DOCUMENTING SICKNESS ABSENCE: THE ROLE OF STIGMA

Accurately recording the reasons for employees' sickness absence will help organizations identify trends to target interventions and implement additional support. Evidence that the true causes of absence are not necessarily documented, particularly in relation to mental health, therefore gives cause for concern. Employees may be particularly reluctant to disclose a mental health complaint if their job is insecure, if their manager is perceived to be unsupportive, or if workplace relationships are dysfunctional (Brohan et al., 2012; Brouwers et al., 2020). The continued stigmatization of mental health problems is illustrated by evidence that employees perceive taking sick leave for a *physical* ailment as more legitimate, compared to taking sick leave for a mental health issue. For example, from a survey of 1,000 employees from different sectors, 40 per cent indicated they would find it easier to take time off work for a physical health problem, and 21 per cent reported they would feel embarrassed to take sick leave for mental illness (Canada Life, 2019). Moreover, individuals can experience more intense feelings of shame following absence for a mental health issue than a physical condition (Knapstad et al., 2014), and co-workers may have more negative attitudes towards them (Edwards & Kotera, 2020).

Mental health stigma seems particularly widespread in occupations with a culture of invincibility, where disclosing difficulties might be seen as a sign of weakness or otherwise disadvantage employees (Turner & Jenkins, 2019). A recent study that examined attitudes towards sickness absence in the police, for example, found that absence for mental health issues was often considered not 'bona fide' or even as 'malingering', and officers in this position often felt marginalized (Bell et al., 2022). Research with prison officers also suggests that being absent for a stress-related illness may not be viewed as legitimate, and can even be considered 'lame' or 'lazy' (Kinman et al., 2019). Such findings are a major cause for concern, as anxiety, stress, and depression are particularly common reasons for sickness absence and ill-health-related early retirement in these sectors (Edwards & Kotera, 2020; Hargreaves et al., 2018; Moran et al., 2022). Moreover, an organizational culture that stigmatizes mental health problems can encourage dysfunctional presenteeism, with serious implications for the wellbeing and performance of employees. Raising awareness about common mental disorders can foster more supportive, compassionate organizational cultures, and encourage early support-seeking and the facilitation of reasonable adjustments that can help avoid long-term sickness absence.

THE CAUSES OF SICKNESS ABSENCE: A WIDER PERSPECTIVE

Clearly, the frequency and duration of sickness absence will be strongly influenced by the type of illness experienced, the symptoms and their severity, and whether it is short-term or chronic, episodic or more enduring, as well as the employee's general health. It is increasingly recognized, however, that health status is not necessarily a direct determinant of absence, especially for longer-term spells (Goorts et al., 2020). This is illustrated by research conducted in six European countries, where workers with moderate disabilities had lower levels of sickness absence than those who were not disabled (García-Serrano & Malo, 2014). Such findings may be explained by several factors, such as adjustments being in place to remove any disadvantages related to disabilities, or for people with chronic health issues to use sickness absence more strategically. Nonetheless, the limitations of a purely biomedical approach in explaining the complexity of sickness absence behaviours are increasingly recognized, and the advantages of a model that acknowledges the role played by social and relational factors acknowledged (Miraglia & Johns, 2021; Striker & Kusideł, 2018). As well as health status, the influences on sickness absence can be considered at the following levels:

(a) *the macro level*, including the unemployment rate and opportunities for alternative employment; and the availability of healthcare, sickness certi-fication practices, and social insurance systems;
(b) *the organizational level*, such as the sector, job type, and size of the organization, the terms and conditions of employment, industrial rela-tions, workforce availability and turnover, human resource policies and practices, and the provision of occupational health services;
(c) *the individual level*, which includes sociodemographic factors (such as gender, age, education, family income, and caring responsibilities), job-related factors (such as status, tenure and contract type, skill level, job demands, control and support, job engagement, and satisfaction), as well as personal lifestyle, experiences of negative life events, coping style, and personality traits.

Although the above influences on sickness absence behaviour are clearly inter-connected, they are typically investigated independently rather than at a more holistic level. How an employee's health status interacts with the requirements of their job role will influence whether or not they can continue working. For example, relevant health status factors include the extent to which any pain, fatigue, incapacity or injury, or treatment regime constrain the employee's ability to execute their duties, and their ability to accommodate set working hours (e.g., do a full day's work), required working patterns (e.g., shift work), and/or locations of work (e.g., commuting or business travel). Their personal financial situation, sickness absence record, and entitlement to sick pay and other benefits will also be key factors. Moreover, working may be therapeutic for some people, providing a distraction from pain, or a sense of purpose. Some of these issues, and how they might interact, are discussed further below.

Organizational Size and Sector

Larger and medium-size organizations typically report a higher level of absence (Tu et al., 2021), linked to their tendency to offer more generous sick pay schemes, and experience lower employee engagement than smaller businesses (Preece, 2019; Van der Wel, 2011). Globally, higher levels of absence are found in the public sector (Bureau of Labour Statistics, 2023; DHS, 2023; ONS, 2023), with potential explanations including the greater use of performance-related pay, and less generous sickness benefits in the private sector that might encourage attendance (Baker-McClearn et al., 2010; Dale-Olsen, 2012). The public sector also employs more women, who, overall, have a higher rate of sickness absence than men (ONS, 2023). Much of the observed gender variance in absence can be explained by differences in psychosocial work environment exposures (Labriola et al., 2011). Nonetheless, insight is needed into how gender socialization and stereotypes influence sickness absence behaviours and cultures, particularly in sectors such as the emergency services where absence might be less socially 'acceptable' for men.

Another potential explanation for higher sickness absence among public sector employees is their greater vulnerability to work-related illness or injury, especially for those working in the emergency and security services (who are exposed to criminal behaviour and violence), and in healthcare (who experience more psychosocial stressors and musculoskeletal complaints) (Demou et al., 2018; HSE, 2023). Stress-related absence is particularly common in the public sector, with one UK study finding that 70 per cent of more than 200 public sector organizations surveyed included stress (particularly due to heavy workloads) in their top causes of long-term absence, compared to 38 per cent of private sector organizations (CIPD, 2020). Such findings reinforce the need for public sector organizations, particularly where workers face known occupational hazards, to implement primary-level interventions to support worker wellbeing (see Teoh et al., 2023; see also the chapter by Watson et al. in this collection). As well as improving health and reducing sickness absence, such interventions can increase retention, which is a particular concern in sectors such as health and social care, and the emergency and security services, that are experiencing staffing shortages globally (Police Executive Research Forum, 2021; Shembavnekar et al., 2022).

Poor-Quality and Precarious Work

A higher rate of sickness absence is typically found in lower socioeconomic groups, particularly for mental health issues (ONS, 2022). The longstanding Whitehall II study, which investigates the social and occupational influences on the health of more than 10,000 UK civil servants, found the risks of absence among the lowest grades to be between three and six times greater than those in senior and management grades (North et al., 1993). Highlighting the socioeconomic variation in sickness absence rates in healthcare, a prospective cohort study found that cleaners, porters, and nursing assistants, were absent more frequently and for a longer duration than doctors (Kristensen et al., 2010). Such findings can be explained not only by the long-established social gradient in health status, but also the psychosocial risks that characterize low-quality work, such as rapid pace, low control and support, and lack of variety (Marmot, 2020). These issues are discussed further later in this chapter.

An increase in atypical working arrangements, such as zero-hours contracts and agency work, has been documented in many countries (Equality and Human Rights Commission, 2018). While the adverse effects of precarious work on health (particularly mental health) have been demonstrated, there is some evidence that temporary employees are less likely to take sick leave than those on permanent contracts (Benach et al., 2014; De Cuyper & De Witte, 2010). Insecure workers experiencing health problems can face particular challenges, with a poor sickness absence record increasing the risk of job termination (Reuter et al., 2019; Virtanen et al., 2006). The high level of sickness presenteeism often found among temporary workers, particularly those with limited entitlement to sick pay, suggests that working during illness and injury, and delaying treatment to protect employment, are common (Reuter et al., 2019). The sustained growth in insecure work since the pandemic (ONS, 2023) means that insight is needed into the mechanisms by which it impacts on health and sickness absence. Several 'core' pathways have been identified that can inform interventions, including uncertainty about income, unreliable working patterns, devalued status within the workplace, and concerns about future employment (Irvine & Rose, 2022).

Individual Risk Factors

Sickness absence behaviours are also strongly influenced by characteristics of the employee (such as attitudes and orientations to work, traits, and behaviours) and their working environment (such as psychosocial stressors, and the sickness absence culture). Positive affective states, such as job engagement, meaningfulness, and satisfaction, appear to be powerful predictors of absence. A study of manufacturing workers (Rongen et al., 2014) found that low engagement at baseline predicted low work ability (i.e., the self-perceived capacity to meet job demands) and long-term sickness absence six months later, after controlling for health behaviours and work characteristics. Moreover, based on over 60,000 observations from four occupational groups in Denmark, low affective commitment and job meaningfulness were found to increase long-term sickness absence 18 months later (Clausen et al., 2014).

Specific personality traits, such as conscientiousness and agreeableness, have been associated with lower levels of sickness absence (Raynik et al., 2020; Shan et al., 2021). Such links could be explained by the task-directed, achievement-oriented nature of conscientious employees (Løset, 2022), and that more agreeable workers may be reluctant to burden their colleagues with additional workload caused by their absence. It should be noted, however, that while such characteristics may be beneficial for organizations over the short term, the observed tendency for conscientious and agreeable employees to work while sick may increase the risk of more serious health problems and longer absence over time (Armon et al., 2012). Findings that the effects of personality traits on sickness absence are moderated by occupation type, age, and attitudes towards the job (Løset & Von Soest, 2023) highlight the complexity of these associations, with further research required.

Specific coping styles have also been linked with sickness absence, with a lower level found among employees with an active problem-solving style, and a higher level found in those using avoidant and emotional coping (Schreuder et al., 2011; Van Rhenen et al., 2008). There is also evidence that workers can use short-term sickness absence to help them recover from work overload and manage fatigue. This may be particularly common among those who do emotionally demanding work, with 54 per cent of more than 5,000 Australian nurses and midwives reporting that they had taken a 'mental health' day to help alleviate the pressure they experienced (Lamont et al., 2017). These findings suggest that short-term absence might be used as a way of protecting wellbeing under conditions of high emotional demand, or where demands have been cumulative. This should be further investigated using daily diary methods, for example, that could identify associations over time.

Organizational Risk Factors

Several organizational-level factors have been identified as key determinants of sickness absence. Sickness absence culture is defined as 'a set of shared understandings about absence legitimacy in a given organization and the established custom and practice of employee absence behaviour and its control' (Johns & Nicholson, 1982, p. 136). Absence cultures can have a powerful influence, with newly appointed employees often 'learning' appropriate sickness behaviours from their colleagues and, to a lesser extent, their managers (Brady et al., 2023; Duff et al., 2015). Strong relationships have been reported between group- and individual-level absence, after controlling for factors found to predict sick leave prevalence, such as gender, seniority, and attitudes towards work (Duff et al., 2015; Martocchio & Judge, 1994). The effects of sickness absence norms in shaping individual behaviours are particularly powerful in teams that are highly task-interdependent and cohesive (ten Brummelhuis et al., 2016). Other studies observe that colleagues can also give people 'unofficial permission' to take sick leave even when they are not unwell – for example, by reassuring them that they 'deserve' a break from work pressure; this is particularly likely if the employee is considered disadvantaged in some way, or if there is a shared sense of dissatisfaction with management (Lorentzen & Pukstad, 2021). These findings suggest that examining sickness absence norms at a collective as well as an individual level can provide more insight into the mechanisms underpinning decisions to take sick leave or remain working.

Working hours have also been examined as a potential predictor of sickness absence, with longitudinal studies suggesting that the effects are cumulative. Observations of the working patterns of nearly 2,000 healthcare employees over three years found that working 12-hour shifts at least 75 per cent of the time was associated with both short- and long-term spells of absence (Dall'Ora et al., 2018). Long shifts are commonplace in healthcare and believed to reduce staffing costs; but these findings suggest that any financial benefits may be undermined by short staffing, or paying agency staff to cover for absent colleagues. Other studies of healthcare workers have found that short intervals between shifts, and being on-call, can also increase the risk of absence (Ropponen et al., 2022). This is likely to be due to chronic fatigue resulting from lack of recovery, found to increase the risk of long-term sickness absence by over one-third (Sagherian et al., 2019), with effects observed up to one year later (Kim et al., 2023). As well as damaging for employees, high sickness absence is costly and disruptive; moreover, long-term sickness among healthcare practitioners increases the risk of them leaving the labour market (Palmer & Rolewicz, 2023). This is a particular concern given the post-pandemic recruitment and retention crisis in healthcare in the UK that is set to continue, which has been linked to high workloads, burnout, and concerns over the quality of care (Nursing & Midwifery Council, 2023).

Psychosocial Aspects of Work

The implications of poor-quality work for health were discussed above. Strong links between specific psychosocial work characteristics and sickness absence have been identified. An overview of the key risk factors was provided by Slany et al. (2014), who examined associations between 25 work factors and long-term absence in more than 32,000 employees from 34 European countries. Across all countries, job demands (quantitative and emotional), limited opportunities for development and promotion, poor-quality social relationships, and experiences of workplace violence were some of the independent predictors of absence, with low meaningfulness, inflexibility, and work–life conflict also influential. A prospective cohort study that examined the additive effects of several workplace psychosocial hazards (i.e., demands, role conflict, and bullying) found an exposure–response relationship with long-term sickness absence (Lunen et al., 2023).

Other studies have considered the organizational-level risks for sickness absence in greater depth, with their findings having strong potential to inform interventions to tackle the risks at the source, improve employee health and wellbeing and, in turn, reduce sickness absence. The quality of interpersonal relationships at work appears highly influential in predicting absence, with disrespectful, undermining, and intimidatory behaviours having particularly powerful effects. For example, a review of 17 studies examining associations between exposure to workplace bullying and sick leave highlighted an increased risk in all but one (Nielsen et al., 2016). In contrast, the provision of social support, perceptions of fair treatment, and a sense of mutual cooperation can reduce the number of sick days taken (Koskenvuori et al., 2021; Nyberg et al., 2008; Van Dierendonck et al., 2002).

Leadership style also has a profound impact on the workplace sickness absence culture, with leaders being powerful role models for absence behaviours, both absenteeism and presenteeism (Dietz et al., 2020). They also have a strong influence over the formulation of absence management policies and how they are implemented. A transformational leadership style (that encourages employee empowerment) and an attentive style (that involves active listening and participation) appear to be protective, whereas an autocratic, dictatorial approach can increase the risk of sick leave (Nyberg et al., 2008; Westerlund et al., 2008). Other studies suggest that a transformational style is particularly effective in reducing illegitimate sickness absence, while also discouraging sickness presenteeism (Frooman et al., 2012; George et al., 2017). These findings suggest that encouraging a more transformational and attentive approach might reduce unnecessary sickness absence without increasing presenteeism, as well as potentially improving employee wellbeing and satisfaction.

Using Theoretical Frameworks

While associations between key stressors such as job demands, control, and support, and sickness absence, have been identified, an understanding of how these variables might interact can inform strategies to improve health, reduce sickness absence, and support return to work. The findings of longitudinal cohort studies using theoretical models of work-related wellbeing will be particularly helpful. Using the job strain model (Karasek, 1979), Haveraaen et al. (2017) found that employees in active jobs (that combine high demand with high control) and passive jobs (that combine low demands with low control) returned to work sooner than those in high-strain jobs (that combine high demands and low control). The importance of job control is also highlighted by de Jonge et al. (2010), where the effects of emotional demands on sickness absence depended on the extent of control available to the employee two years previously. The iso-strain model (where high demands are combined with low control and support; Johnson & Hall, 1988) has also been found to predict short- and long-term sickness absence, as well as multiple absence spells over time (Trybou et al., 2014).

Other longitudinal studies have used the effort–reward imbalance (ERI) model (Siegrist, 2002) to predict sickness absence, with an imbalance between employees' perceptions of their work-related efforts and the rewards they receive, increasing the risk of absence prospectively (Head et al., 2007; Schreuder et al., 2010). The ERI model includes overcommitment, an individual difference variable defined as 'a set of attitudes, behaviours and emotions that reflect excessive striving in combination with a strong desire to be approved of and esteemed' (Siegrist, 2002, p. 55). Overcommitment is predicted to have direct effects on employee wellbeing, but also to intensify the negative effects of an effort–reward imbalance (Siegrist, 2002). While lower levels of overcommitment have been found among employees who are absent more frequently (Schreuder et al., 2010), there is mixed evidence for its interactive effects. Montano and Peter (2021), for example, found that an ERI increased the risk of absence among employees over time, but a combination of a high ERI and high overcommitment was associated with *less* rather than more sick leave. Such findings might be explained by the high job involvement found among overcommitted employees, and their reluctance to withdraw from work obligations, even under high effort/low reward conditions (Kinman & Jones, 2008). Nonetheless, as overcommitment substantially increases the risk of poor health (Siegrist & Li, 2016), employees who are highly overcommitted to work may not be healthier, but instead more inclined to work while they are sick.

Conservation of Resources theory (COR; Hobfoll, 1989) also has potential to explain the mechanisms underlying sickness absence by identifying the resources (both organizational and individual) that can reduce the risk. COR theory posits that people are motivated to maintain their current resources and, through experience and learning, identify new resources to manage threats to their wellbeing. Employees lacking resources are more vulnerable to health problems (Bakker & Demerouti, 2007), and COR theory maintains that exposure to adverse working conditions can intensify the threat to their health, potentially increasing the risk of sickness absence. Research reviewed in this chapter suggests that workplace resources such as a supportive culture, autonomy, and flexibility may be particularly helpful in mitigating the risks. More insight is needed into the organizational- and individual-level resources that can reduce sickness absence by improving wellbeing. The ability to work at home when experiencing health problems could enable employees to work within their limitations and avoid taking sick leave. This issue is discussed further in the next section.

SICKNESS PRESENTEEISM

Sickness presenteeism describes situations where an employee attends work despite feeling unwell (Johns, 2010). Presenteeism is widely believed to be more common, and potentially more damaging than absenteeism, but is considerably more challenging to quantify (Bryan et al., 2022). An annual survey of human resource professionals (CIPD, 2023) indicated that the number who had observed presenteeism in their organization had more than tripled since 2010. It is unclear, however, whether this trend reflects a growing tendency to work while unwell, or an increased awareness of the signs and risks of presenteeism within organizations. Moreover, as working while not fully fit is not necessarily detrimental to wellbeing and can be beneficial, the need to differentiate between *dysfunctional* and *therapeutic* presenteeism has been identified (Karanika-Murray & Biron, 2020).

How an organization's sickness culture can shape employees' attitudes and behaviours was discussed earlier, and the role played by the presenteeism climate can be particularly powerful (Ferreira et al., 2022). Dysfunctional presenteeism can be tolerated (or even encouraged) in organizations that normalize working while sick, where managers role model such behaviour, and where it is considered a sign of dedication and commitment (Johns, 2010). It can also be reinforced in working environments that encourage competition between employees, reward those with exemplary attendance, use sickness records as promotion criteria, or penalize those with 'unsatisfactory' attendance (Kinman, 2019). Organizations may also inadvertently foster a climate of presenteeism where workloads are chronically high, jobs are highly specialized or insecure, and sickness absence cover is unavailable (Kinman, 2019). There is reason to believe that the potential for presenteeism has increased further in the aftermath of the pandemic, due to a range of factors such as concerns about job insecurity, a desire to demonstrate commitment or indispensability, and the perceived pressure to be 'always on' and available (Ferreira et al., 2022; Kinman & Grant, 2021).

Reviews of the literature have identified other organizational- and individual-level factors that predict dysfunctional presenteeism. These include aspects of the job (such as 'hard-line' sickness absence policies, lack of support and resources, and poor-quality relationships), and characteristics of the employee (such as financial concerns, high engagement, feeling indispensable, and having a strong work ethic) (Garrow, 2016; Kinman, 2019; Miraglia & Johns, 2021). Nonetheless, the factors that encourage people to work while sick are to some extent shaped by their working context. This is illustrated by studies of two very different occupational groups. For prison officers (Kinman et al., 2019), the key predictors of presenteeism were pressure from managers, stigmatization of sick leave, lack of compassionate leadership, job insecurity, feelings of guilt, and a sense of duty to colleagues and prisoners. For academic employees, however, the most powerful risk factors included role overload, an inability to reschedule meetings and teaching and renegotiate deadlines, concerns about negative evaluations from students, boredom, and, most importantly, fear of a backlog of work on their return (Kinman & Wray, 2022).

Recent conceptualizations of presenteeism recognize that working while not fully fit is not necessarily damaging and can be therapeutic. Work has many psychosocial benefits – it offers opportunities for purposeful activity and social contact that can improve self-esteem and mental health, and distract people from minor symptoms (Warr, 1999). A key factor in determining whether working while unwell facilitates or impairs recovery, however, is the extent to which working conditions, such as tasks, timing, and locations, can be adjusted (Roe & Van Diepen, 2011). The health-performance framework developed by Karanika-Murray and Biron (2020) helpfully differentiates between different aspects of presenteeism, highlighting the potential advantages as well as the drawbacks. Their model identifies four aspects of presenteeism: functional (where people continue working without further taxing their health), dysfunctional (where working leads to a deterioration in health and performance), overachieving (a compulsion to continue working due, for example, to over-commitment and a drive to maintain performance), and therapeutic (where people are supported to work within their limits).

Although presenteeism can be desirable for individuals and organizations, growing awareness of its negative implications has led to calls for it to be considered a potentially 'self-endangering' behaviour (Steidelmuller et al., 2020), a health and safety risk (Demerouti et al., 2009), and a serious public health problem (Homrich et al., 2020). Research findings show that, in some circumstances, presenteeism can not only delay recovery, but also increase the risk of subsequent health problems and sickness absence (e.g., Bergström et al., 2009; Skagen & Collins, 2016). There is also evidence that dysfunctional presenteeism can threaten work performance via impaired cognitive and social skills, potentially leading to serious errors and accidents (Niven & Ciborowska, 2015; White-Means et al., 2022). This is a particular concern in safety-critical work, and where employees are responsible for the wellbeing of members of the public.

Presenteeism is particularly prevalent in healthcare, where working conditions found to encourage such behaviour, such as high pressure, long hours, and short staffing, are endemic (Kinman & Grant, 2021). Attendance pressure among healthcare professionals can also be intensified by a strong sense of responsibility for the welfare of others, and public perceptions of healthcare professionals as self-sacrificing 'heroes' who 'soldier on' through illness (Mohammed et al., 2021; White-Means et al., 2022). Nonetheless, evidence that working while sick can threaten the wellbeing and safety of patients as well as healthcare professionals (Widera et al., 2010) means that increased awareness of the risks is essential in the post-pandemic workplace.

A higher risk of presenteeism has also been found among remote workers (CIPD, 2023; Steidelmuller et al., 2020). The increased flexibility typical of home-based work can allow people to work within the constraints of their illness, and enable those with disabilities and long-term conditions to remain in the workforce (Ruhle & Schmoll, 2021). Nonetheless, there is evidence that remote workers can experience pressure to continue working while they are unwell – there may be higher expectations for their productivity; they may feel the need to 'prove' their availability and engagement; and disconnecting from work can be more challenging if there are no physical boundaries between the work and personal domains (Ruhle & Schmoll, 2021). The rapid growth in remote working arrangements following the pandemic means that organizations should be aware of how dysfunctional virtual presenteeism can manifest itself, the risks of such behaviour, and how it might affect employee wellbeing and productivity.

Whether presenteeism is therapeutic or dysfunctional can be difficult to establish, particularly when interactions between managers and employees are online. Organizations should conduct risk assessments for remote workers, and provide guidance on how to work in a healthy and sustainable way, emphasizing the importance of boundary-setting and withdrawing from work communications when experiencing health difficulties (see also the chapter by Chan and Kinman in this collection). Providing more choice and control over working patterns is also likely to be helpful, as a lower level of presenteeism is typically found among people who can 'self-schedule' working hours (Böckerman & Laukkanen, 2009). Recent evidence that presenteeism is more prevalent among employees working remotely on a full-time basis (Shimura et al., 2021) suggests that the widespread introduction of hybrid patterns might discourage presenteeism. More longitudinal studies are needed, however, to identify the mechanisms linking particular working patterns, and functional and dysfunctional types of presenteeism.

While it might be tempting for organizations to overlook or even encourage dysfunctional presenteeism, particularly during an economic crisis where organizations are struggling to maintain productivity and reduce costs, it should be recognized that the long-term risks for employee wellbeing and performance can over-ride any short-term gains. This is particularly important given the rapid growth of sectors such as healthcare, and in precarious and remote working arrangements, where the risk of presenteeism is particularly high.

There is reason for optimism, however, as the number of organizations taking steps to discourage people from working while unwell is steadily increasing (CIPD, 2023). The health-performance framework (Karanika-Murray & Biron, 2020) discussed above can help managers differentiate between adaptive and potentially damaging presenteeism; but identifying why a particular employee is working while sick, and whether or not they should be encouraged to do so, will be challenging.

MANAGING SICKNESS ABSENCE AND RETURN TO WORK

A multi-level approach is needed to manage sickness absence behaviours effectively, with interventions at each of the primary, secondary, and tertiary levels. Nonetheless, particular focus is needed on developing organizational initiatives (Ståhl et al., 2022). There is evidence that organizations that take a targeted, strategic approach to wellbeing are likely to see reduced levels of sickness absence (CIPD, 2022). Absence management procedures should be reviewed to ensure they are appropriate and equitable, and their implementation is consistent but flexible. This is particularly important, as policies and practices that are considered unfair or punitive can encourage employees to engage in dysfunctional presenteeism to avoid sanctions, or stressful 'back to work' processes (Kinman & Clements, 2019). Sick pay systems should also be reviewed, as limited entitlement can force employees to continue working during illness, or return to work too soon (Johns, 2010). Insight into the sickness climate and behavioural norms of an organization, particularly in relation to leadership styles, will also help determine whether a culture change is required. Strategies should also be implemented to reduce stigma surrounding ill health, and enhance knowledge and understanding, particularly relating to mental health. Such interventions might include sharing personal stories, social networking, 'lunch and learn' sessions, and expert-led workshops (Ammendolia et al., 2016).

The most effective organizational intervention to improve sickness absence is prevention; that is, improving health and wellbeing. The benefits of encouraging healthy behaviours – such as regular exercise, adequate sleep, and maintaining a work–life balance – in reducing sickness absence have been identified (Ammendolia et al., 2016). As work-related stress is a particularly common reason for absence, the key causes should be identified and minimized wherever possible, alongside secondary-level interventions to enhance employees' coping abilities. Regular risk assessments can also inform interventions by pinpointing the factors that might increase sickness absence or dysfunctional presenteeism; whereas organizational data can identify groups that might be at particular risk, to target additional support.

The advantages of a multi-stakeholder approach to preventing and managing sickness absence behaviours are recognized (Ståhl et al., 2022). This can facilitate knowledge exchange and enhance cooperation between line managers, employees, human resources, trade union representatives, and occupational health providers. A review of occupational health provision is strongly recommended, as early contact can reduce sickness absence by preventing health problems from escalating (Kant et al., 2008). It is particularly helpful for occupational health practitioners to work closely with line managers and employees to encourage functional presenteeism, by negotiating reasonable, personalized adjustments to avoid sickness absence, or to facilitate a sustainable return to work. Nonetheless, occupational health provision is inconsistent in some countries and sectors, and particularly lacking in smaller organizations and among self-employed and temporary workers (Nicholson, 2022). Line managers have a key role to play in absence management, as well as in supporting the wellbeing of employees more generally. They need training to help them recognize the early signs of health problems (whether in person or online), and to identify dysfunctional presenteeism, as well as the knowledge required to refer employees for expert support if needed.

A safe, productive, and sustainable return to work following long-term absence is more likely if employees receive appropriate support during their absence and after their return. Predictors of success include (1) the development of a return-to-work policy with input from all stakeholders, (2) the use of a tailored approach that accommodates employees' specific needs, (3) the formulation of a personalized return-to-work plan, (4) maintaining communication between employees and managers and other key people and providing regular updates, and (5) identifying barriers to returning and reducing any risks found (Institute of Occupational Safety and Health, n.d.). Also recognized is the need to take a flexible approach to return-to-work planning that is responsive to any fluctuations in employees' day-to-day functioning – for example, in relation to long Covid (CIPD, 2022; SOM, 2022). Insight is needed into how best to support a sustainable return to work that considers the wide-ranging pattern of symptoms that characterizes long Covid and their varying impact. Some insight has been gained into the return-to-work experiences and needs of people with long Covid (e.g., Kohn et al., 2022), and the need for tailored rehabilitation programmes has been identified (Brehon et al., 2022), but longitudinal studies are needed to inform best practice and improve outcomes.

The IGLOO model (Nielsen et al., 2018) is particularly helpful in identifying the multi-level, interacting factors that promote or impede a successful and sustainable return to work. A number of resources have been identified across the IGLOO levels that can help employees returning from long-term sick leave to remain working and be productive. Examples at each level are: *Individual* (e.g., creating structure during the working day to maintain employees' focus and concentration), *Group* (receiving feedback on their performance from colleagues, getting help with challenging tasks, and being treated as one of the team), *Leader* (gaining ongoing support and access to reasonable adjustments, with managers being available but not intrusive), *Organizational* (flexible working practices and absence policies, the availability of counselling, and demonstrating care through support), and *Overarching* (the wider social context, such as the sickness absence climate).

Improving return-to-work processes is particularly important for mental health problems; not only are they a common cause of long-term absence, but there is also a high risk of relapse, leading to recurrent spells of absence and subsequent exit from work (Koopmans et al., 2011). A study using longitudinal interpretative phenomenological analysis drew on the IGLOO framework to gain insight into employees' experiences when returning to work following long-term absence for common mental disorders (Nielsen & Yarker, 2023). The findings identified three trajectories following their return: *Thrivers*, *Survivors*, and *Exiteers*. These trajectories were influenced by factors at the *Individual* level (the employee wishing to make a valuable contribution and not let people down; and the ability to engage in task, relational, and cognitive job crafting), at the *Group* level (the availability of emotional and instrumental social support), at the *Leadership* level (ongoing support from the line manager; adjustments made to the work, the timing, or the location that accommodated their needs; being seen as a valuable worker; and being trusted to do a good job), and at the *Organizational* level (effective sickness absence policies, and support for mental health). Reflecting the importance of management training highlighted above, line managers' understanding of common mental disorders was found to be a key facilitator of successful return to work.

CONCLUSION

Sickness absenteeism and dysfunctional presenteeism are extremely costly for organizations, particularly during times of turbulence and uncertainty. Interventions are therefore needed that reflect the complex, multi-layered influences on sickness absence behaviours. This chapter highlights the value in seeing absenteeism and presenteeism not as a function of the objective level of sickness among employees, but shaped by their perceptions of their health, their demographic background and individual characteristics, the type of job they do, and a range of other contextual and psychosocial factors. Conceptualizing sickness absence as a process, or journey, that unfolds over time is likely to be particularly helpful in unravelling this complexity. For example, employees in an organization that is downsizing are at risk of work overload and job insecurity that can, over time, lead to stress and exhaustion that, in turn, can impair their immune function and increase their vulnerability to disease, therefore increasing the risk of sickness absence. Identifying the potential impact on employee health and absenteeism of any organizational change, and providing support at an early stage, would therefore be recommended.

It should also be recognized that identifying and reducing illegitimate sickness absence, without inadvertently encouraging dysfunctional presenteeism, will be challenging. In particular, organizations should resist seeing sickness absence from a normative perspective – that is, something essentially 'bad' that must be reduced or can be eliminated – as this is likely to foster a culture that expects and rewards dysfunctional presenteeism. Research findings suggest that people do not use sickness absence or presenteeism to manage health problems, but instead tend to use both (Miraglia & Johns, 2021). Insight is therefore needed into the factors that influence employees' decisions to take time off sick or to continue working, and whether or not any presenteeism is therapeutic or dysfunctional. As with sickness absence highlighted above, such decisions could be viewed as a process where, for example, someone experiencing chronic health problems may initially take time off sick to recover, but for several reasons, such as work overload, job insecurity, withdrawal of sick pay, overcommitment to the job, or feelings of guilt, resumes work too soon, or continues working during subsequent bouts of illness. In turn, this reduces their opportunities to recover, exacerbating their existing health problems and/or potentially causing further difficulties such as exhaustion and burnout over time, thus increasing the risk of future spells of sickness. Conversely, an individual with a long-term condition may find engaging in work is therapeutic via a sense of purpose and meaning, or through distraction; and, while not performing at 100 per cent, is still providing some valuable work performance. These examples indicate that one-size-fits-all policies and occupational health procedures may not always be appropriate, and instead a person-centred approach is required.

Some of the steps that organizations can take to manage sickness absence behaviours more effectively have been identified in this chapter. Also highlighted is the value in taking a multi-level, context-specific approach to facilitating return to work that recognizes the importance of support at the individual, group, leadership, and organizational level, and the need for mutual understanding and cooperation between multiple stakeholders. This approach will help identify the barriers to a successful and sustainable return to work, and the resources that are likely to be helpful.

REFERENCES

Ammendolia, C., Côté, P., Cancelliere, C., Cassidy, J. D., Hartvigsen, J., Boyle, E., Soklaridis, S., Stern, P., & Amick, B., III. (2016). Healthy and productive workers: Using intervention mapping to design a workplace health promotion and wellness program to improve presenteeism. *BMC Public Health, 16*(1), 1–18. https://doi.org/10.1186/s12889-016-3843-x

Appleby, J. (2021). NHS sickness absence during the Covid-19 pandemic. *BMJ, 372.* https://doi.org/10.1136/bmj.n471

Armon, G., Shirom, A., & Melamed, S. (2012). The big five personality factors as predictors of changes across time in burnout and its facets. *Journal of Personality, 80,* 403–427. https://doi.org/10.1111/j.1467-6494.2011.00731.x

Australian Institute of Health and Welfare. (2022). *Long Covid in Australia – a review of the literature.* https://www.aihw.gov.au/reports/covid-19/long-covid-in-australia-a-review-of-the-literature/summary

Baker-McClearn, D., Greasley, K., Dale, J., & Griffith, F. (2010). Absence management and presenteeism: The pressures on employees to attend work and the impact of attendance on performance. *Human Resource Management Journal, 20*(3), 311–328. https://doi.org/10.1111/j.1748-8583.2009.00118.x

Bakker, A. B., & Demerouti, E. (2007). The job demands-resources model: State of the art. *Journal of Managerial Psychology, 22*(3), 309–328. https://doi.org/10.1108/02683940710733115

Bell, S., Palmer-Conn, S., & Kealey, N. (2022). "Swinging the lead and working the head": An explanation as to why mental illness stigma is prevalent in policing. *The Police Journal, 95*(1), 4–23. https://doi.org/10.1177/0032258X211049009

Benach, J., Vives, A., Amable, M., Vanroelen, C., Tarafa, G., & Muntaner, C. (2014). Precarious employment: Understanding an emerging social determinant of health. *Annual Review of Public Health, 35,* 229–253. https://doi.org/10.1146/annurev-publhealth-032013-182500

Bergström, G., Bodin, L., Hagberg, J., Lindh, T., Aronsson, G., & Josephson, M. (2009). Does sickness presenteeism have an impact on future general health? *International Archives of Occupational and Environmental Health, 82,* 1179–1190. https://doi.org/10.1007/s00420-009-0433-6

Black, C., & Frost, D. (2011). *Health at work: An independent review of sickness absence.* UK Stationery Office. https://assets.publishing.service.gov.uk/media/5a7a1163e5274a319e7779eb/health-at-work.pdf

Böckerman, P., & Laukkanen, E. (2009). Presenteeism in Finland: Determinants by gender and sector. *Ege Academic Review, 9*(3). https://dergipark.org.tr/en/pub/eab/issue/39872/473085

Brady, H. D., McGrath, D., & Dunne, C. P. (2023). Sick leave determinants in the healthcare sector (Part I): A review of contextual factors. *Brown Hospital Medicine, 2*(1). https://doi.org/10.56305/001c.57688

Brehon, K., Niemeläinen, R., Hall, M., Bostick, G. P., Brown, C. A., Wieler, M., & Gross, D. P. (2022). Return-to-work following occupational rehabilitation for long COVID: Descriptive cohort study. *JMIR Rehabilitation and Assistive Technologies, 9*(3), e39883. https://doi.org/10.2196/39883

Brohan, E., Henderson, C., Wheat, K., Malcolm, E., Clement, S., Barley, E. A., Slade, M., & Thornicroft, G. (2012). Systematic review of beliefs, behaviours and influencing factors associated with disclosure of a mental health problem in the workplace. *BMC Psychiatry, 12,* 1–14. https://doi.org/10.1186/1471-244X-12-11

Brouwers, E. P. M., Joosen, M. C. W., Van Zelst, C., & Van Weeghel, J. (2020). To disclose or not to disclose: A multi-stakeholder focus group study on mental health issues in the work environment. *Journal of Occupational Rehabilitation, 30,* 84–92. https://doi.org/10.1007/s10926-019-09848-z

Bryan, M. L., Bryce, A. M., & Roberts, J. (2021). The effect of mental and physical health problems on sickness absence. *The European Journal of Health Economics, 22,* 1519–1533. https://doi.org/10.1007/s10198-021-01379-w

Bryan, M. L., Bryce, A. M., & Roberts, J. (2022). Dysfunctional presenteeism: Effects of physical and mental health on work performance. *The Manchester School, 90*(4), 409–438. https://doi.org/10.1111/manc.12402

Bureau of Labor Statistics. (2023). *Paid leave benefits.* https://www.bls.gov/charts/employee-benefits/paid-leave-sick-vacation-days-by-service-requirement.htm

Canada Life. (2019). *29 million employees have been into work while ill.* https://www.canadalife.co.uk/news/29-million-employees-have-been-into-work-while-ill/

Chartered Institute of Personnel and Development. (2020). *Health and wellbeing at work – public sector.* https://www.cipd.org/globalassets/media/comms/news/ggpublic-sector-summary_tcm18-73787.pdf

Chartered Institute of Personnel and Development. (2022). *Working with long Covid: Guidance for people professionals.* https://www.cipd.org/uk/knowledge/guides/long-covid-guides/

Chartered Institute of Personnel and Development. (2023). *Health and wellbeing at work 2023.* https://www.cipd.org/globalassets/media/knowledge/knowledge-hub/reports/2023-pdfs/8436-health-and-wellbeing-report-2023.pdf

Clausen, T., Burr, H., & Borg, V. (2014). Do psychosocial job demands and job resources predict long-term sickness absence? An analysis of register-based outcomes using pooled data on 39,408 individuals in four occupational groups. *International Archives of Occupational and Environmental Health, 87*(8), 909–917. https://doi.org/10.1007/s00420-014-0936-7

Cooper, C., & Bevan, S. (2014). Business benefits of a healthy workforce. In A. Day, K. Kelloway, & J. Hurrell (Eds.), *Workplace well-being: How to build psychologically healthy workplaces* (pp. 27–49). Wiley.

Dale-Olsen, H. (2012). Sickness absence, performance pay and teams. *International Journal of Manpower, 33*(3), 284–300. https://doi.org/10.1108/01437721211234165

Dall'Ora, C., Ball, J., Redfern, O., Recio-Saucedo, A., Maruotti, A., Meredith, P., & Griffiths, P. (2019). Are long nursing shifts on hospital wards associated with sickness absence? A longitudinal retrospective observational study. *Journal of Nursing Management, 27*(1), 19–26. https://doi.org/10.1111/jonm.12643

Davis, H. E., Assaf, G. S., McCorkell, L., Wei, H., Low, R. J., Re'em, Y., Redfield, S., Austin, J. P., & Akrami, A. (2021). Characterizing long COVID in an international cohort: 7 months of symptoms and their impact. *EClinicalMedicine, 38.* https://doi.org/10.1016/j.eclinm.2021.101019

Davis, H. E., McCorkell, L., Vogel, J. M., & Topol, E. J. (2023). Long COVID: Major findings, mechanisms and recommendations. *Nature Reviews Microbiology, 21*(3), 133–146. https://doi.org/10.1038/s41579-022-00846-2

De Cuyper, N., & De Witte, H. (2010). Temporary employment and perceived employability: Mediation by impression management. *Journal of Career Development, 37*(3), 635–652. https://doi.org/10.1177/0894845309357051

De Jonge, J., Van Vegchel, N., Shimazu, A., Schaufeli, W., & Dormann, C. (2010). A longitudinal test of the demand–control model using specific job demands and specific job control. *International Journal of Behavioral Medicine, 17,* 125–133. https://doi.org/10.1007/s12529-010-9081-1

Demerouti, E., Le Blanc, P. M., Bakker, A. B., Schaufeli, W. B., & Hox, J. (2009). Present but sick: A three-wave study on job demands, presenteeism and burnout. *Career Development International, 14*(1), 50–68. https://doi.org/10.1108/13620430910933574

Demou, E., Smith, S., Bhaskar, A., Mackay, D. F., Brown, J., Hunt, K., Vargas-Prada, S., & Macdonald, E. B. (2018). Evaluating sickness absence duration by musculoskeletal and mental health issues: A retrospective cohort study of Scottish healthcare workers. *BMJ Open, 8*(1). https://doi.org/10.1136/bmjopen-2017-018085

Dietz, C., Zacher, H., Scheel, T., Otto, K., & Rigotti, T. (2020). Leaders as role models: Effects of leader presenteeism on employee presenteeism and sick leave. *Work & Stress, 34*(3), 300–322. https://doi.org/10.1080/02678373.2020.1728420

Direct Health Solutions. (2023). *Absence management and wellbeing report.* https://www.dhs.net.au/2023-absence-management-wellbeing-report

Duff, A. J., Podolsky, M., Biron, M., & Chan, C. C. (2015). The interactive effect of team and manager absence on employee absence: A multilevel field study. *Journal of Occupational and Organizational Psychology, 88*(1), 61–79. https://doi.org/10.1111/joop.12078

Edwards, A. M., & Kotera, Y. (2020). Mental health in the UK police force: A qualitative investigation into the stigma with mental illness. *International Journal of Mental Health and Addiction, 19*, 1116–1134. https://doi.org/10.1007/s11469-019-00214-x

Equality and Human Rights Commission. (2018). *Progress on socio-economic rights in Great Britain.* https://www.equalityhumanrights.com/sites/default/files/progress-on-socio-economic-rights-in-great-britain.pdf

Ferreira, A. I., Mach, M., Martinez, L. F., & Miraglia, M. (2022). Sickness presenteeism in the aftermath of COVID-19: Is presenteeism remote-work behavior the new (Ab) normal? *Frontiers in Psychology, 12*, 748053. https://doi.org/10.3389/fpsyg.2021.748053

Frooman, J., Mendelson, M. B., & Kevin Murphy, J. (2012). Transformational and passive avoidant leadership as determinants of absenteeism. *Leadership & Organization Development Journal, 33*(5), 447–463. https://doi.org/10.1108/01437731211241247

García-Serrano, C., & Malo, M. Á. (2014). How disability affects absenteeism: An empirical analysis for six European countries. *International Labour Review, 153*(3), 455–471. https://doi.org/10.1111/j.1564-913X.2014.00210.x

Garrow, V. P. (2016). *Presenteeism: A review of current thinking.* Institute for Employment Studies. https://www.employment-studies.co.uk/resource/presenteeism-review-current-thinking

George, R., Chiba, M., & Scheepers, C. B. (2017). An investigation into the effect of leadership style on stress-related presenteeism in South African knowledge workers. *SA Journal of Human Resource Management, 15*(1), 1–13. https://hdl.handle.net/10520/EJC-749fda2b7

Goorts, K., Boets, I., Decuman, S., Du Bois, M., Rusu, D., & Godderis, L. (2020). Psychosocial determinants predicting long-term sickness absence: A register-based cohort study. *Journal of Epidemiological Community Health, 74*(11), 913–918. http://dx.doi.org/10.1136/jech-2020-214181

Hargreaves, J., Husband, H., & Linehan, C. (2018). *Police workforce, England and Wales, 31 March 2018.* UK Home Office. https://assets.publishing.service.gov.uk/media/5b4e2794e5274a72fb2fb088/hosb1118-police-workforce.pdf

Haveraaen, L. A., Skarpaas, L. S., & Aas, R. W. (2017). Job demands and decision control predicted return to work: The rapid-RTW cohort study. *BMC Public Health, 17*(1), 1–8. https://doi.org/10.1186/s12889-016-3942-8

Head, J., Kivimäki, M., Siegrist, J., Ferrie, J. E., Vahtera, J., Shipley, M. J., & Marmot, M. G. (2007). Effort–reward imbalance and relational injustice at work predict sickness absence. *Journal of Psychosomatic Research*, *63*(4), 433–440. https://doi.org/ 10.1016/j.jpsychores.2007.06.021

Health and Safety Executive. (2023). *Labour force survey: Self-reported work-related ill health and workplace injuries*. https://www.hse.gov.uk/statistics/lfs/index.htm

Hobfoll, S. E. (1989). Conservation of resources: A new attempt at conceptualizing stress. *American Psychologist*, *44*(3), 513. https://psycnet.apa.org/doi/10.1037/0003 -066X.44.3.513

Høeg, T. B., Ladhani, S., & Prasad, V. (2023). How methodological pitfalls have created widespread misunderstanding about long COVID. *BMJ Evidence-Based Medicine*. https://doi.org/10.1136/bmjebm-2023-112338

Homrich, P. H. P., Dantas-Filho, F. F., Martins, L. L., & Marcon, E. R. (2020). Presenteeism among health care workers: Literature review. *Revista Brasileira de Medicina do Trabalho*, *18*(1), 97–102. https:// doi .org/ 10 .5327 %2FZ1679443520200478

Institute of Occupational Safety and Health. (n.d.). *Return to work*. https:// iosh .com/health-and-safety-professionals/improve-your-knowledge/occupational-health -toolkit/ return -to -work/ #: ~: text = In %20the %20return %2Dto %2Dwork ,monitor %20the%20workers

Irvine, A., & Rose, N. (2022). How does precarious employment affect mental health? A scoping review and thematic synthesis of qualitative evidence from Western economies. *Work, Employment and Society*, *38*(2), 418–441. https:// doi .org/ 10 .1177/ 09500170221128698

Johns, G. (2010). Presenteeism in the workplace: A review and research agenda. *Journal of Organizational Behavior*, *31*(4), 519–542. https:// doi .org/ 10 .1002/ job .630

Johns, G., & Miraglia, M. (2015). The reliability, validity, and accuracy of self-reported absenteeism from work: a meta-analysis. *Journal of Occupational Health Psychology*, *20*(1), 1–14. https://psycnet.apa.org/doi/10.1037/a0037754

Johns, G., & Nicholson, N. (1982). The meanings of absence: New strategies for theory and research. *Research in Organizational Behavior*, *4*, 127–172.

Johnson, J. V., & Hall, E. M. (1988). Job strain, workplace social support, and cardiovascular disease: A cross-sectional study of a random sample of the Swedish working population. *American Journal of Public Health*, *78*(10), 1336–1342. https:// doi.org/10.2105/AJPH.78.10.1336

Kant, I., Jansen, N. W., Van Amelsvoort, L. G., Van Leusden, R., & Berkouwer, A. (2008). Structured early consultation with the occupational physician reduces sickness absence among office workers at high risk for long-term sickness absence: A randomized controlled trial. *Journal of Occupational Rehabilitation*, *18*, 79–86. https://doi.org/10.1007/s10926-007-9114-z

Karanika-Murray, M., & Biron, C. (2020). The health-performance framework of presenteeism: Towards understanding an adaptive behaviour. *Human Relations*, *73*(2), 242–261. https://doi.org/10.1177/0018726719827081

Karasek, R. A., Jr. (1979). Job demands, job decision latitude, and mental strain: Implications for job redesign. *Administrative Science Quarterly*, *24*(2), 285–308. https://doi-org.ezproxy.lib.bbk.ac.uk/10.2307/2392498

Kim, M., Kim, J., Yang, S., Lee, D. W., Park, S. G., Leem, J. H., & Kim, H. C. (2023). The relationship between fatigue and sickness absence from work. *Annals of*

Occupational and Environmental Medicine, 35. https://doi.org/10.35371%2Faoem.2023.35.e32

Kinman, G. (2019). Sickness presenteeism at work: Prevalence, costs and management. *British Medical Bulletin, 129* (1), 69–78. https://doi.org/10.1093/bmb/ldy043

Kinman, G., Clements, A. J., & Hart, J. (2019). When are you coming back? Presenteeism in UK prison officers. *The Prison Journal, 99*(3), 363–383. https://doi.org/10.1177/0032885519838019

Kinman, G., & Grant, C. (2021). *Presenteeism during the Covid-19 pandemic*. Society of Occupational Medicine. https://www.som.org.uk/Presenteeism_during_the_COVID-19_pandemic_May_2021.pdf

Kinman, G., & Jones, F. (2008). A life beyond work? Job demands, work-life balance, and wellbeing in UK academics. *Journal of Human Behavior in the Social Environment, 17*(1–2), 41–60. https://doi.org/10.1080/10911350802165478

Kinman, G., & Wray, S. (2022). "Better than watching daytime TV": Sickness presenteeism in UK academics. *Studies in Higher Education, 47*(8), 1724–1735. https://doi.org/10.1080/03075079.2021.1957813

Knapstad, M., Øverland, S., Henderson, M., Holmgren, K., & Hensing, G. (2014). Shame among long-term sickness absentees: correlates and impact on subsequent sickness absence. *Scandinavian Journal of Public Health, 42*(1), 96–103. https://doi.org/10.1177/1403494813500590

Kohn, L., Dauvrin, M., Detollenaere, J., Primus-de Jong, C., Maertens de Noordhout, C., Castanares-Zapatero, D., Cleemput, I., & Van den Heede, K. (2022). Long COVID and return to work: A qualitative study. *Occupational Medicine, 74*(1), 29–36. https://doi.org/10.1093/occmed/kqac119

Koopmans, P. C., Bültmann, U., Roelen, C. A., Hoedeman, R., Van der Klink, J. J., & Groothoff, J. W. (2011). Recurrence of sickness absence due to common mental disorders. *International Archives of Occupational and Environmental Health, 84*, 193–201. https://doi.org/10.1007/s00420-010-0540-4

Koskenvuori, M., Pietiläinen, O., Elovainio, M., Rahkonen, O., & Salonsalmi, A. (2021). A longitudinal study of changes in interactional justice and subsequent short-term sickness absence among municipal employees. *Scandinavian Journal of Work, Environment & Health, 47*(2), 136–144. https://doi.org/10.5271%2Fsjweh.3927

Kristensen, T., Jensen, S., Kreiner, S., & Mikkelsen, S. (2010). Socioeconomic status and duration and pattern of sickness absence. A 1-year follow up study of 2331 hospital employees. *BMC Public Health, 10*(643). https://doi.org/10.1186/1471-2458-10-643

Labriola, M., Holte, K. A., Christensen, K. B., Feveile, H., Alexanderson, K., & Lund, T. (2011). The attribution of work environment in explaining gender differences in long-term sickness absence: Results from the prospective DREAM study. *Occupational and Environmental Medicine, 68*(9), 703–705. https://doi.org/10.1136/oem.2010.060632

Lamont, S., Brunero, S., Perry, L., Duffield, C., Sibbritt, D., Gallagher, R., & Nicholls, R. (2017). "Mental health day" sickness absence amongst nurses and midwives: Workplace, workforce, psychosocial and health characteristics. *Journal of Advanced Nursing, 73*(5), 1172–1181. https://doi.org/10.1111/jan.13212

Lorentzen, S., & Pukstad, E. (2021). Sickness absence culture: A scoping review. Arctic University of Norway. https://munin.uit.no/bitstream/handle/10037/25499/thesis.pdf?sequence=2

Løset, G. K. (2022). *Sickness absence and the role of personality, human values and attitudes: Experimental and longitudinal studies*. PhD Thesis. https://www.duo.uio .no/bitstream/handle/10852/96731/PhD-Loeset-2022.pdf?sequence=1&isAllowed= y

Løset, G. K., & Von Soest, T. (2023). Big five personality traits and physician-certified sickness absence. *European Journal of Personality*, *37*(2), 239–253. https://doi.org/ 10.1177/08902070211065236

Lunen, J. C., Rugulies, R., Sørensen, J. K., Andersen, L. L., & Clausen, T. (2023). Exploring exposure to multiple psychosocial work factors: Prospective associations with depression and sickness absence. *European Journal of Public Health*, *33*(5), 821–827. https://doi.org/10.1093/eurpub/ckad118

Lyttelton, T., & Zang, E. (2022). Occupations and sickness-related absences during the COVID-19 pandemic. *Journal of Health and Social Behavior*, *63*(1), 19–36. https:// doi.org/10.1177/00221465211053615

Marmot, M. (2020). Health equity in England: The Marmot Review 10 years on. *BMJ*, *368*. https://doi.org/10.1136/bmj.m693

Martocchio, J. J., & Judge, T. A. (1994). A policy-capturing approach to individuals' decisions to be absent. *Organizational Behavior and Human Decision Processes*, *57*(3), 358–386. https://doi.org/10.1006/obhd.1994.1020

Miraglia, M., & Johns, G. (2021). The social and relational dynamics of absenteeism from work: A multilevel review and integration. *Academy of Management Annals*, *15*(1), 37–67. https://doi.org/10.5465/annals.2019.0036

Mohammed, S., Peter, E., Killackey, T., & Maciver, J. (2021). The "nurse as hero" discourse in the COVID-19 pandemic: A poststructural discourse analysis. *International Journal of Nursing Studies*, *117*, 103887. https:// doi .org/ 10.1016/j .ijnurstu.2021.103887

Montano, D., & Peter, R. (2021). The causal structure of the effort-reward imbalance model and absenteeism in a cohort study of German employees. *Occupational Health Science*, *5*(4), 473–492. https://doi.org/10.1007/s41542-021-00097-2

Moran, D., Jones, P. I., Jordaan, J. A., & Porter, A. E. (2022). Nature contact in the carceral workplace: greenspace and staff sickness absence in prisons in England and Wales. *Environment and Behavior*, *54*(2), 276–299. https:// doi .org/ 10.1177/ 00139165211014618

National Health Service. (2023). *Home page*. https://www.nhs.uk

Nicholson, P. (2022). *Occupational health: The value proposition*, SOM https://www .som .org .uk/ sites/ som .org .uk/ files/ Occupational_Health_The_Value_Proposition _March_2022.pdf

Nielsen, K., & Yarker, J. (2023). Thrivers, survivors or exiteers: A longitudinal, inter-pretative phenomenological analysis of the post-return-to-work journeys for workers with common mental disorders. *Applied Psychology*, *73*(1), 267–295. https:// doi .org/10.1111/apps.12479

Nielsen, K., Yarker, J., Munir, F., & Bültmann, U. (2018). IGLOO: An integrated framework for sustainable return to work in workers with common mental disorders. *Work & Stress*, *32*(4), 400–417. https://doi.org/10.1080/02678373.2018.1438536

Nielsen, M. B., Indregard, A. M. R., & Øverland, S. (2016). Workplace bullying and sickness absence: A systematic review and meta-analysis. *Scandinavian Journal of Work, Environment & Health*, *42*(5), 359–370. https:// www .jstor .org/ stable/ 43999304

Niven, K., & Ciborowska, N. (2015). The hidden dangers of attending work while unwell: A survey study of presenteeism among pharmacists. *International Journal of Stress Management, 22*(2), 207–221. https://psycnet.apa.org/doi/10.1037/a0039131

North, F., Syme, S., Feeney, A., Head, J., Shipley, M., & Marmot, M. (1993). Explaining socioeconomic differences in sickness absence: The Whitehall II Study. *BMJ, 6*(306), 361–366. https://doi.org/10.1136%2Fbmj.306.6874.361

Nursing & Midwifery Council. (2023). *Registration data reports.* https://www.nmc.org.uk/about-us/reports-and-accounts/registration-statistics/

Nyberg, A., Westerlund, H., Magnusson Hanson, L. L., & Theorell, T. (2008). Managerial leadership is associated with self-reported sickness absence and sickness presenteeism among Swedish men and women. *Scandinavian Journal of Public Health, 36*(8), 803–811. https://doi.org/10.1177/1403494808093329

Office for National Statistics. (2022). *Economic activity.* https://www.ons.gov.uk/employmentandlabourmarket/peoplenotinwork/economicinactivity

Office for National Statistics. (2023). *Sickness absence in the UK labour market 2022.* https://www.ons.gov.uk/employmentandlabourmarket/peopleinwork/labourproductivity/articles/sicknessabsenceinthelabourmarket/2022

Organisation for Economic Co-operation and Development. (2023). *Health statistics.* https://www.oecd.org/health/health-data.htm

Palmer, B., & Rolewicz, L. (2023). *All is not well: Sickness absence in the NHS in England.* Nuffield Trust. https://www.nuffieldtrust.org.uk/resource/all-is-not-well-sickness-absence-in-the-nhs-in-england

Police Executive Research Forum. (2021). *Survey on police workforce trends.* https://www.policeforum.org/workforcesurveyjune2021

Preece, R. (2019). Sickness absence. In J. Hobson & J. Smedley (Eds.), *Fitness for work: The medical aspects* (pp. 184–206*)*. Oxford University Press.

Rayner, C., & Campbell, R. (2021). Long Covid implications for the workplace. *Occupational Medicine, 71*(3), 121–123. https://doi.org/10.1093/occmed/kqab042

Raynik, Y. I., König, H. H., & Hajek, A. (2020). Personality factors and sick leave days: Evidence from a nationally representative longitudinal study in Germany. *International Journal of Environmental Research and Public Health, 17*(3), 1089. https://doi.org/10.3390/ijerph17031089

Reuter, M., Wahrendorf, M., Di Tecco, C., Probst, T. M., Ruhle, S., Ghezzi, V., Barbaranelli, C., Iavicoli, S., & Dragano, N. (2019). Do temporary workers more often decide to work while sick? *International Journal of Environmental Research and Public Health, 16*(10), 1868. https://doi.org/10.3390/ijerph16101868

Roe, R. A., & Van Diepen, B. (2011). Employee health and presenteeism: The challenge for human resource management. In A. Antoniou & C. Cooper (Eds.), *New directions in organizational psychology and behavioral medicine* (pp. 239–258). Taylor & Francis.

Rongen, A., Robroek, S., Schaufeli, W., & Burdorf, A. (2014). The contribution of work engagement to self-perceived health, work ability, and sickness absence beyond health behaviors and work-related factors. *Journal of Occupational and Environmental Medicine, 56*(8), 892–897. https://doi.org/10.1097/jom.0000000000000196

Ropponen, A., Koskinen, A., Puttonen, S., Ervasti, J., Kivimäki, M., Oksanen, T., ... & Karhula, K. (2022). Association of working hour characteristics and on-call work with risk of short sickness absence among hospital physicians: a longitudinal cohort study. *Chronobiology International, 39*(2), 233-240. https://doi.org/10.1080/07420528.2021.1993238

Ruhle, S. A., & Schmoll, R. (2021). COVID-19, telecommuting, and (virtual) sickness presenteeism: Working from home while ill during a pandemic. *Frontiers in Psychology, 12,* 734106. https://doi.org/10.3389/fpsyg.2021.734106

Sagherian, K., Geiger-Brown, J., Rogers, V. E., & Ludeman, E. (2019). Fatigue and risk of sickness absence in the working population. *Scandinavian Journal of Work, Environment & Health, 45*(4), 333–345. https://www.jstor.org/stable/26746260

Schreuder, J. A., Roelen, C. A., Koopmans, P. C., Moen, B. E., & Groothoff, J. W. (2010). Effort–reward imbalance is associated with the frequency of sickness absence among female hospital nurses: A cross-sectional study. *International Journal of Nursing Studies, 47*(5), 569–576. https://doi.org/10.1016/j.ijnurstu.2009.10.002

Schreuder, J. A. H., Plat, N., Magerøy, N., Moen, B. E., Van der Klink, J. J. L., Groothoff, J. W., & Roelen, C. A. M. (2011). Self-rated coping styles and registered sickness absence among nurses working in hospital care: A prospective 1-year cohort study. *International Journal of Nursing Studies, 48*(7), 838–846. https://doi.org/10.1016/j.ijnurstu.2010.12.008

Shan, G., Wang, S., Wang, W., Guo, S., & Li, Y. (2021). Presenteeism in nurses: Prevalence, consequences, and causes from the perspectives of nurses and chief nurses. *Frontiers in Psychiatry, 11,* 584040. https://doi.org/10.3389/fpsyt.2020.584040

Shembavnekar, N., Buchan, J., Bazeer, N., Kelly, E., Beech, J., Charlesworth, A., McConkey, R., & Fisher, R. (2022). *NHS workforce projections 2022.* https://www.health.org.uk/publications/nhs-workforce-projections-2022

Shimura, A., Yokoi, K., Ishibashi, Y., Akatsuka, Y., & Inoue, T. (2021). Remote work decreases psychological and physical stress responses, but full-remote work increases presenteeism. *Frontiers in Psychology, 12,* 730969. https://doi.org/10.3389/fpsyg.2021.730969

Siegrist, J. (2002). Effort-reward imbalance at work and health. In P. L. Perrewe & D. C. Ganster (Eds.), *Research in occupational stress and well being, Vol. 2: Historical and current perspectives on stress and health* (pp. 261–291). Emerald Group.

Siegrist, J., & Li, J. (2016). Associations of extrinsic and intrinsic components of work stress with health: A systematic review of evidence on the effort-reward imbalance model. *International Journal of Environmental Research and Public Health, 13*(4), 432. https://doi.org/10.3390/ijerph13040432

Skagen, K., & Collins, A. M. (2016). The consequences of sickness presenteeism on health and wellbeing over time: A systematic review. *Social Science & Medicine, 161,* 169–177. https://doi.org/10.1016/j.socscimed.2016.06.005

Slany, C., Schütte, S., Chastang, J. F., Parent-Thirion, A., Vermeylen, G., & Niedhammer, I. (2014). Psychosocial work factors and long sickness absence in Europe. *International Journal of Occupational and Environmental Health, 20*(1), 16–25. https://doi.org/10.1179/2049396713Y.0000000048

Society of Occupational Medicine. (2022). *Long Covid and return to work – what works?* https://www.som.org.uk/sites/som.org.uk/files/Long_COVID_and_Return_to_Work_What_Works_0.pdf

Srikanth, S., Boulos, J. R., Dover, T., Boccuto, L., & Dean, D. (2023). Identification and diagnosis of long COVID-19: A scoping review. *Progress in Biophysics and Molecular Biology, 182,* 1–7. https://doi.org/10.1016/j.pbiomolbio.2023.04.008

Ståhl, C., Gustavsson, I. N., Jonsdottir, I. H., & Akerstrom, M. (2022). Multilevel, risk group-oriented strategies to decrease sickness absence in the public sector: Evaluation of interventions in two regions in Sweden. *International Archives of*

Occupational and Environmental Health, 95(6), 1415–1427. https:// doi .org/ 10 .1007/s00420-022-01864-6

Steidelmüller, C., Meyer, S. C., & Müller, G. (2020). Home-based telework and presenteeism across Europe. *Journal of Occupational and Environmental Medicine, 62*(12), 998–1005. https://doi.org/10.1097%2FJOM.0000000000001992

Striker, M., & Kusideł, E. (2018). Determinants of employee absence differentiation. *Acta Universitatis Lodziensis. Folia Oeconomica, 1*(333), 39–56. https://doi.org/10 .18778/0208-6018.333.03

Ten Brummelhuis, L. L., Johns, G., Lyons, B. J., & ter Hoeven, C. L. (2016). Why and when do employees imitate the absenteeism of co-workers? *Organizational Behavior and Human Decision Processes, 134*, 16–30. https:// doi .org/ 10 .1016/ j .obhdp.2016.04.001

Teoh, K., Dhensa-Kahlon, R., Christensen, M., Frost, F., Hatton, E., & Nielsen, K. (2023). *Organisational interventions to support staff wellbeing*. Society of Occupational Medicine. https:// www .som .org .uk/ sites/ som .org .uk/ files/ Organisational_Interventions_to_Support_Staff_Wellbeing_in_the_NHS.pdf

Trybou, J., Germonpre, S., Janssens, H., Casini, A., Braeckman, L., Bacquer, D. D., & Clays, E. (2014). Job-related stress and sickness absence among Belgian nurses: A prospective study. *Journal of Nursing Scholarship, 46*(4), 292–301. https:// doi .org/10.1111/jnu.12075

Tu, T., Maguire, K., & Shanmugarasa, T. (2021). *Sickness absence and health in the workplace: Understanding employer behaviour and practice*. DWP Research Report. https:// assets .publishing .service .gov .uk/ government/ uploads/ system/ uploads/ attachment_data/file/1003911/sickness-absence-and-health-in-the-workplace-report .pdf

Turner, T., & Jenkins, M. (2019). "Together in work, but alone at heart": Insider perspectives on the mental health of British police officers. *Policing: A Journal of Policy and Practice, 13*(2), 147–156. https://doi.org/10.1093/police/pay016

Van der Wel, K. (2011). Long-term effects of poor health on employment: The significance of life stage and educational level. *Sociology of Health and Illness*. https://doi .org/10.1111/j.1467-9566.2011.01346.x

Van Dierendonck, D., Le Blanc, P. M., & Van Breukelen, W. (2002). Supervisory behavior, reciprocity and subordinate absenteeism. *Leadership & Organization Development Journal, 23*(2), 84–92. https://doi.org/10.1108/01437730210419215

Van Rhenen, W., Schaufeli, W. B., Van Dijk, F. J., & Blonk, R. W. (2008). Coping and sickness absence. *International Archives of Occupational and Environmental Health, 81*, 461–472. https://doi.org/10.1007/s00420-007-0238-4

Virtanen, M., Kivimaki, N., Vahtera, J., Elovainio, M., Sund, R., Virtanen, P. & Ferrie, J. (2006). Sickness absence as a risk factor for job termination, unemployment, and disability pension among temporary and permanent employees. *Occupational and Environmental Medicine, 63*(3), 212–217. https://doi.org/10.1136/oem.2005.020297

Warr, P. (1999). Well-being and the workplace. In G. Kahneman, N. Diener, & N. Schwarz (Eds.), *Well-being: Foundations of hedonic psychology* (pp. 392–412). SAGE.

Westerlund, H., Nyberg, A., Bernin, P., Hyde, M., Oxenstierna, G., Jäppinen, P., ... & Theorell, T. (2010). Managerial leadership is associated with employee stress, health, and sickness absence independently of the demand-control-support model. *Work, 37*(1), 71–79. https://doi.org/10.3233/WOR-2010-1058

Whitaker, S. C. (2001). The management of sickness absence. *Occupational and Environmental Medicine, 58*(6), 420–424. http://dx.doi.org/10.1136/oem.58.6.420

White-Means, S. I., Warren, C. L., & Osmani, A. R. (2022). The organizational impact of presenteeism among key healthcare workers due to the COVID-19 pandemic. *The Review of Black Political Economy*, *49*(1), 20–40. https://doi.org/10.1177/00346446211065175

Widera, E., Chang, A., & Chen, H. L. (2010). Presenteeism: A public health hazard. *Journal of General Internal Medicine*, *25*, 1244–1247. https://doi.org/10.1007/s11606-010-1422-x

9. Sustaining and embedding: a strategic and dynamic approach to workplace wellbeing[1]

David Watson, Rachel Nayani, Olga Tregaskis, and Kevin Daniels

Much of the current literature on health and wellbeing interventions focuses on discrete interventions and individual health and wellbeing outcomes (Burgess et al., 2020), underpinned by rational models of planned change (cf. Mintzberg, 1994), with a tendency to view the organization as a field or context within which workplace health and wellbeing practices take place (Russell et al., 2016), rather than seeing an intervention as one element of a stream of organizational actions that address multiple, sometimes conflicting, priorities (Fuller et al., 2019). In contrast, in the current chapter, we outline a model of how organizations sustain and embed patterns of workplace wellbeing practices over the longer term, in coherent and strategic programmes.

The rationale for a model concerned with longer-term strategic health and wellbeing programmes is three-fold. First, best practice guidelines for workplace health and wellbeing advocate the use of multiple health and wellbeing practices, addressing both prevention and rehabilitation, that are actively managed and subject to continuous improvement processes, rather than stand-alone interventions (International Organization for Standardization, 2018; LaMontagne et al., 2014). Second, and consistent with best practice guidelines, quantitative surveys of organizational practices (Batorsky et al., 2016; Mattke et al., 2015) and case study evidence (Daniels et al., 2022b; Johnson et al., 2018; Jordan et al., 2003) indicate some organizations do indeed adopt multiple health and wellbeing practices in managed and evolving programmes. Third, to help organizations sustain employee health and wellbeing over the longer term, it is important to understand how organizations adjust their health and wellbeing activities to changing environments and priorities, both during periods of slow, incremental change and during turbulent periods of radical change.

Our model provides a complementary perspective to intervention research. Intervention research is primarily focused on understanding whether, how, why, and in which circumstances specific interventions (e.g., job redesign), or combinations of interventions (e.g., job redesign introduced alongside health promotion and resilience training), have effects (Fridrich et al., 2015; Nielsen & Miraglia, 2017; Nielsen & Randall, 2013). Our complementary perspective focuses on how programmes of interventions develop, evolve, and change over time. This complementary perspective is able to subsume the practices that are part of a planned organizational approach that form the basis of the vast majority of studies on interventions (Daniels et al., 2021). The perspective is also able to incorporate workplace health and wellbeing practices that emerge from outside of a planned approach and of the awareness of key managerial decision makers, but that become subsumed into the overall programme over time.

The chapter proceeds as follows. First, to frame the gap in our understanding of health and wellbeing programmes that our complementary approach addresses, we provide a brief overview of research on the implementation of specific interventions. We then introduce the major elements of our model. Finally, we consider how rapid organizational change and turbulence can affect organizational actions around worker health and wellbeing. Rapid change and turbulence may bring, or be caused by, new threats to employee health and wellbeing. However, organizations may also struggle to maintain a focus on employee health and wellbeing during periods of turbulence and rapid change because of competing priorities (e.g., organizational survival) and/or resource constraints.

THE CASE FOR COMPLEMENTING INTERVENTION RESEARCH

Classifications of workplace health and wellbeing practices (e.g., Daniels et al., 2021; LaMontagne et al., 2007; Richardson & Rothstein, 2008) typically differentiate between: (1) primary interventions focused on job/organizational redesign, (2) primary interventions focused on workplace health promotion, (3) secondary interventions focused on training individuals to manage their exposure to risks, (4) tertiary interventions focused on rehabilitation of workers that have developed health conditions, and (5) multicomponent interventions that combine elements of other interventions.

Intervention research, focused on examining the effects of specific and discrete interventions or combinations of interventions, is important for several reasons. First, with appropriate counter-factuals, intervention studies have the potential to provide some of the most robust, ecologically valid inferences on the causes of different facets of health and wellbeing in working-age adults (cf. Cook et al., 1990). For example, randomized control trials or quasi-experiments of job redesign can potentially provide robust evidence on whether psychosocial hazards are causes of poor psychological wellbeing. Second, intervention research can provide sound evidence-based arguments to aid decision makers (e.g., governments, organizational managers) in deciding on what types of interventions can be effective in workplaces. Third, if intervention studies also analyse the impact on a range of indicators of productivity, including factors such as absence or staff turnover (Daniels et al., 2022a; Patey et al., 2021), the cost-effectiveness of interventions can be established, providing an economic case for choosing some interventions ahead of others. Finally, with appropriate analyses of the processes of implementation, intervention studies can provide decision makers with guidance on how best to implement and manage specific interventions (e.g., Murta et al., 2007).

Intervention research does indicate that a range of interventions can be effective in protecting and promoting workers' health and wellbeing, although these benefits are dependent on how the interventions were implemented (Daniels et al., 2021; Egan et al., 2009; Fridrich et al., 2015; Nielsen & Randall, 2013). Implementation is 'the dynamic process of adapting the program to the context of action while maintaining the intervention's core principles' (Herrera-Sánchez et al., 2017, p. 4). In a systematic review covering all of the categories of workplace health and wellbeing interventions identified above, Daniels et al. (2021) identified a number of critical success factors for interventions to produce beneficial effects for workers' health and wellbeing.

One of the factors identified by Daniels et al. (2021) was that tangible changes in workplaces were required for interventions to produce benefits. Put another way, managerial rhetoric, and statements to the effect that 'action will be taken in the future', are insufficient to produce benefits. Tangible actions may unlock the theoretical mechanisms that underpin intervention design; that is, interventions may work as they were intended to.[2] However, Daniels et al. (2021) found evidence that a range of other processes could explain why interventions have beneficial effects. Studies indicate that interventions can have benefits through unintended mechanisms, including promoting self-care (Daniels et al., 2022b; Fitzhugh et al., in press), changes in workplace norms around health behaviours (Daniels et al., 2021, 2022b), and a range of social processes that promote social support, social identity and psychological safety (Daniels et al., 2021, 2022b; Haynes et al., 2022; Musgrove, 2023). In their review, Daniels et al. (2021) also found that other factors related to successful implementation of workplace health and wellbeing interventions were 'continuity of effort and adaptation of interventions, supported by functional learning and governance structures' (p. 11). Another important finding was that a range of barriers to implementation did not necessarily prevent interventions from having beneficial effects. Barriers included constrained resources, wider economic pressures, and unfavourable attitudes held by workers, or middle or senior managers.

The main factors that support implementation of specific interventions, identified by Daniels et al. (2021), might generalize to whole programmes of practices that evolve over time (Daniels et al., 2022b). Indeed, within evolving programmes, some of the mechanisms that promote the success of specific interventions could be magnified in wider programmes by consistent and authentic signalling by the organization of the importance of worker health and wellbeing (Nayani et al., 2022; see below). However, there are also reasons to suspect that applying lessons from intervention research to wider programmes may not provide the whole picture (Daniels et al., 2022b). What applies to a specific intervention may not apply to a wider programme of practices that evolves over time – perhaps many years.[3] This pertains not just to the added complexity of managing a programme of practices as compared to time-limited discrete interventions, but also to phasing-out interventions that are no longer needed, and introducing new interventions as they are needed, or as they emerge as solutions to previously intractable problems. Further, over extended periods of time, organizations themselves will change and evolve, and there needs to be some exploration of how changing workplace health and wellbeing practices come to be accommodated with changes in other aspects of the organization.

In contrast, intervention research is concerned with investigating specific and pre-defined interventions with a limited timeframe,[4] within which the organization is assumed to be in a steady state excepting any changes made directly to implement the intervention (Russell et al., 2016). Any other organizational changes that occur during the limited timeframe of an intervention study may be treated as 'contextual noise', or a nuisance that has affected the fidelity with which an intervention was implemented, rather than a naturally occurring aspect of organizations. Further, by focusing on a specific intervention, researchers may understandably conclude that contextual factors led to failure to implement the focal intervention, yet not notice that another health and wellbeing intervention was implemented instead to suit changing circumstances. Indeed, researchers may not even be engaged in the field after the focal intervention for the research has been abandoned.

In sum, although there are clear advantages for pursuing research on specific interventions, there is also a case for examining how programmes of health and wellbeing practices develop, are sustained, and evolve over extended periods. This is because it cannot be assumed that findings from intervention research can be readily transferred to wider programmes, and/or that other factors need to be considered. Moreover, by examining health and wellbeing programmes over the longer term, it may become more readily apparent how organizations are able to negotiate any tensions that occur between evolving workplace health and wellbeing programmes, and other dynamic aspects of organizations.

A MODEL OF IMPLEMENTING WORKPLACE HEALTH AND WELLBEING PROGRAMMES

To develop our understanding of the actions organizations can take to protect and enhance worker health and wellbeing over the longer term, we developed a model that, compared to traditional intervention research, is focused more on the organization and the range of practices (discrete interventions) that could be integrated into a programme of workplace health and wellbeing practices (see Daniels et al., 2022b for a more detailed explanation of the model). Some of these practices could be focused on the entire organization; others on specific locations, departments, or occupational or demographic groups. Figure 9.1 illustrates the model.

One important basis of the model was the recognition that organizational strategies reflect a pattern in a stream of decisions, behaviours, and practices (Mintzberg & Waters, 1985, p. 257). Following Mintzberg and Waters, and

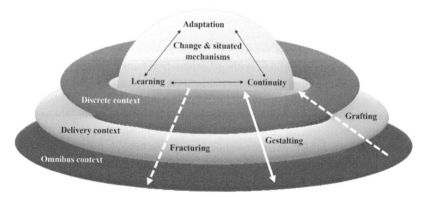

Source: Adapted from Daniels, K., Tregaskis, O., Nayani, R., & Watson, D. (2022b). *Achieving sustainable workplace wellbeing.* Springer Nature.

Figure 9.1 *A model of how organizations implement and sustain workplace health and wellbeing programmes*

Fuller et al.'s (2019) application of these ideas to workplace safety, we recognize that workplace health and wellbeing strategies do not need to follow rational planning approaches advocated in much of the intervention literature (see Daniels et al., 2022b, chapter 2 for a review). Rather, some planned practices may never be realized; and some practices may emerge from the behaviours of organizational actors without explicit planning, but may come to be adopted when recognized as useful by key decision makers.[5] Therefore, we can conceptualize a strategic approach to workplace health and wellbeing as one that reflects an ongoing pattern of health and wellbeing practices in a workplace, that is formally managed to a greater or lesser extent, and can include elements that are planned, some elements that are never implemented even if planned, and some unplanned elements that are brought into an overall organizational approach to health and wellbeing. Importantly, the definition of a strategic approach to workplace health and wellbeing as an *ongoing* pattern of practices implies dynamism, rather than just the introduction of discrete interventions.

At the centre of the model are continuity, learning, and adaptation. These are three key processes identified by Daniels et al. (2021) that explain how a health and wellbeing practice or series of connected practices are implemented, and the consequent activation of contextually situated mechanisms. Continuity, learning, and adaptation are reciprocally related. For example, efforts directed towards continuity and learning enable adaptations to unanticipated and/or changing circumstances. Adaptations enable further continuity and further learning. It is activated mechanisms that confer health and wellbeing benefits to workers; although, as noted above, these mechanisms may or may not reflect the mechanisms intended by the practice's designers. Without continuity, learning, and adaptation, other contextual factors, such as senior manager or line manager antipathy, resource constraints, or disruptions, can inhibit either implementation and/or the activation of mechanisms. In the following sections, we outline some of the key, novel components of the model in more detail. These relate to levels of context, grafting, fracturing, and Gestalting.

Levels of Context

Drawing from intervention research (e.g., Fridrich et al., 2015; Nielsen & Randall, 2013), our model also builds on Johns' (2006) distinction between discrete and omnibus contexts. The omnibus context represents the wider organization and its environment (operational procedures, overall strategy, economic conditions). The implementation of specific health and wellbeing practices represents the discrete context (such as service provider characteristics and employee attitudes to the intervention). For specific practices, it is the discrete context where tangible changes activate mechanisms, supported by continuity, adaptation, and learning.

However, our model is concerned with implementation (and possibly modification or withdrawal) of multiple practices over time. Therefore, in between the omnibus and discrete contexts, we introduce the notion of the delivery context. The delivery context is the space through which multiple practices are implemented and co-ordinated by key actors (e.g., occupational health and human resources professionals, other managers and workers with responsibilities for health and wellbeing). Governance structures and consultative processes in the delivery context provide the means to transfer learning from implementing other health and wellbeing practices (i.e., other discrete contexts, past or present – for example, other practices, from other locations) to a given discrete context (i.e., a specific, current intervention) so that it is adapted. Moreover, governance structures and consultative processes in the delivery context are a means of capturing learning from a focal intervention, to apply to future interventions. In this way, capabilities can be developed through longevity of programmes (see also Thiele Schwarz et al., 2016; Zollo & Winter, 2002), so that resources (financial and material, symbolic and discursive) can be leveraged to aid more efficient implementation.

We (Daniels et al., 2022b) have identified a range of implementation and co-ordination functions of the delivery context. These relate to: the preparatory work of needs assessments, informing relevant stakeholders of the actions that will be taken, programme planning, ensuring appropriate levels of resourcing, communications and information provision, co-ordinating multiple practices or service providers, incorporating practices initiated by workers and not included in initial programme plans, managing the tension between implementing standardized practices across an organization and tailoring practices to specific groups or locations, and monitoring progress.

However, we (Daniels et al., 2022b) also identified political and symbolic functions of the delivery context, which relate to the political and symbolic processes required to initiate and implement change (see, for example, Gersick, 1991; Johnson, 1987, 1990; Westover, 2010). One of most straightforward political tactics relates to involvement of a range of stakeholders in programme design and/or implementation. Involvement is important for tailoring and adapting (Cherns, 1987), but is also important for discerning the acceptability of different options to different stakeholder groups, as a means of signalling the importance of health and wellbeing to stakeholders (Johnson, 1987), and as a means of overcoming resistance through co-opting resistant stakeholders into learning and governance structures (Swan & Fox, 2010). As key enablers or blockers of change (Balogun, 2006; Currie & Proctor, 2005), we identified another symbolic tactic of programme designers – promoting early-adopting line managers of new practices as role models to other managers. Routinized practices can symbolize what is important and valued by an organization (Johnson, 1987; Schein, 1985). Regular consultations around wellbeing (e.g., staff question and answer sessions, toolbox talks), and incorporation of health and wellbeing concerns into other organizational routines (e.g., performance appraisals in our study; Kaizen procedures in Thiele Schwarz et al., 2016), can perform these symbolic functions, and therefore help with implementation of a range of health and wellbeing practices.

The delivery context itself can influence worker health and wellbeing over and above that of the constituent components. Organizations that adopt multiple health and wellbeing practices send stronger signals of care for employee health and wellbeing. In turn, such signals may influence workers to adopt healthier behaviours through changing workplace norms (Jia et al., 2018), and improve perceptions of organizational support (Haynes et al., 2022), that enhance (psychological) wellbeing. Such signals can be magnified if accompanied by management actions that communicate, reinforce, and legitimize the implementation of workplace health and wellbeing practices (Bowen & Ostroff, 2004). Examples might be senior managers giving speeches about their own wellbeing and being visibly engaged in programme governance.

Grafting, Fracturing, and Gestalting

The delivery context is also the space in which factors in the omnibus context and discrete contexts are reconciled. Mechanisms and variables that might be important in the discrete context of health and wellbeing practices must be aligned with, or take account of, influences of the omnibus context, but this is not a uni-directional relationship. There are three processes that link the discrete context to the omnibus context through the delivery context. These are *grafting, fracturing*, and *Gestalting*.

Grafting is defined as adapting a health and wellbeing practice (or practices) so that it is implemented in a way that is compatible with other organizational procedures, practices, and structures. That is, the omnibus context influences the discrete context. Grafting enables multiple objectives to be pursued in ways that are compatible with each other (e.g., productivity, wellbeing), rather than in conflict with each other. Ensuring compatibility with existing procedures, practices, and structures has been recommended in prior reviews and conceptual models focused on workplace wellbeing interventions (e.g., Daniels et al., 2017; Knight et al., 2019; Nielsen & Noblet, 2018; Thiele Schwarz, et al., 2021), as well as in several generic models of organizational change (e.g., Armenakis et al., 1993; Kotter, 1995). Grafting also appears to be the default approach adopted in organizations to the implementation of health and wellbeing practices (Daniels et al., 2022b), presumably because it offers the route of least resistance to implementation.

Examples of grafting include the use of existing meeting structures to discuss how to improve health and wellbeing (Thiele Schwarz et al., 2017), formalizing an already informal peer support process by having peer supporters nominated by colleagues (Busch et al., 2017), developing interventions to ensure compatibility with existing social norms or routines (Braganza et al., 2018), and adding a decision aid to the usual diagnostics used by occupational health physicians (Volker et al., 2015, 2017). In our empirical research

(Daniels et al., 2022b), we found grafting can also involve repurposing existing practices or resources for health and wellbeing practices, such as staff intranets, meetings, or meeting rooms.

Fracturing is defined as changing the organization to be compatible with a health and wellbeing practice (or practices) by replacing old processes, structures, and structures with new ones. That is, the omnibus context is influenced by the discrete context, so that there is a break with existing ways. Fracturing is about seeking conflict. Conflict may be inevitable during change (Johnson, 1990), but also seen as manageable (Westover, 2010). Fracturing itself may therefore represent changing organizational practices. For example, in our research we found examples of redesigning performance appraisals systems or even entire human resources systems (Daniels et al., 2022b). Other examples include openly challenging behavioural norms around, for example, existing work routines (Chapleau et al., 2011), or other workers' performance (Daniels et al., 2022b). Fracturing may be more salient where harmful behaviours and norms are prevalent (e.g., unsafe working practices, abusive supervision, long-hours cultures). One example from the literature is an intervention that included training in how to challenge others' unsafe behaviours in a high-hazard manufacturing environment (Tregaskis et al., 2013).

Gestalting is defined as bringing different wellbeing practices and other organizational procedures, practices, and structures together for simultaneous change, in order to meet common goals or interpretation and hence reduce conflict. That is, the omnibus and discrete contexts mutually influence each other. Gestalting processes may be focused on sensemaking/sensegiving (from the work of Weick, 1995); that is, through visionary and symbolic leadership (Westley & Mintzberg, 1989), and experiential learning (Lewin, 1944/1952; Burnes & Cooke, 2013). One example in our research was an organization that incorporated health and wellbeing as a core value of the business, and therefore part of the underpinning business model (Daniels et al., 2022b). Other examples include bringing together corporate social responsibility and wellbeing initiatives under a single steering group (Daniels et al., 2022b), integrative workshops to bring together elements of a complex intervention (Thiele Schwarz et al., 2017), and bringing different stakeholder groups together in communities of practice for shared learning (Mabry et al., 2018). In addition, having an integrated, coherent, and communicated health and wellbeing strategy is itself an example of Gestalting.

It should be noted that grafting, fracturing, and Gestalting are not mutually exclusive, but can co-occur or occur in sequence. For example, workplace health promotion may have a role to play in triggering changes to cultural norms around health and wellbeing (fracturing existing norms), therefore making it easier/more acceptable to implement more complex practices around job and process design (grafting onto new norms).

It is possible to think of grafting, fracturing, and Gestalting as means of managing tensions and conflicts between workplace health and wellbeing practices and other organizational processes. It is also possible to think of these processes as reflecting means of managing the tensions and conflicts between the logics underpinning the choices in regard to addressing employee health and wellbeing, and the logics underpinning other choices concerning organizational processes. Following Prahalad and Bettis (1986), we view *logics* as organizational actors' cognitive schemas of the organization and its environment, goals, and priorities. Different logics can be shared to a greater or lesser extent across an organization or across separate groups (Daniels et al., 2002). Because organizations, their environments, and their employees change, so do different logics (including logics related to health and wellbeing), so that there is a continual need to find ways of managing the tensions and conflicts between health and wellbeing logics and other competing logics. One approach to managing tensions between logics is to make material changes to health and wellbeing practices or other organizational processes. However, given that logics are social-psychological phenomena, stakeholders can also deploy symbolic and discursive devices to manage tensions (Lawrence & Phillips, 2019).

HEALTH AND WELLBEING PROGRAMMES DURING PERIODS OF DISRUPTION

One reason organizations may adopt workplace health and wellbeing strategies is to develop a sense of reciprocal exchange between employees and the employer. In this line of thinking, if an employer provides a workplace that protects or even enhances employee health and wellbeing (through the way the work is organized, social relations at work, terms and conditions, as well as overt wellbeing- or health-focused practices such as mindfulness training), then employees will respond positively with enhanced commitment, motivation, and performance (Guest, 2017). However, during times of turbulence in the omnibus context, positive and progressive approaches to employment relations can come under threat (Dobbins & Dundon, 2017), with employers shifting towards their own interests at the expense of employee interests – for example, through intensification of work (Cook et al., 2016; Johnstone & Wilkinson, 2018).

In respect of workplace health and wellbeing practices, it is widely thought that external shocks in the omnibus context can 'derail' those practices (cf. Biron & Karanika-Murray, 2015). This may be because external shocks impose resource constraints, or influence how organizations prioritize goals (e.g., survival may become more important). A more fundamental reason is that shocks may surface competing logics, so that decisions about where to allocate scarce resources, or what to prioritize, reflect health and wellbeing logics less than competing logics (Daniels et al., 2022b). Although external shocks can affect the implementation of workplace health and wellbeing practices, it may not always be the case that external shocks do so, if organizations adapt their internal processes to the external shocks in a way that does not threaten health and wellbeing practices (Daniels et al., 2021). There is a key role here for the delivery context, in how the discrete contexts of specific practices or the wider omnibus context are adjusted, and whether these adjustments enable continuity, learning, and adaptation. The adjustments may require different elements of grafting, fracturing, or Gestalting.

In respect of mainstream occupational intervention research, it may also be the case that shocks appear to derail health and wellbeing practices because of how intervention studies are designed. Interventions that are the focus of a specific study may be abandoned because they are no longer suitable for a changed organizational context; but other health and wellbeing practices more suited to the changed context may be introduced as substitutes. Such substitution may not be noticed by intervention researchers who have a specific focus and remit.

The COVID-19 pandemic presented an opportunity to study the effects of external shocks on workplace health and wellbeing programmes. Perhaps uniquely, the COVID-19 pandemic affected organizations' economic priorities (business continuity, survival), while at the same time presenting very salient challenges for the health and wellbeing of employees (e.g., the virus itself, fear of the virus, various mental health challenges associated with lockdowns, homeworking/schooling). As part of our ongoing research, during the first lockdown in the UK in March 2020, we had already started fieldwork to examine how organizations develop, implement, and sustain workplace health and wellbeing programmes (see Nayani et al., 2022). The study has revealed that, although some organizations do struggle with maintaining a focus on health and wellbeing during external shocks, others actively develop their programme of practices to be suited to changing contexts.

Nayani et al. (2022) found that underpinning employee perceptions of whether their employer had genuine concerns for their health and wellbeing was the authenticity with which employers acted towards worker health and wellbeing. Organizations that are authentic about worker health and wellbeing match espoused values with tangible actions and practices (Cording et al., 2014; Hahl, 2016; Lehman et al., 2019), and this contrasts with organizations who merely pay 'lip service' to employee wellbeing (Guest, 2017, p 33). Nayani et al. found that organizations that appeared to maintain health and wellbeing strategies through the pandemic did so through an effortful process of 'authenticity work' – namely, such organizations notice changes to employee concerns about their health and wellbeing, and understand and act on new health and wellbeing concerns.

Authenticity work can ensure health and wellbeing programmes are developed to match new circumstances (see the discussion on learning and adaptability above), but also have symbolic value for the importance of employee health and wellbeing, because adapting and changing practices is effortful. Authenticity work underpins the construct of 'authenticity building', which is defined as 'past and present activities through which organizations channel efforts to be interpreted as authentic in their concern for their employees' interests' (p. 1150), which implies that authenticity work is an ongoing process. In this respect, authenticity building is part of the process of continuity of specific practices, but also underpins continuity, learning, and adaptation of the delivery context. Authenticity work and authenticity building may also be required to realize the benefits of the signalling effects of health and wellbeing practices.

From the point of view of some organizations' responses to the COVID-19 pandemic, organizational shocks are not terminal for workplace health and wellbeing practices. Rather, shocks can provide an opportunity for organizations to demonstrate authentic care for employees, through adapting their health and wellbeing programmes to both the changing circumstances and employee concerns.

CONCLUSIONS

An approach focused on workplace health and wellbeing strategies is complementary to research focused on interventions. A focus on strategy – especially because it needs to include unpredictable elements, practices that were not implemented as planned (or at all), and practices that were never intended to be implemented – necessarily implies using alternative methods to those used in intervention research (Patey et al., 2021). Such alternative methods could include longitudinal case studies that capture longer-term changes, not just in espoused strategies, but also from the organizational cultural elements associated with sustained strategies and their development (Johnson, 1987; cf. Dollard & Karasek, 2010).

Focusing on health and wellbeing strategies enables new research approaches and new research questions. As well as examining the factors that sustain and embed programmes of practices over an extended period, other questions could relate to, for example: how tensions with other organizational processes, goals, and logics are managed over extended periods, especially as competing logics evolve, or events make competing logics more salient; how new practices emerge, become noticed by key decision makers, and become incorporated (or not) into an overall strategic programme; and how a strategic health and wellbeing programme influences the whole organization, including organizational culture, and any other factors that may promote health and wellbeing that are not tied specifically to a single intervention.

To restate earlier points, many organizations adopt multiple health and wellbeing practices in coherent programmes, and many organizations now find themselves in a state of flux. Adopting a strategic lens to workplace health and wellbeing enables research on how programmes are managed and can be best adapted to other organizational changes. This is especially relevant for the turbulent times in which we find ourselves in the current post-COVID-19 era.

NOTES

1. Acknowledgement: This work was supported by Economic and Social Research Council Grants ES/N003586/1 and ES/S012648/1.
2. If interventions work in the manner intended, this provides ecologically valid evidence for the theory or model underpinning intervention design.
3. Although we are unaware of any research data on the topic of longevity of health and wellbeing programmes, some of the organizations we have worked with or are otherwise familiar with have pursued health and wellbeing strategies over several years, in some cases decades.
4. This may reflect either the resource constraints of intervention research and/ or that a typical intervention study is concerned with whether a specific intervention works, how it may work, and how it can be made to work. In the latter case, researchers may, resources permitting, only stay in the field for as long as it reasonable for an intervention to have an effect. In the case of interventions included in Daniels et al.'s (2021) review, some 70 per cent of studies had a follow-up assessment at 12 months or less, 92 per cent had a follow-up assessment at 24 months or less, and 99 per cent had a follow-up assessment at 48 months or less.
5. We prefer the term 'health and wellbeing practice' to the term 'health and wellbeing intervention' in this context. This reflects both that such practices need not be planned 'interventions' as such and that the interventions literature itself is concerned with formal evaluation by scientific research teams. In many organizations, formal evaluation by scientific research teams or consultants may be the exception, and many organizations may not even evaluate the effects of specific practices in ways that would be considered scientifically appropriate.

REFERENCES

Armenakis, A. A., Harris, S. G., & Mossholder, K. W. (1993). Creating readiness for organizational change. *Human Relations, 46*, 681–703.
Balogun, J. (2006). Managing change: Steering a course between intended strategies and unanticipated outcomes. *Long Range Planning, 39*, 29–49.

Batorsky, B., Van Stolk, C., & Liu, H. (2016). Is more always better in designing workplace wellness programs? A comparison of wellness program components versus outcomes. *Journal of Occupational and Environmental Medicine, 58,* 987–993.

Biron, C., & Karanika-Murray, M. (2015). From black and white to colours: Moving the science of organizational interventions for stress and well-being forward. In C. Biron & M. Karanika-Murray (Eds.), *Derailed organizational interventions for stress and wellbeing: Confessions of failure and solutions for success* (pp. 275–282). Springer.

Bowen, D. E., & Ostroff, C. (2004). Understanding HRM–firm performance linkages: The role of the "strength" of the HRM system. *Academy of Management Review, 29,* 203–221.

Braganza, S., Young, J., Sweeny, A., & Brazil, V. (2018). oneED: Embedding a mindfulness- based wellness programme into an emergency department. *Emergency Medicine Australasia, 30,* 678–686.

Burgess, M. G., Brough, P., Biggs, A., & Hawkes, A. J. (2020). Why interventions fail: A systematic review of occupational health psychology interventions. *International Journal of Stress Management, 27,* 195–207.

Burnes, B., & Cooke, B. (2013). Kurt Lewin's Field Theory: A review and re-evaluation. *International Journal of Management Reviews, 15,* 408–425.

Busch, C., Koch, T., Clasen, J., Winkler, E., & Vowinkel, J. (2017). Evaluation of an organizational health intervention for low-skilled workers and immigrants. *Human Relations, 70,* 994–1016.

Chapleau, A., Seroczynski, A. D., Meyers, S., Lamb, K., & Haynes, S. (2011). Occupational therapy consultation for case managers in community mental health: Exploring strategies to improve job satisfaction and self-efficacy. *Professional Case Management, 16,* 71–79.

Cherns, A. (1987). Principles of sociotechnical design revisited. *Human Relations, 40,* 153–161.

Cook, H., MacKenzie, R., & Forde, C. (2016). HRM and performance: The vulnerability of soft HRM practices during recession and retrenchment. *Human Resource Management Journal, 26,* 557–571.

Cook, T. D., Campbell, D. T., & Peracchio, L. (1990). Quasi experimentation. In M. D. Dunnette & L. M. Hough (Eds.), *Handbook of industrial and organizational psychology* (2nd ed., Vol. 1) (pp. 491–576). Consulting Psychologists Press.

Cording, M., Harrison, J. S., Hoskisson, R. E., & Jonsen, K. (2014). Walking the talk: A multistakeholder exploration of organizational authenticity, employee productivity, and post-merger performance. *Academy of Management Perspectives, 28,* 38–56.

Currie, G., & Procter, S. J. (2005). The antecedents of middle managers' strategic contribution: The case of a professional bureaucracy. *Journal of Management Studies, 42,* 1325–1356.

Daniels, K., Gedikli, C., Watson, D., Semkina, A., & Vaughn, O. (2017). Job design, employment practices and well-being: A systematic review of intervention studies. *Ergonomics, 60,* 1177–1196.

Daniels, K., Johnson, G., & De Chernatony, L. (2002). Task and institutional influences on managers' mental models of competition. *Organization Studies, 23*(1), 31–62.

Daniels, K., Russell, E., Michaelides, G., Nasamu, E., & Connolly, S. (2022a). The measurement of wellbeing at work. In L. M. Lapierre & C. Cooper (Eds.), *Organisational stress and wellbeing* (pp. 347–386). Cambridge University Press.

Daniels, K., Tregaskis, O., Nayani, R., & Watson, D. (2022b). *Achieving sustainable workplace wellbeing*. Springer Nature.

Daniels, K., Watson, D., Nayani, R., Tregaskis, O., Hogg, M., Etuknwa, A., & Semkina, A. (2021). Implementing practices focused on workplace health and psychological wellbeing: A systematic review. *Social Science and Medicine, 227,* 113888.

Dobbins, T., & Dundon, T. (2017). The chimera of sustainable labour–management partnership. *British Journal of Management, 28,* 519–533.

Dollard, M. F., & Karasek, R. A. (2010). Building psychosocial safety climate. In J. Houdmont & S. Leka (Eds.), *Contemporary occupational health psychology: Global perspectives on research and practice* (Vol. 1) (pp. 208–233). Wiley.

Egan, M., Bambra, C., Petticrew, M., & Whitehead, M. (2009). Reviewing evidence on complex social interventions: Appraising implementation in systematic reviews of the health effects of organisational-level workplace interventions. *Journal of Epidemiology & Community Health, 63,* 4–11.

Fitzhugh, H., Michaelides, G., Daniels, K., Connolly, S., & Nasamu, E. (in press). Mindfulness for performance and wellbeing in the police: Linking individual and organizational outcomes. *Review of Public Personnel Administration.* https://doi.org/10.1177/0734371X231155794

Fridrich, A., Jenny, G. J., & Bauer, G. F. (2015). The context, process, and outcome evaluation model for organisational health interventions. *BioMed Research International,* 414832.

Fuller, P., Randall, R., Dainty, A., Haslam, R., & Gibb A. (2019). Applying a longitudinal tracer methodology to evaluate complex interventions in complex settings. *European Journal of Work and Organizational Psychology, 28,* 443–452.

Gersick, C. J. (1991). Revolutionary change theories: A multilevel exploration of the punctuated equilibrium paradigm. *Academy of Management Review, 16,* 10–36.

Guest, D. E. (2017). Human resource management and employee well-being: Towards a new analytic framework. *Human Resource Management Journal, 27,* 22–38.

Hahl, O. (2016). Turning back the clock in baseball: The increased prominence of extrinsic rewards and demand for authenticity. *Organization Science, 27,* 929–953.

Haynes, N. J., Vandenberg, R. J., Wilson, M. G., DeJoy, D. M., Padilla, H. M., & Smith, M. L. (2022). Evaluating the impact of the live healthy, work healthy program on organizational outcomes: A randomized field experiment. *Journal of Applied Psychology, 107,* 1758–1780.

Herrera-Sánchez, I. M., León-Pérez, J. M., & León-Rubio, J. M. (2017). Steps to ensure a successful implementation of occupational health and safety interventions at an organizational level. *Frontiers in Psychology, 8,* 2135.

International Organization for Standardization. (2018). BS 45002-1:2018. *Occupational Health and Safety Management Systems: General Guidelines for the Application of ISO 45001 – Guidance on managing occupational health.*

Jia, Y., Fu, H., Gao, J., Dai, J., & Zheng, P. (2018). The roles of health culture and physical environment in workplace health promotion: A two-year prospective intervention study in China. *BMC Public Health, 18,* 457.

Johns, G. (2006). The essential impact of context on organizational behavior. *Academy of Management Review, 31,* 386–408.

Johnson, G. (1987). *Strategic change and the management process.* Blackwell.

Johnson, G. (1990). Managing strategic change: The role of symbolic action. *British Journal of Management, 1,* 183–200.

Johnson, S., Robertson, I., & Cooper, C. L. (2018). *Work and well-being.* Palgrave Macmillan.

Johnstone, S., & Wilkinson, A. (2018). The potential of labour–management partnership: A longitudinal case analysis. *British Journal of Management, 29*, 554–570.

Jordan, J., Gurr, E., Tinline, G., Giga, S. I., Faragher, B., & Cooper, C. L. (2003). *Beacons of excellence in stress prevention: Research report 133*. HSE Books.

Knight, C., Patterson, M., & Dawson, J. (2019). Work engagement interventions can be effective: A systematic review. *European Journal of Work and Organizational Psychology, 28*, 348–372.

Kotter, J. P. (1995). Leading change: Why transformation efforts fail. *Harvard Business Review, 73*(2), 59–67.

LaMontagne, A. D., Keegel, T., Louie, A. M., Ostry, A., & Landsbergis, P. A. (2007). A systematic review of the job-stress intervention evaluation literature, 1990–2005. *International Journal of Occupational and Environmental Health, 13*, 268–280.

LaMontagne, A. D., Martin, A., Page, K. M., Reavley, N. J., Noblet, A. J., Milner, A. J., Keegel, T., & Smith, P. M. (2014). Workplace mental health: developing an integrated intervention approach. *BMC Psychiatry, 14*, 1–11.

Lawrence, T. B., & Phillips, N. (2019). *Constructing organizational life: How social-symbolic work shapes selves, organizations, and institutions*. Oxford University Press.

Lehman, D. W., O'Connor, K., Kovács, B., & Newman, G. E. (2019). Authenticity. *Academy of Management Annals, 13*, 1–42.

Lewin, K. (1944/1952). Constructs in field theory. In D. Cartwright (Ed.), *Field theory in social science: Selected theoretical papers by Kurt Lewin* (pp. 30–42). Social Science Paperbacks.

Mabry, L., Parker, K. N., Thompson, S. V., Bettencourt, K. M., Haque, A., Luther Rhoten, K., Wright, R. R., Hess, J. A., & Olson, R. (2018). Protecting workers in the home care industry: Workers' experienced job demands, resource gaps, and benefits following a socially supportive intervention. *Home Health Care Services Quarterly, 37*, 259–276.

Mattke, S., Kapinos, K., Caloyeras, J. P., Taylor, E. A., Batorsky, B., Liu, H., Van Busum, K. R., & Newberry, S. (2015). Workplace wellness programs: Services offered, participation, and incentives. *Rand Health Quarterly, 5*, 7.

Mintzberg, H. (1994). *The rise and fall of strategic planning*. Free Press.

Mintzberg, H., & Waters, J. A. (1985). Of strategies, deliberate and emergent. *Strategic Management Journal, 6*, 257–272.

Murta, S. G., Sanderson, K., & Oldenburg, B. (2007). Process evaluation in occupational stress management programs: A systematic review. *American Journal of Health Promotion, 21*, 248–254.

Musgrove, H. (2023). *Employer insight report: Supporting people with disabling long-term health conditions to sustain work*. Ernst & Young.

Nayani, R., Baric, M., Patey, J., Fitzhugh, H., Watson, D., Tregaskis, O., & Daniels, K. (2022). Authenticity in the pursuit of mutuality during crisis. *British Journal of Management, 33*, 1144–1162.

Nielsen, K., & Miraglia, M. (2017). What works for whom in which circumstances? On the need to move beyond the "what works?" question in organizational intervention research. *Human Relations, 70*, 40–62.

Nielsen, K., & Randall, R. (2013). Opening the black box: Presenting a model for evaluating organizational-level interventions. *European Journal of Work and Organizational Psychology, 22*, 601–617.

Nielsen, K. M., & Noblet, A. (2018). Organizational interventions: Where we are, where we go from here? In K. Nielsen & A. Noblet (Eds.), *Organizational interven-*

tions for health and well-being: A handbook for evidence-based practice (pp. 1–21). London.

Patey, J., Nasamu, E., Nayani, R., Watson, D., Connolly, S., & Daniels, K. (2021). Evaluating multicomponent wellbeing strategies: Theoretical and methodological insights. In T. Wall, C. Cooper, & P. Brough (Eds.), *The SAGE handbook of organisational wellbeing* (pp. 478–493). SAGE.

Prahalad, C. K., & Bettis, R. A. (1986). The dominant logic: A new linkage between diversity and performance. *Strategic Management Journal, 7*, 485–501.

Richardson, K. M., & Rothstein, H. R. (2008). Effects of occupational stress management intervention programs: A meta-analysis. *Journal of Occupational Health Psychology, 13*, 69–93.

Russell, J., Berney, L., Stansfeld, S., Lanz, D., Kerry, S., Chandola, T., & Bhui, K. (2016). The role of qualitative research in adding value to a randomised controlled trial: Lessons from a pilot study of a guided e-learning intervention for managers to improve employee wellbeing and reduce sickness absence. *Trials, 17*, 396.

Schein, E. H. (1985). *Organizational culture and leadership*. Wiley.

Swan, E., & Fox, S. (2010). Playing the game: Strategies of resistance and co-optation in diversity work. *Gender, Work & Organization, 17*, 567–589.

Thiele Schwarz, U. von, Lundmark, R., & Hasson, H. (2016). The dynamic integrated evaluation model (DIEM): Achieving sustainability in organizational intervention through a participatory evaluation approach. *Stress and Health, 32*, 285–293.

Thiele Schwarz, U. von, Nielsen, K., Edwards, K., Hasson, H., Ipsen, C., Savage, C., Abildgaard, J. S., Richter, A., Lornudd, C., Mazzocato, P., & Reed, J. E. (2021). How to design, implement and evaluate organizational interventions for maximum impact: The Sigtuna Principles. *European Journal of Work and Organizational Psychology, 30*, 415–427.

Thiele Schwarz, U. von, Nielsen, K. M., Stenfors-Hayes, T., & Hasson, H. (2017). Using kaizen to improve employee well-being: Results from two organizational intervention studies. *Human Relations, 70*, 966–993.

Tregaskis, O., Daniels, K., Glover, L., Butler, P., & Meyer, M. (2013). High performance work practices and firm performance: A longitudinal case study. *British Journal of Management, 24*, 225–244.

Volker, D., Zijlstra-Vlasveld, M. C., Anema, J. R., Beekman, A. T. F., Brouwers, E. P. M., Emons, W. H. M., Van Lomwel, A. G. C., & Van der Feltz-Cornelis, C. M. (2015). Effectiveness of a blended web-based intervention on return to work for sick-listed employees with common mental disorders: Results of a cluster randomized controlled trial. *Journal of Medical Internet Research, 17*, e116.

Volker, D., Zijlstra-Vlasveld, M. C., Brouwers, E. P. M., & Van der Feltz-Cornelis, C. M. (2017). Process evaluation of a blended web-based intervention on return to work for sick-listed employees with common mental health problems in the occupational health setting. *Journal of Occupational Rehabilitation, 27*, 186–194.

Weick, K. E. (1995). *Sensemaking in organizations*. SAGE.

Westley, F., & Mintzberg, H. (1989). Visionary leadership and strategic management. *Strategic Management Journal, 10*, 17–32.

Westover, J. H. (2010). Managing organizational change: Change agent strategies and techniques to successfully managing the dynamics of stability and change in organizations. *International Journal of Management and Innovation, 2*, 45–51.

Zollo, M., & Winter, S. G. (2002). Deliberate learning and the evolution of dynamic capabilities. *Organization Science, 13*, 339–351.

10. Using digital tools to improve well-being and work performance in agile work

Emma Russell and Christine Grant

The digital revolution at work has significantly influenced the demands, goals, and priorities of today's global, flexible, knowledge-based workforce (Angelici & Profeta, 2020; Derks et al., 2014; Olson-Buchanan et al., 2016; Schmidtner et al., 2021; Wang et al., 2021). For knowledge workers[1] today, access to colleagues, clients, and work itself has been enabled by information and communication technologies (ICTs), digital software, and work-extendable devices (Derks et al., 2014). This has afforded workers liberation from traditional work patterns restricted by time, place, and role (Jeyasingham, 2016; Russell and Grant, 2020; Schmidtner et al., 2021). Such workers are known as 'agile workers', characterized by their ability to flexibly adopt working patterns and innovative practices to service the needs of the organization, and accommodate their own personal preferences (Russell & Grant, 2020). Agile working goes beyond offering remote or hybrid work-from-home opportunities. It offers a real alternative for people to work when, where, and how they want to, and to adapt their working patterns when things change (Russell & Grant, 2020).

Engagement with ICTs is a central enabler of agile working. Given the exponential growth in the use of and access to ICTs in recent years (Forbes, 2019; Radicati Group, 2021), agile working has become a reality for substantial numbers of knowledge workers. Organizations need to provide the infrastructure, knowledge, and policies to accommodate requests for flexibility and to support and promote agile working (Kossek & Kelliher, 2023). As market and service environments change, organizations and their workers need to be able to respond in a dynamic and timely fashion; ICTs help to align working practices with changing environments (Orlikowski, 1992). For example, during the pandemic, when medical appointments moved online, ICTs enabled clinical specialists (general practitioners [GPs], physiotherapists, etc.) to work from home, and at different times, and continue to have contact with digitally connected patients (Murphy et al., 2021; Taylor et al., 2021).

In this chapter, we focus on ICTs as essential for enabling agile working, and indicate how use of ICTs impacts the effectiveness and well-being of agile workers, from a psychological perspective. We focus primarily on agile workers, mindful that not all work can be managed and delivered flexibly in relation to time, place, and role. Workers' use of ICTs in more traditional settings may face different challenges and/or may be heavily controlled and monitored, with choice over how, when, and where to work being significantly limited (Franken et al., 2021; Kelliher & Anderson, 2010). We do not explicitly refer to such workers in this chapter, but recommend the Digit Blog (Digital Futures at Work Research Centre, n.d.) for accessing concise summaries of how low-autonomy, low-status workers (platform-based gig workers, care workers, etc.) engage with new technology, and the impact this has on their work. We begin by outlining the ICTs that have had the most impact on agile working, and identify reasons for their rise in popularity. Despite the manifold benefits that have led to their adoption, we then describe how these ICTs have the potential to undermine work well-being and performance, justified by theoretical frameworks. We discuss how ICTs can – when used effectively – also have a liberating and equalizing effect for people, including those with neurodivergence and/or disability and/or low socio-economic status. In particular, we reflect on how to build resources for digital, agile workers, and refer to the efficacy of new policies and practices that have been designed to make working life better (e.g., the four-day week, hybrid working, community-based co-working). We consider who has benefitted from new forms of digital, agile work, and argue that to make ICTs work for all, we need to remove one-size-fits-all approaches. Insight is needed into the organizational and individual factors that ensure digital, agile work provides benefits for all.

THE RISE IN POPULARITY OF ICTS FOR AGILE WORKING

ICTs relate to the intrinsic software that enables work to be communicated and information shared (email, Slack, WhatsApp, MS Teams, Zoom and Cloud data-sharing systems, etc.), delivered via digital devices and hardware (computers, laptops, tablets, smartphones, smartwatches, etc.; Demerouti et al., 2014; Garrett & Danziger, 2008; Park & Jex, 2011). ICTs provide the means to be connected to work at any time and in any location, assuming the infrastructure is available to support this (Diaz et al., 2012; D'Mello, 2020). This capability provides significant advantages for agile workers, such as being able to adopt flexible working hours and working places, and to undertake tasks and work activities in different (often more efficient) ways (Diaz et al., 2012; Madden & Jones, 2008).

Work-based ICTs became most notably widespread during the early to mid-2000s as broadband, Wi-Fi, 3G, and 4G revolutions allowed instantaneous communication beyond the traditional workplace environs (Korunka & Vartiainen, 2017). ICTs were quickly adopted by knowledge workers and organizations, impressed with the efficiencies and conveniences promised (Dabbish et al., 2005). For the first time, work could be delivered and information transmitted in a highly flexible and convenient way, and at low cost to organizations (Dawley & Anthony, 2003; Middleton & Cukier, 2006). Masses of information could be made available to multiple users at the click of an email, whilst projects and tasks (with audit trails) could be organized on easily accessible platforms, the precursors to Slack and Teams (Levy, 2019). Workers began to find that they could easily connect with, and access, colleagues and clients across time zones, nations, and settings, allowing for the formation of new relationships and access to expertise (D'Mello, 2020; Grant et al., 2018, 2020).

Within a few years, the very nature of knowledge work was changing with the digitalization of communication at work; being available, accessible, and contactable through ICT use became an inherent part of daily work activities (Wajcman & Rose, 2011). ICTs were no longer viewed as 'add-ons' to everyday working life, but – for agile workers – were essential tools for enabling work, consequently contributing to substantial changes in working cultures and work arrangements (Wajcman & Rose, 2011). Yet, accompanying these rapid changes, not all organizations responded at pace or considered the impact on worker well-being. Although many organizations introduced agile working policies in accordance with government legislations, many failed to introduce any direct guidance (Grant et al., 2018), meaning that some workers were left floundering as they tried to work out the best way to accommodate these massive digital changes. And then came the COVID-19 pandemic …

During the pandemic, homeworking – enabled by the now-widespread adoption of ICTs and enforced government lockdowns – increased rapidly, characterizing 46 per cent of the UK working population by March/April 2020 (Office for National Statistics [ONS], 2020). The effects appear to have endured post-pandemic; by 2022, 38 per cent of the UK working population were still working remotely (ONS, 2022). Many organizations reported moving towards hybrid ways of working, with 60/40 per cent of time being spent in the work/non-work environment respectively (Charalampous et al., 2022). Latest figures indicate a drop in working from home full-time to 16 per cent of workers, with hybrid working increasingly becoming the more popular option for 28 per cent of workers (ONS, 2023). For many people, the COVID-19 pandemic significantly changed how ICTs were utilized, allowing greater access for workers who had previously either not used digital tools for remote working, or had done so in a more limited or occasional way (Franken et al., 2021; Wang et al., 2021).

Different types of ICTs also began to rise in popularity, with Teams, Zoom, and other virtual meeting platforms becoming more prolific (Williams, 2021). Further, messaging apps, such as WhatsApp, that were seldom used outside of the social sphere rose in popularity for colleagues wanting to stay connected (Deloitte, 2023; Mishna et al., 2021). This expansion in the variety of ICTs available also accompanied the erosion of barriers between work and home. For some, this has costs for well-being, increasing the potential for professional/personal boundary infringements, and encouraging over-working (Basile & Beauregard, 2020; Russell et al., 2023). For others, this has been found to help with improving work collaborations and increasing social capital for workers, especially those in demanding jobs who need to feel supported by colleagues, even when the working day has finished (Ren et al., 2023; Russell et al., 2023). In the next section, we consider some of the paradoxes of ICTs and how the very flexibility, convenience, and accessibility they offer has facilitated a rise in problematic behaviours and dysfunctional practices that are changing the very nature of work and working cultures (Belkin et al., 2020; Brown et al., 2014).

THE PARADOX OF ICTS

It has long been understood that ICTs offer a 'double-edged sword' in terms of costs and benefits to workers (Boswell & Olson-Buchanan, 2007; Dawley & Anthony, 2003; Madden & Jones, 2008; Middleton & Cukier, 2006; O'Kane & Hargie, 2007). Most of the research relating to this has focused on work email and smartphone use (Barley et al., 2011; Derks et al., 2014; Mazmanian et al., 2005, 2013; Russell & Woods, 2020; Russell et al., 2023). Whilst work email and smartphones are lauded for the ease and convenience they afford for autonomous, flexible, and connected working, they are damned in equal measure for encouraging resource-depleting issues associated with 'always-on' cultures, interruptions, constant connectivity, and an inability to switch off (Hassard & Morris, 2022; Russell & Woods, 2020; Russell et al., 2017). The impact of ICTs on work performance and well-being alike must therefore be carefully considered (Russell et al., 2023).

For example, email has the advantage of providing a quick and easy method to send digital messages, provide information, and disseminate work tasks to a wide range of contacts (Russell et al., 2023). This is beneficial in that many tasks can be coordinated and resolved within a short timeframe. However, a significant disadvantage is the continual and persistent interruption to work flow produced by emails constantly arriving (Addas & Pinsonneault, 2018; Chen & Karahanna, 2018). Thus, on the one hand, email is productive in that work can be completed quickly. On the other hand, it means constant vigilance so that important messages are not missed (Russell et al., 2017). This 'fear of missing out' (FOMO) is the psychological feeling state that an unread email can engender; in reality, constantly checking work emails is detrimental to both work performance and well-being (Budnick et al., 2020; Dabbish & Kraut, 2006; Russell et al., 2017; Russell et al., 2022c; Russell et al., 2023).

Further, whilst receiving and answering emails outside of usual working hours can, in some cases, provide a means to work more flexibly (Mazmanian et al., 2005, 2013), it can also be intrusive by over-stepping work time and place boundaries, permitting overwork cultures, and enhancing pressure to respond in non-work time (Barley et al., 2011; Belkin et al., 2016; Braun et al., 2019). With the emergence of more synchronous ICTs (e.g., instant messaging via Slack and Teams), and tools such as WhatsApp being used with colleagues (Deloitte, 2023), there is emerging evidence of an escalation of such problems, and increasing reports of worker burnout and resistance to using technology, as people struggle to cope with new ICT demands (Russell et al., 2021; Russell et al., 2022c).

To counter this, organizations have tried to develop policies such as the 'right to disconnect', the four-day week, and 'email free Fridays'. Evidence suggests, however, that restricting access to work email is not an effective solution for improving well-being and work performance, and can have the opposite effect on some groups of workers who have different priorities, job roles, and caring responsibilities (Russell & Bevan, 2022; Russell et al., 2022a; Russell et al., 2023). Primarily, the issue with these policies is that they are 'one size fits all' applications. In agile work, flexibility in access to when, where, and how people work is required to support individual circumstances (Russell & Bevan, 2022; Russell et al., 2022a). Organizations need to help workers to manage their digital boundaries appropriately and ensure that people have time to switch off each day, without dictating when and how this should work. The benefits and disadvantages of ICTs are summarized in Table 10.1.

It is clear that ICTs have offered agile workers many benefits, but that they also come at a cost to well-being and work performance. In the next sections, we refer to psychological theories that explain why ICTs were adopted as initially helpful to agile workers, and why/how they may also cause problems.

APPLYING PSYCHOLOGICAL THEORIES TO EXPLAIN THE IMPACT OF ICT USE ON AGILE WORKERS

Psychological theories of well-being provide a framework for understanding how the use of ICTs can support effective agile working, and lead to improvements in well-being and work performance. The Conservation of Resources (COR) theory explains that people are motivated to protect, acquire, and invest

Table 10.1   The pros and cons of ICTs for agile workers

Agile theme	The ICT paradox	
	Benefits	Disadvantages
Flexibility	Convenient to use re time and place	'Always-on' cultures (time boundaries break down); overwork and work intensification
Information dissemination	Low-cost dissemination of information to multiple end-users	Information overload
Project management	Organize projects, resources, and tasks	'Fear of missing out' and increased vigilance (resource-depleting); requires self-moderation
Connectivity	Connect with more people across time and place barriers; always accessible	Constant connectivity (too accessible); excessive interruptions; requires well-being recovery activity
Independent working	Provides greater autonomy and control over work	Loss of visibility and social isolation; lack of direction for early career professionals
Relationships	Form and nurture new relationships and networks	More transient relationships; relationship management effortful
Productivity	Efficient; productive; task-focused	Informal; social rapport building reduced
Work and non-work activity	Can fit work around non-work activities	Boundary intrusions and infringements – 'work creep'
Innovation and creativity	Can access diverse range of colleagues and experts to optimize innovation and creativity	Innovation can be stifled by only using more formalized methods of communication; video calling, etc.
Diversity and inclusion	Supports greater inclusion from a wider and more diverse group	ICT can be overwhelming and increase fatigue for some, so it requires effort to learn how best to communicate using these methods

key resources to achieve valued goals at work and beyond (Hobfoll, 1989; Hobfoll et al., 2018). Resources can include objects (e.g., personal computer or smartphone), personal characteristics (e.g., self-esteem or optimism), energies (e.g., time or money), and conditions (e.g., social support) that are commonly valued within a culture (Hobfoll, 2001). Because of the value ascribed to resources, when these are threatened, lost, or cannot be gained (following investment), this can be a source of psychological distress; people will often be compelled to engage in coping activities to both prevent and respond to this (Chwaszcz et al., 2022; Dunahoo et al., 1998; Hobfoll, 1989).

ICTs are considered to be an essential resource in modern knowledge work. For agile workers in particular, ICTs enable access to work in a timely, convenient, and portable manner, and support the achievement of goals for delivering work in a flexible and responsive way. Utilizing ICTs as resources also means that other resources can be protected or acquired, such as work–life balance (ten Brummelhuis & Bakker, 2012), knowledge acquisition (Catalano et al., 2021), and positive working relationships (Nurmi, 2011). Using ICTs may also help agile workers to fulfil their psychological needs. According to Self-Determination Theory (Ryan & Deci, 2017), when people feel that their three psychological needs – autonomy, relatedness, and competence – are being satisfied, they will experience heightened well-being, motivation, and work performance (Deci et al., 2017; Gillet et al., 2016; Ryan, 1995; Van den Broeck, 2016).

In undertaking their work, people try to regulate their activity towards the satisfaction of these needs, which is easier for those who have more resources (e.g., support, feedback, job control; Deci et al., 2017). ICTs could be considered useful for helping people to engage in autonomous self-regulation, to carry out their jobs in the way that best fits them and helps them meet their goals. Further, ICTs may directly impact the extent to which psychological needs are supported and satisfied. For example, for *relatedness* needs, being able to quickly communicate and respond to others can strengthen relationships in organizations and help people feel a sense of belonging (Gagne et al., 2022). In relation to *competence* needs, the ability to access and get on with work, through using ICTs, can improve performance and outputs (Lüthje & Thiele, 2020; Mano & Mesch, 2010). In relation to *autonomy* needs, using ICTs can free people up to work in an agile way, liberating them from traditional work structures and enhancing their flexibility in terms of place, time, and role (Chen & Karahanna, 2018; Chesley & Johnson, 2015; Collins et al., 2015; Estévez-Mujica & Quintane, 2018).

APPLYING PSYCHOLOGICAL THEORY TO EXPLAIN THE PARADOX OF ICT USE FOR AGILE WORKING

The double-edged sword of ICT use (Potter et al., 2022) can also be explained using psychological theories. Having constant access to work – anytime, anyplace, anywhere – means that more effort, energy, and time resources may be spent on work than ever before. We are seeing an escalation in work intensification (doing more in work hours) and extensification (doing more out-of-hours), brought about by the availability of ICTs and the infrastructure to support 24/7 use (Hassard & Morris, 2022). This is resource-depleting, and can negatively impact the extent to which people are able to relax and recover from work or enjoy a healthy work–life balance (Braukmann et al., 2018; Russell et al., 2023). If people feel tethered to their devices (Ferguson et al., 2016), and unable to resist the constant allure of work via ICTs, then intrinsic and autonomous motivation will become eroded. In such cases, people may become more externally regulated by the cultures in which they work (Deci et al., 2017) and norms of being 'always on' (McDowall & Kinman, 2017). Gagne et al. (2022) suggest that ICTs may: (1) encourage more superficial and isolated work relationships, (2) result in excessive communications that overwhelm or even deskill people, and (3) reduce decision latitude via ICT algorithms and uncertainty. Relatedness, competence, and autonomy needs satisfaction may thus be respectively hindered. Framing our use of ICTs in the context of psychological need satisfaction and resource loss, gain, and conservation activity can help us to better understand the paradoxical impact on well-being and work performance (Russell et al., 2023).

The impact of ICTs has been fundamental in supporting the era of agile working, improving efficacy, flexibility, and well-being; but only when this is accompanied by adequate resources to help support psychological needs for autonomy, competence, and relatedness. In the next section we turn to understanding how different groups of agile workers may benefit from the provision of different resources in relation to ICT use. In our research, we have uncovered the importance of tailoring ICTs to meet the different needs and demands of different agile workers, to foster both effectiveness and well-being.

USING ICTS TO MAKE AGILE WORKING WORK FOR ALL

ICTs and new technologies have enabled many workers to be included in and have access to work (Kelly & Mutebi, 2023). In many ways, ICTs have an equalizing effect, and have therefore been welcomed by previously 'invisible' or under-represented groups of workers (Raja, 2016). For example, some disabled people with mobility problems may previously have struggled to obtain resources to work in an agile way. With the advent of ICTs and the recent surge in agile working, people have been able to switch on and off to work when they feel physically and mentally able to, in places and at times that suit them best (Grant et al., 2022b; Raja, 2016). In the recent 'Remote4All' research, disabled and neurodivergent workers reported on the ICT support and infrastructure they need (Grant et al., 2022b). These workers had previously felt 'invisible' at work; that is, disabled and neurodivergent workers were dispersed, working from home and/or at different times, depending on their health conditions, whereas able-bodied and neurotypical workers tended to be physically and temporally co-located.

To improve visibility and increase interaction with colleagues and line managers, many disabled/neurodivergent workers have embraced the provision of ICT platforms like Teams and Zoom (Grant et al., 2022b). Indeed, scholars suggest that the specific skills and talents of neurodivergent workers means they may be especially well suited to working in an increasingly digitalized workplace, offering specialist knowledge resources, and engaging in agile working in a way that supports the satisfaction of their psychological needs (LeFevre-Levy et al., 2023). Noteworthy here though is that different ICTs impact disabled and neurodivergent workers in different ways. Whilst text-based communications (email/messaging) might be preferable for people who find excessive social cues distracting (e.g., from video communications), for others the absence of social cues in text-based messages can be problematic (Sklar, 2020). The key to increasing satisfaction of autonomy, relatedness, and competence needs for these groups is to tailor the tools to fit the needs of the worker.

Other research has examined how workers with low socio-economic status (SES) requested, and were given access to, agile working opportunities (D'Mello et al., 2022). These workers showed a good understanding of the required resources to support their work, and articulated useful suggestions about how ICT resources could be used more efficiently to optimize access. For example, the use of online self-rostering shift systems was considered to be a useful resource for allowing flexibility, and enabling opportunities to work at times that suited both worker and organization. However, many low-SES workers reported that – potentially because of their lower status – effective and regular communication with managers was absent, and they struggled to obtain appropriate software, devices, and other technological resources to support their agile work. This left them feeling under-appreciated, under-resourced, and resentful. In many cases this was said to undermine well-being, and lead to intentions to quit (D'Mello et al., 2022).

Another study with agile workers found that those who develop 'professional intimacy' with their teams and leaders enjoyed better well-being and effectiveness (Russell et al., 2022b). In this study, when temporally and physically dispersed, workers needed professional intimacy (feeling mutual trust, reciprocal connectedness, warmth, and interpersonal support) to be fostered using ICT resources. Managers who provided regular opportunities to meet online and engage in informal chats and exchanges in this way also benefitted from a more satisfied and supported workforce (Russell et al., 2022b).

In the absence of in-person work, it can be easy for teams to lose a sense of belongingness and trust in each other (Malhotra et al., 2007). Encouraging regular Zoom/Teams/WhatsApp drop-ins was found to be essential for reinforcing connections between colleagues. However, as noted above, careful management of ICT use is required. If use of ICTs means an over-stepping of boundaries (e.g., contact beyond appropriate hours, insistence on 'screens on' when people are in private spaces), trust and professional intimacy can be eroded, with detrimental repercussions for work and well-being (Russell et al., 2022b; Sobande, 2022).

These empirical studies indicate that, as we move to a more agile working environment, it is increasingly important for both organizations and leaders to support the shift, not only in the provision of tools and equipment to enable effective ICT use, but also the shift in work practices, and appreciation of different workers' contributions. In the current post-COVID period, the issue of agile (or remote) working, for example, is being increasingly debated, with some organizations requiring workers to return to their offices on a full-time basis, citing a detrimental lack of collaboration opportunities and innovation in remote forms of working (Parry et al., 2022). This may well be because organizations have failed to put infrastructure in place to support remote collaborations. In other words, it may have been poor management and deficient resource provision that created such problems, rather than specifically the place of work, or use of digital tools, that hindered progress (Parry et al., 2022; Russell et al., 2022b). Time and effort need to be spent on listening to and communicating with all workers, to understand their personal needs and circumstances, so that these can be accommodated and actioned (Forbes et al., 2020; Malhotra et al., 2007). It is also essential that employers consider fully the implications for an inclusive workplace. It was found in a UK National Health Service (NHS) survey that 84 per cent of disabled workers would prefer to keep on working from home post-pandemic, and to retain flexibility in their working styles (NHS Employers, 2022). Therefore, rather than simply resting on the laurels of pre-lockdown 'tried and tested' working arrangements, if organizations want to be responsive, flexible, and adaptive to ever-changing market and societal needs then digital infrastructure and resources are required to facilitate agile working. In addition, managers need to be educated about how best to support and nurture a dispersed, diverse, and agile workforce, so that both they and the organization can flourish (Parry et al., 2022).

WHAT NEXT FOR ICTS AND AGILE WORKING?

We have examined how ICTs offer a range of benefits in relation to ease, convenience, and access, enabling flexible work, inclusion of previously marginalized groups, efficient task and project management, and the fostering of new relationships. We have also seen that these same ICTs can create circumstances whereby trust and a sense of belongingness is eroded, and working life becomes more intensive and extensive, with repercussions for burnout, exhaustion, and work–home conflict. Inequalities also appear to still exist when it comes to enabling access to ICTs as an agile working resource. To combat some of these issues, we are interested to see the emergence of new working arrangements being piloted – for example, the four-day working week trials, hybrid and e-working, and the rise in community-based co-working hubs. Here, ICTs are used to enable agility in time and place of work, whilst also trying to redress the balance in terms of work–life harmony and engagement with others.

The 4-Day Week Trials

Schor et al. (2022) have undertaken a wide-scale study trialling 33 organizations (903 employees) moving to a four-day week (with no reduction in pay). Four-day weeks can follow different patterns – from working only on four days to working for 0.8 of a full-time contract spread across different days (Spencer, 2022). In most cases, workers are expected to retain a 1.0 full-time workload, and receive the equivalent pay of a 1.0 full-time worker. The premise here is that, even though maintaining pay and productivity in the face of reduced time availability might seem counter-intuitive, the extra time off work can provide an opportunity for rest and relaxation, allowing workers to recover well-being resources (Sonnentag & Fritz, 2007). Further, in order to meet productivity requirements, researchers have suggested that unnecessary activities (e.g., needless meetings, water-cooler moments) can be cut out, leading to efficiency savings (Delaney & Casey, 2022).

Initial findings from the most recent four-day-week trials indicate high levels of satisfaction for both employers and employees with the scheme (Schor et al., 2022). Out of the 33 organizations that took part, 27 plan to continue with the four-day week, and none of the organizations intend to return to a five-day week. Employees cited job satisfaction, productivity, and well-being improvements as beneficial outcomes from the scheme (Schor et al., 2022). However, to ensure the four-day week works effectively and is sustainable, scholars are suggesting that organizations carefully monitor the extent to which it creates a more intensified work experience (Delaney & Casey, 2022; Russell et al., 2022a; Spencer, 2022). For example, maintaining the same level of workload, truncated into four rather than five days, will inevitably lead to overload (Russell et al., 2022a), especially if more intensive work involves excessive use of screens and technology (Rae, 2023). It could also mean that people of low SES choose to use their 'day off' to engage in other paid work, negating the rest and recovery benefits that 'day 5' might otherwise bring (Spencer,

2022). Further, allowing organizations to 'own' the employee's time on day 5 could mean that – via ICTs – people can still be contacted, reducing the psychological detachment from work that the four-day week has been designed to address (Russell et al., 2022a; Spencer, 2022). More research, especially into the physiological and psychological implications of different four-day-week arrangements, can help to uncover what approaches are likely to work best (Rae, 2023; Russell et al., 2022a).

Hybrid Working and E-Working Arrangements

In developing a post-pandemic 'new normal' of agile working, researchers are suggesting that the preference seems to be for a hybrid model, where days are split between home and office working, helping to increase in-person contact, and reduce social and professional isolation, whilst also retaining the productivity and well-being gains (Charalampous et al., 2022; Franken et. al., 2021). The use of ICTs has enabled different forms and types of working to emerge, such as hybrid working; but it is important also to consider how these new forms of working may affect workers' cognitive load to manage the necessary changes in location and working methods. A way of monitoring the quality of workers' e-work lives is to utilize the E-Work Life Scale (Charalampous et al., 2022; Grant et al., 2018). This scale has four key dimensions relating to (1) work–life interference, (2) flexibility, (3) organizational trust, and (4) productivity. This measure enables organizations, managers, and workers to gain an understanding of how well employees are managing their work on each of these dimensions. Measuring these key factors is essential to understand the impact of e-work on well-being, and to ensure the best possible outcomes for remote/agile workers.

Community-Based Co-Working Hubs

To address issues around social isolation, co-working hubs have been enjoying a resurgence in recent years (Mossa, 2020). Working in a local or regional hub has been found to ameliorate some of the feelings of isolation experienced by agile workers (Bosworth et al., 2023; Charalampous et al., 2018; Merrell et al., 2022). In particular, where these hubs are embedded in local communities and rural settings, they have been found to help satisfy the key psychological needs for autonomy, competence, and relatedness, along with other human needs such as the need to attain work respite in the natural world (Merrell et al., 2022). Researchers suggest that since the global pandemic has redesigned our work–life habits, co-working is now vital for harnessing creativity and collaboration (Mossa, 2020), and for improving networking opportunities (Bosworth et al., 2023; Weijs-Perrée et al., 2019). Co-working hubs appear to offer a flexible solution for organizations who wish to offer their workers a more agile work experience, whilst also fostering new collaborations, relationships, and community embeddedness (Bosworth et al., 2023). Research is needed, however, to evaluate the implications of co-working for the well-being and productivity of remote workers.

SUMMARY

It is clear that research into the use of ICTs in relation to agile working is reporting paradoxical impacts on well-being and efficacy (Charalampous et al., 2021; D'Mello et al., 2022; Russell et al., 2023; Tramontano et al., 2021). It is evident that there is no 'one size fits all' when it comes to finding solutions; but the above studies offer alternative working arrangements to accommodate, facilitate, and promote digital, agile working in these fast-paced, changing times. Organizations need to provide the structures, policies, and training to ensure that a move to different working arrangements will benefit workers' productivity and well-being; and researchers are encouraged to undertake more intervention studies to test whether new practices work.

In addition to providing managerial and organizational support, developing specific competencies for agile workers should also be promoted. For example, Grant and Clarke (2020) found five competency areas to support effective agile working and to aid digital resilience: (1) *social and relational competencies*, supporting the need for a well-developed network of social and work contacts; (2) *trust competencies*, ensuring autonomous and trusting relationships are developed with peers, colleagues, and line managers; (3) *knowledge competencies* – that is, adapting and developing skills to manage technology effectively; (4) *personal efficiency competencies*, in being self-aware and able to prioritize and manage tasks effectively; and (5) *self-care competencies* – that is, awareness of health needs and the ability to find appropriate coping strategies. Encouraging organizations to offer training and support to develop these in workers can help build a workforce that is properly equipped to deal with the modern challenges of digital, agile work.

CONCLUDING THOUGHTS

Extending the right to flexible working is a policy priority for international governments across the world (World Economic Forum, 2023). Most recently, the UK Government has passed the *Employment Relations (Flexible Working) Act* (2023). Our research has found that ICTs are paramount to facilitating a move to more agile working for many workers. In this chapter, we reviewed theories of psychological resources and needs, and the body of research from the past 20 years, to outline how the rise of ICTs has had both an exponentially positive and negative effect on working life and well-being. We hope that our summary can highlight to scholars, organizations, and policy makers how ICTs can now be optimized to facilitate healthy and effective agile work for all. In increasingly turbulent, fast-paced, and challenging times, where the nature of work has changed dramatically, the optimization of digital tools to aid timely and inclusive adjustments is now more relevant and important than ever before.

NOTE

1. Knowledge workers have high degrees of expertise and education and are involved in the creation and distribution of knowledge (Davenport, 2005; Field & Chan, 2018; Mattern et al., 2021). Knowledge workers have greater access to time and place flexibility, compared to other workers, and have more job autonomy (Ojala & Pyöriä, 2018).

REFERENCES

Addas, S., & Pinsonneault, A. (2018). E-mail interruptions and individual performance: Is there a silver lining? *MIS Quarterly, 42*(2), 381–405.

Angelici, M., & Profeta, P. (2020). Smart-working: Work flexibility without constraints. *CESifo Working Paper No. 8165.* https://ssrn.com/abstract=3556304 or http://dx.doi.org/10.2139/ssrn.3556304

Barley, S. R., Meyerson, D. E., & Grodal, S. (2011). E-mail as a source and symbol of stress. *Organization Science, 22*(4), 887–906.

Basile, K. A., & Beauregard, T. A. (2020). Boundary management: Getting the work-home balance right. In E. Russell & C. Grant (Eds.), *Agile working and well-being in the digital age* (pp. 35–46). Palgrave Macmillan.

Belkin, L. Y., Becker, W. J., & Conroy, S. A. (2016). Exhausted, but unable to disconnect: After-hours email, work-family balance and identification. *Academy of Management Proceedings, 2016*(1), 10353.

Belkin, L. Y., Becker, W. J., & Conroy, S. A. (2020). The invisible leash: The impact of organizational expectations for email monitoring after-hours on employee resources, well-being, and turnover intentions. *Group & Organization Management, 45*(5), 709–740.

Boswell, W., & Olson-Buchanan, J. (2007). The use of communication technologies after hours: The role of work attitudes and work-life conflict. *Journal of Management, 33*, 592–610.

Bosworth, G., Whalley, J., Fuzi, A., Merrell, I., Chapman, P., & Russell, E. (2023). Rural co-working: New network spaces and new opportunities for a smart countryside. *Journal of Rural Studies, 97*, 550–559.

Braukmann, J., Schmitt, A., Ďuranová, L., & Ohly, S. (2018). Identifying ICT-related affective events across life domains and examining their unique relationships with employee recovery. *Journal of Business and Psychology, 33*(4), 529–544.

Braun, S., Bark, A. H., Kirchner, A., Stegmann, S., & Dick, R. van. (2019). Emails from the boss – curse or blessing? Relations between communication channels, leader evaluation, and employees' attitudes. *International Journal of Business Communication, 56*(1), 50–81.

Brown, R., Duck, J., & Jimmieson, N. (2014). E-mail in the workplace: The role of stress appraisals and normative response pressure in the relationship between e-mail stressors and employee strain. *International Journal of Stress Management, 21*(4), 325–347.

Budnick, C. J., Rogers, A. P., & Barber, L. K. (2020). The fear of missing out at work: Examining costs and benefits to employee health and motivation. *Computers in Human Behavior, 104*, 106161.

Catalano, A. J., Torff, B., & Anderson, K. S. (2021). Transitioning to online learning during the COVID-19 pandemic: Differences in access and participation among students in disadvantaged school districts. *The International Journal of Information and Learning Technology, 38*(2), 258–270. https://doi.org/10.1108/IJILT-06-2020-0111

Charalampous, M., Grant, C. A., & Tramontano, C. (2021). It needs to be the right blend: A qualitative exploration of remote e-workers' experience and well-being at work, *Employee Relations, 44*(2), 335–355.

Charalampous, M., Grant, C. A., & Tramontano, C. (2022). Getting the measure of remote e-working: A further validation of the E-Work Life Scale. *Employee Relations, 45*(1), 45–68.

Charalampous, M., Grant, C. A., Tramontano, C., & Michailidis, E. (2018). Systematically reviewing remote e-workers' well-being at work: A multi-dimensional approach. *European Journal of Work and Organisational Psychology, 28(1)*, 51–73.

Chen, A., & Karahanna, E. (2018). Life interrupted: The effects of technology mediated work interruptions on work and nonwork outcomes. *MIS Quarterly, 42*(4), 1023–1042.

Chesley, N., & Johnson, B. E. (2015). Technology use and the new economy: Work extension, network connectivity, and employee distress and productivity. *Work and Family in the New Economy (Research in the Sociology of Work), 26*, 61–99.

Chwaszcz, J., Bartczuk, R. P., Niewiadomska, I., & Sławska-Jaroszewska, P. (2022). Quality of life and prosocial or antisocial coping with resource deprivation: A cross-sectional study of people at risk of social exclusion. *PLOS One, 17*(9), e0275234.

Collins, E. I. M., Cox, A. L., & Wootton, R. (2015). Out of work, out of mind? Smartphone use and work-life boundaries. *International Journal of Mobile Human Computer Interaction (IJMHCI), 7*(3), 67–77.

D'Mello, D. (2020). E-resistance: Making active choices for technology management. In C. Grant & E. Russell (Eds.), *Agile working and well-being in the digital age* (pp. 77–90). Palgrave Macmillan.

D'Mello, D., Tibbutt, H., & Russell, E. (2022). *Feeling seen, being heard, taking action: appreciation in addressing the agile working needs of workers with lower socioeconomic status.* agiLab Research Report, University of Sussex.

Dabbish, L. A., & Kraut, R. E. (2006). Email overload at work: an analysis of factors associated with email strain. *Proceedings of the 2006 20th Anniversary Conference on Computer Supported Cooperative Work – CSCW '06*, 431–440.

Dabbish, L. A., Kraut, R. E., Fussell, S., & Kiesler, S. (2005). Understanding email use: Predicting action on a message. *Proceedings of the SIGCHI Conference on Human Factors in Computing Systems*, 691–700.

Davenport, T. H. (2005). *Thinking for a living: How to get better performances and results from knowledge workers.* Harvard Business Press.

Dawley, D. D., & Anthony, W. P. (2003). User perceptions of e-mail at work. *Journal of Business and Technical Communication, 17*(2), 170–200.

Deci, E. L., Olafsen, A. H., & Ryan, R. M. (2017). Self-determination theory in work organizations: The state of a science. *Annual Review of Organizational Psychology and Organizational Behavior, 4*, 19–43.

Delaney, H., & Casey, C. (2022). The promise of a four-day week? A critical appraisal of a management-led initiative. *Employee Relations, 44*(1), 176–190.

Deloitte. (2023). *ACS Australia's Digital Pulse: A new approach to building technology skills.* https:// www .deloitte .com/ au/ en/ services/ economics/ perspectives/ australias-digital-pulse.html

Demerouti, E., Derks, D., Lieke, L., & Bakker, A. B. (2014). New ways of working: Impact on working conditions, work-family balance, and well-being. In C. Korunka & P. Hoonakker (Eds.), *The impact of ICT on quality of working life* (pp. 123–141). Springer.

Derks, D., Van Mierlo, H., & Schmitz, E. B. (2014). A diary study on work-related smartphone use, psychological detachment and exhaustion: examining the role of the perceived segmentation norm. *Journal of Occupational Health Psychology, 19*(1), 74–84.

Diaz, I., Ciaburu, D. S., Zimmerman, R. D., & Boswell, W. R. (2012). Communication technology: Pros and cons of constant connection to work. *Journal of Vocational Behavior, 80*, 500–508.

Digital Futures at Work Research Centre. (n.d.). *Digit Blog: Views and analysis from the Digit community on how digital technologies are changing work.* https:// digit -research.org/blog/

Dunahoo, C. L., Hobfoll, S. E., Monnier, J., Hulsizer, M. R., & Johnson, R. (1998). There's more than rugged individualism in coping, Part 1: Even the Lone Ranger had Tonto. *Anxiety, Stress and Coping, 11*(2), 137–165.

Employment Relations (Flexible Working) Bill 2022–23. House of Commons Library. https://commonslibrary.parliament.uk/research-briefings/cbp-9648/

Estévez-Mujica, C. P., & Quintane, E. (2018). E-mail communication patterns and job burnout. *PLOS One, 13*(3), e0193966.

Ferguson, M., Carlson, D., Boswell, W., Whitten, D., Butts, M. M., & Kacmar, K. M. (2016). Tethered to work: A family systems approach linking mobile device use to turnover intentions. *Journal of Applied Psychology, 101*(4), 520.

Field, J. C., & Chan, X. W. (2018). Contemporary knowledge workers and the boundaryless work–life interface: Implications for the human resource management of the knowledge workforce. *Frontiers in Psychology, 9*, 2414.

Flexible Working Legislation (2014). *The Flexible Working Regulations 2014.* https:// www.legislation.gov.uk/uksi/2014/1398/made

Forbes, S., Birkett, H., Evans, L., Chung, H., & Whiteman, J. (2020). *Managing employees during the COVID-19 pandemic: Flexible working and the future of work.* https://kar.kent.ac.uk/85918/1/managerial-experiences-during-covid19-2020 -accessible.pdf

Franken, E., Bentley, T., Shafaei, A., Farr-Wharton, B., Onnis, L. A., & Omari, M. (2021). Forced flexibility and remote working: Opportunities and challenges in the new normal. *Journal of Management & Organization, 27*(6), 1131–1149.

Gagné, M., Parker, S. K., Griffin, M. A., Dunlop, P. D., Knight, C., Klonek, F. E., & Parent-Rocheleau, X. (2022). Understanding and shaping the future of work with self-determination theory. *Nature Reviews Psychology, 1*(7), 378–392.

Garrett, R. K., & Danziger, J. N. (2008). IM = Interruption Management? Instant messaging and disruption in the workplace. *Journal of Computer-Mediated Communication, 13*(1), 23–42.

Gillet, N., Fouquereau, E., Lafrenière, M.-A. K., & Huyghebaert, T. (2016) Examining the roles of work autonomous and controlled motivations on satisfaction and anxiety as a function of role ambiguity. *The Journal of Psychology, 150*(5), 644–665. https:// doi.org/10.1080/00223980.2016.1154811

Grant, C., Charalampous, M., & Tramontano, C. (2022a, November 21). Disability, neurodivergence and remote working: what employers need to know. *Digit Blog.* https:// digit -research .org/ blog _article/ disability -neurodivergence -and -remote -working-what-employers-need-to-know/

Grant, C., Charalampous, M., & Tramontano, C. (2022b). *Disability, neurodiversity, and remote e-working: Promoting the creation of an inclusive workplace. "Remote for All" (R4All).* https:// digit -research .org/ research/ innovation -fund/ disability -neurodiversity-and-remote-eworking/

Grant, C., & Clarke, C. (2020). Digital resilience: A competency framework for agile workers. In C. Grant & E. Russell (Eds), *Agile working and well-being in the digital age* (pp. 117–130). Palgrave Macmillan.

Grant, C. A., Wallace, L. M., Spurgeon, P. C., Tramontano, C., & Charalampous, M. (2018). Construction and initial validation of the E-Work Life Scale to measure remote e-working. *Employee Relations, 41*(1), 16–33.

Hassard, J., & Morris, J. (2022). The extensification of managerial work in the digital age: Middle managers, spatio-temporal boundaries and control. *Human Relations, 75*(9), 1647–1678.

Hobfoll, S. E. (1989). Conservation of resources: A new attempt at conceptualizing stress. *American Psychologist, 44*(3), 513–524.

Hobfoll, S. E. (2001). The influence of culture, community, and the nested-self in the stress process: Advancing conservation of resources theory. *Applied Psychology, 50(3)*, 337–421.

Hobfoll, S. E., Halbesleben, J., Neveu, J. P., & Westman, M. (2018). Conservation of resources in the organizational context: The reality of resources and their consequences. *Annual Review of Organizational Psychology and Organizational Behavior, 5*, 103–128.

Jeyasingham, D. (2016). Open spaces, supple bodies? Considering the impact of agile working on social work office practices. *Child & Family Social Work, 21(2)*, 209–217.

Kelliher, C., & Anderson, D. (2010). Doing more with less? Flexible working practices and the intensification of work. *Human Relations, 63(1)*, 83–106.

Kelly, R., & Mutebi, N. (2023). *Invisible disabilities in education and employment.* UK Parliament POST Report. https://post.parliament.uk/research-briefings/post-pn -0689/

Korunka, C., & Vartiainen, M. (2017). Digital technologies at work are great, aren't they? The development of information and communication technologies (ICT) and their relevance in the world of work. In N. Chmiel, F. Fraccaroli, & M. Sverke (Eds.), *An introduction to work and organizational psychology* (pp. 102–120). Wiley.

Kossek, E. E., & Kelliher, C. (2023). Making flexibility more i-deal: Advancing work-life equality collectively. *Group & Organization Management, 48(1)*, 317–349.

LeFevre-Levy, R., Melson-Silimon, A., Harmata, R., Hulett, A. L., & Carter, N. T. (2023). Neurodiversity in the workplace: Considering neuroatypicality as a form of diversity. *Industrial and Organizational Psychology, 16*(1), 1–19.

Levy, P. (2019, January 25). Slack: How the messaging app could change after an IPO. *The Conversation*. https://theconversation.com/slack-how-the-messaging-app-could -change-after-an-ipo-110324

Lüthje, C., & Thiele, F. (2020). Communication floods–emails in scholarly communication. *SCM Studies in Communication and Media, 9*(3), 367-393.

Madden, M., & Jones, S. (2008). *Networked workers*. Pew Research Center Publications. http://www.pewresearch.org/pubs/966/

Malhotra, A., Majchrzak, A., & Rosen, B. (2007). Leading virtual teams. *Academy of Management Perspectives, 21*(1), 60–70.

Mano, R. S., & Mesch, G. S. (2010). E-mail characteristics, work performance and distress. *Computers in Human Behavior, 26*(1), 61–69.

Mazmanian, M., Orlikowski, W. J., & Yates, J. (2013). The autonomy paradox: The implications of mobile email devices for knowledge professionals, *Organization Science, 24*(5), 1337–1357.

Mazmanian, M. A., Orlikowski, W. J., & Yates, J. (2005). CrackBerries: The social implications of ubiquitous wireless e-mail devices. In C. Sørensen, Y. Yoo, K. Lyytinen, & J. I. DeGross (Eds.), *Designing ubiquitous information environments: Socio-technical issues and challenges* (Vol. 185). IFIP – The International Federation for Information Processing.

McDowall, A., & Kinman, G. (2017). The new nowhere land? A research and practice agenda for the 'always on' culture. *Journal of Organizational Effectiveness: People and Performance, 4*(3), 256–266.

Merrell, I., Füzi, A., Russell, E., & Bosworth, G. (2022). How rural coworking hubs can facilitate well-being through the satisfaction of key psychological needs. *Local Economy, 36*(7–8), 606–626.

Middleton, C. A., & Cukier, W. (2006). Is mobile email functional or dysfunctional? Two perspectives on mobile email usage. *European Journal of Information Systems, 15*(3), 252–260.

Mishna, F., Milne, E., Bogo, M., & Pereira, L. F. (2021). Responding to COVID-19: New trends in social workers' use of information and communication technology. *Clinical Social Work Journal, 49*, 484–494.

Mossa, A. (2020). The case of co-working spaces for fulfilling agile working and worker needs. In C. Grant & E. Russell (Eds), *Agile working and well-being in the digital age* (pp. 157–167). Palgrave Macmillan.

Murphy, M., Scott, L. J., Salisbury, C., Turner, A., Scott, A., Denholm, R., Lewis, R., Iyer, G., Macleod, J., & Horwood, J. (2021). Implementation of remote consulting in UK primary care following the COVID-19 pandemic: A mixed-methods longitudinal study. *British Journal of General Practice, 71*(704), e166–e177.

NHS Employers. (2022, March 21). *NHS Disabled staff experiences during COVID-1*. https://www.nhsemployers.org/publications/nhs-disabled-staff-experiences-during -covid-19-report

Nurmi, N. (2011). Coping with coping strategies: how distributed teams and their members deal with the stress of distance, time zones and culture. *Stress and Health, 27*(2), 123–143.

Office for National Statistics (2020). Coronavirus and homeworking in the UK. https:// www.ons.gov.uk/employmentandlabourmarket/peopleinwork/employmentandempl oyeetypes/bulletins/coronavirusandhomeworkingintheuk/april2020

Office for National Statistics. (2022). *Is hybrid working here to stay?* https:// www.ons.gov.uk/employmentandlabourmarket/peopleinwork/employmentandempl oyeetypes/articles/ishybridworkingheretostay/2022-05-23

Office for National Statistics. (2023). *Characteristics of homeworkers, Great Britain: September 2022 to January 2023*. https:// www .ons .gov .uk/ employ mentandlab ourmarket/ peopleinwork/ employm entandempl oyeetypes/ articles/ c haracteris ticsofhomeworkersgreatbritain/september2022tojanuary2023#:~:text=Being%20in %20a%20single%2Dadult,their%20property%20outright%20(23%25)

Ojala, S., & Pyöriä, P. (2018). Mobile knowledge workers and traditional mobile workers: Assessing the prevalence of multi-locational work in Europe. *Acta Sociologica, 61*(4), 402–418.

O'Kane, P., & Hargie, O. (2007). Intentional and unintentional consequences of substituting face-to-face interaction with e-mail: An employee-based perspective. *Interacting with Computers, 19*(1), 20–31.

Olson-Buchanan, J. B., Boswell, W. R., & Morgan, T. J. (2016). The role of technology in managing the work and nonwork interface. In T. D. Allen & L. T. Eby (Eds.), *The Oxford handbook of work and family* (pp. 333–348). Oxford University Press.

Orlikowski, W. J. (1992). The duality of technology: Rethinking the concept of tech-nology in organizations. *Organization Science, 3(3)*, 398-427.

Park, Y., & Jex, S. M. (2011). Work–home boundary management using communi-cation and information technology. *International Journal of Stress Management, 18*(2), 133–152.

Parry, J., Young, Z., Bevan, S., Veliziotis, M., Baruch, Y., Beigi, M., Bajorek, Z., Richards, S., & Tochia, C. (2022). *Work after lockdown: No going back – What we have learned from working from home through the COVID-19 pandemic.* https://eprints.soton.ac.uk/456151/2/7379_UoS_WorkAfterLockdownReport_am4 _280222_v8.pdf

Potter, R. E., Dollard, M., Pignata, S., Zadow, A., & Lushington, K. (2022). Review of practice & policy strategies for managing digital communication and ICT use in Australian universities. *Computers in Human Behavior Reports, 5*, 100160.

Radicati Group. (2021). *Email statistics report 2021–2025*. https://www.radicati.com/ wp/ wp -content/ uploads/ 2020/ 12/ Email -Statistics -Report -2021 -2025 -Executive -Summary.pdf

Rae, C. (2023, March 2). What the 4-day week does to your brain. *Digit Blog.* https:// digit-research.org/blog_article/what-does-the-4-day-week-do-to-your-brain/

Raja, D. S. (2016). *Bridging the disability divide through Digital Technology.* World Bank Report. https:// thedocs .worldbank .org/ en/ doc/ 123481461249337484 -0050022016/ original/ WDR16BPBridg ingtheDisabilityDivi dethroughD igitalTech nologyRAJA.pdf

Ren, S., Hu, J., Tang, G., & Chadee, D. (2023). Digital connectivity for work after hours: Its curvilinear relationship with employee job performance. *Personnel Psychology, 76*(3), 731–757.

Russell, E., & Bevan, S. (2022, January 24). Is the "right to disconnect" a red herring? *Digit Blog.* https:// digit-research.org/ blog_article/is-the-right-to-disconnect-a-red -herring/

Russell, E., & Grant, C. (2020). Introduction to agile working and well-being in the digital age. In C. Grant and E. Russell (Eds.), *Agile working and well-being in the digital age* (pp. 3–17). Palgrave Macmillan.

Russell, E., Jackson, T., & Banks, A. (2021). Classifying computer-mediated commu-nication (CMC) interruptions at work using control as a key delineator. *Behavior & Information Technology, 40*(2), 191–205.

Russell, E., Jackson, T. W., Fullman, M., & Chamakiotis, P. (2023). Getting on top of work-email: A systematic review of 25 years of research to understand effective work-email activity. *Journal of Occupational and Organizational Psychology* (online ahead of print). doi: 10.1111/joop.12462.

Russell, E., Jaser, Z., & McCloskey, J. (2022b). *Leading an agile workforce in the NHS: Professional intimacy as a key resource for leaders to support effectiveness and well-being in agile working.* agiLab Research Report, University of Sussex, Sussex.

Russell, E., Murphy, C., & Terry, E. (2022a, May 27). What leaders need to know before trying a 4-day work week. *Harvard Business Review.* https://hbr.org/2022/05/what-leaders-need-to-know-before-trying-a-4-day-work-week

Russell, E., & Woods, S. A. (2020). Personality differences as predictors of action-goal relationships in work-email activity. *Computers in Human Behavior, 103*, 67–79.

Russell, E., Woods, S. A., & Banks, A. P. (2017). Examining conscientiousness as a key resource in resisting email interruptions: Implications for volatile resources and goal achievement. *Journal of Occupational and Organizational Psychology, 90*(3), 407–435.

Russell, E., Woods, S. A., & Banks, A. P. (2022c). Tired of email? Examining the role of extraversion in building energy resources after dealing with work-email. *European Journal of Work and Organizational Psychology, 31*(3), 440–452.

Ryan, R. M. (1995). Psychological needs and the facilitation of integrative processes. *Journal of Personality, 63*(3), 397–427.

Ryan, R. M., & Deci, E. L. (2017). *Self-determination theory: Basic psychological needs in motivation, development, and wellness.* Guilford Publications.

Schmidtner, M., Doering, C., & Timinger, H. (2021). Agile working during COVID-19 pandemic. *IEEE Engineering Management Review, 49*(2), 18–32.

Schor, J. B., Wen, F., Kelly, O., Gu, G., Bezdenezhnykh, T., & Bridson-Hubbard, N. (2022). *The four-day week: Assessing global trials of reduced work time with no reduction in pay.* 4 Day Week Global.

Sklar, J. (2020, April 24). Coronavirus zoom fatigue is taking the brain: Here's why that happens. *National Geographic.* https://www.nationalgeographic.com/science/article/coronavirus-zoom-fatigue-is-taxing-the-brain-here-is-why-that-happens

Sobande, F. (2022, July 5). Feeling at home at work? Inequalities, inclusiveness, and changing work environments. *Digit Blog.* https://digit-research.org/blog_article/feeling-at-home-at-work-inequalities-inclusiveness-changing-work/

Sonnentag, S., & Fritz, C. (2007). The Recovery Experience Questionnaire: Development and validation of a measure for assessing recuperation and unwinding from work. *Journal of Occupational Health Psychology, 12*(3), 204–221.

Spencer, D. A. (2022). A four-day working week: Its role in a politics of work. *The Political Quarterly, 93*(3), 401–407.

Taylor, A., Caffery, L. J., Gesesew, H. A., King, A., Bassal, A. R., Ford, K., Kealey, J., Maeder, A., McGuirk, M., Parkes, D., & Ward, P. R. (2021). How Australian health care services adapted to telehealth during the COVID-19 pandemic: A survey of telehealth professionals. *Frontiers in Public Health, 9*, 648009.

Ten Brummelhuis, L. L., & Bakker, A. B. (2012). A resource perspective on the work–home interface: The work–home resources model. *American Psychologist, 67*(7), 545.

Tramontano, C., Grant, C. A., & Clarke, C. (2021). Development and validation of the e-Work Self-Efficacy Scale to assess digital competencies in remote working. *Computers in Human Behaviour Reports, 4*(August–December), 100129. https://doi.org/10.1016/j.chbr.2021.100129

Van den Broeck, A., Ferris, D. L., Chang, C. H., & Rosen, C. C. (2016). A review of self-determination theory's basic psychological needs at work. *Journal of Management, 42*(5), 1195–1229.

Wajcman, J., & Rose, E. (2011). Constant connectivity: Rethinking interruptions at work. *Organization Studies, 32*(7), 941–961.

Wang, B., Liu, Y., Qian, J., & Parker, S. K. (2021). Achieving effective remote working during the COVID-19 pandemic: A work design perspective. *Applied Psychology, 70*(1), 16–59.

Weijs-Perrée, M., Van de Koevering, J., Appel-Meulenbroek, R., & Arentze, T. (2019). Analysing user preferences for co-working space characteristics, *Building Research & Information, 47*(5), 534–548.

Williams, N. (2021). Working through COVID-19: "Zoom" gloom and "Zoom" fatigue. *Occupational Medicine, 71*(3), 164.

World Economic Forum. (2023, August 4). *The UK's new flexible working law and why WFH is here to stay for the global workforce.* https:// www .weforum .org/ agenda/2023/08/flexible-working-law-rights/

11. Working patterns and wellbeing

Jo Yarker, Rachel Lewis, Sophie Walker, and Rodrigo Rodriguez Fernandez

INTRODUCTION

Globalization – that is, the movement of products, services, people, and knowledge across boundaries – continues to change the way we work. While globalization has long been a focus for researchers, their efforts have largely focused on the mechanics of supply chain processes (e.g., Kano et al., 2020), or on navigating the complexities of business structures and international regulations (Reiche et al., 2019), with less focus placed on the impact of global work on people. Research examining the impact of global work has, until relatively recently, largely focused on talent acquisition, and navigating international and organizational cultures (Anlesinya et al., 2019). The national and international travel restrictions imposed by governments across the world in response to the COVID-19 pandemic brought about a rapid change to the way global work is done. Almost overnight, those who could work from home were required to do so, bringing a hiatus to the daily commute for millions of people; and those who travelled internationally for work were quickly required to find alternative ways of working.

Business or corporate travel accounts for 20 per cent of the global tourism spend, amounting to more than $740 billion worldwide (Statista, 2022), with a full recovery to pre-pandemic volume anticipated by late 2024 (Deloitte, 2023). With growing focus on environmentalism, geo-political tensions being at a high since the Cold War, increased costs of fuel and commodities making travel more expensive, and many businesses being financially depleted following the pandemic, there is growing evidence that some businesses are looking to contain their risk and to source materials and labour more locally, to help them manage turbulent times. While these changes are yet to be realized, they are certain to bring changes for our global workforce.

Advances in technology have afforded organizations many benefits, with instant messaging, video conferencing, and digital conferencing platforms making it easier to collaborate and meet without the need for travel. However, such advances are not without cost. Workers are taking out-of-hours work calls, or attending meetings across time zones, with increasing regularity (Savić, 2020); and with growing recognition that face-to-face meetings can reduce friction in working relationships (Bartik et al., 2020) and buffer the negative impacts of social isolation (Galanti et al., 2021), workers who traditionally travelled for their work but no longer do so are now likely to be exposed to new risks. (See also the chapter by Russell and Grant in this collection.)

This chapter brings together research on factors impacting wellbeing for three very different groups of employees who travel with or for work: business travellers, remote rotational workers, and hybrid workers. We present three studies, all of which adopted the evidence-based practice model as described by Briner et al. (2009), taking a three-phased approach to gather the best available evidence, including: (1) a systematic literature review, (2) interviews with key stakeholders and travelling employees, and (3) a survey of travelling employees. The findings from the initial two stages of the research were used to create a model, which informed the design of the final employee survey, which, in turn, informed recommendations for practical intervention and change to support employee wellbeing. Our work demonstrates that the evidence-based practice model facilitates the perspectives of a wide range of stakeholders on developing solutions, and therefore enables the creation of clearer and more targeted guidance and recommendations for employees, their managers, and their organizations. We propose a practice of *evidence-based wellbeing at work* (EB WaW) to act as a catalyst to improve health and wellbeing at work. Such an approach is likely to be ever more important in times of uncertainty and turbulence, when there is less tolerance for test-and-learn approaches, and resources must be used wisely.

USING AN EVIDENCE-BASED PRACTICE APPROACH TO IMPROVE WELLBEING AT WORK

As the demand for interventions and activities to protect and promote the wellbeing of employees has grown, so too have the concerns about 'wellbeing washing' (i.e., businesses publicly supporting wellbeing but taking no action to benefit the workforce), and 'snake oil' (i.e., deceptive marketing, where a product or activity is claimed to provide a proven remedy but has no evidence or backing). The growing acceptance that taking action to support wellbeing not only complies with legislation but makes good business sense is welcome across the community. Yet, there is less understanding of how best to act, with many interventions failing to deliver the intended outcomes. There has been a rapid rise in brief 'wellbeing webinars'; an over-reliance on individual interventions – to promote sleep or nutrition, for example – but less acknowledgement of the need to take an integrated and systemic approach to address problems at source. Recent frameworks and guidelines, such as the World Health Organization's *Guidelines for Mental Health at Work* (WHO, 2022), and the *ISO 45003 Guidelines for Managing Psychosocial Risk*, aim to encourage organizations to adopt an integrated approach to wellbeing at work, and consider the activities that can promote, develop, and protect staff wellbeing. These guidelines draw on evidence and, aligned to the implementation of these guidelines, there is need for practitioners to adopt an evidence-based approach when implementing interventions to improve wellbeing at work. Such an approach has greater potential to improve the quality of decision-making regarding the implementation of interventions and increase the likelihood that they will be successful.

'Evidence-based practice is about making decisions through the conscientious, explicit and judicious use of the best available evidence from multiple sources' (Barends et al., 2014, p. 1). It is not a new phenomenon. The movement for 'evidence-based medicine' has been widely advocated to improve decision-making when making decisions about individual patients, making explicit the need to consider and critically evaluate the clinical literature when doing so (Masic et al., 2008). Such an approach requires a different skill set of clinicians; one that moves beyond traditional practice approaches to medicine, to searching and interrogating literature and drawing on multiple sources of evidence. An evidence-based practice approach has also been advocated in management and, more specifically, in human resource management, with organizations such as the Centre for Evidence-based Management (CEBMa) that promote the use of evidence-based practice to help organizational managers make better decisions.

An evidence-based approach encourages practitioners to draw from multiple sources of evidence to inform decisions, noting four key sources: scientific evidence (e.g., published literature), organizational evidence (e.g., survey data, facts, figures, policies), stakeholder evidence (e.g., values and concerns of those affected by the decisions, such as workers), and professional experience (e.g., professional experience and judgement). In practice, not all evidence is of good quality, or available to the researcher or practitioner. To that end, there is a need to focus on the best available evidence, carefully consider its trustworthiness, and provide transparency in data sources. In reviewing the evidence in its entirety and considering carefully how best to synthesize the findings, an evidence-based practice approach can support a better understanding of the situation, and inform specific and appropriate recommendations to address workforce challenges. It is particularly important in informing approaches to help organizations develop policies and practices to manage uncertainty, where limiting the unknown variables is likely to be of benefit.

We have long applied evidence-based practice approaches within our own work to improve wellbeing at work. Most often, our starting point is a systematic review of the evidence, enabling us to develop a strong understanding of what is known, and what is not yet known, in the broader field. Wellbeing at work is often 'owned' by multiple stakeholders within an organization, with responsibilities for a duty of care, safeguarding, employee engagement, and performance variously falling to professionals across disciplines of health and safety, occupational health, human resources, workforce planning, engagement, and wellbeing. This brings two important considerations for evidence-based practice in the context of wellbeing at work: first, the need to review, critically examine, and synthesize broad and often disconnected evidence bases; and second, to include a broad and comprehensive sample of stakeholders to ensure that all perspectives are fully considered, and concerns and opportunities incorporated into final decisions.

In the following case studies, evidence-based practice has been applied, each demonstrating how drawing on evidence from different perspectives reveals new and important findings to inform decision-making that, in turn, impacts the wellbeing of workers.

The Impact of International Business Travel on Wellbeing

The first case study relates to the psychological impact of international business travel. The research was conducted in the year before the pandemic (2018) and, at the time, demonstrated that there was an increasing need for business travel as a result of globalization and international growth. For example, the number of UK business trips in 2016 were 502.8 million, rising from 488.1 million in 2015 (Global Business Travel Association Foundation, 2015).

Despite international business travel generally being seen as essential for global business, and advantageous for employees' career progression, research findings demonstrate that it can also be deleterious to health. Most research in this area focuses on the physical health risk to the traveller (e.g., frequent flyer radiation, infectious disease, and cardiovascular disease risk markers). It has also been found (e.g., Rundle et al., 2017; Willis et al., 2017) to be associated with behavioural and psychological issues (such as sleep disorders, stress, increased alcohol consumption, and obesity), as well as social or relational outcomes (such as lack of opportunity to detach from work, distance from support networks, and increased work–family conflict). Research by Donald et al. (2005) found that frequent business travellers made three times as many claims for psychological treatment as non-travellers, and had lower psychological wellbeing, poorer work–life balance, and lower productivity than non-travelling colleagues (Rundle et al., 2017).

The link between the psychological health of employees and organizational success is now unequivocal; therefore, given the climate of increasing business travel, it was timely and necessary to understand how and why it may be psychologically harmful, and how organizations could better support and protect their travelling employees. The research comprised four stages: first, a systematic evidence review of the academic literature was undertaken across three search engines, along with a hand-search of practitioner literature, which resulted in 21 papers which were narratively synthesized to identify key themes. Second, eight interviews were conducted with key stakeholders to examine the psychological implications of international business travel, with a particular focus on contributory factors at the organizational, individual, and social levels. Interviews were transcribed and subjected to thematic analysis. The themes identified from the first two stages informed the design of stage three, a survey distributed to international business travellers via our client to their own client base, existing networks, and social media. The number of completed survey responses were 195, with an even split by gender, an average age of 41, and representation from a wide range of sectors (including professional, scientific, technical, manufacturing, and financial). The majority of participants were based in, and travelled predominantly to, Europe, followed by those based in and travelling predominantly to the US, Latin America, and Australasia. Finally, data from all stages were synthesized and recommendations developed.

The evidence review identified that, to date, academic literature had largely focused on the implications of business travel for the family/social aspects of life, in terms of relationship disruption and work–life conflict, and how these interact with employee stress, anxiety, depression, and emotional exhaustion. By combining the data from the sources, however, international business travel was found to impact on employee psychological outcomes in four ways: emotional, family/social, behavioural/physical/psychosomatic, and job/travel-related.

Emotional outcomes

Forty-one per cent of business travellers reported that their mood suffered while on business trips. Nearly one-third (31 per cent) experienced emotional exhaustion on a weekly basis, and just over one-quarter (27 per cent) experienced depression.

Family/social outcomes

The majority (67 per cent) of respondents experienced work–family conflict, with 81 per cent reporting that they had less connection than usual with family and friends while away. Interestingly, perceptions of work–life balance were divided, with an even split (40 per cent vs. 39 per cent) reporting having sufficient balance overall vs. not.

Behavioural/physical/psychosomatic outcomes

Changes in alcohol consumption were found to be common (with 46 per cent of business travellers drinking more), and a reduction in health-promoting behaviours (with 76 per cent less likely to eat a balanced diet, 76 per cent less likely to exercise, and 73 per cent less likely to have good-quality sleep). Although not explored in the academic literature, a strong outcome that emerged at the interview stage was that of risk-taking behaviour, suggesting that when business travellers were away, the perceived anonymity and lack of responsibility could affect their behaviour: 'We behave as if no-one is watching.' Indeed, the survey responses concurred with this finding, with around a third (32–35 per cent) of respondents reporting being more or much more likely to engage in risky behaviours while away, ranging from eating in potentially unhygienic places, travelling to unsafe areas, and travelling in vehicles without adequate protection, such as seatbelts. Nine per cent of respondents reported being more likely to start a relationship with a new sexual partner, and 2 per cent to use drugs while away from home. Although the interview data found that risk-taking was thought to be a largely male domain ('When boys are away, boys will play'), only small, isolated gender effects were found in the survey responses.

Outcomes related to the job

The majority of business travellers (78 per cent) saw their working hours significantly increase while they were away. Over a third (37 per cent) of respondents did not feel that they had sufficient choice or control over their business trip. The impact of lack of control emerged strongly from interviews, with interviewees describing feeling 'powerless in the air travel experience', having little warning about or ability to plan their trips, and feeling a lack of control over the frequency of their trips or the duration of travel. Despite these largely negative outcomes, respondents described feeling engaged with their work in general (67 per cent), and seeing business travel as an opportunity for adventure and exploration (74 per cent) and for freedom from home life (59 per cent). This outlook on business travel is likely to explain the positive work–life conflict findings reported by this group.

Several factors were found to moderate respondents' experience of business travel and wellbeing outcomes. The strongest individual protective factor was work engagement, whereby travellers who were more engaged typically reported less depression and low mood when they were away. Business travellers that took exercise and had good-quality sleep were less likely to suffer from stress, but those who worked longer hours had less opportunity to participate in these health-promoting behaviours. Interestingly, working hours were found to have a protective effect in reducing the likelihood of risk behaviours. Other factors also reduced the likelihood of risk-taking behaviours, such as employee engagement, perceptions of control over the trip, and support from family and friends.

Further, increased alcohol consumption by respondents was associated with both lower-quality sleep and increased stress. Conversely, the strongest barrier to wellbeing outcomes was emotional exhaustion (an element of burnout), with findings suggesting that if travellers were emotionally exhausted, they were more likely to report stress, anxiety and depression, and work–family conflict. Data from all sources found that gender interacted with outcomes, with female business travellers reporting poorer psychological health when travelling than males, with their experiences reflecting prevailing social norms and expectations around gender (such as the expectation to retain childcare responsibilities while away).

At a social level, respondents who had supportive families and friends they could talk to about their mental health tended to be more engaged (and therefore, in turn, had less depression and low mood); and those who had a good work–life balance were less likely to suffer from emotional exhaustion. Conversely, other interviewees reported a lack of spousal support, and spousal frustration towards the business traveller that meant that they would face negativity upon returning and would be asked to take on more responsibility (compensatory behaviours) in the home, to 'pay back' the spouse for their additional load.

The study findings suggested that some organizational resources (such as real-time information on travel destinations, access to high-quality hotel accommodation, and business-class travel or lounges) were linked with better wellbeing outcomes. The findings also brought the concept of 'bleisure' (where a business trip is preceded or followed by a leisure trip) to the foreground, with respondents who were able to engage in this being less likely to experience anxiety. The relationship found between 'bleisure' and anxiety could be mediated by control, in that having the choice or flexibility to extend a business trip would increase feelings of autonomy, or the anticipation of having a break to recharge following the trip. It must, however, be considered that those being offered 'bleisure' were already more 'privileged' travellers, for instance in terms of status and seniority. Although organizational resources were contributing factors, it was clear from the study (including the previous research) that the main contributing factor to negative psychological outcomes was the increased pressure and workload associated with international business travel. This came from a lack of work-time regulations (e.g., working across different time zones while working abroad), a difference in routine, a lack of physical and psychological boundaries between work and personal life, and the knowledge that work 'at home' would be accumulating while they were away.

The findings of this work informed a free-to-access report and a toolkit of materials that were aimed at enabling organizations and employers, managers and business travellers, together with their colleagues, friends, and families, to better support and protect the mental health of this population. The report itself was downloaded over 1000 times, with 100 hard copies, and was presented to over 30 organizations, with exposure via the global press reaching in excess of 12 million. The work formed the strategic underpinning for a suite of resources and products for International SOS, to support the psychological health of international business travellers. The findings have provided a platform for organizations to support the psychological health of their business travellers, informing practical strategies to help them respond more rapidly in an increasingly turbulent environment.

This case study has two key conclusions. Firstly, it highlights the importance of gaining information from multiple sources when addressing an issue of concern. If focusing purely on academic literature, insights such as the propensity for risk and behaviour change when away, and the importance of organizational resources and job design for travellers, would not have been gained. These insights not only provide organizations, managers, and travellers with clear recommendations and practical actions, but also address a previously unexplored security and financial risk. Secondly, by applying evidence-based approaches to wellbeing at work, findings are more likely to be accessible and relevant to organizations – meaning that they are likely, as seen by this case study, to achieve a wider reach, and ultimately bring about greater change and support for the intended workers.

Health and Wellbeing of Remote Rotational Workers

The second case study relates to people doing remote rotational work. This is defined as a method of employing people in remote areas by transporting them directly to the work site (according to a pre-set work pattern), as opposed to relocating employees and their families permanently. The work is often labelled according to the mode of transport, such as 'Fly-in-fly-out' (FIFO), 'Drive-in-drive-out' (DIDO), or 'Sail-in-sail-out' (SISO). Workers include those employed in the oil and gas industries, within mining and offshore sectors, as well as maritime workers and seafarers. Remote rotational work is a lucrative business for many employees, employers, and communities; and indeed, endeavours in offshore oil and gas, as well as mining, play an important role in the global and local economy – for instance, mining contributed to 29 per cent of the gross state product of Western Australia in 2016–2017 (Parker et al., 2018).

Despite its potential positive impact upon the economy, there is evidence that remote rotational work can be deleterious to employee psychological health. Mental health issues such as elevated levels of depression, anxiety, and burnout are particularly prevalent in this occupational group when compared to the general population, with work–family conflict, alcohol and drug use, and suicide risk also being commonly identified (Parker et al., 2018; Xiao et al., 2017).

This case study was conducted during 2019–2020, and obtained data on the perceptions of remote rotational workers and their employers from a wide range of sectors globally. Its aim was to synthesize the findings, develop new insights, and deliver practical recommendations for organizations employing remote rotational workers. The timing of the research also enabled the gathering of the unique experiences and impacts of working through the pandemic for remote rotational workers. Insights gained will help organizations build a culture of psychological safety that will support the wellbeing and effectiveness of rotational workers during turbulent and uncertain times.

The research comprised four stages aligned with the evidence-based approach described above: first, a systematic evidence review resulted in 36 papers; second, ten interviews were conducted with key stakeholders and employees to examine the psychological implications of remote rotational work, with a particular focus on contributory factors at the organizational, individual, and social levels. Interviews were transcribed and subjected to thematic analysis. Third, a survey was distributed to remote rotational workers via our client to their own client base, existing networks, and social media. Responses were received from 172 workers, largely male, who were split between mining, offshore, and seafaring/maritime industries, and dispersed across the world. Finally, data from all stages were synthesized and recommendations developed.

The evidence review identified that previous research exploring the mental health of rotational workers has focused on one occupational group, one location, or one psychological outcome. Findings from across the four data sources obtained during the research process revealed that remote rotational work impacted psychological outcomes in four ways: emotional; family, social, and work–life; physical, behavioural, and psychosomatic; and job and organizational-related outcomes.

Emotional outcomes
Some participants reported being satisfied with the excitement of rotational work; but others emphasized the emotional toll of remote work. Over half of the sample indicated that their mood deteriorated during rotation, while 40 per cent reported experiencing suicidal thoughts some, or all, of the time. Experiences of emotional exhaustion, both on shift and when returning home, were reported, as well as isolation and loneliness.

Family, social, and work–life outcomes

While some respondents indicated that their family benefited from the structure of remote work, for many, family and social relations were strained, with reports of children experiencing behavioural problems or other negative impacts due to their absence from the family; and strained relationships with partners, sometimes leading to marital dissolution. Notably, however, nearly all of our participants reported being satisfied with the support they gained from family and friends.

Physical, behavioural, and psychosomatic outcomes

Complaints of fatigue, insomnia, and cardiovascular and cognitive concerns were common among rotational workers; and the extent to which they engaged in healthy behaviours varied. Over a third took less exercise, while 76 per cent reported that they consumed less alcohol on rotation than at home. Overall, risk-taking behaviours, such as unprotected sex and taking recreational drugs, were seen to decrease while on rotation. It is likely that these responses are shaped by the type of work done, which is often safety-critical, and the isolated locations where alcohol may not be permitted or they may be located away from the wider public (e.g., on an oil platform).

Job and work outcomes

Most remote rotational workers (84 per cent) perceived high levels of job control, and support from their co-workers, managers, and their back-to-backs (the name given to the person the rotational worker swaps places with, performing the same role). Despite this finding, only around half (56 per cent) felt engaged in their work, with one respondent in six being actively disengaged.

A number of factors were found to facilitate health and wellbeing outcomes among remote rotational workers. At the individual level, those who had a positive attachment to work were more motivated to comply with safety regulations, and tended to report higher levels of wellbeing. Gender also played a role, with women more likely to develop social support networks during rotations, and access mental health service provisions in general. These findings are in line with findings from the wider working population. Older workers, and those who had worked for longer in a remote rotational role, tended to report more depleted wellbeing, suggesting a cumulative negative effect of rotational work over time.

Social factors were found to be important across the different occupational groups. Having an infrastructure that enabled meetings, socializing, and exercising, and being able to access a range of social activities, were seen by respondents as key facilitators to creating community and promoting health and wellbeing. Workers who felt that they had sufficient autonomy during their time off- and on-site typically reported higher levels of wellbeing.

Interestingly, for many, the transition from offshore work to family life was not characterized by rest, but by the pursuit of other activities, including childcare and home-related tasks. Unlike the evidence review, the interview data highlighted the importance of family support while being on rotation. Maintaining daily contact with family members, and making plans for family activities upon returning home, were crucial, with many employees describing the process of planning every day of their off-rotation time as a key coping mechanism.

A wide range of organizational factors were reported to positively impact on respondents' psychological health. Satisfaction with the on-shift/off-shift patterns, flexibility within the shift patterns, and compatibility with workers' lifestyles were all associated with intention to stay in the organization and with lower levels of burnout. There was evidence to suggest that a 14-day swing shift (i.e., seven night shifts followed by seven day shifts) enabled better circadian rhythm adjustment following the second week than a 14-night fixed shift. This could, in turn, provide better leisure time recovery during the off-shift period. Having job autonomy and control over decision-making was found to be particularly important for psychological health and engagement in remote rotational workers. Those who felt that they were working in a supportive culture and climate – where the organization was committed to supporting employee physical and mental health, and where pay and organizational security were rated more positively – reported lower levels of work pressure and stress, better sleep and rest, and better psychological health. Furthermore, feeling part of the company, and working for an organization that had a good induction process and training, were both negatively related to turnover intentions.

While supervisor and peer support were important, support from colleagues was considered particularly valuable. In particular, the notion of the 'back-to-back' was emphasized; as mentioned above, this term refers to the person who the remote rotational worker swaps places with when starting the on-rotation phase. A positive relationship with their back-to-back was seen by workers as a crucial resource, from both an instrumental and emotional point of view. Respondents considered a 'good' relationship to involve effective communication, clear handovers, and a well-aligned way of working between each party. Being able to depend on each other in times of difficulty was also found to be important for mental health.

Rotational work is often a male-dominated, macho environment (Shortland, 2020), where voicing mental health issues is frowned upon. Indeed, our study found that mental health stigma was highly prevalent, and a stronger predictor of distress, burnout, reduced wellbeing, and suicide risk than experiences of bullying. Interviewees described a fluctuating psychological process, where emotional 'highs' were experienced towards the end of the on-rotation and at the beginning to middle of the off-rotation, and lows in the first week(s) of returning from being off-rotation and the last week(s) of being off-rotation. Overall, there was a consensus among respondents that their employers were generally ill-equipped to support their mental wellbeing and mental health. While interviewees highlighted the increased support received during the COVID-19 pandemic, they expressed some cynicism that this was not borne out of concern for them, but due to client, economic, and global pressure.

The findings of this research were translated into practical recommendations for organizations, for managers of remote rotational workers, and for remote rotational workers themselves, to inform practice. Like the first study described above, the research was disseminated through a free-to-access report and a series of global webinars and workshops. This case study highlights the importance of two things: first, the need for multi-level interventions, comprising systemic changes to culture, policy, and practice, with initiatives targeting line managers and co-workers, and where workers themselves and their families can take specific actions to protect and promote mental health. Second, while a number of shared themes was found, the different data sources highlighted a range of barriers and facilitators. Significant gaps in our understanding would have remained had we interrogated the research question using one lens alone. These findings will help organizations employing remote rotational workers to provide targeted, more accessible support during their rotation and their 'down time'; and, in turn, ensure that they are better able to respond effectively during times of turbulence. The findings further endorse the value of adopting an evidence-based approach, to allow for the triangulation of data to inform interventions, driving deeper insights and practical recommendations.

Health and Wellbeing of Hybrid Workers

The final study explores the wellbeing outcomes and expectations of hybrid workers, specifically examining how they differ by working pattern, sector, and locality. The last three years have seen a huge proliferation in the number of employees working, some or all of the time, away from a traditional workplace; and data suggest that the trend is likely to remain for the years ahead (Microsoft, 2022). In this period, there has also been a change in employee expectations, with a far greater number now prioritizing flexibility and wellbeing over more traditional sources of motivation such as pay and performance. Examples include findings that 93 per cent of workers see physical, emotional, and mental wellbeing to be as important as pay (Deloitte & Swinburne, 2022); and 53 per cent of workers were more likely to prioritize health and wellbeing over work than before the pandemic (Microsoft, 2022). Some organizations have embraced the change with proactive moves to redesign office space and implement initiatives and programmes enabling employees to work flexibly. For others, the focus has been on returning to more traditional working practices, and for these, the issue of flexibility has resulted in a growing disconnect. The pandemic has seen already common conditions such as depression and anxiety rise by over 25 per cent in recent years (WHO, 2022), and this increase has also been experienced in the workplace. Although evidence suggests that employees and leaders are increasingly prioritizing wellbeing, only a minority have increased their budget for this key area, or have a strategy in place (Business in the Community, 2021).

The need for wellbeing support for hybrid employees is clear. Firstly, managing wellbeing risks for employees who are not visible, and are working in a range of environments (from those who work from home to working overseas, or nomadically), presents far greater challenges to organizations compared to managing those working in in-person environments. Secondly, evidence suggests that the flexibility of hybrid working that employees are increasingly requesting, in part to protect their wellbeing, may in fact be deleterious to wellbeing for some. As one example, hybrid workers may be less likely to maintain physical and psychological boundaries (Yang et al., 2023); and work demands for hybrid workers have been found to exceed those for non-hybrid workers, being associated with a 28 per cent increase in after-hours work, and a 14 per cent increase in weekend work (Microsoft, 2022). (See also the chapter by Chan and Kinman in this collection.) Finally, in a more flexible workplace, the range of working patterns that fall under 'hybrid' are many and varied, and it is likely that the needs and experiences of each worker will differ. This research is still in its infancy; and studies typically consider hybrid employees as a homogenous group, thereby reducing the ability to develop clear guidance about how best to support their wellbeing. Our research, conducted in 2022 on a global sample of employers and employees, sought to provide a bridge between the increasing disconnect between employers and employees regarding hybrid working, and bring together our understanding of the link between working patterns and wellbeing.

Our research approach involved the same four stages as the previous case studies: first, a review of reviews, synthesizing findings from six systematic reviews, 117 studies across 15 countries, and 12 research reports; and second, interviews with key stakeholders from six organizations. Third, an employee survey was developed drawing on a model developed from the data collected in stages one and two, setting out the wellbeing outcomes of hybrid workers, factors affecting those outcomes, and their perceptions and expectations of organizational support. The sample comprised 1,069 employees from 62 countries and 33 different industries/sectors, with an equal split between hybrid and non-hybrid workers. The factors that acted as barriers and facilitators to a range of outcomes were examined, and differences between demographic characteristics were investigated. Finally, findings from all data sources were synthesized.

For some, hybrid work enhances wellbeing, while for others it can be a negative experience. In our research, hybrid work was classified into seven categorizations following the Chartered Institute of Personnel and Development (2021) classification from the *Flexible Working* report. A complex pattern of outcomes of hybrid work emerged when looking across data sources. Four broad categories were identified: emotional (e.g., wellbeing and burnout), social (e.g., improved family time and invasion of space), psychosocial (e.g., health-related behaviours such as eating and drinking), and job-related outcomes (e.g., turnover, absenteeism, and career development). The picture was mixed, however, with both positive and negative findings emerging across all four outcome categories, indicating that workers experience hybrid work differently.

An examination of the barriers and facilitators aimed to elucidate why hybrid work can bring benefits for some and harm to others. Interviews with stakeholders and workers indicated that individual factors, such as addictive behaviours, being at an early career stage (where work relationships and job knowledge are not yet established), and a lack of space to work from home, were barriers to wellbeing; while those who had a capacity to manage boundaries thrived. Concerns about social isolation were also noted. Clear communication, a strong feedback culture, and trust were believed to facilitate psychological health. At the organizational level, role ambiguity, time pressure, lack of equity, and poor technology were negatively associated with the outcomes. Interviewees reported that autonomy, clarity, support, and flexibility enabled them to work effectively in a hybrid environment.

The survey findings highlighted that wellbeing continues to present a significant issue for hybrid workers: 40 per cent of the sample reported burnout, and over 60 per cent had lower levels of wellbeing than would be expected in a working population. However, the reason for such findings were not explained by working pattern, as no significant difference was found between the wellbeing of hybrid and non-hybrid workers. While this does not mean that working patterns will not have positive or negative effects for certain individuals, does not appear to be a wellbeing advantage for any specific working pattern overall. Future research needs to identify the occupational, individual difference, and behavioural and contextual factors that predict distress and wellbeing among hybrid workers, in order to inform interventions for this growing population.

Our research identified several consistencies in the experience of work and health across workers globally. Working hours were reported to be the biggest wellbeing concern for all workers, as these had the most powerful impact on outcomes, specifically job stress. For all workers, regardless of their working pattern, providing job clarity, prioritizing health and safety, ensuring fair and equitable treatment, and encouraging both colleague and manager support were key factors in enabling positive outcomes such as job satisfaction, well-being, and reduced stress. The line manager relationship, both for instrumental (such as providing resources and job clarity) and emotional support (such as being able to talk about wellbeing), appears particularly important for realizing the success of hybrid working. Overall, providing support, adequate resources, training, and development to line managers continues to be vital for both well-being and self-reported productivity in this population.

While hybrid working itself does not have universally positive effects, con-sistent with other research findings, workers who were able to choose where they work reported higher job satisfaction in general. Moreover, those who were able to work from a different country, other than that in which they were officially based, typically reported higher work engagement and productivity, and being less likely to want to leave their job. These workers were also clearer about their responsibilities, more satisfied with communication from their manager, and more likely to disclose mental health difficulties, as well as reporting higher autonomy. These findings suggest that a recent move by some organizations to increase levels of geographical flexibility for workers is likely to have a positive effect and aid employee retention, and likely to be of particular value to those organizations in sectors or locations where there are skills shortages. This also links to our finding that workers with a support network in the country where they are working see improved wellbeing, which could be facilitated through more geographical flexibility, allowing workers to move closer to their support network. In accordance with the findings of previ-ous research where voluntariness (i.e., the ability to choose one's own pattern of work) has a positive impact for employees, this finding further emphasizes the importance of choice and control as protective factors for wellbeing.

Different levels of remote working were found to have different advan-tages. Our findings showed that, while more frequent remote working helps individuals to save money, and was associated with greater autonomy, those who spend some time in the workplace, particularly at a 50/50 split, were more likely to perceive greater psychosocial support and be more likely to talk about wellbeing, thus providing additional resources both to fulfil their role and to protect their wellbeing. In our study, hybrid workers typically placed more importance on work adjustments and flexibility to support their wellbeing, followed closely by management support, suggesting that positive work prac-tices are considered more effective than other interventions in this situation. Hybrid workers were also notably less interested in training and development opportunities.

In comparing results for men and women across hybrid and non-hybrid working patterns, women without access to hybrid working were more likely to report that their working pattern cost them more money, they did not have a choice in this pattern, and they did not perceive it as fair. This finding may support the identification of inequity issues within organizations and allow for more focused tracking of engagement. The findings also show considerable differences between how senior leaders experience hybrid working and how their more junior colleagues experience it. The survey responses suggest that key differences in job satisfaction, the quality of technology available in the physical workplace, development opportunities, and satisfaction with manager support are likely to explain previous research findings suggesting that senior leaders may be more keen to return to a non-hybrid pattern of work (e.g., Microsoft, 2022), while managers and employees in their organization are more likely to see hybrid working as being preferable for the same reasons, enjoying the freedom and reduced commuting time associated with hybrid work. Acknowledging differences and increasing mutual understanding of the different positions taken by senior leaders and employees will be key to making informed decisions that suit workers in different roles within an organization.

There are considerable differences between global areas about which well-being interventions are perceived as useful by workers; yet our research found that workers are united by a common concern regarding workload and working hours. While every worker must take some responsibility for their own health and wellbeing – for example, managing their boundaries, and engaging in healthy behaviours – this research highlights the complexity of hybrid working in a global context, and has implications for practice. Firstly, by demonstrating the significant roles that job design and organizational culture have in support-ing workers to work well, there is a need for organizations to fully consider how psychosocial factors are identified and managed. Secondly, the complex and individualized impact of remote work highlights the need for organiza-tions to increase opportunities for workers to have choice over their schedules, and to support managers in providing appropriate support to hybrid workers.

The research report provided practical recommendations for organizations and for managers, and aimed to provide clarity for organizations to support them in decision-making around the duty of care and support requirements of employees. The findings, disseminated through a free-to-access report, and a suite of global webinars, conferences, and workshops, demonstrate the need for future research; and multi-level interventions that consider different working patterns, and global and generational differences. Like the two previ-ous studies outlined in this chapter, the findings have important implications for helping organizations to offer their employees control over their working patterns that will help them navigate the post-pandemic challenges.

CONCLUSION

This chapter has focused on three different samples of employees who have something in common – they are less visible to employers and managers than those who are purely on-site in the office or workplace-based, and they face specific risks to wellbeing because of the pattern of their work. The use of an evidence-based approach to wellbeing at work enabled a richer understanding of the complex, and multi-level, factors impacting on the experience of work and wellbeing of those who are working off-site or in a hybrid pattern, and revealed practical and actionable solutions to mitigate any challenges they face. All three case studies highlighted the need for a focus on preventative measures and job design, particularly around ensuring greater autonomy (whether that be on deciding duration of business trips and accommodation on trips, decision-making around shifts, or determining working hours and/or location of work), and enhancing support and social connections both inside and outside work (for instance, from organizations, managers, colleagues, and friends and family). Being 'less visible', all three groups highlighted the importance of effective organizational communications, of providing opportunities for employee voice, and of promoting value and appreciation at work. Above all, there was a recognition from the research that a systemic approach to supporting these workers was needed, with interventions at the organizational and the team level rather than merely focusing on the individual. Although presenting perhaps a more complex picture, using this methodology facilitates a more structured approach, emphasizing shared responsibility for support.

OUR CALL TO ACTION: EVIDENCE-BASED WELLBEING AT WORK AS A MODEL FOR POSITIVE CHANGE

In response to the growing concerns about 'wellbeing washing', and the need for organizations to be better equipped to manage uncertainty and turbulence, we propose that evidence-based wellbeing at work (EB WaW) be used as a model for positive change. This model proposes gathering evidence from four sources: scientific evidence (e.g., published literature), organizational evidence (e.g., survey data, facts, figures, and policies), stakeholder evidence (e.g., values and concerns of those affected by the decisions, such as workers), and professional experience; and explicitly, transparently, and critically synthesizing this evidence into targeted guidance and recommendations for employees, their managers, and organizations.

The advantages of this evidence-based approach to wellbeing at work are five-fold:

- Focusing on just one source of data, such as either academic data or organizational data, risks excluding key factors and insights which, without integration, could derail solutions and cause interventions to fail.
- Wellbeing in organizations is often 'owned' by multiple stakeholders with multiple insights and aims. Using a participative approach to data gathering ensures that all perspectives are considered, and therefore increases buy-in and the perceived relevance of findings.
- Addressing wellbeing demands an integrated and systemic approach, involving shared responsibility for change. This is hard to achieve if research and its findings have a narrow focus.
- In a world where employees and employers are time-poor, there is a need to communicate and disseminate evidence clearly and widely to shape interventions. Using a methodology which incorporates a number of voices, and which therefore appeals to multiple stakeholders, is likely to achieve this aim.
- Organizations have a financial, ethical, and moral imperative to protect and support wellbeing at work, particularly in turbulent times. Doing so will help them retain and attract high-quality talent, and maintain productivity.

To take action that makes a tangible difference to the way workers are protected and supported, practitioners need to be able to make decisions using the best available evidence. A shift to an evidence-based wellbeing at work approach will require changing the mindsets, and the building of new skill sets, for many involved in the field of wellbeing at work. However, there is promise that using an evidence-based wellbeing at work model will, as demonstrated in other disciplines such as medicine and management, increase the likelihood that we can achieve a positive change.

REFERENCES

Anlesinya, A., Dartey-Baah, K., & Amponsah-Tawiah, K. (2019). A review of empirical research on global talent management. *FIIB Business Review, 8*(2), 147–160.

Barends, E., Rousseau, D. M., & Briner, R. B. (2014). *Evidence-based management: The basic principles*. Centre for Evidence-Based Management. https://cebma.org/assets/Uploads/Evidence-Based-Practice-The-Basic-Principles.pdf

Bartik, A. W., Cullen, E. L., Glaeser, M., L., & Stanton, C. (2020). What jobs are being done at home during the COVID-19 crisis? Evidence from firm-level surveys. *NBER Working Paper* 27422. National Bureau of Economic Research.

Bjerkan, A. M. (2011). Work and health: A comparison between Norwegian onshore and offshore employees. *Work, 40*(2), 125.

Briner, R. B., Denyer, D., & Rousseau, D. M. (2009). Evidence-based management: concept cleanup time? *Academy of Management Perspectives, 23*(4), 19–32.

Business in the Community. (2021). *What if your job was good for you: A once in a life-time opportunity to transform mental health and wellbeing at work.* https://www.bitc .org.uk/report/what-if-your-job-was-good-for-you/?v=16520398

Chartered Institute of Personnel and Development. (2021). *Flexible working: Lessons from the pandemic report, April 2021.* https://www.cipd.org/globalassets/media/ knowledge/ knowledge -hub/ reports/ flexible -working -lessons -from -pandemic -report_tcm18-92644.pdf

Deloitte. (2023). Corporate transport study 2023. https://www2.deloitte.com/ us/ en/ insights/focus/transportation/corporate-travel-study-2023.html

Deloitte & Swinburne (2022). *Reset, restore, reframe – Making fair work FlexWork.* https:// www .deloitte .com/ au/ en/ services/ risk -advisory/ perspectives/ making -fair -work-flexwork.html

Donald, I., Taylor, P., Johnson, S., Cooper, C., Cartwright, S., & Robertson, S. (2005). Work environments, stress and productivity: An examination using ASSET. *International Journal of Stress Management, 12*, 409–423.

Galanti, T., Guidetti, G., Mazzei, E., Zappalà, S., & Toscano, F. (2021). Work from home during the COVID-19 outbreak: The impact on employees' remote work productivity, engagement, and stress. *Journal of Occupational and Environmental Medicine, 63*(7), e426.

Global Business Travel Association Foundation. (2015). *Business travel spending to rise nearly 5% in 2015, but "erratic" economic drivers limit growth.* PR Newswire. https:// www .prnewswire .com/ news -releases/ business -travel -spending -to -rise -nearly -5 -percent -in -2015 -but -erratic -economic -drivers -limit -growth -300109491 .html

Kano, L., Tsang, E. W., & Yeung, H. W. C. (2020). Global value chains: A review of the multi-disciplinary literature. *Journal of International Business Studies, 51*, 577–622.

Masic, I., Miokovic, M., & Muhamedagic, B. (2008). Evidence based medicine-new approaches and challenges. *Acta informatica medica: AIM: Journal of the Society for Medical Informatics of Bosnia & Herzegovina: casopis Drustva za medicinsku informatiku BiH, 16*(4), 219–225.

Microsoft. (2022). *2022 Work trend index: Annual report – Great expectations: Making hybrid work.* https://ms-worklab.azureedge.net/files/reports/2022/pdf/2022 _Work_Trend_Index_Annual_Report.pdf

Parker, S. K., Fruhen, L., Burton, C., McQuade, S., Loveny, J., Griffin, M., & Esmond, J. (2018). *Impact of FIFO work arrangements on the mental health and wellbeing of FIFO workers.* Australia: University of Western Australia.

Reiche, B. S., Lee, Y. T., & Allen, D. G. (2019). Actors, structure, and processes: A review and conceptualization of global work integrating IB and HRM research. *Journal of Management, 45*(2), 359–383.

Rundle, A. G., Revenson, T. A., & Friedman, M. (2017). Business travel and behavioural and mental health. *Journal of Occupational and Environmental Medicine, 60*(7), 612–616.

Savić, D. (2020). COVID-19 and work from home: Digital transformation of the workforce. *Grey Journal (TGJ), 16*(2), 101–104.

Shortland, S. (2020). International rotational assignments: Women's challenge to occupational gender segregation. *Career Development International, 25*(7), 693–714.

Statista. (2022). *Global business travel - statistics & facts*. https://www.statista.com/topics/2439/global-business-travel-industry/#topicOverview

Willis, C., Ladkin, A., Jain, J., & Clayton, W. (2017). Present while absent: Home and business tourist gaze. *Annals of Tourism Research*, 6348–6359.

World Health Organization. (2022). *Guidelines for mental health at work*.

Xiao, J., Huang, B., Shen, H., Liu, X., Zhang, J., Zhong, Y., Wu, C., Hua, T., & Gao, Y. (2017). Association between social support and health-related quality of life among Chinese seafarers: A cross-sectional study. *PLOS One*, *12*(11), e0187275.

Yang, E., Kim, Y., & Hong, S. (2023). Does working from home work? Experience of working from home and the value of hybrid workplace post-COVID-19. *Journal of Corporate Real Estate*, *25*(1), 50–76. https://doi.org/10.1108/JCRE-04-2021-0015

12. Work structures, work cultures and wellbeing in turbulent times

Ida Bagus Gede Adi Permana, Sudong Shang, and Peter J. Jordan

INTRODUCTION

The recent COVID-19 epidemic had a wide-ranging impact, but many argue that the turbulence it created has been experienced before. The Spanish flu (Bishop, 2020), world wars (Drucker, 2012), global depression (Amaral & MacGee, 2002), and financial crises (Helleiner, 2011) have all been disruptive and generated unrest and conflict. While the social turbulence caused by such events has undoubtedly been dramatic, the recent pandemic has arguably created an unprecedented degree of change to work practices and employees' experiences of the workplace, profoundly influencing work structures and culture. Specifically, change during the pandemic has been associated with dramatic and short-term structural decisions that were required to maintain outputs, in a work environment where businesses are more integrated in terms of work processes and reliant on international supply chains (Carroll & Conboy, 2020). Change in this context has been influenced by advances in technology (Carroll & Conboy, 2020), changing personal expectations about the quality of work and life (Adisa et al., 2022), and emerging views on work–life balance (Ninaus et al., 2021; Shirmohammadi et al., 2022), resulting in significant and ongoing transformation to the workplace.

To accommodate this transformation, both managers and employees have been, and are still, engaged in a process of adjusting and adapting work practices (Caringal-Go et al., 2022; Cascio, 2000). For example, employees are increasingly adjusting their work habits and routines to accommodate the transition from in-person to virtual work settings (Sander et al., 2021). Additionally, the pandemic offered many workers increased autonomy, which then increased their responsibility and accountability for their work productivity (Pass & Ridgway, 2022). This recent shift in work structure and culture observed in numerous work environments has highlighted another pertinent issue: the potential negative implications of these changes in relation to well-being for both employees and managers (Faupel & Süß, 2019).

In this chapter, we review the common ways in which organizations have responded to turbulence through reforming work structures and culture, and we consider the subsequent impact of these reforms on the wellbeing of employees and managers. By conducting this review, we aim to gain deeper insights into how organizations foster their adaptive capacity to transform their work structures and cultures, with the aim of ultimately sustaining their performance and simultaneously protecting or enhancing employee wellbeing.

The recent pandemic resulted in rapid changes to work structure and culture to address the challenges that the crisis precipitated (Stephens et al., 2020). Many of these changes had a direct impact on the division of labor, division of authority, grouping of units, and coordination, which are all components of organizational structure (Mintzberg, 1980). The time-sensitive nature of the change that organizations embarked upon during this crisis (as there was a major threat to physical health) meant that little time was allowed for considering the human consequences of these changes, particularly in relation to the impact on work culture and employee wellbeing. Technological changes, such as remote access to work communication networks, occurred almost immediately, as they were essential for task performance (Ninaus et al., 2021). What was not considered were the challenges that would emerge for some employees around the lack of boundaries between their work and home domains (Chan et al., 2023). As a result, the widespread adoption of remote work following the pandemic has had an unintended significant impact on employee engagement and communication (Soga et al., 2022; Venkatesan, 2021). The hybrid work models, where employees could work a combination of days in the office and days remotely, increased work location flexibility, but sometimes at a human cost. For instance, Galanti et al. (2021) found that moving to remote work reduced both employees' wellbeing and productivity, particularly for those with less work experience. Jackman et al. (2022) argue that the initial reduction in wellbeing and productivity was reversed once employees adjusted to the new working contexts and patterns. Given these mixed findings, considering changes to the ways in which we work, and the structure of work itself, is important for understanding employees' experiences of work, and in particular the potential for the work culture to change with those experiences.

Extensive research on work culture indicates that it typically evolves slowly over time and is often resistant to change (Cameron & Quinn, 2011). Organizational culture is defined as a set of common beliefs, values, conventions, and attitudes that form organizational members' mental schema (Alvesson, 2002; Smircich, 1983). Researchers argue that organizational culture shapes how members perceive and understand their surroundings, as well as how they behave within them (Frontiera, 2010). While there is a broad assumption that employees' behaviors and work practices emerge from organizational assumptions, beliefs, and values (Schein, 1983), there is also an argument that changes to the artifacts of an organization, such as the way in which work is structured, may actually influence the experienced or practiced (as opposed to the espoused or publicly stated) culture of an organization (Jacobides, 2007; Warrick, 2017). This has been evidenced during the COVID-19 pandemic, where rapid adjustments in work structure are beginning to catalyze shifts in work culture. Gaining insight into how changes to work structure may precipitate cultural change is important, because it provides a valuable approach to assessing and understanding employees' experiences in a turbulent environment, and how these might affect their wellbeing and productivity.

The COVID-19 pandemic has significantly highlighted the issue of employee wellbeing in response to the stress created by the crisis (Chan et al., 2023). Research has revealed that the ongoing changes in work structure and culture have led to additional stress (beyond the effects of the pandemic) among both employees and managers (Carnevale & Hatak 2020). While limited attention has been paid to how structural changes might impact employees' performance, prospects, and overall presence within the organization, the impact of structure on wellbeing is clearly a phenomenon worthy of a deeper examination. A good place to start this journey is to understand the impact of turbulence on work structures.

TURBULENCE AND WORK STRUCTURE

Reviewing the literature on work structure reveals the multi-faceted nature of this construct. Taken literally, work structure can be examined at an organizational level in terms of the levels and arms of the organization that complete tasks (Mintzberg, 1980), typically discussed as departmentation and span of control. *Departmentation* refers to how an organization organizes its jobs to coordinate work (Yousaf et al., 2021), while the term *span of control* describes the number of people who report to a manager (Jensen et al., 2023). Changes to organizations that have experienced turbulence can impact on both departmentation (as service delivery and lines of coordination change to adapt to the turbulence) and span of control (e.g., as the removal of restrictions on co-location as a framework for supervision results in the span of control being wider for managers, as they expand their responsibilities to include additional remote workers). Changes to each of these factors can cause disruption in a workplace (Delfino et al., 2021).

At a micro level, work structure is reflected in work design and reporting, and working relationships including delegation (e.g., Hackman & Oldham, 1980). Work/job design refers to the structure and method by which tasks are completed by individuals, focusing on the core work activities that individuals carry out as part of their daily contributions to the organization (Oldham & Fried, 2016; Truxillo et al., 2012). In terms of working relationships, delegation involves granting authority to different individuals (typically from a superior to a subordinate) for the execution of specific tasks (Xiong Chen & Aryee, 2007). Again, in turbulent times, both work design and delegation can be changed to allow for adaptation. For instance, specialized jobs may be broadened to design tasks that require less interpersonal coordination (e.g., making individuals responsible for an entire process to complete a task). Similarly, more delegation may be required during turbulence to allow decision-making to be expedited (Al-Dabbagh, 2020). All these aspects of structure can be impacted in response to a crisis. Given the above, compared to the macro-level factors, the micro-level factors are more directly related to employees' work experiences, and hence are the focus of this review.

From a historical perspective, the earliest roots of job design theory are associated with scientific management and Taylorism, emphasizing efficiency through approaches like time and motion studies, along with the use of 'piecework' for motivation (Barley & Kunda, 1992). Historically, the understanding of job design was promoted by the turbulence stemming from the broad adoption of Fordism (mass production of goods in the early 20th century; Pruijt, 1997). Subsequently, attention in work design shifted to exploring productivity concerns, with research investigating the impacts of improving environmental and social conditions on employees' motivation, satisfaction, comfort, and productivity (Oldham & Fried, 2016; Sander et al., 2019). Again, the research on work design was promoted by the turbulence created by the notion of 'welfare capitalism', a new focus on workers in the economy at the time of the Hawthorne studies (Hassard, 2012). In more recent studies focusing on work structure, the emphasis has turned towards approaches such as job enlargement and enrichment, to enhance employees' levels of motivation and satisfaction (Winkelhaus et al., 2022). Additionally, researchers have examined specific task attributes to understand their influence on work perceptions and behavior (Afsar & Umrani, 2020).

In response to a new focus on employee wellbeing, and a recognition of the importance of meaningful work, Hackman and Oldham (1980) developed a comprehensive theory of job design, the Job Characteristics Model (JCM). According to the JCM, jobs incorporate a combination of multiple tasks, autonomy, feedback, importance, and identity that can have a direct effect on work motivation, job satisfaction, overall performance, responsibility, and knowledge of outcomes (Hackman & Oldham, 1980). A crucial aspect of job design is fostering interactions among organizational members to receive feedback from peers and create opportunities for camaraderie (Rush, 2022), which places a strong emphasis on the quality of working relationships in the workplace (Kurland & Bailey, 1999; Rush, 2022). Certainly, for organizations operating in turbulent times, there is a need for effective communication and feedback, which, as Zhong et al. (2023) noted, are essential mechanisms that allow society and organizations to move forward during a crisis. As job design decisions are introduced to adapt to new demands, a key issue is ensuring communication and feedback processes are developed to allow employees to understand the new work environment, and enable them to maintain performance under the new structures.

COVID-19 AND WORK STRUCTURES

The COVID-19 pandemic has led to a heightened dependence on information and communication technology (ICT) for both job-related tasks and overall organizational performance (Chan et al., 2023). Work structures have been influenced by the enhanced use of new and evolving technology (for instance, improvements in video conferencing) in response to the COVID-19 pandemic (Ninaus et al., 2021). As a result, the structures that organizations relied on to complete work have, in many cases, become more technical (Chan et al., 2023) and, therefore, less personal. Meetings, which were a prime source of information-sharing and decision-making in organizations, are now often facilitated virtually using video conferencing tools (Sander & Bauman, 2020). Pataki-Bittó and Kapusy (2021) noted that the use of tools like Zoom and Microsoft Teams skyrocketed during the pandemic, allowing employees to conduct virtual meetings and collaborative sessions, and facilitating the practices of remote work and working from home (e.g., Chan et al., 2023). The debate over the relative efficacy of face-to-face meetings and virtual meetings in relation to information-sharing and decision-making is unresolved, with research exploring the impact on employees of online fatigue (Shockley et al., 2021), poor meeting etiquette, and gender discrimination (Gupta, 2020), which can have negative implications for employee wellbeing. As a response to the pandemic, these technologies were essential; but, in turn, they were also found to generate job stress (Arias-Pérez & Vélez-Jaramillo, 2022) across a range of organizations, including sales (Ojha et al., 2021), manufacturing (Puriwat & Hoonsopon, 2022), and high-technology firms (Wang et al., 2021), due to their rapid development and deployment.

One evident concern during the crisis was the merging of work and personal spaces due to the widespread implementation of remote work. Although this process was found to have a direct impact on reducing work–family conflict in some cases (Schieman et al., 2021), in other cases it was mixed in outcomes, increasing and decreasing work–family conflict (Vaziri et al., 2020). It could also have a negative impact on the dynamics of employee relationships (Contreras et al., 2020). Research indicates that for some workers, remote work can be associated with a sense of isolation and reduced social interactions among employees, which can have a negative impact on teamwork and collaboration (Pyöriä, 2011). However, it is important to note that the extent of these effects can vary depending on an individual's occupation and specific job, and the nature of the organization. For instance, employees who have opportunities to provide and obtain support from colleagues may experience less isolation, which in turn can facilitate team collaboration as they are more likely to reach out to share ideas (Carnevale & Hatak, 2020).

From an organizational standpoint, remote work can also negatively affect the process of employees learning about new tasks or addressing novel challenges within the organization, due to the lack of direct interaction and collaboration with colleagues (Pianese et al., 2023; Waight et al., 2022). Consequently, both employees and organizations encountered challenges in adapting to new work structures, with a subsequent impact on employee interaction and collaboration in a remote work environment. As noted earlier, however, this relationship can be ameliorated by organizational support from colleagues and supervisors.

In terms of the way in which tasks are structured and work is designed, Gajendran and Harrison (2007) noted that remote work could be optimized for employees who are better able to understand information technology, and who are self-organizing. So, although the COVID-19 pandemic created conditions that may have been stressful for some employees, for others this turbulence offered opportunities for engaging in work structures that better suited their skills and abilities. In terms of work design, it appears that autonomy becomes an important element for the new structure of work, and can enable employees who are confident in their ability to use ICT to thrive in the turbulence, coping better with isolation and the issues that remote communication engenders. That said, research also suggests that some employees feel less confident in their ability and willingness to perform at the same level when working remotely, compared to what they could achieve if they worked in the same location as their manager (Kaplan et al., 2018). Jentjens and Cherbib (2023) confirm this effect post-pandemic, and ascribe it to changes in trust of managers which then impacts on the self-efficacy of employees.

Since the height of the pandemic, work structure has been in the process of transitioning into a hybrid model that, for many, combines remote and on-site work. As a result, the frequency and format of communication in reporting relationships, both between managers and employees and among employees, has changed. According to Verma et al. (2023), the emergence of the hybrid workplace is a response to evolving employee expectations and needs that became more prominent during the COVID-19 pandemic. Many companies have implemented a permanent hybrid work approach, offering employees the flexibility to choose between remote work and office attendance, accommodating diverse work preferences and providing a balance between remote and face-to-face interactions (Gratton, 2021). Consequently, many organizations are reconfiguring office spaces to align with this hybrid model of work (Surma et al., 2021). This involves emphasizing collaborative working spaces which enable employees to engage in meaningful discussions and interactions. The evolution of work structure, from traditional offices to the rapid adoption of remote work, followed by the emergence of hybrid work models throughout the stages of the pandemic, highlight organizational adaptability and the evolving expectations of employees. Indeed, we suggest that meeting these expectations may contribute to organizations retaining talent (Maylett & Wride, 2017).

Although turbulence of the type generated by the COVID-19 pandemic had a direct effect on work structures, as we noted earlier, there can be a concomitant effect on work culture. In the next section, we examine the overall impact of turbulence on work cultures.

TURBULENCE AND WORK CULTURE

As noted earlier, *culture* is a widely employed term used to depict the characteristics of a given context, such as national cultures, social cultures, and workplace cultures (Geertz, 1973). In relation to workplace culture, Schein (1983) contends that this manifests as three aspects: beliefs or underlying assumptions, espoused values, and artifacts (actual behaviors and physical manifestations). The key here is that these views imply a unified culture throughout an organization. Other research, however, argues that a homogenous work culture does not exist, and that cultures can give rise to subcultures – for example, the occurrence of different work cultures at different work sites (Van Mannen, 1992). Indeed, amid the COVID-19 pandemic and its aftermath, the overall cultural coherence within an organization is likely to have undergone a degree of dilution due to the adoption of remote work arrangements. This separation of employees into two distinct groups – workers able to work mostly from home as a dominant work pattern, and those who could not (e.g., frontline workers) – may potentially foster the emergence of two distinct subcultures within the organization (Chan et al., 2023).

Culture reveals the basic assumptions that an organization adopts, to make sense of and to resolve contextual issues through external adaptation. It becomes apparent in organizational artifacts, and through internal integration can emerge as values and assumptions (Schein, 2010). Schein (2010) noted that culture is a sense-making vehicle to allow employees to understand themselves as part of the organization. While changes in culture at the deeper levels of values and assumptions are difficult to modify (Spicer, 2020), culture as norms and behavioral artifacts occurs at the surface level and can, therefore, change relatively easily. Within this literature there is a broad assumption that values and assumptions drive the artifacts of an organization.

During turbulence, however, we note that work structure is likely to change employees' work practices and experiences, which subsequently may drive the change of work culture. This is classically seen in the notion of *unwritten ground rules*. Simpson (2004) argued that a company's values are driven by the behaviors and activities of its employees, which he refers to as unwritten ground rules, which can be contrasted with espoused or stated culture. In this context, Dellaportas et al. (2007) described how the practices of a major bank changed its culture from a conservative profit-driven entity to an institution that supported a culture that valued high risk. This change was created in part by the turbulence generated by internal, national, and international competition for increasing profits. Schoemaker and Day (2021) argue that an openness to cultural change is vital for organizations experiencing turbulence, whether it be from challenges from competitors, changes to market conditions, or innovations in the field. It should be acknowledged that when organizations face turbulence, culture itself does not drive behaviors and structures. Responses to contextual events (e.g., the pandemic) can drive changes in structures (and associated employee behaviors) that require cultural change for these responses to be successful.

COVID-19 AND WORK CULTURE

The COVID-19 pandemic has transformed work culture across a range of organizations, particularly in relation to employees' work processes, individual work expectations, and norms in the workplace. Regarding the changes to work structure, many individuals within the work environment have altered ingrained routines encompassing everyday behaviors and decisions, to maintain their productivity during this event. Specifically, employees have altered their communication methods and choices, with an increasing reliance on digital technologies and platforms (sometimes against personal preferences for face-to-face interactions) to complete tasks remotely (Verma et al., 2023). Similarly, in many organizations, paperwork and managerial approval for activities have been minimized to enable employees to be more autonomous (Grant & Ashford, 2008). The increased utilization of ICT has enabled workers to perform their tasks, communicate, and collaborate with others more effectively, and accordingly become more autonomous. At the same time, ICT has created additional challenges, such as technical problems, cyber threats, reduced opportunities for social interaction and feedback, and blurred work–life boundaries (Waizeneggera et al., 2020). Clearly, if an organization's values are more accurately reflected in its practices, rather than in broad statements about those values, changes to such practices are likely to impact on its culture.

Indeed, as noted earlier, the autonomy that some individuals experience in working from home away from direct managerial supervision may engender a culture based on initiative, autonomous decision-making, and managerial trust, rather than on risk management and frequent checking of decisions, which may be more likely to occur in a face-to-face office environment.

Francisco (2007) noted that 'the way we do things around here' is a clear manifestation of the culture of an organization. In developing his argument, Francisco discusses emergent cultures as those that develop based on the common practices and normative behaviors of an entity. In essence, major changes of organizational artifacts (such as changes to organizational structures), and new ways in which individuals behave, force organizations to readjust their experienced culture to fit the new environmental realities (Verma et al., 2023). Indeed, this may cause a dissonance between the espoused culture and the practiced culture of an organization. For instance, during the pandemic, some organizations that espoused family and people-focused values as a part of their culture also engaged in retrenching and outsourcing jobs, thus changing the structure of the organization (Tu et al., 2021), and suggesting a different actual culture in practice.

The pandemic also changed the expectations and norms regarding work outcomes and processes, forcing workers to cope with changing demands, increasing uncertainty, and ambiguity (Venkatesan, 2021). In response, many employees have been reported to show more self-regulation, initiative, creativity, resilience, trust, empathy, and support in their work (Triest & Williams, 2024). These changes have required employees to adopt a more flexible and adaptive mindset towards their work, by acquiring new skills and competencies (Surma et al., 2021). Furthermore, there is evidence that the pandemic has influenced employees' perspectives of their work (Spicer, 2020), for many necessitating a reconsideration of their motivations, desires, and satisfaction in relation to their jobs. Additionally, many employees who work remotely, or who engage in a hybrid work pattern, have had to redefine their roles in both their work and personal life domains, requiring greater efforts to balance work with health, family, community, and leisure (Shirmohammadi et al., 2022) in response to changing work structures. These cognitive adjustments impact work-related decisions and actions, encompassing engagement levels, tenure within organizations, job changes, and career planning (Pataki-Bittó & Kapusy, 2021). Changes to these artifacts of organizations are an indication of a changing culture which is underpinned by values that prioritize individual decision-making, autonomy, and responsibility.

WELLBEING, WORK STRUCTURES AND CULTURES

While changes in structures are often determined by organizations as operational decisions to maintain productivity during crises or in the face of turbulence (Sahut & Lissillour, 2023), this does not imply that wellbeing is not an important issue for organizations. Wellbeing is an individual self-perception regarding affective states, and constructive sentiments and emotions such as job/life satisfaction or self-realization (Loon et al., 2019). The impact of employee wellbeing on organizational performance, and being a preferred employer, is significant (Huettermann & Bruch, 2019). Despite this finding, operational decisions often fail to consider the wide-ranging impact of their structural decisions on employees and their wellbeing, and the unintended consequences that can arise.

The nature of social and economic turbulence is to create stress, based on the uncertainty associated with the turbulence (Weinberg & Cooper, 2011). Change, and in particular work structural change and the uncertainty this can generate, is a major source of stress (Stranks, 2005). Research that examines employees' reactions to changes in the way in which work is structured reveals that they tend to engage in more impersonal and hostile communication and be less empathic towards their team members, which can increase stress experiences (Chai & Park, 2022; Derks et al., 2016). On this basis, acknowledging the cumulative nature of stress (Evans et al., 2012), we argue that the stress caused by organizational decision-making, particularly in relation to changing structures, may be exacerbated in turbulent times, and have a negative impact on employee wellbeing.

These types of operational decisions, however, while necessary for the survival of organizations, also need to consider the sustainability of employees. Structural change may be necessary, but the way in which these changes are made, and the ongoing ways in which the new structure is managed, directly influences workers' wellbeing. We argue that the interaction of structure and culture can have a significant effect on the wellbeing of employees. Boxall and Macky (2014) noted that work processes that encourage high involvement and engagement are linked to positive employee wellbeing. Unfortunately, many of the structural decisions made during turbulent times require quick decisions which often do not allow for employees' involvement or engagement in the change process. While changes in structure may threaten employee wellbeing, a culture that focuses simultaneously on employee motivation and on employee experiences of change can help enhance organizational wellbeing, even during turbulent times (Johnston et al., 2020).

Research suggests that many employees found it difficult to adapt to new ways of working during the COVID-19 pandemic (Carnevale & Hatak, 2020).

Bordia et al. (2004) described these types of challenges as a specific type of organizational transformation. Change and turbulence exposes organizations to ambiguity, uncertainty, and operational challenges (Bordia et al., 2004). Uncertainty is a subjective experience of being unable to accurately anticipate anything, and it is commonly felt throughout organizational transition (Rafferty & Griffin, 2006). It can be exacerbated when linked to societal uncertainty related to financial and economic pressures and serious threats to health (Lu & Lin, 2021). Uncertainty may lead to emotional discomfort, anxiety, and stress, all of which may impair coping and wellbeing (Ashford, 1988). Additionally, market changes or financial restrictions introduce uncertainty by impacting an organization's stability and capacity to make strategic decisions (DesJardine et al., 2019). During these times, employees may also be concerned about their job security and financial stability (Montani & Stagliano, 2022), which are additional sources of stress.

CONCLUSION

The recent pandemic has provided valuable information about how turbulence in society and business can impact on employees' experience of work. During the pandemic, many organizations were forced to change the way they organized their work. Moreover, organizations were frequently obliged to redesign their work structures to accommodate the introduction of remote work, which allowed them to maintain business operations and their competitiveness during the crisis (Sahut & Lissillour, 2023). What was not expected was that, after the immediate crisis was over, many of the structural changes adopted by organizations have become embedded as standard procedures. For many workers, working from home provided the autonomy to be more flexible in completing their work, and helped them improve their work–life balance, with further benefits from reductions in the time and cost of commuting (Angelici & Profeta, in press; Russell et al., 2009). From an organizational viewpoint, structural change addressed the initial challenges of maintaining productivity and performance during the crisis. New knowledge drawn from implementing these changes resulted in a realization that working from home allows productivity to be maintained, while offering reduced capital infrastructure costs and operational costs (Brough & O'Driscoll, 2010; Kinman et al., 2020). These changes could not be achieved without the appropriate structural decisions to support them. What was not considered, however, was the subsequent long-term impact for workers' wellbeing. That said, we note this is gradually being acknowledged by many organizations, and attention is now being paid to providing organizational and co-worker support to enable employees to work remotely in a healthy, sustainable, and productive way.

The evidence we have offered so far suggests that new or innovative organizational structures do not automatically emerge in turbulence. Rather, organizations use well-known ways of structuring to respond flexibly to the context. At the core of these decisions is the operational stability and continuing operations of businesses. However, these decisions can have a direct impact on the wellbeing of employees.

Connection is a basic human need that influences work dynamics (Strom & Mills, 2021), and it can be disrupted during turbulent events. Work can be performed online (Waizeneggera et al., 2020), or through virtual meetings (Sander & Bauman, 2020), but research suggests this is not fully equivalent to in-person contact (Duffy & McEuen, 2010). While some remote workers prefer solitude (Smith et al., 2003), others may experience isolation and be at a higher risk of experiencing mental health issues (Morgan et al., 2020). For instance, extroverted workers can suffer from a lack of co-worker interactions, and be at greater risk of experiencing burnout and poorer wellbeing (Maslach et al., 2001). This may be exacerbated depending on the type of work done, and other workplace psychosocial hazards that they might experience (Wray & Kinman, 2022). On the other hand, some structural changes are likely to improve employee wellbeing by, for example, providing a more flexible workplace that does not automatically start and finish the working day with stressful commutes to and from work (Rissel et al., 2014).

Changed work structures that arise during turbulent periods will likely favor certain individuals while putting others at a disadvantage. Research has shown that changes to work structures, such as the surge in remote work during the pandemic (Baumann & Sander, 2021, noting an increase from 8 percent to 35 percent of the US workforce), may have adverse implications for employee wellbeing (Charalampous et al., 2019). Structural change, however, is not a simple temporary response by organizations with a return to the previous structure at the end of the crisis. For example, Galanti et al. (2021) anticipated the possibility of a continued rise in remote work post-pandemic after the cost-benefits of this structure were assessed. Should some of these changes to work structure persist, or become further optimized (Sahut & Lissillour, 2023), the organization should actively oversee these changes to safeguard employee wellbeing.

This could be achieved, for example, with a multi-level strategy which involves establishing a culture that supports this type of work, and by individuals being encouraged to develop appropriate coping skills required to work successfully under the new structure. For instance, at the individual level, remote workers may lack the skills or training to use ICT effectively, to manage boundaries between work and personal life, and to manage their time efficiently when the workplace is also the home (Golden & Veiga, 2008); these are all factors which can be addressed through organizational training and support. Employees working remotely may also communicate less effectively and empathically with their team members, which can place them at a higher risk of experiencing stress and mental ill-health (Chai & Park, 2022; Derks et al., 2016). Therefore, it is essential to provide appropriate guidance for communication and support between workers. At the organizational level, to cope with these structural changes, organizations need to develop a supportive environment for employees that promotes psychological and physical wellbeing, based on research evidence. This approach can help employees to mitigate some of the potentially adverse impacts of remote work such as reduced wellbeing, limited learning opportunities, and diluted organizational culture (Kulik, 2021).

The adoption of a culture which helps to maximize employee engagement and organizational performance (Pataki-Bittó & Kapusy, 2021) can result in a better employee experience during change. A culture which encourages managers to consider the quality of the work experience during such times, by evaluating employee attitudes, feelings, and behaviors towards work, organization, and technology, enables a more holistic focus on wellbeing. This, in turn, will help managers engage employees in co-designing flexible work environments (Surma et al., 2021), with the structures to respond to turbulent times in the future.

REFERENCES

Adisa, T. A., Antonacopoulou, E., Beauregard, T. A., Dickmann, M., & Adekoya, O. D. (2022). Exploring the impact of COVID-19 on employees' boundary management and work–life balance. *British Journal of Management, 33*(4), 1694–1709. https://doi.org/10.1111/1467-8551.12643

Afsar, B., & Umrani, W. A. (2020). Transformational leadership and innovative work behavior: The role of motivation to learn, task complexity and innovation climate. *European Journal of Innovation Management, 23*(3), 402–428. https://doi.org/10.1108/EJIM-12-2018-0257

Al-Dabbagh, Z. S. (2020). The role of decision-maker in crisis management: A qualitative study using grounded theory (COVID-19 pandemic crisis as a model). *Journal of Public Affairs, 20*(4), e2186. https://doi.org/10.1002/pa.2186

Alvesson, M. (2002). *Understanding organizational culture*. SAGE.

Amaral, P. S., & MacGee, J. C. (2002). The Great Depression in Canada and the United States: A neoclassical perspective. *Review of Economic Dynamics, 5*, 45–72. https://doi.org/10.1006/redy.2001.0141

Angelici, M., & Profeta, P. (in press). Smart working: Work flexibility without constraints. *Management Science*. https://doi.org/10.1287/mnsc.2023.4767

Arias-Pérez, J., & Vélez-Jaramillo, J. (2022). Understanding knowledge hiding under technological turbulence caused by artificial intelligence and robotics. *Journal of Knowledge Management, 26*(6), 1476–1491. https://doi.org/10.1108/JKM-01-2021-0058

Ashford, S. J. (1988). Individual strategies for coping with stress during organizational transitions. *Journal of Applied Behavioral Science, 24*(1), 19–36. https://doi.org/10.1177/0021886388241005

Barley, S. R., & Kunda, G. (1992). Design and devotion: Surges of rational and normative ideologies of control in managerial discourse. *Administrative Science Quarterly, 37*(3), 363–399. https://doi.org/10.2307/2393449

Baumann, O., & Sander, E. J. (2021). Psychological impacts of remote working under social distancing restrictions. In D. Wheatley, I. Hardill, & S. Buglass (Eds.), *Handbook of research on remote work and worker well-being in the post-COVID-19 era* (pp. 1–17). IGI Global. https://doi.org/10.4018/978-1-7998-67548.ch001

Bishop, J. (2020, June 18). Economic effects of the Spanish flu. *The Bulletin.* https://www.rba.gov.au/publications/bulletin/2020/jun/economic-effects-of-the-spanish-flu.html

Bordia, P., Hunt, E., Paulsen, N., Tourish, D., & DiFonzo, N. (2004). Uncertainty during organizational change: Is it all about control? *European Journal of Work and Organizational Psychology, 13*(3), 345–365. https://doi.org/10.1080/13594320444000128

Boxall, P., & Macky, K. (2014). High-involvement work processes, work intensification and employee well-being. *Work, Employment and Society, 28*(6), 963–984. https://doi.org/10.1177/0950017013512714

Brough, P., & O'Driscoll, M. P. (2010). Organizational interventions for balancing work and home demands: An overview. *Work & Stress, 24*(3), 280–297. https://doi.org/10.1080/02678373.2010.506808

Cameron, K. S., & Quinn, R. E. (2011). *Diagnosing and changing organizational culture: Based on the competing values framework* (3rd ed.). Jossey-Bass.

Caringal-Go, J. F., Teng-Calleja, M., Bertulfo, D. J., & Manaois, J. O. (2022). Work-life balance crafting during COVID-19: Exploring strategies of telecommuting employees in the Philippines. *Community, Work & Family, 25*(1), 112–131. https://doi.org/10.1080/13668803.2021.1956880

Carnevale, J. B., & Hatak, I. (2020). Employee adjustment and well-being in the era of COVID-19: Implications for human resource management. *Journal of Business Research, 116*, 183–187. https://doi.org/10.1016/j.jbusres.2020.05.037

Carroll, N., & Conboy, K. (2020). Normalising the "new normal": Changing tech-driven work practices under pandemic time pressure. *International Journal of Information Management, 55*, 102186. https://doi.org/10.1016/j.ijinfomgt.2020.102186

Cascio, W. F. (2000). Managing a virtual workplace. *Academy of Management Perspectives, 14*(3), 81–90. https://doi.org/10.5465/ame.2000.4468068

Chai, D. S., & Park, S. (2022). The increased use of virtual teams during the COVID-19 pandemic: Implications for psychological well-being. *Human Resource Development International, 25*(2), 199–218. https://doi.org/10.1080/13678868.2022.2047250

Chan, X. W., Shang, S., Brough, P., Wilkinson, A., & Lu, C. Q. (2023). Work, life and COVID-19: A rapid review and practical recommendations for the post-pandemic workplace. *Asia Pacific Journal of Human Resources, 61*(2), 257–276. https://doi.org/10.1111/1744-7941.12355

Charalampous, M., Grant, C. A., Tramontano, C., & Michailidis, E. (2019). Systematically reviewing remote e-workers' well-being at work: A multidimensional approach. *European Journal of Work and Organizational Psychology, 28*(1), 51–73. https://doi.org/10.1080/1359432X.2018.1541886

Contreras, F., Baykal, E., & Abid, G. (2020). E-leadership and teleworking in times of COVID-19 and beyond: What we know and where do we go. *Frontiers in Psychology*, *11*, 590271. https://doi.org/10.3389/fpsyg.2020.590271

Delfino, G. F., & Van Der Kolk, B. (2021). Remote working, management control changes and employee responses during the COVID-19 crisis. *Accounting, Auditing & Accountability Journal*, *34*(6), 1376–1387. https://doi.org/10.1108/AAAJ-06-2020-4657

Dellaportas, S., Cooper, B. J., & Braica, P. (2007). Leadership, culture and employee deceit: The case of the National Australia Bank. *Corporate Governance: An International Review*, *15*(6), 1442–1452. https://doi.org/10.1111/j.1467-8683.2007.00597.x

Derks, D., Bakker, A. B., Peters, P., & Van Wingerden, P. (2016). Work-related smartphone use, work-family conflict and family role performance: The role of segmentation preference. *Human Relations*, *69*(5), 1045–1068. https://doi.org/10.1177/0018726715601890

DesJardine, M., Bansal, P., & Yang, Y. (2019). Bouncing back: Building resilience through social and environmental practices in the context of the 2008 global financial crisis. *Journal of Management*, *45*(4), 1434–1460. https://doi.org/10.1177/0149206317708854

Drucker, P. (2012). *Managing in turbulent times*. Routledge.

Duffy, C., & McEuen, M. B. (2010). *The future of meetings: The case for face-to-face*. Cornell Hospitality Industry Perspectives. https://ecommons.cornell.edu/server/api/core/bitstreams/e7d8cab3-fe84-4991-972a-658b1ba0b9c9/content

Evans, G. W., Becker, F. D., Zahn, A., Bilotta, E., & Keesee, A. M. (2012). Capturing the ecology of workplace stress with cumulative risk assessment. *Environment and Behavior*, *44*(1), 136–154. https://doi.org/10.1177/0013916510389981

Faupel, S., & Süß, S. (2019). The effect of transformational leadership on employees during organizational change: An empirical analysis. *Journal of Change Management*, *19*(3), 145–166. https://doi.org/10.1080/14697017.2018.1447006

Francisco, S. (2007). The way we do things around here: Specification versus craft culture in the history of building. *American Behavioral Scientist*, *50*(7), 970–988. https://doi.org/10.1177/0002764206298322

Frontiera, J. (2010). Leadership and organizational culture transformation in professional sport. *Journal of Leadership and Organizational Studies*, *17*(1), 71–86. https://doi.org/10.1177/1548051809345253

Gajendran, R. S., & Harrison, D. A. (2007). The good, the bad, and the unknown about telecommuting: Meta-analysis of psychological mediators and individual consequences. *Journal of Applied Psychology*, *92*(6), 1524–1541. https://doi.org/10.1037/0021-9010.92.6.1524

Galanti, T., Guidetti, G., Mazzei, E., Zappalà, S., & Toscano, F. (2021). Work from home during the COVID-19 outbreak: The impact on employees' remote work productivity, engagement, and stress. *Journal of Occupational and Environmental Medicine*, *63*(7), e426. https://doi.org/10.1097/JOM.0000000000002236

Geertz, C. (1973). *The interpretation of cultures: Selected essays*. Basic Books.

Golden, T. D., & Veiga, J. F. (2008). The impact of extent of telecommuting on job satisfaction: Resolving inconsistent findings. *Journal of Management*, *35*(6), 1416–1438. https://doi.org/10.1177/0149206304271768

Grant, A. M., & Ashford, S. J. (2008). The dynamics of proactivity at work. Research in *Organizational Behavior*, *28*, 3–34. https://doi.org/10.1016/j.riob.2008.04.002

Gratton, L. (2021). Four principles to ensure hybrid work is productive work. *MIT Sloan Management Review*, 62(2), 11A–16A.

Gupta, A. H. (2020, April 14). It's not just you: In online meetings, many women can't get a word in. *New York Times*. https://www.nytimes.com/2020/04/14/us/zoom-meetings-gender.html

Hackman, J. R., & Oldham, G. R. (1980). *Work redesign*. Addison-Wesley.

Hassard, J. S. (2012). Rethinking the Hawthorne studies: The Western Electric research in its social, political and historical context. *Human Relations*, 65(11), 1431–1461. https://doi.org/10.1177/0018726712452168

Helleiner, E. (2011). Understanding the 2007–2008 global financial crisis: Lessons for scholars of international political economy. *Annual Review of Political Science*, 14, 67–87. https://doi.org/10.1146/annurev-polisci-050409-112539

Huettermann, H., & Bruch, H. (2019). Mutual gains? Health-related HRM, collective well-being and organizational performance. *Journal of Management Studies*, 56(6), 1045–1072. https://doi.org/10.1111/joms.12446

Jackman, P. C., Sanderson, R., Haughey, T. J., Brett, C. E., White, N., Zile, A., Tyrrell, K., & Byrom, N. C. (2022). The impact of the first COVID-19 lockdown in the UK for doctoral and early career researchers. *Higher Education*, 84(4), 705–722. https://doi.org/10.1007/s10734-021-00795-4

Jacobides, M. G. (2007). The inherent limits of organizational structure and the unfulfilled role of hierarchy: Lessons from a near-war. *Organization Science*, 18(3), 455–477. https://doi.org/10.1287/orsc.1070.0278

Jensen, D. C., Hansen, A.-K. L., Pedersen, L. D., & Andersen, L. B. (2023). Span of control and ethical leadership in highly professionalized public organizations. *Public Personnel Management*, 52(2), 191–217. https://doi.org/10.1177/00910260221140398

Jentjens, S., & Cherbib, J. (2023). Trust me if you can: Do trust propensities in granting working-from-home arrangements change during times of exogenous shocks? *Journal of Business Research*, 161, 113844. https://doi.org/10.1016/j.jbusres.2023.113844

Johnson, A., Dey, S., Nguyen, H., Groth, M., Joyce, S., Tan, L., Glozier, N., & Harvey, S. B. (2020). A review and agenda for examining how technology-driven changes at work will impact workplace mental health and employee well-being. *Australian Journal of Management*, 45(3), 402–424. https://doi.org/10.1177/0312896220922292

Kaplan, S., Engelsted, L., Lei, X., & Lockwood, K. (2018). Unpackaging manager mistrust in allowing telework: Comparing and integrating theoretical perspectives. *Journal of Business Psychology*, 33, 365–382. https://doi.org/10.1007/s10869-017-9498-5

Kinman, G., Grant, C., Fraser, J., Bell, N., Breslin, G., Colville, T., Kwiatowski, R., Steele, C., Tehrani, N., Thomson, L., Waites, B., Whittaker, L., & MacKey, G. (2020). *Working from home: Healthy sustainable working during the COVID-19 pandemic and beyond*. British Psychological Society. https://pure.ulster.ac.uk/en/publications/working-from-home-healthy-sustainable-working-during-the-COVID-19

Kulik, C. T. (2021). We need a hero: HR and the "next normal" workplace. *Human Resources Management Journal*, 32(1). https://doi.org/10.1111/1748-8583.12387

Kurland, N. B., & Bailey, D. E. (1999). Telework: The advantages and challenges of working here, there, anywhere, and anytime. *Organizational Dynamics*, 28(2), 53–68. https://doi.org/10.1016/S0090-2616(00)80016-9

Loon, M., Otaye-Ebedeb, L., & Stewart, J. (2019). The paradox of employee psycho-
    logical well-being practices: An integrative literature review and new directions
    for research. *The International Journal of Human Resources Management, 30*(1),
    156–187. https://doi.org/10.1080/09585192.2018.1479877

Lu, X., & Lin, Z. (2021). COVID-19, economic impact, mental health, and coping
    behaviors: A conceptual framework and future research directions. *Frontiers in
    Psychology, 12*, 759974. https://doi.org/10.3389/fpsyg.2021.759974

Maslach, C., Schaufeli, W. B., & Leiter, M. P. (2001). Job burnout. *Annual Review of
    Psychology, 52*, 397–422. https://doi.org/10.1146/annurev.psych.52.1.397

Maylett, T., & Wride, M. (2017). *The employee experience: How to attract talent,
    retain top performers, and drive results.* John Wiley & Sons.

Mintzberg, H. (1980). Structure in 5's: A synthesis of the research on organization
    design. *Management Science, 26*(3), 322–341. https://doi.org/10.1287/mnsc.26.3
    .322

Montani, F., & Stagliano, R. (2022). Innovation in times of pandemic: The moderating
    effect of knowledge sharing on the relationship between COVID-19-induced job
    stress and employee innovation. *R&D Management, 52*(2), 193–205. https://doi.org/
    10.1111/radm.12457

Morgan, T., Wiles, J., Moeke-Maxwell, T., Black, S., Park, H. J., Dewes, O., Williams,
    L. A., & Got, M. (2020). "People haven't got that close connection": Meanings of
    loneliness and social isolation to culturally diverse older people. *Aging & Mental
    Health, 24*(10), 1627–1635. https://doi.org/10.1080/13607863.2019.1633619

Ninaus, K., Diehl, S., & Terlutter, R (2021). Employee perceptions of information and
    communication technologies in work life, perceived burnout, job satisfaction and the
    role of work-family balance. *Journal of Business Research, 136*, 652–666. https://
    doi.org/10.1016/j.jbusres.2021.08.007

Ojha, D., Struckell, E., Acharya, C., & Patel, P. C. (2021). Managing environmental
    turbulence through innovation speed and operational flexibility in B2B service
    organizations. *Journal of Business & Industrial Marketing, 36*(9), 1627–1645.
    https://doi.org/10.1108/JBIM-01-2020-0026

Oldham, G. R., & Fried, Y. (2016). Job design research and theory: Past, present
    and future. *Organizational Behavior and Human Decision Processes, 136*, 20–35.
    https://doi.org./10.1016/j.obhdp.2016.05.002

Pass, S., & Ridgway, M. (2022). An informed discussion on the impact of COVID-19
    and "enforced" remote working on employee engagement. *Human Resource
    Development International, 25*(2), 254–270. https://doi.org/10.1080/13678868.2022
    .2048605

Pataki-Bittó, F., & Kapusy, K. (2021). Work environment transformation in the post
    COVID-19 based on work values of the future workforce. *Journal of Corporate Real
    Estate, 23*(3), 151–169. https://doi.org/10.1108/JCRE-08-2020-0031

Pianese, T., Errichiello, L., & da Cunha, J. V. (2023). Organizational control in
    the context of remote working: A synthesis of empirical findings and a research
    agenda. *European Management Review, 20*(2), 326–345. https://doi.org/10.1111/
    emre.12515

Pruijt, H. D. (1997). *Job design and technology: Taylorism vs. anti-Taylorism.*
    Routledge.

Puriwat, W., & Hoonsopon, D. (2022). Cultivating product innovation performance
    through creativity: The impact of organizational agility and flexibility under tech-
    nological turbulence. *Journal of Manufacturing Technology Management, 33*(4),
    741–762. https://doi.org/10.1108/JMTM-10-2020-0420

Pyöriä, P. (2011). Managing telework: Risk, fears and rules. *Management Research Review, 34*, 386–399. https://doi.org/10.1108/01409171111117843

Rafferty, A. E., & Griffin, M. A. (2006). Perceptions of organizational change: A stress and coping perspective. *Journal of Applied Psychology, 91*(5), 1154. https://doi.org/10.1037/0021-9010.91.5.1154

Rissel, C., Petrunoff, N., Wen, L. M., & Crane, M. (2014). Travel to work and self-reported stress: Findings from a workplace survey in south west Sydney, Australia. *Journal of Transport & Health, 1*(1), 50–53. https://doi.org/10.1016/j.jth.2013.09.001

Rush, D. (2022, June 2). Elon Musk tells employees to return to office or "pretend to work" elsewhere. *The Guardian.* https://www.theguardian.com/technology/2022/jun/01/elon-musk-return-to-office-pretend-to-work-somewhere-else

Russell, H., O'Connell, P. J., & McGinnity, F. (2009). The impact of flexible working arrangements on work–life conflict and work pressure in Ireland. *Gender, Work & Organization, 16*(1), 73–97. https://doi.org/10.1111/j.1468-0432.2008.00431.x

Sahut, J. M., & Lissillour, R. (2023). The adoption of remote work platforms after the COVID-19 lockdown: New approach, new evidence. *Journal of Business Research, 154*, 113345. https://doi.org/10.1016/j.jbusres.2022.113345

Sander, E. J., & Baumann, O. (2020). 5 reasons why Zoom meetings are so exhausting. *The Conversation.* https://theconversation.com/5-reasons-why-zoom-meetings-are-so-exhausting-137404

Sander, E. J., Caza, A., & Jordan, P. J. (2019). The physical work environment and its relationship to stress. In O. Ayoko & N. Ashkanasy (Eds.), *Organizational behaviour and the physical environment* (pp. 268–284). Routledge.

Sander, E. L. J., Rafferty, A., & Jordan, P. J. (2021). Escaping the cubicle: Exploring the physical work environment of the home. In D. Wheatley, I. Hardill, & S. Buglass (Eds.), *Handbook of research on remote work and worker well-being in the post-COVID-19 era* (pp. 181–201). IGI Global. https://doi.org/10.4018/978-1-7998-6754-8.ch011

Schein, E. H. (1983). The role of the founder in creating organizational culture. *Organizational Dynamics, 12*(1), 13–28. https://doi.org/10.1016/0090-2616(83)90023-2

Schein, E. H. (2010). *Organizational culture and leadership.* Jossey-Bass.

Schieman, S., Badawy, P. J., A. Milkie, M., & Bierman, A. (2021). Work-life conflict during the COVID-19 pandemic. *Socius, 7*, 1–19. https://doi.org/10.1177/23780231209882 85

Schoemaker, P. J., & Day, G. (2021). Preparing organizations for greater turbulence. *California Management Review, 63*(4), 66–88. https://doi.org/10.1177/00081256211022039

Shirmohammadi, M., Au, W. C., & Beigi, M. (2022). Remote work and work life balance: Lessons learned from the COVID 19 pandemic and suggestions for HRD practitioners. *Human Resource Development International, 25*(2), 163–181. https://doi.org/10.1080/13678868.2022.2047380

Shockley, K. M., Gabriel, A. S., Robertson, D., Rosen, C. C., Chawla, N., Ganster, M. L., & Ezerins, M. E. (2021). The fatiguing effects of camera use in virtual meetings: A within-person field experiment. *Journal of Applied Psychology, 106*(8), 1137–1155. https://doi.org/10.1037/apl0000948

Simpson, S. (2004). Unwritten ground rules: The way we really do things around here. In C. Taylor (Ed.), *The power of culture: Driving today's organisation.* McGraw Hill.

Smircich, L. (1983). Organizations as shared meanings. In L. Pondy, P Frost, G. Morgan, & T. Dandrige (Eds.), *Organizational symbolism* (pp. 55–65). JAI.

Smith, P. J., Murphy, K. L., & Mahoney, S. E. (2003). Towards identifying factors underlying readiness for online learning: An exploratory study. *Distance Education, 24*(1). https://doi.org/10.1080/01587910303043

Soga, L. R., Bolade-Ogunfodun, Y., Mariani, M., Nasr, R., & Laker, B. (2022). Unmasking the other face of flexible working practices: A systematic literature review. *Journal of Business Research, 142*, 648–662. https://doi.org/10.1016/j.jbusres.2022.01.024

Spicer, A. (2020). Organizational culture and COVID-19. *Journal of Management Studies, 57*(8), 1737–1740. https://doi.org/10.1111/joms.12625

Stephens, K. K., Jahn, J. L., Fox, S., Charoensap-Kelly, P., Mitra, R., Sutton, J., Waters, E. D., Xie, B., & Meisenbach, R. J. (2020). Collective sensemaking around COVID-19: Experiences, concerns, and agendas for our rapidly changing organizational lives. *Management Communication Quarterly, 34*(3), 426–457. https://doi.org/10.1177/0893318920934890

Stranks, J. (2005). *Stress at work*. Routledge.

Strom, K., & Mills, T. (2021). Enacting affirmative ethics through auto theory: Sense-making with affect during COVID-19. *International Journal of Qualitative Studies in Education, 37*(3), 660–675. https://doi.org/10.1080/09518398.2022.2127024

Surma, M. J., Nunes, R. J., & Rook, C. (2021). Assessing employee engagement in a post-COVID-19 workplace ecosystem. *Sustainability, 13*(20). https://doi.org/10.3390/su132011443

Triest, S., & Williams, C. (2024). Following the chain of command? How managers balance benefits and risks in granting autonomy to employees. *European Management Journal, 42*(1), 89–97. https://doi.org/10.1016/j.emj.2022.08.007

Truxillo, D. M., Cadiz, D. M., Rineer, J. R., Zaniboni, S., & Fraccaroli, F. (2012). A lifespan perspective on job design: Fitting the job and the worker to promote job satisfaction, engagement, and performance. *Organizational Psychology Review, 2*(4), 340–360. https://doi.org/10.1177/2041386612454043

Tu, Y., Li, D., & Wang, H. J. (2021). COVID-19-induced layoff, survivors' COVID-19-related stress and performance in hospitality industry: The moderating role of social support. *International Journal of Hospitality Management, 95*, 102912 https://doi.org/10.1016/j.ijhm.2021.102912

Van Maanen, J. (1992). Displacing Disney: Some notes on the flow of culture. *Qualitative Sociology, 15*(1), 5–35. https://doi.org/10.1007/BF00989711

Vaziri, H., Casper, W. J., Wayne, J. H., & Matthews, R. A. (2020). Changes to the work–family interface during the COVID-19 pandemic: Examining predictors and implications using latent transition analysis. *Journal of Applied Psychology, 105*(10), 1073–1087. https://doi.org/10.1037/apl0000819

Venkatesan, M. (2021). Engagement and efficiency of remote higher education: An economics perspective. In D. Wheatley, I. Hardill, & S. Buglass (Eds.), *Handbook of research on remote work and worker well-being in the post-COVID-19 era* (pp. 67–80). IGI Global. https://doi.org/10.4018/978-1-7998-6754-8

Verma, A., Venkatesan, M., Kumar, M., & Verma, J. (2023). The future of work post COVID-19: Key perceived HR implications of hybrid workplaces in India. *Journal of Management Development, 42*(1), 13–28. https://doi.org/10.1108/JMD-11-2021-0304

Waight, C. L., Kjerfve, T. N., Kite, A., & Smith, B. (2022). Connecting and relating in Brazil: Implications of remote work. *Human Resource Development International*, *25*(2), 231–253. https://doi.org/10.1080/13678868.2022.2048435

Waizeneggera, L., McKennab, B., Caic. W., & Bendz, T. (2020). An affordance perspective of team collaboration and enforced working from home during COVID-19. *European Journal of Information Systems*, *29*(4), 429–442. https://doi.org/10.1080/0960085X.2020.1800417

Wang, M. C., Chen, P. C., & Fang, S. C. (2021). How environmental turbulence influences firms' entrepreneurial orientation: The moderating role of network relationships and organizational inertia. Journal of Business & Industrial Marketing, *36*(1), 48–59. https://doi.org/10.1108/JBIM-05-2019-0170

Warrick, D. D. (2017). What leaders need to know about organizational culture. *Business Horizons*, *60*(3), 395–404. http://dx.doi.org/10.1016/j.bushor.2017.01.011

Weinberg, A., & Cooper, C. (2011). *Stress in turbulent times*. Springer.

Winkelhaus, S., Grosse, E. H., & Glock, C. H. (2022). Job satisfaction: An explorative study on work characteristics changes of employees in Intralogistics 4.0. *Journal of Business Logistics*, *43*(3), 343–367. https://doi.org/10.1111/jbl.12296

Wray, S., & Kinman, G. (2022). The psychosocial hazards of academic work: An analysis of trends. *Studies in Higher Education*, *47*(4), 771–782. https://doi.org/10.1080/03075079.2020.1793934

Xiong Chen, Z., & Aryee, S. (2007). Delegation and employee work outcomes: An examination of the cultural context of mediating processes in China. *Academy of Management Journal*, *50*(1), 226–238. https://doi.org/10.5465/amj.2007.24162389

Yousaf, Z., Majid, A., & Yasir, M. (2021). Is polychronicity a panacea for innovative work behavior among nursing staff? Job embeddedness and moderating role of decentralization. *European Journal of Innovation Management*, *24*(1), 173–189. https://doi.org/10.1108/EJIM-06-2019-0172

Zhong, W., Hu, Q., & Kapucu, N. (2023). Robust crisis communication in turbulent times: Conceptualization and empirical evidence from the United States. *Public Administration*, *101*(1), 158–181. https://doi.org/10.1111/padm.12855

13. An integrated approach to managing wellbeing in the workplace

Karina Nielsen, Cristina Di Tecco, Jo Yarker, and Michela Vignoli

Mental health is a major challenge in the modern workplace. Prior to the COVID-19 pandemic, it was estimated that in the Organisation for Economic Co-operation and Development (OECD) countries, stress, anxiety, and depression affected approximately 15 per cent of employees (OECD, 2014). For approximately half of this group, long-term sickness absence is the consequence (OECD, 2014). Mental health in the workplace is costly. A recent report revealed that in the UK, mental health issues cost UK employers £34.9 billion; the breakdown of these costs were: £10.6 billion due to sickness absence, £21.2 billion due to presenteeism (working while ill), and £3.1 billion due to employees leaving employment due to mental health issues (Parsonage & Saini, 2019). Post-pandemic, these figures have only increased, with mental health cost estimates of £53–56 billion (Hampson et al., 2022). Together, these figures call for a comprehensive integrative approach to promoting and protecting mental health in the workplace.

The turbulence created by the COVID-19 pandemic highlights even more the importance of organizations having robust policies, practices, and procedures in place that enable quick adaptions to changes in the environment. In the present chapter, we consider these organizational adaptions, and develop a research agenda based on three case studies, to promote a multi-faceted, integrated approach to manage employee mental health and wellbeing. We propose that resilience is key to managing turbulences in the environment, and present the Integrated Organizational Mental Health Resilience Framework (IOMHRF). We have developed this framework based on three case studies that were conducted at the height of the COVID-19 pandemic. The first case study outlines a preventative approach, and demonstrates the importance of developing robust policies and practices on how to prevent poor mental health in the workplace. The second case study presents an approach to addressing emerging mental health issues, ensuring mental health provision fits with the needs of employees emerging in turbulent times. The third case study makes a case for flexible approaches to novel diseases, which require multi-level coordinated approaches to ensure sustainable employment for vulnerable workers.

The first two case studies occurred in the healthcare sector, where employees experienced a dual turbulence, as individuals living through the COVID-19 pandemic and as workers employed in a sector that was put under extreme pressure during the pandemic. Resources were moved from other departments to the emergency units where COVID-19 patients were treated for multiple issues (Della Monica et al., 2022; Jonsdottir et al., 2021). Healthcare professionals were among the employees at greatest risk of exposure to COVID-19, and their commitment at the forefront of the health emergency exposed them to a growing operational and emotional overload (Della Monica et al., 2022; Gualano et al., 2021), resulting in long-term pressure on healthcare staff. This is due to excessive workloads during the pandemic with employees being overworked, but also with the long waiting lists in other areas (Van Ginneken et al., 2022). This resulted in increases in physical, operational, and emotional strain for healthcare employees (Clemente-Suárez et al., 2021).

The third case study focuses on 'long COVID', as an example of an emerging disease that requires a novel approach to workplace support to enable employees to stay at work. According to estimates, one in ten COVID-19 patients experience symptoms which last for 12 weeks or longer. This has been termed 'long COVID' (World Health Organization, 2021). It has been suggested that the younger population is more likely to suffer long-term health consequences due to long COVID than to die of COVID-19 (Briggs & Vassall, 2021). Reuschke and Houston (2022) estimated that 0.5 per cent of the working population suffered from long COVID in March 2022, and 3.7 per cent of the workforce suffering from long COVID had left employment. Efforts to manage long COVID focus on the assessment and treatment of the disease, rather than on the support needed to retain long COVID employees in the workplace (Akbarialiabad et al., 2021; NHS England, 2021). Long COVID has significantly impacted the working population, and thus requires the development of appropriate strategies for how to effectively manage it and similar viruses in the workplace.

PROTECTING AND PROMOTING MENTAL HEALTH AND WELLBEING IN THE WORKPLACE

Interventions to prevent harm, and to protect and promote mental health and wellbeing in the workplace, require attention to the full range of mental health and wellbeing states that employees experience; and they should ideally address both work-related and other mental health problems (LaMontagne et al., 2014; Petrie et al., 2018). For employees with no history of mental health problems, prevention is the most important. For those with developing mental health problems, early intervention is most beneficial; and for those with diagnosable disorders, access to support and treatment is key. Strategies to address these illustrative scenarios (and more) should be multi-faceted, and performed by a range of workplace stakeholders (e.g., employers, unions, occupational health professionals, business service providers; Petrie et al., 2018).

Interventions are often classified as primary, secondary, or tertiary. Primary interventions aim at modifying or eliminating the causes of poor mental health and wellbeing, by reducing the negative impact of the working environment on mental health and wellbeing (Randall & Nielsen, 2010). These types of interventions are also known as organizational interventions, occupational health interventions, job re-design interventions, psychosocial interventions, or work environment interventions (Randall & Nielsen, 2010). They aim to improve employee mental health and wellbeing through making changes to the way work is organized, designed, and managed (Nielsen, 2013). Common examples of such changes include introducing flexible working practices and work time scheduling, or changing job tasks (Fox et al., 2021). Such interventions may also take a participatory approach to changing working conditions, whereby employees, managers, and other organizational stakeholders (e.g., human resources [HR]), jointly decide what changes to make (Fox et al., 2021).

Secondary interventions aim to reduce the severity of poor mental health symptoms before they reach a critical stage (Randall & Nielsen, 2010). Such interventions aim to break or weaken the link between the exposure to adverse working conditions and their impact on employee mental health, by changing employees' reactions to the environment, and enabling them to feel, think, and/ or behave differently in the workplace. The focus of secondary interventions is on providing employees with the skills to manage the adverse conditions they face in the workplace. Secondary interventions often take the form of training (Randall & Nielsen, 2010), and include, for example, mindfulness training, stress management training, or training on job crafting.

Tertiary interventions are reactive, and aim to improve poor mental health for employees who have 'fallen off the cliff' and are returning to work after long-term sickness absence (Randall & Nielsen, 2010). These interventions often take the form of rehabilitation or return-to-work support (LaMontagne et al., 2014), and include making work adjustments to keep employees at work. Support is provided to enable returned employees to manage their symptoms while working, and thus avoid them taking sick leave (Joyce, 2013).

A framework that combines these three threads, and delivers provision and evaluation of the impact across all three threads to ensure employee mental health and wellbeing, is particularly pertinent in times of turbulence and insecurity. We thus suggest that, during turbulent times, effective strategies to protect and promote mental health and wellbeing include: (1) protecting mental health by reducing work-related and other risk factors for mental health problems, also known as the *preventative approach*; (2) promoting mental health and wellbeing by developing the positive aspects of work, as well as employee strengths and positive capacities; and (3) responding to mental health problems as they manifest at work regardless of cause (work-related or otherwise; LaMontagne et al., 2014). An integrated approach to managing mental health and wellbeing is vital in times of instability and uncertainty, when employees with no history of mental health problems are at risk of developing new illnesses; and those with pre-existing mental health issues are at risk of their condition worsening (Neelam et al., 2021).

Events such as the COVID-19 pandemic have had a profound influence on the world of work, and this calls for a revised research agenda on how we can more effectively prevent harm and promote and protect mental health in the workplace. In this chapter, we draw on three case studies, conducted during the pandemic, to suggest a new framework for managing employee mental health and wellbeing during turbulent times. The case studies focus on primary, secondary, and tertiary interventions, respectively. In the following sections, we first discuss the key results of these three case studies, and then consider them together in a framework for the improved promotion and protection of mental health and wellbeing in the workplace.

PREVENTING HARM AND POOR MENTAL HEALTH AND WELLBEING DURING TURBULENT TIMES

The first case study was a primary intervention in the Italian healthcare sector, aimed at investigating how healthcare organizations manage psychosocial risk factors assessment to create healthier workplaces. The existing literature on primary interventions has largely focused on employees as the targets of such interventions. However, such interventions often employ a participatory approach to ensure the changes to work policies, practices, and procedures address the most pertinent psychosocial risks (Nielsen & Randall, 2015). To enable the participatory approach, it is recommended that a steering group is established that oversees the intervention process and the subsequent actions that are developed and implemented. Key members of such steering groups are managers, and representatives from HR and occupational health and safety, with the latter representing the interests of employees (Nielsen et al., 2010). It is also recommended that a project champion takes overall responsibility for driving the intervention process; such champions also play a key role in ensuring the steering groups function well (Nielsen et al., 2010). Despite the important role of these key actors in relation to the effectiveness of the intervention, there is a lack of studies focusing on the experiences of target key stakeholders such as steering group members.

In this case study, we focused on the experiences of the health and safety representative, and the project champion – an internal occupational health consultant – to better understand how they perceived the challenges and opportunities of implementing a primary intervention during times of turbulence and uncertainty. We term this process evaluation – of steering group members' reflections of the overall intervention process – a 'meta-process evaluation'. We conducted qualitative interviews with the health and safety representative and the internal consultant on the steering group; each interview lasted approximately 100 minutes, and was recorded and transcribed ad verbum. The interviews explored their perceptions of each phase of the intervention (Nielsen et al., 2010).

Primary interventions comprise five phases – preparation, screening, action planning, implementation, and evaluation – occurring in a continual process; and it is important to understand how each phase influences the intervention's outcomes. We used a realist evaluation approach (Pawson & Tilley, 1997), which is a theory-driven approach that attempts to answer three main questions: what works, for whom, and in which circumstances (Nielsen & Abildgaard, 2013). This approach allows researchers to gain insight into the complex processes of organizational interventions; and the approach may be used to develop supportive activities to ensure successful implementation of the intervention (Nielsen & Randall, 2013).

Two different hospitals in one trust employing 3,656 workers conducted a psychosocial risk management process, a process required by the Italian national safety law. The employees were categorized into 57 homogeneous groups (groups of employees exposed to similar psychosocial work conditions), based on operative units of 30 to 230 employees in each unit. The results of the interviews with the health and safety representative, and the project champion, showed a main overarching influence of the pandemic on all the aspects related to the psychosocial risk management process. Specifically, because of the outbreak of the pandemic, the main and only focus of the organization was related to the physical safety of the employees, with less of a focus on mental health and wellbeing. Organizational communication focused entirely on the risks of contracting COVID-19. During turbulent and insecure times, it is important also to consider how organizational changes such as moving staff across departments, allocating them new responsibilities, and exposing them to high risks influence employees' mental health and wellbeing (de Jong et al., 2016).

The interviews focused on two main categories of issues related to the intervention: technical and managerial issues. Technical issues related to the intervention primarily concerned risk assessment. The interviews revealed issues related to the tools to conduct the risk assessment; that is, the survey and the feedback tools provided by the Italian workers' compensation authority, the

National Institute for Insurance against Accidents at Work (INAIL). Collecting data such as sickness absence rates, injuries, and incidents, is time-consuming, and requires specific and highly proficient data management skills that are not always present in an organization. The Italian approach to psychosocial risk management requires the steering groups to identify homogenous groups. Survey results are then analyzed based on these homogenous groups, and the results reported back to the organizations. However, in practice, the homogenous groups were often not easy to identify on the official organizational charts, making it difficult to develop appropriate action. For example, the steering group identified a homogenous group of nurses that rotated between different departments of the hospital (and thus had different managers and work practices and procedures), which meant that it was difficult to understand the results of this group as they had very different work experiences.

The safety representative and the project champion felt that the databases and software used by the organizations should be developed, to allow for the consideration of not only the content of the work (e.g., whether an employee is a nurse or a doctor), but also of the potential different exposure to psychosocial risks in the workplace (for example, if the person rotates between departments or not). This is extremely important for the success of the organizational intervention process, as it would improve the accurate definition of the homogenous groups at the beginning of the project. As noted, these groups were often based on formal organizational structures, and not on employees' actual exposure to psychosocial risks. Such flexibility is particularly important during turbulent times, where staff may be moved to emergency departments at short notice and be allocated new work responsibilities.

The managerial issues related to the intervention, identified from the interviews, focused on communication and management of the interventions. Communication has been identified as an important aspect of many organizational interventions (e.g., Cox et al., 2000; Nielsen, 2024). Accordingly, our interviews indicated that communication can directly influence the psychosocial risk management process at many different levels. Communication influenced participants' engagement, as many employees were concerned about the anonymity of their responses to the online survey, and thus the survey failed to produce satisfactory response rates. In response to these concerns, the process was adjusted to include the distribution of paper and pencil questionnaires. This result highlights the important role of the members of the steering group in defining a good communication plan that involves managers and supervisors disseminating the relevant information about the process, and why employee involvement is relevant.

Another important aspect raised was the management of the initiatives related to the action planning and implementation phases of the intervention. Participants reported challenges related to defining initiatives based on the results of the first phases, for two main reasons. First, not all the members of the steering group agreed on what should be the initiatives, how they should be implemented, and whom they should target. This disagreement can easily occur, as each member of the steering group represents the interests of different groups. Second, once the initiatives have been decided, the line managers, if not involved directly, could negatively influence the success of the initiatives, jeopardizing the success of the entire process (Christensen et al., 2019).

These results emphasize how organizational interventions are complex. One solution is the development of meta-process evaluation instruments, such as the semi-structured interviews conducted as part of this study. Meta-process evaluation may assist organizations in achieving the intervention goals. In addition, monitoring step-by-step actions could also counteract the change of people in specific roles, as career transitions are becoming more and more frequent (De Vos et al., 2021). The use of the meta-process evaluation instruments should be accompanied by a culture of monitoring the process, and by making suitable adjustments to the process to ensure long-term learning about how to best manage psychosocial risks.

SUPPORTING EMPLOYEES AT RISK FOR POOR MENTAL HEALTH AND WELLBEING

The second case study was a secondary intervention in the healthcare sector in Italy, due to the impact of the pandemic on this sector. Particularly during the first phase of the COVID-19 pandemic, there was a need for immediate interventions, to provide individualized psychological support for healthcare employees. The adoption of secondary interventions, such as individualized psychological support, is crucial to protect the mental health of healthcare workers. Their mental wellbeing is at risk due to organizational and contextual factors that cannot be immediately modified through primary prevention measures. Secondary interventions help to cope with stress, maintain the effectiveness of the healthcare professionals, reduce the risk of burnout, and foster resilience in an extremely challenging and uncertain work environment.

In response to this need, INAIL, in collaboration with the Italian Council of the Order of Psychologists, implemented an initiative aimed at providing psychological support to healthcare professionals, to enable them to manage stress and prevent burnout. The main strategies employed related to individual employees' coping, adaption, and recovery, and developing interventions appropriate to the situation. Healthcare organizations were encouraged to establish internal emergency units with a taskforce of psychologists. Units aimed to provide psychological and psychosocial interventions to support and assist the healthcare employees, by listening to their needs and responding to their psychological problems.

The targets of this secondary intervention were all healthcare employees working on the frontline, who had a high risk of contracting COVID-19. The intervention was promoted with the aim of foreseeing needs and mental problems that may arise in healthcare employees during the COVID-19 pandemic. This intervention aligned with the recommendations of the European Strategy on Health and Safety at Work 2021–2027 (European Commission, 2021), which calls for anticipating emerging risks for employees. Moreover, the purpose of the intervention was to provide psychological support and tools to the employees, and to respond to the emergency by taking advantage of resources already present at the local level.

An anonymized psychological triage checklist was developed to collect data about the support delivered to healthcare professionals. The checklist consisted of three main sections: (1) to collect information on the organization and the psychologists involved in the unit; (2) to profile the applicant, including personal details, role, and work unit; and (3) to register the main psychological problems that the applicants were experiencing due to the direct and/or indirect exposure to the pandemic event. In particular, the psychologists reported information about previous mental illness and/or psychopharmacological treatments, which type of reaction to COVID-19 the applicant reported (e.g., anxiety, depression, psychosomatic disorders), and the main psychological resources adopted in terms of coping styles (e.g., task-focused, emotion-focused, avoidance-focused; Endler & Parker, 1990). A summary of the key points, actions provided, and indications for eventual follow-up interviews were also reported in each checklist.

Data collected using the checklist were shared with INAIL's researchers for an in-depth analysis about the mental health level of the healthcare employees, their common reactions to the COVID-19 emergency, the personal resources put in place, and the main interventions and actions implemented. Data were collected from February to December 2020, from 556 employees who approached the psychological support unit in their own hospital. Findings highlighted that moderate and severe anxiety symptoms were the most frequent reactions to COVID-19, followed by depression and psychosomatic symptoms. The experience of previous psychological illness was an important predictor of depression, anxiety, and psychosomatic symptoms during the pandemic; thus, the pandemic had a higher impact for individuals with latent mental disorders (Clemente-Suárez et al., 2021).

No significant differences were found between those working in COVID-19 and non-COVID-19 units. This result is consistent with other studies reporting that direct contact with patients with COVID-19 was not associated with worse mental health outcomes among healthcare employees; but nurses reported more psychosomatic disorders compared to physicians (Tamrakar et al., 2021; Tiete et al., 2021).

Different reactions in terms of psychological resources also emerged. Emotion-focused and avoidance coping styles were associated with higher levels of anxiety and psychosomatic disorders, while only an emotion-focused coping style was associated with higher levels of depression. Although we were unable to directly assess the effectiveness of the psychological support for the employees' health, this type of secondary intervention demonstrates practical implications in terms of the interventions that may be adopted by the hospitals. Actions orientated to support employees, such as training courses, improved communication, and psychotherapy, were implemented. Moreover, evidence from these data helps to identify sensitive and at-risk groups, and manage mental health in the post-COVID turbulent times.

This case study illustrates how secondary-level interventions aim to improve employees' resources, and should be considered essential when potential sources of stress, burnout, and depression cannot be eliminated at the source; or the situation requires employees to work in highly demanding conditions, as is the case of healthcare employees during the pandemic.

PROMOTING SUSTAINABLE RETURN TO WORK FOR EMPLOYEES WITH LONG COVID

The third case study focused on the need for a tertiary intervention for employees experiencing long COVID across a range of occupational sectors. Common symptoms of long COVID include fatigue, breathlessness, muscle pain, joint pain, headache, cognitive impairment, memory loss, anxiety, and sleep disorders (Akbarialiabad et al., 2021). As a new condition, with no clearly established pathogenesis and agreed treatment plan, employees with long COVID faced (and many continue to face) periods of great uncertainty, as they wait for a diagnosis and a treatment plan to support them in recovering their health and sustaining their work performance. We interviewed a sample of 14 employees with long COVID, and conducted roundtable focus groups with 43 professionals who supported these and other employees with long COVID. These professionals included occupational health and human resource practitioners, employment support and vocational rehabilitation professionals, physiotherapists, occupational therapists, and line managers. The interviews aimed to identify the specific needs for the return to work and the retention of employees with long COVID. Interviews were transcribed and comprehensive verbatim notes were taken during the focus groups. Thematic analysis was conducted to analyse the data, using the Individual, Group, Leader, Organizational, and overarching context (IGLOo) Framework (Nielsen et al., 2018) as a guiding heuristic, followed by inductive analysis to identify discrete sub-themes.

Our findings highlighted the struggle experienced by employees with long COVID. The experiences described by employees, and those providing them with support, echoed the experiences of employees with other long-term health conditions, particularly employees with fluctuating conditions. Thus, it was clear that pathways to diagnosis are slow, access to support is variable, and the disconnect between healthcare and work is not conducive to supporting employees to stay in, or return to, work.

At the individual level, employees and professionals described how recovery accelerated following the formal acceptance of reduced work functioning. Many employees described transitioning through a period of denial and frustration, setting unrealistic and unkind expectations of themselves, noting that pacing and energy management required self-discipline. Those that recovered well were those who were able to put in place clear boundaries between work and home, enabling them to rest and restore themselves and thereby preventing relapse.

At the group level, colleagues played a vital role in restoring employees' confidence through the provision of practical support, such as stepping in to support employees with difficult work tasks, or with tasks requiring significant personal energy. Notably, professionals described how, where work groups were nuanced in supporting wellbeing more broadly, routinely discussing mental health and wellbeing needs, these groups were seen to be more proactive in their support of the employee with long COVID.

At the leader level, many of the barriers and facilitators to work sustainability reported by the employees with long COVID were similar to those identified in relation to work sustainability for employees with mental ill health (Nielsen & Yarker, 2022, 2023a). Too often, line managers expected employees to return (prematurely) to full workloads, often including lagged work that had built up in their absence. Professionals reported that many line managers were impatient, frustrated by their employee's slow and fluctuating recovery; and waited for their employees to present a formal diagnosis with a clear specification for work adjustments before fully realizing the employee's needs and adjusting their work. Work sustainability was found to be facilitated where line managers adopted a symptom-led approach and were flexible and responsive to the day-to-day needs of the employee, and where they regularly checked in with the employee.

At the organizational level, the rigidity of absence management policies and practices was a significant barrier to sustainable work. Many employees and professionals described how absence triggers resulted in them experiencing uncertainty and disciplinary procedures. There was a strong recognition that the changes to the ways of working caused by COVID-19, and the pressures that this placed on HR and health and safety functions within organizations, limited the resources available to support employees' absence management – which is often poorly managed even under normal working circumstances.

External resources were reported to be invaluable for both the employees with long COVID and the professionals supporting them. As a new condition, there was a sense of 'muddling through' and relying on previous experience. Where employees were able to access support from family and friends, in the form of compassionate understanding, or practical support such as helping with food and travel, they described more positive experiences of sustaining their work requirements. External support groups were utilized to source vital learnings on the impact of long COVID on individual health, functioning, and work ability. The most consistent and pervasive challenge identified by these participants was the pathway to diagnosis and support. None of the participants or professionals described an effective and straightforward healthcare pathway. In all instances, employees reported long waiting times to see healthcare professionals, sometimes up to six months; and experiencing disconnected care whereby they were transferred from one specialist to another, without a holistic consideration of the myriad of symptoms they were experiencing. This study was conducted in the middle of the pandemic, and it is noted that long COVID clinics have since been established across the UK. However, it is recognized that access to these clinics is variable and limited (Gorna et al., 2021).

Both employees and professionals noted a lack of understanding of the condition and its impact, which influenced their ability to access resources. Many employees described having a minimal understanding of their condition, and sought resources to accept their situation and focus on recovery. Similarly, their colleagues and line managers also lacked an understanding of long COVID, and their behaviour was reported as a significant barrier to employees with long COVID sustaining work. The impact of this lack of understanding varied, from overlooking the impact of fatigue on the individual's need for regular breaks to open cynicism that long COVID was not a 'real' condition, thereby preventing opportunities for pacing and recovery. Our findings suggest that employers were generally slow to mobilize resources to support employees with long COVID, and any action taken was piecemeal and reactive.

THE INTEGRATED ORGANIZATIONAL MENTAL HEALTH RESILIENCE FRAMEWORK

Together, the three case studies call for the development of an integrated approach to organizational resilience in relation to mental health practices. Organizational resilience in relation to managing mental health in the workplace refers to the organization's ability to anticipate unexpecting events, and to develop effective monitoring systems. Such systems enhance the organization's ability to identify unexpected events sooner, effectively put processes and practices in place to address the challenges of turbulence, and build capabilities for a recovery from unexpected events (Vogus & Sutcliffe, 2007).

In light of the above, we developed the *Integrated Organizational Mental Health Resilience Framework* (IOMHRF). The framework integrates the three types of intervention: primary, secondary, and tertiary. While some larger, well-resourced, organizations may have many interventions at each of these levels in place, our research suggests that gaps remain and limit their resilience to future turbulence.

For each type we discuss the most important factors to consider when aiming to develop organizational resilience. Improving resilience enables organizations to address key challenges and emerge from a situation strengthened and more resourceful (Vogus & Sutcliffe, 2007). It is important to note that there is not a 'one size fits all' formula to achieve organizational resilience, but that it is best that each organization establish its own systems, processes, and functions, to develop the necessary capabilities to most effectively manage turbulence and insecurity (Horne, 1997). Organizational resilience is contingent on policies, practices, and procedures that promote competence and efficacy (Vogus & Sutcliffe, 2007). For an overview of the IOMHRF, see Figure 13.1.

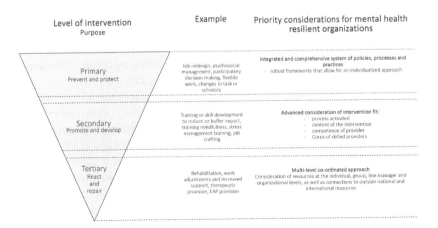

Figure 13.1   *The Integrated Organizational Mental Health Resilience Framework*

We argue that if the mental health and wellbeing of employees is effectively managed, then employees will also be productive (Nielsen et al., 2017). We propose that organizational resilience will occur if organizations develop comprehensive policies, procedures, and practices that balance the need for an individualized and targeted approach that fits the need of the organization to ensure a healthy workforce, together with the need to enable employees to be productive at work and to provide a high-quality service or product.

Primary Interventions

As shown in Figure 13.1, the first level refers to primary interventions. These interventions focus on how work is organized, designed, and managed, and are therefore fundamental to provide better working conditions for employees. Primary interventions can have a preventative function, and thus are especially essential in turbulent times, when organizations experience sudden external events such as pandemics or wars. In these turbulent situations, an organization's health and resilience is crucial to successfully manage contextual demands. For primary interventions to be effective and foster organizational resilience, we argue that it is important to focus on three different but intertwined organizational aspects: policies, procedures, and practices.

At the policy level, it is important that organizations prepare emergency plans. As various kinds of emergencies occur more frequently, organizations should develop these plans so they are ready to be implemented at the appropriate time for the organization to proactively manage emergencies. A plan requires a clear mapping and definition of all the resources (both human and economic) in the organizations that could be involved in an emergency response. In a qualitative study of the dimensions of effective organizational emergency management using the COVID-19 pandemic as a case, Atkinson et al. (2021) identified seven dimensions of effective healthcare emergency management: (1) identification of capable leaders, (2) assurance of institutional support, (3) the design of tiered communications systems, (4) initiation of an incident command system to delineate roles and responsibilities, (5) promotion of collaboration and team building, (6) initiation of training and exercises, and (7) balance between structure and flexibility. These dimensions could usefully provide a framework for organizations of all sizes and sectors to review the resources required across a range of scenarios (e.g., climate change, civil unrest, pandemic) to aid preparedness.

Moreover, as organizations are increasingly complex, it is important to develop organizational interventions which consider both an overall strategy and a multi-level strategy. Primary intervention needs to be integrated into daily business and work practices, so that employee mental health and wellbeing becomes part of day-to-day discussions – for example, as a part of meetings. Thiele Schwarz et al. (2017) suggested integrating mental health and wellbeing considerations into continuous improvement systems. Effective organizational interventions are also based on an understanding of the complexity of mental health and wellbeing. Organizations should understand that mental health and wellbeing interventions are often related to potential stigmatization processes; thus, at the policy level, it is important to provide appropriate initiatives to minimize stigmatization. In many countries, legislation protects against discrimination (e.g., in the UK, The Equality Act, 2010; or the EU [European Union] Directive 2000/78); however, concrete initiatives are needed to ensure the translation of policy into practice at the organizational level.

At the procedure level, it is important that organizations conduct a needs analysis to inform training initiatives aimed at developing skills and competencies, especially of the members of the steering committee who will manage the organizational interventions, and those involved in enacting emergency plans. Procedures should include a clear and dedicated communication plan. Organizational interventions should also include the implementation of procedures that facilitate the monitoring of the activities of the organizational interventions, in order to guarantee that the organizational intervention is occurring as planned, and that all those involved are taking action to successfully deliver the intervention.

Lastly, at the practice level, organizations should provide for the involvement of people from different departments of the organizations at the right time, and should clearly allocate the needed resources for the interventions to be effective. Organizational interventions are long-term processes that require a large amount of time and effort from different employees; thus, specific resources in terms of people involved, dedicated time, and specific competences required should be identified, and managed upstream. Moreover, organizational interventions should sustain the commitment to change of the employees and all the stakeholders involved.

Secondary Interventions

In turbulent times, secondary interventions for protecting mental health and wellbeing are essential, particularly when the sources of poor mental health cannot be immediately managed, eliminated, or mitigated. To be effective, secondary-level interventions should meet their proposed aims. This calls for consideration of four different components of 'intervention fit': (1) the process activated by the intervention, (2) the content of the intervention, (3) the competencies needed for the intervention delivery, and (4) the availability of a corps of resources skilled to deliver the intervention.

First, at the process level, the range of interventions must fit the needs identified to protect employees' mental health and wellbeing. Sometimes secondary interventions are too general, and do not target the issues experienced in the organizations; this includes off-the-shelf components such as general mindfulness training, versus tailored bereavement training. Moreover, it is essential to prioritize time for participation, to ensure employees have enough time in their daily activity to take part in the intervention.

The second aspect of intervention fit is related to the content. Even if the range of interventions fall into the needs identified, the content of the interventions is often too general. Interventions should be tailored to the specific needs identified. As an example, when some issues concerning management support are identified and a training course for line managers is considered, then the training must focus on the specific (supportive) leadership skills needed, and not on leadership styles in general.

A lack of fit of the content is closely related to the third level of fit – namely, the level of competencies of those delivering secondary interventions. Mapping of the competencies of intervention providers would help in case of emergency to identify and immediately activate the correct trainer, as in the case reported above in this chapter. It is important to have an overview of the cross-organizational resource persons that can be activated at short notice. Mapping the competencies present in an organization is a useful exercise to identify who might be best suited to provide tailored emergency training. Co-operative groups could be created by selecting one emergency reference person in each department who, in times of emergency, will engage in a coordinated response. Existing roles such as health and safety or union representatives could be expanded. An intra-departmental group could help in collecting competencies, identifying specific needs, and facilitating communication into the organization; and this could increase the level of awareness of employees of secondary interventions put in place.

Tertiary Interventions

The final level of interventions are the tertiary interventions, addressing the identified health problems of employees. Effective tertiary interventions adopt a multi-level coordinated approach, moving beyond the siloed and reactive provision currently experienced by many employees. In line with the results of our qualitative study, we propose that actions need to be taken at the IGLOo levels (i.e., Individual, Group, Leader, Organizational, and overarching context).

At the individual level, organizations need to offer improved support for employees to stay at work or return to work after long-term sickness absence. This support can take the form of training to build employees' resources. First, interventions should aim to build employees' ability to identify which work adjustments are needed to enable them to manage their symptoms successfully while working, and to communicate their needs to occupational health, HR, and their managers. Second, employees should be offered interventions that help them to develop awareness about self-care strategies, to identify when they risk becoming overwhelmed and at increased risk for relapse. For example, this includes setting boundaries, time management, energy management and pacing, building awareness of and confidence in requesting work adjustments, and job crafting strategies.

At the group level, it is recommended that organizations develop the group's ability to make rapid adjustments to the working conditions, accounting for the potential reduced work functioning of returned employees.

At the leader level, line managers should be trained in understanding the needs of struggling or returned employees, and also which work adjustments are needed to address these needs, post return-to-work, to ensure that employees are supported in the weeks and months following their return. Line managers should develop the competencies to facilitate the discussion about working conditions and how to make ongoing adjustments that meet the needs of the employee at a given point in time, engaging in a dialogue about what changes are required for long-term effective work performance.

At the organizational level, policies, practices, and procedures need to be in place for the lower levels of the IGLOo model to fully support returned employees. This includes raising awareness about the dangers of stigmatizing employees; and allocating resources to enable groups and line managers to make the necessary adjustments to support struggling or returned employees on a flexible and ongoing basis, in order to respond to changing needs. Procedures should be in place that enable groups and line managers to report when issues arise; and tailored, ongoing support should be in place once issues are reported. Furthermore, flexible work policies should be in place that enable struggling or returned employees and their managers to make adjustments as and when they are needed, in recognition of the fluctuations of the health and wellbeing of employees. Existing policies tend to focus on linear recovery, and the pre-return and re-entry periods (Nielsen & Yarker, 2023b).

Organizations should also work with the healthcare system in the overarching context outside the organization, specifically with long COVID clinics. While there is an impetus for employers to better integrate recommendations from healthcare professionals, an effective coordinated approach will not be realized without healthcare professionals placing a greater emphasis on work as a health outcome. This means upskilling healthcare employees to recognize and discuss the impact of symptoms and treatment on cognitive, emotional, and physical functioning, as long COVID affects all bodily functions (Davis et al., 2021). Employees should also be provided with direct and anonymous access to qualified providers to ensure they obtain the necessary support via employee assistance programmes (EAPs). Finally, organizations should liaise with community and charity support groups to provide assurances that employees are not alone, and to identify early emerging trends in the experience and solutions of similar unusual occurrences.

CONCLUSION

It could be argued that the COVID-19 pandemic is a once-in-a-century phenomenon. Yet predictions suggest we will see a range of emergencies in the future, due to climate changes, wars, and other major viruses. It is, therefore, vital that organizations develop resilience in their approach to mental health. Resilient organizations can meet the challenges by seeking and analysing relevant information, loosening control to enable rapid adjustments to meet emerging demands, and reconfiguring resources. We propose that an integrated and multi-level approach to address employee mental health and wellbeing is required to provide organizations with a robust foundation – integrating primary, secondary, and tertiary interventions – that organizations can quickly adapt to emergencies. The Integrated Organizational Mental Health Resilience Framework outlines the priority considerations required to enable organizations to prevent harm, and promote and protect employee mental and wellbeing, in times of both stability and turbulence.

REFERENCES

Akbarialiabad, H., Taghrir, M. H., Abdollahi, A., Ghahramani, N., Kumar, M., Paydar, S., Razani, B., Mwangi, J., Asadi-Pooya, A. A., Malekmakan, L., & Bastani, B. (2021). Long COVID, a comprehensive systematic scoping review. *Infection, 49*, 1163–1186. https://doi.org/10.1007/s15010-021-01666-x

Atkinson, M. K., Cagliuso, N. V., Hick, J. L., Singer, S. J., Bambury, E. A., Hayirli, T. C., Kuznetsova, M., & Biddinger, P. D. (2021). Moving forward from COVID-19: Organizational dimensions of effective hospital emergency management. *Health Security, 19*(5), 508–520.

Briggs, A., & Vassall, A. (2021). Count the cost of disability caused by COVID-19. *Nature, 593*, 502–505.

Christensen, M., Innstrand, S. T., Øystein Saksvik, P., & Nielsen, K. (2019). The line manager's role in implementing successful organizational interventions. *Spanish Journal of Psychology, 1*(22), E5. https://doi.org/10.1017/sjp.2019.4

Clemente-Suárez, V. J., Martínez-González, M. B., Benitez-Agudelo, J. C., Navarro-Jiménez, E., Beltran-Velasco, A. I., Ruisoto, P., Diaz Arroyo, E., Laborde-Cárdenas, C. C., & Tornero-Aguilera, J. F. (2021). The impact of the COVID-19 pandemic on mental disorders: A critical review. *Int J Environ Res Public Health, 18*(19), 10041. https://doi.org/10.3390/ijerph181910041. PMID: 34639341; PMCID: PMC8507604.

Cox, T., Griffiths, A., Barlow, C., Randall, R., Thomson, I., & Rial-Gonzalez, E. (2000). *Organisational interventions for work stress*. HSE Books.

Davis, H. E., Assaf, G. S., McCorkell, L., Wei, H., Low, R. J., Re'em, Y., Redfield, S., Austin, J. P., & Akrami, A. (2021). Characterizing long COVID in an international cohort: 7 months of symptoms and their impact. *EClinicalMedicine, 38*, 101019.

De Jong, B. A., Dirks, K. T., & Gillespie, N. (2016). Trust and team performance: A meta-analysis of main effects, moderators, and covariates. *Journal of Applied Psychology, 101*(8), 1134–1150.

De Vos, A., Jacobs, S., & Verbuggen, M. (2021). Career transitions and employability. *Journal of Vocational Behavior, 126*, 103457. https://doi.org.10.1016/j.jvb.2020.103475

Della Monica, A., Ferrara, P., Dal Mas, F., Cobianchi, L., Scannapieco, F., & Ruta, F. (2022). The impact of Covid-19 healthcare emergency on the psychological well-being of health professionals: A review of literature. *Ann Ig, 34*(1), 27–44.

Directive 2000/78. *Official Journal of the European Communities*. https://eur-lex.europa.eu/LexUriServ/LexUriServ.do?uri=OJ:L:2000:303:0016:0022:EN:PDF

Endler, N. S., & Parker, J. D. (1990). Multidimensional assessment of coping: A critical evaluation. *Journal of Personality and Social Psychology, 58*(5), 844–854. https://doi.org/10.1037/0022-3514.58.5.844

Equality Act. (2010). https://www.gov.uk/guidance/equality-act-2010-guidance

European Commission. (2021). *Communication from the Commission to the European Parliament, the Council, the European Economic and Social Committee and the Committee of the Regions Empty. EU Strategic Framework on Health and Safety at Work 2021–2027. Occupational Safety and Health in a Changing World of Work.* COM(2021) 323 final. Brussels, 28.6.2021.

Fox, K. E., Johnson, S. T., Berkman, L. F., Sianoja, M., Soh, Y., Kubzansky, L. D., & Kelly, E. L. (2021). Organisational- and group-level workplace interventions and their effect on multiple domains of worker well-being: A systematic review. *Work & Stress, 36*(1), 30–59. https://doi.org/10.1080/02678373.2021.1969476

Gorna, R., MacDermott, N., Rayner, C., O'Hara, M., Evans, S., Agyen, L., Nutland, W., Rogers, N., & Hastie, C. (2021). Long COVID guidelines need to reflect lived experience. *The Lancet, 397*(10273), 455–457.

Gualano, M. R., Sinigaglia, T., Lo Moro, G., Rousset, S., Cremona, A., Bert, F., & Siliquini, R. (2021). The burden of burnout among healthcare professionals of intensive care units and emergency departments during the COVID-19 pandemic: A systematic review. *International Journal of Environmental Research and Public Health, 18*(15), 8172.

Hampson, E., Polner, A., Assal, V., & Abrahams N. (2022). *Mental health and employers: The case for investment – Pandemic and beyond.* Deloitte. https://www2.deloitte.com/content/dam/Deloitte/uk/Documents/consultancy/deloitte-uk-mental-health-report-2022.pdf

Horne, J. F., III. (1997, April). The coming age of organizational resilience. *Business Forum, 22*(2/3), 24.

Jonsdottir, I. H., Degl'Innocenti, A., Ahlstrom, L., Finizia, C., Wijk, H., & Akerstrom, M. (2021). A pre/post analysis of the impact of the COVID-19 pandemic on the psychosocial work environment and recovery among healthcare workers in a large university hospital in Sweden. *Journal of Public Health Research, 10*(4), jphr-2021.

Joyce, J. (2013). Facing the challenge of mental ill health in the workplace. *Journal of Public Mental Health, 12*(2), 93–97.

LaMontagne, A. D., Shann, C., & Martin, A. (2018). Developing an integrated approach to workplace mental health: A hypothetical conversation with a small business owner. *Annals of Work Exposure and Health, 62*(suppl_1), S93–S100. doi: 10.1093/annweh/wxy039. PMID: 30212883. https://academic.oup.com/annweh/article/62/Supplement_1/S93/5096681

Neelam, K., Duddu, V., Anyim, N., Neelam, J., & Lewis, S. (2021). Pandemics and pre-existing mental illness: A systematic review and meta-analysis. *Brain, Behavior, & Immunity-Health, 10*, 100177. https://doi.org/10.1016/j.bbih.2020.100177

NHS England. (2021). *Post-COVID syndrome (long COVID)*. https://www.england
.nhs.uk/coronavirus/post-covid-syndrome-long-COVID/#five-point-plan

Nielsen, K. (2024). Improving employee well-being through improving working
conditions: A review on how we can make participatory organizational interventions work. In L. E. Tetrick, G. G. Fisher, M. T. Ford, & J. Campbell Quick (Eds.),
Handbook of occupational health psychology (3rd ed., pp. 449–466). American
Psychological Association.

Nielsen, K. (2013). How can we make organizational interventions work? Employees
and line managers as actively crafting interventions. *Human Relations, 66,*
1029–1050.

Nielsen, K., & Abildgaard, J. S. (2013). Organizational interventions: A research-based
framework for the evaluation of both process and effects. *Work & Stress, 27,*
278–297. https://doi.org/10.1080/02678373.2013.812358

Nielsen, K., Nielsen, M. B., Ogbonnaya, C., Känsälä, M., Saari, E., & Isaksson, K.
(2017). Workplace resources to improve both employee well-being and performance: A systematic review and meta-analysis. *Work & Stress, 31*(2), 101–120.

Nielsen, K., & Randall, R. (2013). Opening the black box: Presenting a model for evaluating organizational interventions. *European Journal of Work and Organizational
Psychology, 22*(5), 601–617. https://doi.org/10.1080/1359432X.2012.690556

Nielsen, K., & Randall, R. (2015). Addressing the fit of planned interventions to the
organizational context. In M. Karanika-Murray & C. Biron (Eds.), *Derailed organizational stress and well-being interventions: Confessions of failure and solutions for
success* (pp. 107–118). Springer.

Nielsen, K., Randall, R., Holten, A.-L., & González, E. R. (2010). Conducting
organizational-level occupational health interventions: What works? *Work & Stress,
24*(3), 234–259. https://doi.org/10.1080/02678373.2010.515393

Nielsen, K., & Yarker, J. (2022). Employees' experience of supervisor behaviour:
A support or a hindrance on their return-to-work journey with a CMD? A qualitative
study. *Work & Stress, 37*(4), 487–508. https://doi.org/10.1080/02678373.2022
.2145622

Nielsen, K., & Yarker, J. (2023a). What can I do for you? Line managers' behaviors
to support return to work for workers with common mental disorders. *Journal of
Managerial Psychology, 38*(1), 34–46.

Nielsen, K., & Yarker, J. (2023b). Thrivers, survivors or exiteers: A longitudinal, inter-
pretative phenomenological analysis of the post-return-to-work journeys for workers
with common mental disorders. *Applied Psychology: An International Review,
73*(1), 267–295. https://doi.org/10.1111/apps.12479

Nielsen, K., Yarker, J., Munir, F., & Bültmann, U. (2018). IGLOO: An integrated
framework for sustainable return to work in workers with common mental disorders.
Work & Stress, 32(4), 400–417.

Organisation for Economic Co-operation and Development. (2014). *Making mental
health count: The social and economic costs of neglecting mental health care.*
OECD Health Policy Studies, OECD Publishing.

Parsonage, M., & Saini, G. (2017). *Mental health at work.* Centre for Mental Health.

Pawson, R., & Tilley, N. (1997). An introduction to scientific realist evaluation. In E.
Chelimsky & W. R. Shadish (Eds.), *Evaluation for the 21st century: A handbook*
(pp. 405–418). SAGE. https://doi.org/10.4135/9781483348896.n29

Petrie, K., Joyce, S., Tan, L., Henderson, M., Johnson, A., Nguyen, H., Modini,
M., Groth, M., Glozier, N., & Harvey, S. B. (2018). A framework to create more

mentally healthy workplaces: A viewpoint. *Australian & New Zealand Journal of Psychiatry*, *52*(1), 15–23. https://doi.org/10.1177/0004867417726174

Randall, R., & Nielsen, K. (2010). Interventions to promote well-being at work. In S. Leka & J. Houdmont (Eds.), *Occupational health psychology: A key text* (pp. 88–123). Wiley-Blackwell.

Reuschke, D., & Houston, D. (2022). The impact of Long COVID on the UK work-force. *Applied Economics Letters*, *30*(18), 2510–2514.

Tamrakar, P., Pant, S. B., & Acharya, S. P. (2021). Anxiety and depression among nurses in COVID and non-COVID intensive care units. *Nurs Crit Care*, *28*. https://doi.org/10.1111/nicc.12685

Thiele Schwarz, U. von, Nielsen, K., Stenfors-Hayes, T., Hasson, H. (2017). Using Kaizen to improve employee wellbeing: Results from two organizational interven-tion studies. *Human Relations*, *70*(8), 966–993.

Tiete, J., Guatteri, M., Lachaux, A., Matossian, A., Hougardy, J. M., Loas, G., & Rotsaert, M. (2021). Mental health outcomes in healthcare workers in COVID-19 and non-COVID-19 care units: A cross-sectional survey in Belgium. *Frontiers in Psychology*, *11*. https://doi.org/10.3389/fpsyg.2020.612241

Van Ginneken, E., Siciliani, L., Reed, S., Eriksen, A., Tille, F., & Zapata, T. (2022). Addressing backlogs and managing waiting lists during and beyond the COVID-19 pandemic. *TEN*, *28*(1), 35.

Vogus, T. J., & Sutcliffe, K. M. (2007)). Organizational resilience: Towards a theory and research agenda. In *2007 IEEE International Conference on Systems, Man and Cybernetics* (pp. 3418–3422). IEEE.

World Health Organization. (2021). *New policy brief calls on decision-makers to support patients as 1 in 10 report symptoms of "long COVID"*. https://www.euro.who.int/en/health-topics/health-emergencies/pages/news/news/2021/02/new-policy-brief-calls-on-decision-makers-to-support-patients-as-1-in-10-report-symptoms-of-long-covid

Index

Note: Further references to contributing authors can be found in their respective chapters in the book.

absenteeism 134–61
absence management 134–61, 242, 249
abusive supervision 64, 87
accommodations provision 82
accountability, leaders 89–90
adaptation processes 167, 173
AET *see* affective events theory
affect 115–16, 125
affect dispersion 125
affective events theory (AET) 118–19, 122
affective states, absence behaviours 140
age/ageing concepts 78
ageing societies 78
agile work 3, 179–99
    see also flexible work; hybrid work
AI *see* artificial intelligence
alcohol consumption 205–6
Alhejji, H. 86
Allen, J. 97
Andrulli, R. 104
anxiety 30–2, 206
Appel-Meulenbroek, R. 67
appraisal theories 116–18
artificial intelligence (AI) 3, 21
asymmetrical interruptions 59
attentive-style leadership 143
authenticity 80, 172
'authenticity building' 173
'authenticity work' 172–3
autism 81–2
autonomy, culture of 228
autonomy needs 185–7
avoidance coping style 248

'back-to-backs' 209, 210

Baillien, E. 100
Bala, H. 99
Barboza-Wilkes, C. 115, 122
behavioural outcomes
    business travel 205–6
    remote rotational work 209
    sickness absence 134–61
Bell, C. 14
Bell, V. 31, 41
belonging 80, 89, 185, 188–9
Berdahl, J. L. 7
betrayal-related moral injury 35, 46
Bettis, R. A. 171
Biggs, A. 2
Billings, J. 2, 44
Biron, C. 146
'bleisure' 206
Bloom, N. 66
border keepers 60
border theory 59–60
Bordia, P. 97, 105, 230
boundary control 58, 62
boundary flexibility 58
boundary flexing 67
boundary management 56–75
    conceptualizations of 58–66
    future research 64–6
    ICT use 188
    implications of 61–4
    operationalizations 58–66
    theoretical underpinnings 59–61
boundary permeability 58
boundary theory 59
Boxall, P. 229
Brewin, C. R. 34, 47
Briner, R. B. 201
Brooks, S. 38
Brough, P. 59–60, 99
Brown, R. L. 79
burnout 2, 36–7, 38
business travel 5, 200, 203–7